AF344270

There & Back.
Africa

Curated by
Danielle Tilkin

La Casa Encendida   31.03.2006
                           11.06.2006

Ammar Bouras

Frédéric Bruly
Bouabré

Mbongeni Richman
Buthelezi

Soly Cissé

Viyé Diba

Modou Dieng

Moustapha Dimé

Touhami Ennadre

Frances Goodman

There & Back.
Africa

Romuald Hazoumé

Bodys Isek Kingelez

Abdoulaye Konaté

William Kentridge

Moshekwa Langa

Otobong Nkanga

Marie Blanche
Ouedraogo

Miguel Petchkovsky

Chéri Samba

Djibril Sy

Emeka Udemba

Organising an exhibition of work by a group of artists from a continent like Africa requires not only detailed knowledge of the subject but also exemplary meditation. In this respect, we have been honoured with the invaluable assistance of Danielle Tilkin, curator of the exhibition, whose insights into the vast web of artistic representations and forms of expression to be found in Africa provide us with the opportunity of discovering the work of several key artists. Different communities, religions and social and artistic modes, plus the dichotomy between past and present, tradition and modernity, all feature in African art. But added to this is the phenomenon of emigration that spread throughout the continent in the wake of World War Two and the emergence of a middle class. These complex factors impact on the force of expression and subtlety of language used by the artists represented here, who display a knowledge acquired through the toing and froing, voluntary or imposed, between one culture and another, between one generation and another.

The exhibition invites viewers to undertake a two-way journey, from South to North, and examine the similarities and differences between the work of those artists who emigrated and the work of those who stayed. It also invites us to reevaluate our concept of what is "African". The works on display represent several generations of artists who have penetrated international circuits in recent years. Frédéric Bruly Bouabré (Ivory Coast) serves as the starting point for a dialogue between the local and the global with works that challenge every possible preconceived idea about tradition and contemporaneity. In turn, these establish a harmonious dialogue with the works of other artists such as William Kentridge (South Africa), Viyé Diba (Senegal) and Touhami Ennadre (Morocco), and with those of younger artists who experiment with the full range of media (photography, video and film), such as Emeka Udemba (Nigeria), Marie Blanche Ouedraogo (Burkina Faso), Otobong Nkanga (Nigeria), Romuald Hazoumé (Benin) and Soly Cissé (Senegal).

We are particularly grateful for the co-operation provided by all the artists. Our thanks are also due to the collectors and loaners, without whose generosity this exhibition would not have been possible. Finally, we warmly congratulate the curator and the entire team of people who have co-ordinated this exhibition and the accompanying catalogue.

Carlos María Martínez Martínez
Managing Director of Obra Social Caja Madrid

"Let's be quite clear: Contemporary Africa is the fruit of colonisation. Let's say it again: colonisation made us aware of this geographic entity we call Africa when it carved up the continent in Berlin in 1885. Let us add this: African nationalism was born out of the colonisers' arrogant nationalism. Finally, colonisation gave us the French language, our main weapon against its damaging effects in Africa."

Time for History, Boniface Mongo-Mboussa[1]

Nowadays, talking about Africa and bringing together a group of artists from all four corners of the continent under this geographical concept remains as controversial as ever. And yet, this is not to deny the different communities and cultures in their social, religious and artistic manifestations, nor to ignore the fact that for centuries these have rubbed shoulders with each other and intermingled, articulating and renewing themselves through the constant exchange and migration of people in a never-ending search, not so much for a present as for a future. Neither is it a question of interpreting artists' output as the manifestation of an identity that may not even be a central theme of their work. It is a quest, a way of relating artists' work with the circumstances of its context. For is art not the outward manifestation of the mindset of a given time? Can it really be appreciated without recourse to history? An artist's vision of the interior or exterior world is influenced by his or her experience. It is inspired by the global, the local and the personal and while it is sometimes immediately comprehensible, more often than not it requires the meticulous decoding of the language in which it is couched.

As has occurred in postcolonial literature with French, English and Portuguese, the visual arts in Africa have inherited a new code of expression, a formal language developed in art schools founded by Europeans in the late 1930s and informal studios established by foreign artists-in-residence. The tuition provided by these was based on an official curriculum that had no place for the study of African aesthetics, which ironically was behind the enormous formal revolution that followed the "discovery" of African art by European artists at the beginning of the twentieth century. Another fact to be borne in mind is the adoption of the great monotheistic religions and Islam in particular, whose restrictions in terms of image revolutionised a whole system of representation. What is left today of the dichotomy between past and present, tradition and contemporaneity, that took several forms during the various colonial, independence and postcolonial periods? Is the question today not the same, namely the place of art when it is no longer at the service of society or religion but obliged to carve a niche for itself in a non-existent local market?

The independence era undoubtedly created a dynamic that was accompanied by an urban explosion and the proliferation of an emerging middle class in search of symbols of modernity. This is illustrated, for example, by the famous photographs

[1] Translator's note: Translated from the French *Le temps de l'Histoire*, published at http://www.africultures.com/anglais/list_article_E.asp, issue number 43, December 2001.

There & Back. Africa

from the period of Seydou Keyta and Malick Sidibé in Mali. Turning their backs on traditional modes, or grafting new ones onto old, numerous artists turned successfully to painting, often abstract, on canvas and board, eclipsing sculpture and finding a receptive, sophisticated local audience including the European expatriates. Others, in the wake of the first wave of emigration after the Second World War, left the continent to pursue their studies abroad.

Nowadays, in these times of globalisation, African artists and the intellectuals and writers who live either in Africa or the cities and countries of their choice, are weary of the vision of an Africa wallowing in self-pity, perpetuated by classical authors and the media, and of what a politican recently described on African television as the "virus of belated navel-gazing." Emboldened by a well-assimilated past and a vision of the future in which they are stakeholders, their work invites us to reflect on this new chapter in history and their efforts to project, if not produce their own version of globalisation.

Judging from the force of expression, the subtle language and the knowledge acquired during their toing and froing, voluntary or imposed, between one culture and another, between one generation and another, the sources and means are inexhaustible, whether in the fields of the visual arts, literature, music, film or architecture. While the contrasts in socio-economic situation between north and south, east and west, often hinder access to new technologies, they are not an obstacle to creativity, which uses all kinds of supports and offers a new style of poetics based on the most heterogeneous materials. "You go beyond the function and come back to the original material," says Viyé Diba about the tendency to recycle the "non-recyclable" that permeates numerous works. This new individual consciousness is not without a certain subversive humour, nor is this particular group, which seems more than capable of tossing the ball back.

The works chosen for this exhibition represent several generations of artists who gained international recognition following the historic *Magiciens de la Terre* (Magicians of the Earth) exhibition held in Paris in 1989. The oldest amongst them is Frédéric Bruly Bouabré, born in 1923 in Zéprégüé, in the central-west region of the present-day Republic of the Ivory Coast. After a short education at the French school, he pursued a number of trades until his retirement in the 1980s. Self-taught, he says his work is directly linked to a revelation he had in 1948: "On 11 March 1948, when the sky opened before my eyes and the seven suns traced a beautiful circle around their Mother-Sun, I became Cheick Nadro" (unforgettable in the Bété language)[2]. Since then, as a means of furthering the universal dissemination of his culture, that of the Bété people, he has observed, analysed and presented in his habitual 10 x 15 cm "index card" format all the relevant knowledge, myths, tales and cosmogonical details, noting "all the little events through which the eternal world invades the ephemeral world."[1] One of his first works was to cre-

[2] The artist interviewed by Yaya Savané and André Magnin.

ate an alphabet for his ethnic group, published in 1958 by Théodore Monod. He then went on to ponder *"La connaissance du monde"* (The knowledge of the world) and to illustrate his "annotations" in fields as varied and universal as philosophy, science, ethics, politics, religions, traditional arts and customs, etc., creating a type of encyclopaedic dictionary in the form of series and groups entitled, for example, *Le Musée du visage africain (Scarifications)*, (The Museum of the African Face (Scarifications)), *Les poids akans à peser l'or* (The Akan Scales for Weighing Gold), *Relevés des signes observés sur noix de cola* (Annotations on Signs Observed on Kola Nuts), and *Relevés des signes observés sur oranges* (Annotations on Signs Observed on Oranges). With his modest means and a humanity tinged with humour, Bruly Bouabré draws us into his quest to understand symbols and their manifestations, where tradition and modernity are fused into one: the present.

A hard, hand-to-mouth present, and a future in which idealism and the folly of forms at the service of social renewal are set to triumph, are contrasting themes in the work of Chéri Samba and Bodys Kingelez, both of whom live in Kinshasa, in the Democratic Republic of Congo. Veterans of the 1989 show *Magiciens de la Terre*, each argues that social renewal necessarily depends on a new political and social consciousness. Chéri Samba demonstrates his social commitment through his "message" pictures and his mockery of politicians, accompanying his images with language, Lingala and French, thereby reaching out not only to a local audience but a transnational one. His often loud palette serves as the perfect complement to his swift drawing and his incisive vision. Meanwhile, Bodys Kingelez builds "super-models" and imagines whole towns for a new generation freed from the yoke of violence and corruption. Made out of cardboard and *papier collé*, his constructions are as fragile as the messages they convey, and are often accompanied by long, eloquent texts written by the artist.

If social and political reflections were central to the work of numerous artists of the independence years, it was above all in South Africa, during the final years of apartheid, that they formed a genuine resistance movement. William Kentridge was born in Johannesburg, where he still lives and works. Raised by a politically-committed family (his father was a famous anti-apartheid lawyer), he studied politics, philosophy, fine arts and, in Paris between 1981-1982, drama. Before returning to drawing, he worked as an actor, stage designer and theatre director, as well as in film. His work draws on literature, history and politics, and explores memory and guilt. It is also influenced by his study of painters such as Max Beckmann, William Hogarth and Goya. He embarked on his series of drawings for *Ubu Tells the Truth*, inspired by Alfred Jarry's character *King Ubu*, around 1996-97, perceiving the latter as "the incarnation of twentieth-century man, his power, his cruelty, his self-pity and his social blindness"[3] and integrating it here with the spectacle of the Truth and Reconciliation Commission, responsible for crime investigation during the apartheid regime. Exploring themes such as truth and responsibility, the film ex-

[3] The artist interviewed by Carolyn Christov-Bakargiev, reproduced in "William Kentridge", Phaidon Press, London, 1999

amines the individual and collective memory of a society in which brutality plunged to its lowest depths. His animation technique has nothing in common with that of specialised studios, but is rather the result of the laborious yet fascinating task of superimposing drawing upon drawing, erasures, shadow and light from which the various scenes, characters, landscapes and so on emerge. For Kentridge, the art of drawing is a metaphor of the way we think; arriving at an image is a process, not a moment frozen in time. Rather than beginning with a screenplay or storyboard, the story unfolds with the drawings, his pacing back and forth between these and the camera, and the shots captured on film. As such, each drawing undergoes numerous transformations, sometimes hundreds of them, until the story moves on to a new scene and the same process begins all over again. *Ubu Tells the Truth* is therefore based on a series of close on thirty charcoal and chalk drawings of varying sizes but also includes photographs and excerpts from documentary films about the riots in Soweto in 1976, where over 700 people lost their lives, and the uprisings of the 1980s.

Viyé Diba, who lives and works in Senegal, is from the same generation. He is represented in the exhibition by the installation *Messe nue,* 2001-2002 (Naked Mass), inspired by a report he heard on radio of the midnight masses that the Catholic Church would organise for the people in the Gbadolite region of the Congo as a means of concealing their nakedness with the night. Abandoned to their fate by corrupt governments, these men, women and children, survivors of wars, genocides, pillages and poverty, forgotten by everyone and without even clothes to their name, are the subject of a profound reflection on the nature of globalisation and universal consciousness in these times of mass-media power and simultaneous information. The chapel, originally conceived as an installation performance, served, like the set of a television studio, as a platform for debates about wars, genocides and other tragedies that weaken Africa, with direct reference to Rwanda. With its huge cross looming over a pile of ragged clothes, the chapel reconstructed for our exhibition is illuminated by hundreds of electric lamps whose light gradually fades away, plunging us into the darkness of our own conscience, beyond religion, in the mere shadows of history. In recreating this scene of disaster, Viyé Diba also reveals his sensitivity to the recycling of materials, both poetic and economic using them in new metaphors to create a dual play between origin and memory.

Mustapha Dimé, also from Senegal, shares the same fascination with recovered materials and uses them to create his own works. However, his choice leads him to a symbology deeply anchored in his culture and to "materials from everyday life"[4] which, rather than alienating the society in which he lives, reach out to people, are things that can be identified with. Calabashes, pestles, nails, *canaris* (clay cooking pots) and pieces of string all form part of his sculpture. Dimé, who had his studio on the most beautiful cape on the Isle de Gorée, was born near Saint-Louis. His first contact with sculpture, which would normally have been precluded by the

[4] The artist interviewed by Thomas McEvilley, "Mustapha Dimé" catalogue, City Hall, Paris.

caste system of his village, occurred as a young boy, when at school he became friendly with children of the lowest caste, woodcutters, from the Lawbé community. At the age of 14, stubbornly overriding his father's forbiddance, he abandoned his village and went to study at the Ecole des Arts Décoratifs in Dakar. There he complemented his technical training with courses in literature, mathematics and French history, from which the famous "Our ancestors the Gauls..."[5] was eventually taken up by his generation as "the rallying cry to express everything wrong with the colonial regime."(00) There were no courses on African aesthetics, not even at the Ecole des Beaux-Arts in Dakar when he subsequently enrolled. Following a sojourn with the Dogon tribe in Mali, he rebelled against these gaps in his education and devoted himself to the study of the cultures of the various regions in Senegal and the Ouolof language, which he then did not master. A member of the Mouride sect, for him sculpture is a way of practising Islam, of acknowledging the creator of the world's visible beauty. Dimé believes in the liberation of humanity through the awakening of memory: "this is why my characters usually look expectant, despite producing the impression of movement."[6] *La grande danse* (The Great Dance), 1995, which features in the exhibition, crystallises his thinking. His filiform characters, nailed, knotted and bound to each other, share the spiritual importance of this expectancy. Moustapha Dimé died in 1998.

Abdoulaye Konaté initially became known in Europe through his installations. His early work made reference to his culture but also to universal themes, as in *La mort, la naissance, la culture* (Death, Birth, Culture) from 1993 and *Lutte contre le HIV* (Fighting HIV) from 1995. He has since gone on to use cloth as his support, arranged in the fashion of wall-hangings from which he cuts out, affixes or meticulously sews on the images or symbols that are central to his theme. These wall-hangings become a kind of altar to exorcism when he incorporates *gris-gris* or juxtaposes objects on the ground, as in *Bosnie, Rwanda, Angola* (Bosnia, Rwanda, Angola) from 1995, where cartridges, a cap, a gun and burnt or torn clothing are strewn on the ground. Intolerance is a reflection at the heart of his work. In his piece *Hommage aux arbitres* (Homage to Referees) from 2006, he uses sport to provide us with a new insight. Football: the way it is covered by the media and the millions of spectators of all ages around the whole world that it mobilises for matches; all that football represents symbolically, with national or regional teams falling over backwards to sign up the best players, whatever their nationality; refereeing, justice and order, but increasingly also violence, aggression, tendentious decisions and the financial issues that corrupt both the players and the sport. In this work by Konaté, the rigour of the composition contrasts with the add-ons and cut-outs – the black silhouettes of the referees, the red and yellow cards, the red lettering – made on the local hand-woven textiles that he has chosen as his support and the hundreds of sewn-on *gris-gris*, intended as protection, that recall Africa. The stadium as a cultural space. One of the only arenas in which Africans are equals alongside all the nations of the world. Abdoulaye Konaté lives and works in

[5] Idem.

[6] Idem.

Bamako and divides his time between his studio and the Conservatoire des Arts that he has directed for several years. He was commissioned to create a work for the opening of the African Cup of Nations (football) held in Bamako in 2002. The gigantic patchwork he produced covered 7,200 square yards.

Of the same generation, Touhami Ennadre, born in 1953 in Casablanca, Morocco, belongs to the group of artists educated in Paris, in his case as a result of his family emigrating there in 1961. In 1977 his works were shown at the exhibition *Tendances actuelles de la photographie en France* (Current Trends in Photography in France) held at the Musée d'Art Moderne de la Ville de Paris. With photography as his medium, he uses his camera to capture images on the spot, totally shunning poses and manipulation. He spends hours in the dark room teasing out the forms, if not to say the spirits out of that black ground, "the intensity and force of which produce light." The "metaphysical black" that gives rise to the expression of an impassioned vision of truth. Whatever his subject – trance-inducing rituals, gay clubs, tramps on the underground or the New Yorkers in despair after 9/11–Touhami Ennadre does not observe, he slides into the skin of his subjects, holding his camera just a few centimetres from a face or body to capture a detail or that moment of "duende" or magic when the temporal becomes eternal. He openly confesses to being "an anti-photographer as well as an anti-painter."[7]

[7]The artist interviewed by François Aubral.

Miguel Petchkovsky, born in Angola in 1956, also studied in Europe, first in Portugal (from 1971 to 1977) and then at the Gerrit Rietveld Academy in Amsterdam, the city where he still lives today. As a multimedia artist, he alternates between the use of video, painting and installation as the supports for his conceptual and formal reflections, which he articulates as the construction/deconstruction of the modernist vision to redefine an artistic practice more in keeping with individual experience. In the diptych *West Side Story,* made in 2004, the questions are raised by the town, the machine, the presence/absence of humanity, and the bolts used in construction. All contemporary elements viewed through what appears to be a metal eye mask. By contrast, in *The Ejaculation of God* and *Modernism,* both from 2005, the reference space/time is articulated via symbols of the past, such as masks or what might be the strings of musical instruments or threads laid out as if waiting to be weaved, emerging from or resting on the surface of the pictures.

Romuald Hazoumé was born in 1962 and lives and works in Porto Novo. Photography is a recent incorporation in his work. Known for his portraits/masks made from all kinds of ordinary recycled materials such as gasoline cans and radio and television sets, with all their connotations, he returned for a while to painting and the use of materials such as sand and earth to analyse Fa divination signs and their interpretation. In this exhibition, photography strikes up a dialogue with his installation *Pièce montée* (Celebration Cake), a pyramid of gasoline cans, revealing the other side of the cake, as it were. In these verdant landscapes, on remote paths and congested roads, there are cans everywhere, empty on the outward journey and full to brimming on the return journey. True masterpieces fashioned by the artisans of death. Fifty-litre cans heated and expanded to double their capacity. Scarred, lacerated and patched, the very image of the poverty on which this business feeds. The street vendors are genuine balancing artists on their bikes and mopeds, not to mention the women that carry them on their heads for hours on the long march from the Nigerian border. Romuald Hazoumé collects these strange cans and piles them up in his garage. Anchored in time, in interminable suffering, they form a silent mural. Whether symbolic objects or not, Hazoumé simply waits for the right moment to issue them with a new form and invest them with his vision of art, life and contemporaneity.

For Mbongeni Richman Buthelezi, born in 1965 in the township of Soweto, near Johannesburg, and other black artists of his generation in South Africa, reality and the need to find alternatives to inaccessible materials have led them to explore the multicoloured plasticity of the little utilitarian bags that litter streets and vacant plots of land. Even today, his studio remains a huge multicoloured palette on which he walks to find the perfect hue and texture, using a welding torch to melt them down and apply them like a painter uses paint. In the post-apartheid years, this medium emphasised the social and political content of the everyday scenes that he depicted, often incorporating newspaper cuttings. More recently, following a period of experimentation with abstract forms, he has returned to figuration, displaying redoubled force in his expression of the emotions and life of his evolving community.

Representing North Africa, Ammar Bouras (b.1964) lives and works in Algiers, where he studied at the Ecole Supérieure des Beaux-Arts. His aesthetic work is underpinned by a political discourse expressed through painting, photography and video images, which he manipulates and fuses into highly arresting multimedia images, in terms both of their content and form. His installations and videos focus on the history of Algeria, war crimes and colonisation, while also analysing the present and the shadow of terrorism, moral repression and fear. Words, thoughts and voices, as much as marks, overlap in a rhythmic sequence of colourful images. Poetics at the service of sombre reality. A repertoire that challenges conventions and places historic consciousness firmly in the foreground.

Soly Cissé was born in 1969 and lives and works in Dakar. The series of drawings on display in this exhibition were inspired by two fortuitous events. The first, the discovery of a new support: a box of unused photographic paper rendered useless by exposition to light. The other, a chance view of a mosaic of television screens. He attacks this black surface with white paint, using his fingers to create characters and animal forms that are simultaneously terrified and terrifying, their profiles and expressions incised in the paint. His vivid, rapid gesture can be discerned in a composition that produces a snapshot effect. Black and white versus white and black. Or, as he says, the encroachment of western civilisation upon Africa.

Emeka Udemba, who was born in Nigeria in 1968 and lives in Germany, addresses the same theme but from the opposite angle, using photography, video and performance to explore his status as an African in Europe. His work, in which he is simultaneously the subject and actor, is shot through with a subversive humour that is reminiscent, in the forms it takes, of that of the writers of his generation. Meanwhile, his installations reveal a reality whose only media appeal lies in the statistics. They make use of explicit symbols, barriers, tunnels, boats and impassable walls between one world and another, between an unbearable present and an imaginary future.

Modou Dieng was born in Senegal in 1970. He currently lives in San Francisco, where he has just completed a course of study at the San Francisco Art Institute. In formal terms, his work is mainly characterised by collage. His superimposition of eclectic elements provides his compositions with texture, colour and relief while at the same time demonstrating his fascination with urban American culture and the role of black Americans in particular. In his tribute to Charlie Parker, city scenes are juxtaposed with racist graffiti and jazz records. His polyfaceted composition invites us to reformulate his images, making them appear and disappear, as if a piece of improvised music.

Moshekwa Langa is from South Africa but has lived in Europe since 1996. Born in 1975, he grew up in the country, in KwaNdebele, one of the territories to which whole black communities were deported for segregation purposes. Any movement outside these so-called homelands required a special permit. The notions of cartography, landscape, the quest for memory, scorned identity and displacement are central to his work, alongside the personal experience of being uprooted and fate. His reflection on the past is occasionally melancholic, expressed via large gouaches with fluid, evanescent forms representing stratified landscapes or vacant-looking people. Collage, installations and photography are skilful additional techniques in his repertoire. The video presented here, *Where do I begin,* is a perfect metaphor of the Myth of Sisyphus. Its powerful poetic symbology transports us to the very heart of the rebellion that convulsed an entire society.

Let us now look at the work of three younger women artists. Frances Goodman is the youngest of this group. Born in Johannesburg in 1975, she attended the University of the Witwatersrand before continuing her studies at Goldsmiths College in London and the Higher Institute for Fine Art (HISK) in Antwerp, Belgium. Her work occupies the realm of the mind, of echoing words and sounds, and the realm of the body, not as an object of desire but of rejection, rebuttal, and as the den of fear, neurosis and psychosis. She presents her mental images through installations, audio monologues and sound sculptures, as well as disconcerting stickers through which she tritely addresses all the prohibitions and clichés of the spaces in which she places them. In her video and sound installation *Voice of Reason,* 2000, a row of red chairs would invite rest and reflection, as in a waiting room, were it not for the fact that the chairs are fitted with headphones for listening to the long monologue, written by the artist, on the subject of her phobia of germs. Her voice is clear and precise. Elbow to elbow, in a calculated promiscuity, bodies are incorporated and connected to the sound. With regard to her use of language and words, the artist remarks that "these are the raw materials of life, the bricks for building human and social relations."[8]

[8]The artist interviewed by James Sey, Arththrob Reviews, Capetown, August 2004.

Marie Blanche Ouedraogo was born in 1971 in Ouagadougou, where she still lives today. Self-taught, she began painting in 1994 and perfected her technique by taking part in several workshops. The interior world she expresses is at the confluence between the local and global, between tradition and modernity. In the series *Recette et Mythe,* 2005 (Recipe and Myth), she brings about the globe/earth/*canari* (African clay cooking pot) transmutation that evokes the history of creation through the symbology of roundness and materials such as ash, red earth, pigment, acrylic and oil applied to cardboard. In these liquid round forms signs of chiefdom, terracotta pots and sperm are juxtaposed with the "coiled system @, the present-day symbol of modernity", like the signs of a divination table. "For me, writing is not static; it's like the lines on a hand, the writing of the gods."

Otobong Nkanga was born in Nigeria in 1974 but lives and works in Amsterdam. She studied at the Ecole des Beaux-Arts in Paris and has recently embarked on the study of drama and dance at DasArts in Amsterdam. Her experimentation with the visual arts is manifested in installations, performances, photography and watercolours. For this exhibition, we have chosen her watercolour series *Delta Stories,* 2005. Created in different formats, these fit together to form a jigsaw puzzle that narrates a story based on the geological and economic metamorphoses of a region, ecological disaster inflicted by human beings, the power of the capitalist system and corrupt political regimes that quash all resistance. It is a story repeated the world over, but which the artist has experienced at close quarters through the writings of the Nigerian author Ken Saro-Wiwa, who was executed as a result of his vigorous campaigns on behalf of the people of Ogoni.

We will close with Djibril Sy for whom memory and the profound reflection on an inescapable present are inextricably linked. As a photojournalist his images question. As works of art they convey poetry, joy but also sadness, violence plus a whole range of nuances that viewers, no doubt, will read into them.

Specificity in universality. This is the sole perspective through which works of art can transgress. No discourse can sustain them beyond words, but their own presence.

Danielle Tilkin

In an article published in 1998 [1], "Les enfants de la postcolonie" (Children of the Postcolony), the Djiboutian writer Abdourahman A. Waberi divided African literary history into four generations: the Pioneer Generation (1910-1930), the Negritude Generation (1930-1960), the Decolonisation Generation, and lastly, in a nod at Salman Rushdie's *Midnight's Children*, the Generation of the Children of the Postcolonial Period, which emerged in the 1990s and to which he ascribes himself.

In his opinion, the latter generation has two distinguishing characteristics: firstly, date of birth because, with a few exceptions, most of its members were born after 1960, the year of decolonisation; and secondly, virtually all the writers of this generation reject their predecessors' third world ideology and consider themselves to be international bastards. This stance ignores the issue of return to the native country, so highly esteemed by Aimé Césaire, and concentrates instead on the issue of arrival in France.Not everyone agrees with this breakdown of generations. In another article, "Littérature et postcolonie" (Literature and Postcolony)[2], Lydie Moudileno, Professor of Postcolonial Studies at the University of Pennsylvania, focuses on the confusion between generation and literary movement. While Abdourahman Ali Waberi announces the birth of a new postcolonial generation, Lydie Moudileno expresses caution, believing that these young writers challenge literary and artistic historiography by their very position at the confluence of different geographical and intellectual territories. It is clearly within this perspective, seeking out the interstices, that the exhibition *There & Back. Africa* must be situated.

It is therefore appropriate to explore the transnational character of contemporary African artistic production, its hybrid nature, its ubiquity (here and there), its temptation to rewrite and remodel tradition; in short, a genuine artistic palimpsest.

Reading and writing Africa in the vacuum

The prospect of capturing African artistic production in a vacuum necessarily refers us to contemporary philosophical and anthropological theories, which deconstruct the idea of Africa as an essence. In his famous 1980's essay *The invention of Africa*[3] the Congolese philosopher Valentin Yves Mudimbe stated that contemporary Africa was an invention of the "colonial library". Paradoxically, it was in that "colonial library" that the African nationalists "took up arms" to produce a genuine "African gnosis", turning contemporary Africa into a joint invention[4]. This thesis has impacted considerably on African studies and has led, in the words of Bogumil Jewsiewicki, to the decolonisation of knowledge about Africa.

From The Belly of the Atlantic[5]

If we leave Africa and cross the Atlantic, it becomes evident that the various "diasporas" have been accompanied by a similar deconstruction. In the case at hand, this is thanks to Paul Gilroy. In his essay *The Black Atlantic: Modernity and Double Consciousness,* he turns the question of origins on its head. Focusing on routes

Africa as a Palimpsest

[1] Abdourahman A. Waberi, "Les enfants de la postcolonie : esquisse d'une nouvelle génération d'écrivains francophones d'Afrique noire", Notre Librairie, no. 135, September-December, 1998.

[2] Lydie Moudileno, " *Littérature et postcolonie»*, Africultures, no. 28, May, 2000.

[3] V. Y. Mudimbe, *The invention of Africa, Gnosis, Philosophy, and the Order of Knowledge*, Bloomington-Indianapolis, Indiana University Press, 1988.

[4] In fact, V. Y Mudimbe believes that since works such as *La philosophie bantoue* by Father Tempels and *Dieu d'eau* by Griaule, African thinkers have managed to invent an Africa that constitutes a defining element in its identity.

[5] I borrow the term from the novel by the Senegalese-born Fatou Diome (*Le ventre de l'Atlantique*, Anne Carrière, 2003).

as opposed to roots, he examines movement, displacement and, consequently, multiple identities. He writes: "I would like to introduce a suggestion that confronts nationalist approaches geared towards ethnic absolutism: cultural historians might do well to consider the Atlantic as a unique and complex subject of analysis in their debates about the modern world, and use this to develop an explicitly transnational and intercultural perspective"[6]. For Paul Gilroy, understanding African-American identity necessarily begins with the slave ship, not the homeland, because the crossing changed the lives of these people and their way of relating with the world. To a certain extent this work continues that of the Martinican poet and philosopher Edouard Glissant. Reared on the poetic and philosophical theories of Deleuze, Segalen and Saint-John Perse, Glissant views the West Indies in the light of the experience on the slave ship, inhabited by what he calls the "naked migrant". In doing so he is obliged to revise and rewrite a number of concepts: the genesis that grants the right to conquer the Other, he counters with a non-essentialist "dignesis"; the systems thinking that imposes the absolute being, he counters with the "archipelagic" thinking; the identity/root that kills the things around it, he counters with the rhizome from which sprouts Relation[7], and so on. This detour around the West Indies takes us back to Africa and, more specifically, to the theories of the Cameroonian historian Achille Mbembe, strongly influenced both by the postmodern theories that prevail on American campuses and by the works of Foucault, Bataille and Fanon.

Africa revisited

His essay *On the postcolony*[8] is now regarded as an indispensable guide to African modernity. He argues that recourse to the notion of the postcolony does away with the clichés (exceptionally frequent in the discourse about Africa), mainly conveyed by the concept of Afro-pessimism, terminology gone mad, by Africanism, which according to Achille Mbembe is doomed to psittacism and is incapable of taking a broad view of Africa, and finally by Afro-radicalism, a reactive system of thinking to the meeting between Africa and the west. *On the postcolony* is therefore a criticism of subaltern studies and postcolonial theories that, even while destroying "imperial knowledge", nevertheless fail to take on board the issues of "self" and "violence between siblings"[9]. In response to the "identity fixation" tendency, Achille Mbembe calls for the African debate to be waged in the "interface between autochthony and cosmopolitanism"[10], which he defines as Afro-politanism. Indeed, we might ask ourselves who is and who is not African, or wonder about the criteria that define a person's Africaneity. For many people, anyone who is "black" must be African. However, all kinds of individuals (Arabs, Europeans, Indians, Afrikaners, Lebanese, Syrians and Indo-Pakistanis) are either associated with or have some link with Africa, and therefore have a claim to African citizenship. This is where Afro-politanism comes in, which is neither negritude nor Pan-Africanism, but a "poetic vision of the world, a specific way of relating with the world that rejects on principle all forms of victimist identity. But this is not to ignore the injustice and

[6] Paul Gilroy. *The Black Atlantic: Modernity and Double Consciousness*, Harvard University Press, 1992.

[7] Edouard Glissant, *The Poetics of Relation*. Translated from the French by Betsy Wing, University of Michigan Press, 1997. See also his latest essay: *La Cochée du lamentin*. Poétique V, 2005.

[8] Achille Mbembe, *On the postcolony. Essay on political imagination in Africa*, Berkely: University of California Press, 2003.

[9] Idem, ibid, p. 11.

[10] Achille Mbembe. *African Modes of Self-Writing*. Translated from the French by Stephen Rendall, published in Public Culture, Volume 14, No. 1, Duke University Press, 2002.

violence that universal laws have inflicted on this continent and its people. Rather, it is a political and cultural stance with regard to nation, race and the issue of difference in general. To the extent that our states are mere inventions (and recent ones at that), there is nothing in their essence that demands our worship. Which is not to say that we are indifferent to their fate."[11]

From theory to artistic practice

If we abandon the theorists and move on to the writers, it becomes evident that this preoccupation with Relation is not new. The poets of the Negritude Movement expressed this approach, couched in the language of the times. They shared the idea that the quest for self had to precede participation in the universal. But their assertion of universality was simultaneously accompanied by a criticism of western hegemony. "Assimilate, not be assimilated"[12] was the creed of the Senegalese poet and president Léopold Sédar Senghor, considered the father of the Negritude Movement and champion of cultural miscegenation. Senghor fiercely defended this notion in the 1930s, at a time when for any African such a claim was the result, at the best, of total alienation and, at the worst, of self-deprecation. Curiously, this was the same Senghor who confessed to being profoundly Serere while celebrating francophony; again, the same Senghor who, while governing the Senegalese, invented the concept of "Normandity" to demonstrate that he was also Norman by virtue of his Norman wife; yet again, the same Senghor who called for solidarity amongst the blacks of the world, all the while asserting his *Saudade* roots based on the fact that his surname was a deformation of the Portuguese word *senhor*. Meanwhile, Martinique-born Aimé Césaire sums up his universality with the following illuminating phrase: there are two ways of getting lost: by segregation in that which is particular or by dilution in that which is universal."[13]

The genuinely curious thing about these quotations is the patent gap between the open mind of the artists and the schematic texts of the critics, who refuse to read their works dialogically.

The local without walls

Let us look, for example, at the Ivorian novelist Ahmadou Kourouma, usually regarded as the orality poet because he "malinkised" the French language. However, the splendid documentary made about him by Joël Calmets[14] demonstrates that his orality, the subject of erudite theses, can be traced back to Céline's *Journey to the End of the Night* and the Malinke proverbs that punctuate his novels are taken from essays written by French ethnologists and missionaries. And here again we meet the famous Africa invention. This explains why the new generation of African writers, discouraged by the way their works are often received, are so critical in the interstices of their texts: warnings, postscripts, interviews and limits that permit them to open the debate. One such in this respect is the Togolese dramatist and novelist Kossi Efoui, who outlines his theatrical project in his work *Récupérations*[15] (Recoveries).

[11] Achille Mbembe. *Afropolitanisme*, www.Africultures.com published 28/12/05.

[12] L.S. Senghor, *Liberté I. Négritude et Humanisme*, Seuil, 1964, p. 39.

[13] Aimé Césaire, *Lettre à Maurice Thorez*, Présence africaine, 1956, p. 21.

[14] Joël Calmets, Ahmadou Kourouma, *Ami-mots*, Production MK2 TV/Arte, 2001.

[15] Kossi Efoui, *Récupérations*, Lansman Carrières, 1992.

The work begins with a quotation from the Cameroonian Blaise Ndjehoya: *"Qui manie deux langues, la maternelle et la colonelle, baise forcément mieux"* (People who use two tongues, their mother tongue and the colonial tongue, are bound to screw better). In this way he not only underlines his dual cultural background (African and French) as a means of banishing the eternal wrench of emigrating, but also asserts the concept of universality in the style of Miguel Torga[16].

The writer, therefore, is one step ahead of the critics, pointing the way forward, demanding tools of analysis beyond the limited vision, where exoticism still prevails, to encompass a much broader view. His novel *La Fabrique des cérémonies*[17] (The Factory of Rituals) pursues this desire to produce rebellious writing. It tells the story of two former students of African origin, Edgar Fall and Urbain Mango, correspondents for *Périple Magazine,* which reports on strong emotions experienced around the world. Running through the writing is a dual parody. On the one hand and somewhat treacherously, it launches an attack on travel accounts (these travels take place in a non-existent Africa, or at least an Africa that no longer exists, like the Soviet Union where the novel's anti-hero, Edgard Fall, attended university). And on the other hand, it warns of the reader of the temptations of succumbing to auto-exoticism. The distance the author takes with regard to this latent trap is mainly perceived through the comic rewriting of invented or real proverbs in which the original sense has been altered to lend this distance. *"Ex Africa semper aliquid novi . De l'Afrique toujours surgit le nouveau. C'est un vieux proverbe dogon traduit par Amadou".* (About Africa there is always something new. This is an ancient Dogon proverb translated by Amadou); *"Glissez, mortels, n'appuyez pas. Proverbe bambara, traduit par Sartre"* (Slip, mortals, don't hold on. Bambara proverb, translated by Sartre), *"Pourquoi faire avec deux doigts ce qu'on peut faire avec un poing. Proverbe mormon"* (Why use two fingers when you can use a fist? Mormon proverb). The author presents a vision of an Africa loyal to its proverbs, its traditions and its "ancestral wisdom", diminished by translations or parodic rewritings.

Another writer for whom criticism is the central theme of his work is A. Waberi. The author of dialogic, erudite texts, Abdourahman Waberi is influenced by the works of those he calls "my two Edwards" (Edward Saïd and Edouard Glissant). From the Palestinian theorist he borrows the central idea that the east is a western invention. Using this premise as his prop and following the example of Edouard Glissant, he goes on to produce an exercise in rewriting. And just as in *Les Indes*[18] (The Indies) Glissant rewrites the *Vents*[19] (Winds) by Saint-John Perse, Abdourahman Waberi juxtaposes his native Djibouti with that of the famous travellers who toured it and then invented it. This is the classic reinterpretation and subsequent rewriting of certain western texts by southern writers. Edward W. Saïd explored this literary process in *Culture and Imperialism*[20], specifically through the relationship between the Kenyan Ngugi Wa Thiongo, the Nigerian Chinua Achebe, the Sudanese Tayeb

[16] "l'universel, c'est le local sans les murs" (the universal is the local without walls), Miguel Torga quoted by Christophe Pradeau and Tiphaine Samoyault in *Où est la littérature mondiale*, Presses Universitaires de Vincennes, 2005.

[17] Kossi Efoui, *La Fabrique des cérémonies*, Seuil, 2001.

[18] Edouard Glissant, *Les Indes*, Editions Falaize, 1956.

[19] Saint-John Perse, *Vents*, Gallimard, 1960.

[20] Edward W. Saïd, *Culture and Imperialism*, Vintage, 1994.

Salih, the Trinidadian V.S. Naipaul and Conrad. Nevertheless, the critical work of Abdourahman Waberi is not concerned exclusively with reinterpretation but simultaneously practises a type of literary transhumance. In African literature, he is one of the few writers with a clear affiliation, whose writings reveal a specific library. For example, Henri Michaux, Arthur Rimbaud, Charles Baudelaire, Omar Khayam, Ibn Arabi, René d'Obaldia, Saint-John Perse, Haadraawi and Cesare Pavese, to name but a few, can all be discerned in his work *Cahier Nomade*[21] (Nomad Notebook).

Africa in the World Republic of Literature

Another two writers reveal the same preoccupation with belonging to world literature and their relation with it. They are Togo-born Sami Tchak and Congo-born Alain Mabanckou. While in the latter this concern is recent, it has always been present in the works of Sami Tchak.

Hard on the trail of *The Life Before Us* by Romain Gary, and even *Journey to the End of the Night* by Louis-Ferdinand Céline, Sami Tchak's *Place des fêtes*[22] (Celebration Square) uses intertextual winks between the narrator and his conspiratorial reader, with whom he shares literary and cultural references from the francophone world, while *Hermina*[23], replete with references to world and Latin American literature, makes recourse to collage, quotations and the dramatisation of the critic as reflected by his subtle comparatist interpretation of the writings of the Mauritian Ananda Devi. By contrast, *La fête des masques*[24] (The Masked Ball) is populated with gay literary figures and is set to the memorable musical rhythm of *Memoirs of Hadrian*[25], which describes the divine emperor inconsolable at the disappearance of Antinous. Meanwhile, Alain Mabanckou (finalist for the Renaudot Award 2005) produces *Verre Cassé*[26] (Broken Glass), a delicious short comedy that is becoming a jubilant anthology of world literature. Albeit rapid and superficial, these portraits nevertheless demonstrate that African writers reveal, time and again, the following truth: that literature breeds literature, because, where art is concerned, genealogies are all too improbable. This almost sick obsession with using intertextuality to get a foothold in world literature has several explanations: criticism of a certain type of critic, who often only advocates cultural and political readings of francophone African literature; the probable technical pirouette of writers trying to avoid the hard test of creating lifelike characters and a good story; and the genuine rootless sensation experienced by these young African writers, most of them having been born following independence and having studied in the west. No longer at ease in either their native or adopted country, these seek refuge in literature, their only homeland, even if they occasionally produce disembodied works. Moreover, their ambiguous engagement with western readers, in reality their only audience, consciously or subconsciously conditions the way they write. This is one of the theses explored by the South African writer J. M. Coetzee in his latest novel, *Elizabeth Costello*, whose eponymous heroine says: "The English

[21] Abdourahman A. Waberi, *Cahier nomade*, Serpents à plumes, 1994.

[22] Sami Tchak, *Place des fêtes*, Gallimard, 2000.

[23] Sami Tchak, *Hermina*, Gallimard, 2003.

[24] Sami Tchak, *La fête des masques*, 2004.

[25] Marguerite Yourcenar, *Memoirs of Hadrian*, first translated from the French by Grace Flick in collaboration with the author, Farrar, Strauss and Giroux, 1963.

[26] Alain Mabanckou, *Verre cassé*, Seuil, 2005.

novel is written in the first place by English people for English people. That is what makes it the English novel. The Russian novel is written by Russians for Russians. But the African novel is not written by Africans for Africans. African novelists may write about Africa, about African experiences, but they seem to me to be glancing over their shoulder all the time they write, at the foreigners who will read them. Whether they like it or not, they have accepted the role of interpreter, interpreting Africa to their readers. Yet how can you explore a world in all its depth if you are having to explain it to outsiders?"[27]

At the centre of extroversion

All of this illustrates what the Beninese philosopher Paulin J. Houtondji calls Africa's extroversion. Approaching the issue from an anthropological and historical perspective, he argues that African discourse does not exercise the same influence on African society as western discourse does on western society. In his opinion, within the international framework of knowledge production, Africans are directly descended from the old colonial informer, nowadays occupying an intermediate position and serving as a liaison between the illiterate or semi-illiterate informers and western anthropologists. For intellectual activity in the third world in general, and in Africa in particular, is characterised by a type of dependence not unlike economic dependence. Paulin Houtondji concludes from this parallelism between economic production and intellectual production that all African intellectual production is not only characterised by a theoretical void but also functions as a product for export. He goes on to argue that "this is not only the case of philosophical production: all African scientific and theoretical production is read more outside than inside Africa. All African literature in French, English or Portuguese serves as a product for export, just like, in different ways, airport art... To a certain extent, discourse adapts to its target audience."[28]

This extroversion is not only inherent to literary production but is a permanent element of art in general. This is best illustrated in the article *Africains sur le marché mondial de l'art* (Africans in the global art market) by the art critic Yacouba Konaté. When journalists commented that most of the participating companies at the Market for African Performing Arts (MASA, in its French initials) played to virtually empty houses, the director replied, "It doesn't matter if there are only twenty people in the audience. If there's a promoter amongst them willing to sign a contract with a company, MASA will have achieved its goal."[29] Controversial at the time and still the subject of hot debate, there is nevertheless much common sense in this response. But instead of praising the MASA director's shrewd insight and entering the debate about extroversion, African audiences, journalists and artists tend to hide behind nationalist sentiments. And yet, this extroversion clearly goes some way to explaining the obsessive quest for identity, the evidence of the split-personality syndrome and the self-justification strategies that underpin contemporary African artistic production, etc. In her diptych *Burn out country*

[27] J.M. Coetzee, *Elizabeth Costello: Eight Lessons*, South Africa, 2003.

[28] Paulin J. Houtondji, *Combats pour le sens, un itinéraire africain*, Foreword by Souleymane Bachir Ndiaye, Édition du Flamboyant, 1997.

[29] Moussa Konaté, *Esprit*, August-September 2005, p. 93.

/bright dark (colour photograph, 2001), the German-Kenyan artist Ingrid Mwangui presents two shots, identical yet different, of the same part of her body, her belly. Ingrid Mwangui uses inversion to represent herself as coloured in Germany and white in Africa, skilfully employing a binary negative/positive effect to focus the spotlight on mixed breeding, with all the ambiguity it implies.

Miscegenation, miscegenations

Discernible at the centre of the diptych is an indelible birthmark on the belly, the place where life develops and the search for self-identity stems, to borrow the expression of the Congolese poet Tchicaya U Tam Si[30]. If Ingrid Mwangui meditates on her biological identity, Zoulikha Bouabdellah questions her dual French-Algerian identity in her video installation *Dansons* (Dance, 2003): on the screen, an oriental body reduced to a pair of swaying hips is wrapped in a cloth with the colours of the French flag and dances to the tune of *La Marseillaise*. But unlike Ingrid Mwangui's diptych, here the body is not used as a physical criterion for indicating origins but in terms of an action associated with specific cultural references. It replaces the "*marchons, marchons*" (Let us march, let us march) of the refrain from the French national anthem with "*dansons, dansons*" (Let us dance, let us dance). Instead of the brusque, linear military march that characterises *La Marseillaise*, the hips sway to the beat of oriental music. Here, dance symbolises both the movement and the connections between the different communities. Gainsbourg's reggae version of *La Marseillaise* inevitably springs to mind. This subversion is also present in the work of Chéri Samba, albeit from a more insolent, radical perspective.

Unlike most African artists, who tie themselves in knots trying to justify or define themselves, Chéri Samba explores the situation of African artists on the international scene. In my work *Désir d'Afrique* [31] (Longing for Africa), I have tried to explain how Chéri Samba uses pictorial strategies, occasionally naively, to attack the art market from a socio-political point of view. If his works are purchased by western institutions (museums, galleries, collectors), can Chéri Samba still be regarded as an African painter? This is the question formulated by his paintings *Pourquoi ai-je signé un contrat* ? (Why did I sign a contract?, 1990) and *Une peinture à défendre* (A Painting to defend, 1993). Are we purchasing a work of art or the work of an African? Why defend the painting of Chéri Samba? By raising all these questions, the Congolese painter mocks and dramatises his dependence, establishing an ambiguity between auto-exoticism and ironic meditation. The text that is always present in his paintings, generating a reciprocal communication between image and comment, between universal artistic language and local tongue (Lingala), enables Chéri Samba to deliberately confuse viewers' interpretations and appraisals. He asserts the legacy of the western self-portrait tradition but adds a local touch, a type of nod at his compatriots, as a means of establishing where he belongs. African literature also reveals the same strategies of avoidance and integration with the global art

[30] Tchicaya U Tam'Si, *Le Ventre, le pain ou la cendre*, Présence Africaine, 1978.

[31] Boniface Mongo-Mboussa, *Désir d'Afrique*, Gallimard, 2001.

market, the same interrogations about identity. In fact, African novelists echo the three types of quest we have just examined.

The miscegenation issue, for a long time largely ignored in African literature, emerged in the 1990s in the novel *Le Chercheur d'Afriques*[32] (The Seeker of Africas) by the Congolese writer Henri Lopes. The work narrates the journey of André Leclerc, a young French-Congolese man who travels to France in search of his father. Once there, he is confronted with several initiation tests: a showdown with his father, Dr. Leclerc, at the latter's surgery, resulting in the death of Leclerc Snr.; an incestuous encounter with his half-sister Fleur… The whole novel is a parody of the myths about miscegenation, extended here to encompass creolisation. The plural of the title, Africas, is a reference to Africa's contribution to music, in contact with the American continent, to film and to historical violence. However, of all the African writers interested in the issue of miscegenation, the French-Senegalese historian Sylvie Kandé particularly stands out. She adopts a highly original approach to miscegenation, beginning with her doctoral thesis on the architecture of Sierra Leone, where she examines the development of a Creole society in the country and raises crucial questions concerning the African diasporas. Is return to Africa possible? If so, under what identity? Clearly, the author's sojourn in the United States has induced her to meditate deeply about this matter, and the result is the extraordinarily profound short story-poem *Lagon Lagunes*[33] (Lake, Lagoons).

Complex, opaque, baroque, *Lagon Lagunes* reconstructs the author's biographical and intellectual journey, set against the backdrop of key historical moments for Africa and its diasporas and all underpinned by awesome erudition. A genuine Borgian labyrinth, *Lagon Lagunes* exalts biological miscegenation, world literature, intertextuality and the male/female interplay, encompassing far more than the single theme of miscegenation. This may well explain why Edouard Glissant was chosen to write the afterword, because miscegenation, but not creolisation, is foreseeable: "Creolisation is the meeting of several different cultural elements in a specific place in the world, giving rise to a new and totally unforeseeable situation in relation to the sum or mere synthesis of these elements."[34] In this respect, *Lagon Lagunes* is a tale about creolisation.

In praise of subversion

The issue of dual identity, in this case cultural, is a common theme in the tales of Ahmadou Kourouma. All his work revolves around tradition and modernity. His first novel, *The Suns of Independence*[35] is situated during the transition from the old African dynasties to the new powers emerging under independence. It is precisely this tension that provides the work with its originality. Throughout the novel, the narrator underlines the equivocal relationship with the French language, using a style of expression that simulates oral discourse, superimposing the Malinke

[32] Henri Lopes, *Le Chercheur d'Afriques*, Seuil, 1990.

[33] Sylvie Kandé, *Lagon Lagunes*, Gallimard. Coll. "Continents noirs", 2000.

[34] Edouard Glissant, *Traité du Tout- Monde*, Paris, Gallimard, 1997.

[35] Ahmadou Kourouma, *The Suns of Independence*, translated from the French by Adrian Adams, 1981.

language on to French syntax. A similar style pervades his third novel, *Waiting for the Vote of the Wild Animals*[36] (1999), an epic tale of Malinke hunters revised and corrected with western novel-writing techniques. Finally, the identity issue is dealt with in *From The Belly of the Atlantic* by the Senegalese novelist Fatou Diome. Here, the split-personality syndrome is handled via a projection in space. The novel describes immigration through football. Its hero, Madické-Maldini, is obsessed with the idea of going to Europe to play alongside his idol and namesake Paolo Maldini, captain of the Squadra Azzura. The novel makes patently clear the dual identity of the hero, portraying both Senegal and France, with the backdrop of the broadcast of the European Cup creating a mirror effect between the two locales.

At a time of galloping migration and the creolisation of Africa, there is little point in examining contemporary artistic production through the prism of authenticity. As Jean-Paul Sartre famously said, existence precedes essence. This is certainly the case with creativity, whatever its nature.

[36] Translator's Note: *Waiting for the Vote of the Wild Animals*, English translation by Carrol F. Coates, 2001, published by University Press of Virginia.

Boniface Mongo-Mboussa

Ammar Bouras

Et + si aff
2004
Video projection
5' 5"

Stridences,
sangcommentaire
2001
Video projection
7' 24"

Un aller simple
2002-2003
Video projection
4' 42"

Ez-zaim, le roi est mort,
vive le roi
2001
Video installation
3' 57"

To earn my living, I worked as a press photographer while studying fine art in Algiers. My trade gave me the opportunity of travelling and exploring my country, which in turn made me eager to go just that little bit further every day. I met new people and struck up friendships with journalists and other press workers.

Since the beginning of the "events" in my country, journalists, intellectuals and anyone else who wants a life have had to keep moving from one place to another, avoid going out, never go to parties and, above all, never develop fixed customs.

You have to make sure you don't draw attention to yourself, wear smart clothes, keep your finger nails clean and tidy, and change your underwear every morning before leaving the house so as not to be ashamed before God or at the hospital.

Visiting my parents, who live in the Ouled Yaha mountains, in the east of Algeria, was a complicated matter. The only place where I knew I would be safe from falling into a trap was the south of the country, which I adopted for its beauty and the safety it offered. But I missed the mountains.

One-way only

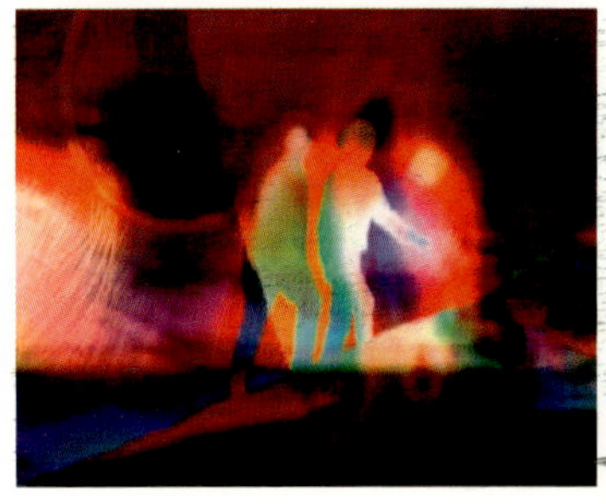

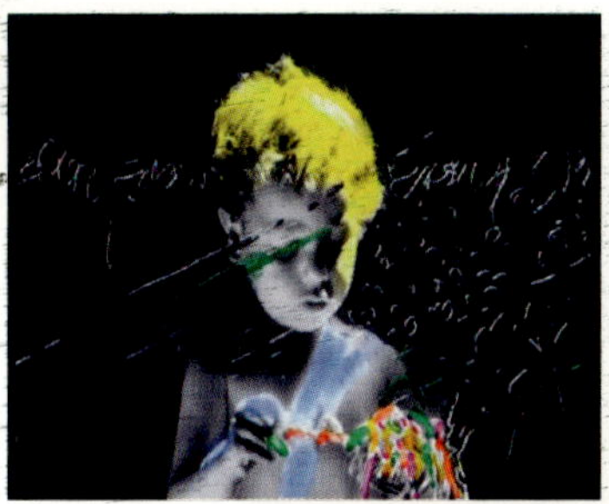

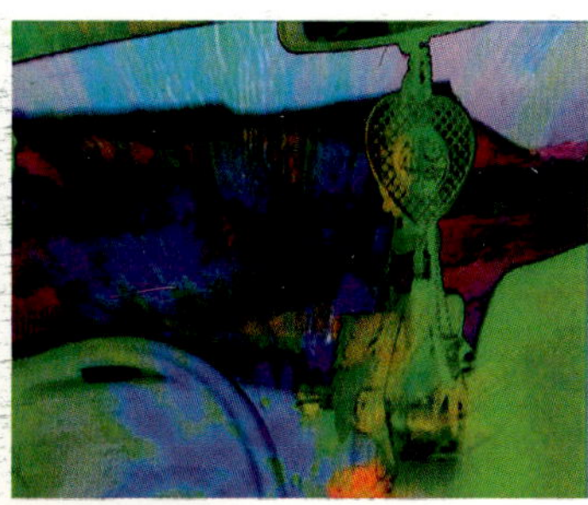

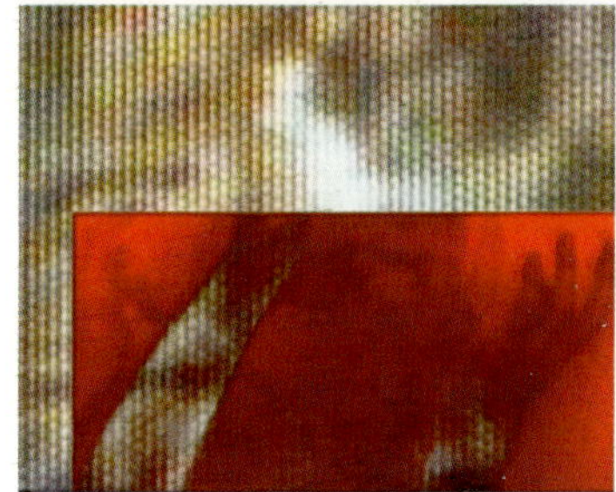

Kharja oua lem yaâoud is the title of my video in Arabic. In English, the literal translation would be something like: "He left never to return".

I chose to call it "Un aller simple" (One-way only) because it's the story of a journalist who paid for the right to express himself and live with his own life.

It's the story of a traveller who changes his place of residence and customs to erase all the traces of his former life.

It's the story of young people who spend whole nights outside consulates to apply for visas that are never granted, in the hope of being able to live somewhere else.

It's the story of the women who doll themselves up (although they don't need to) and take to the street, every single day...

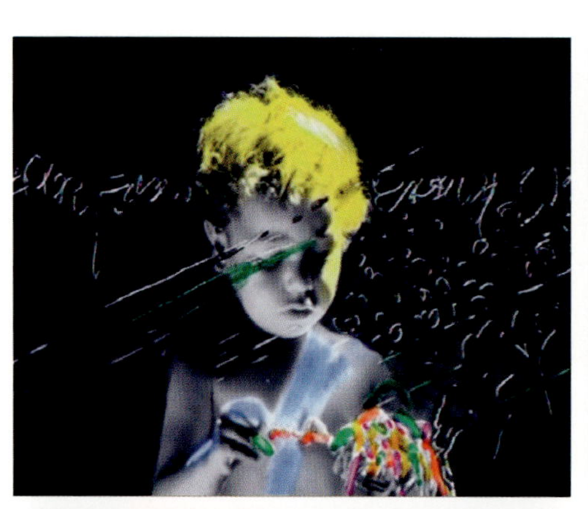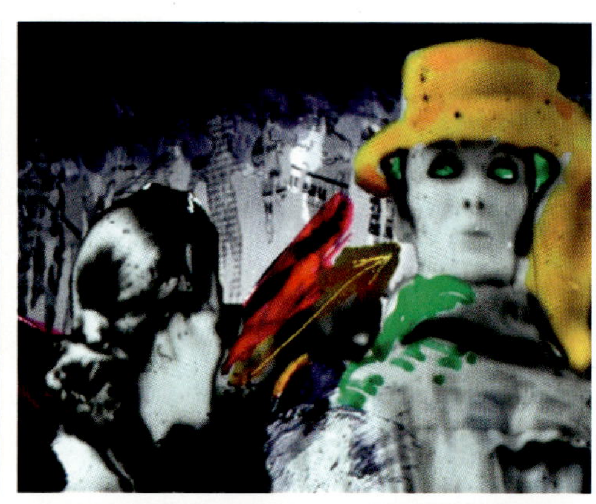
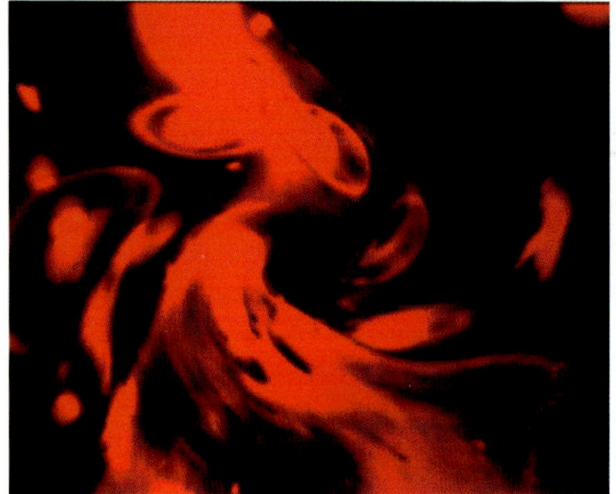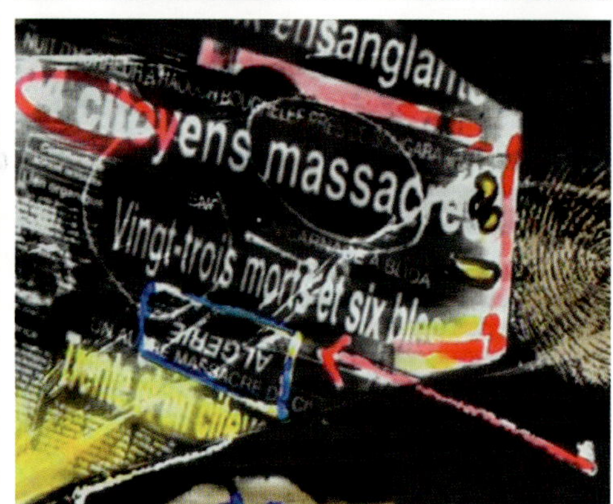

ensanglanté
4 citoyens massacrés
Vingt-trois morts et six blessés
ALGÉRIE

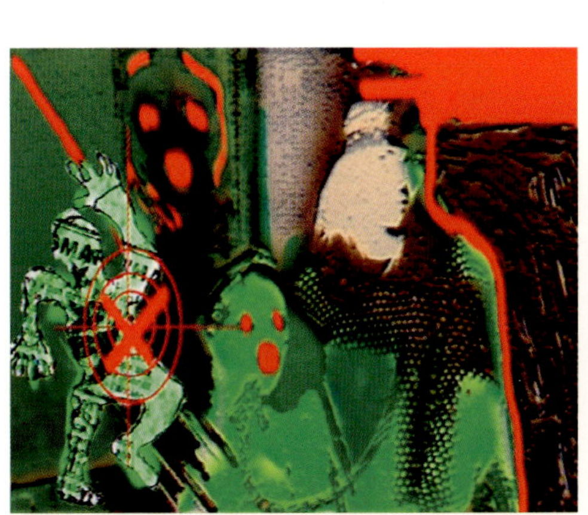
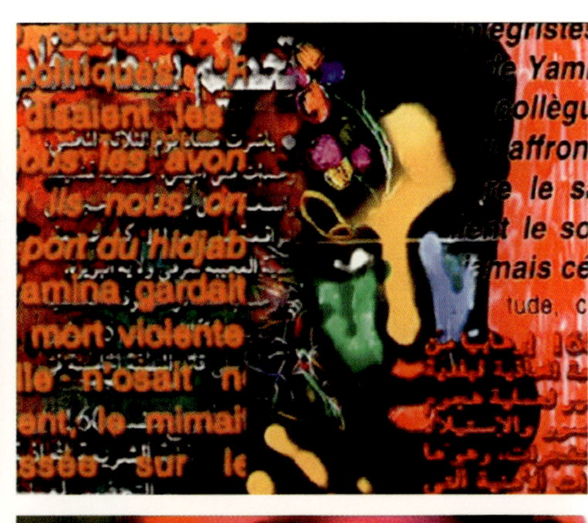
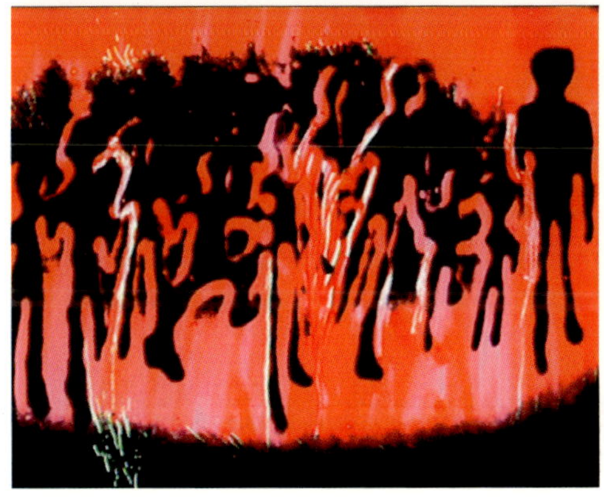
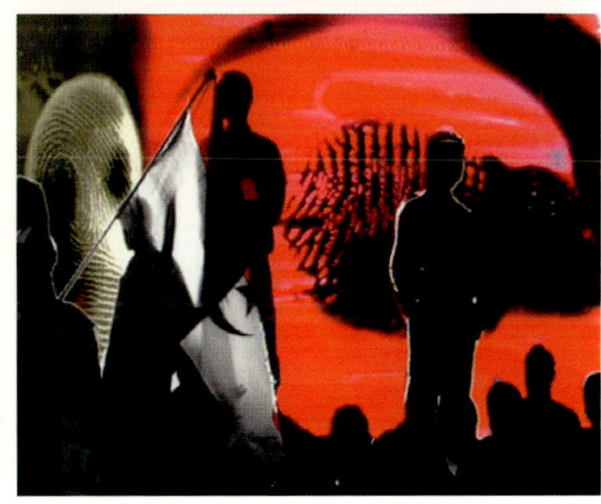

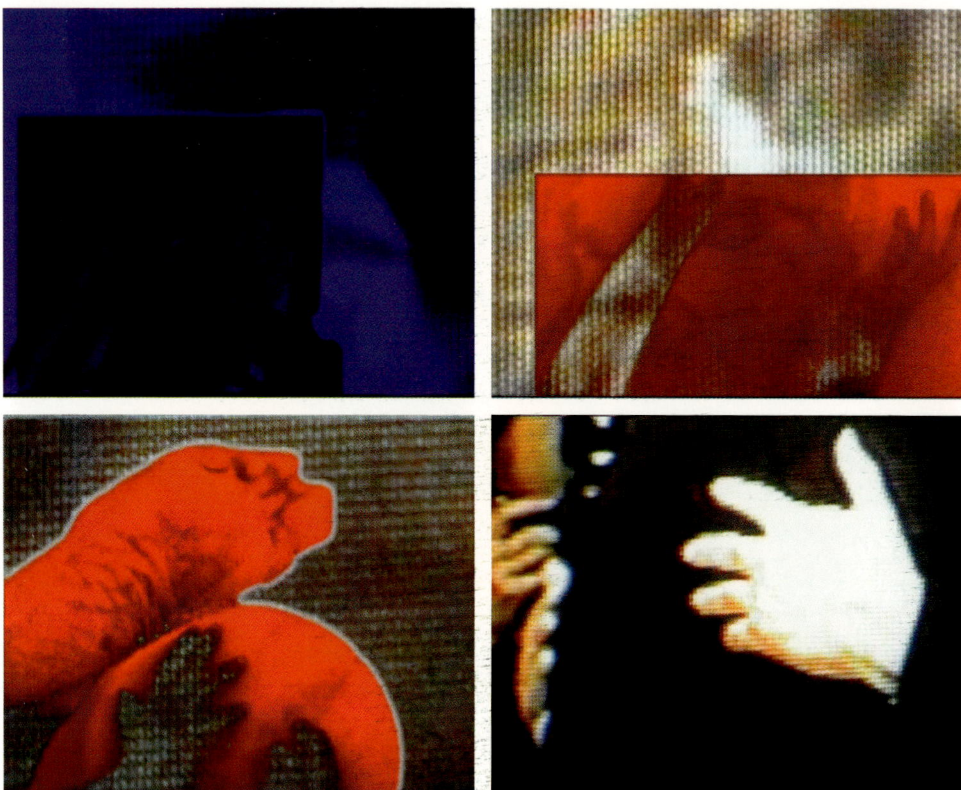

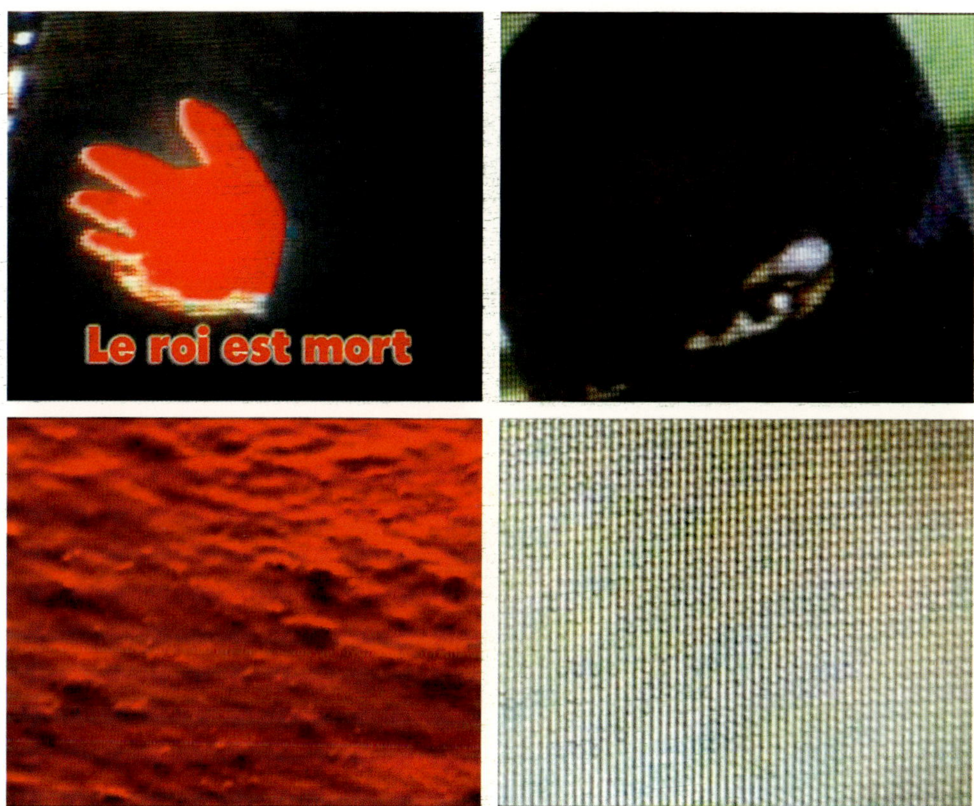
Le roi est mort

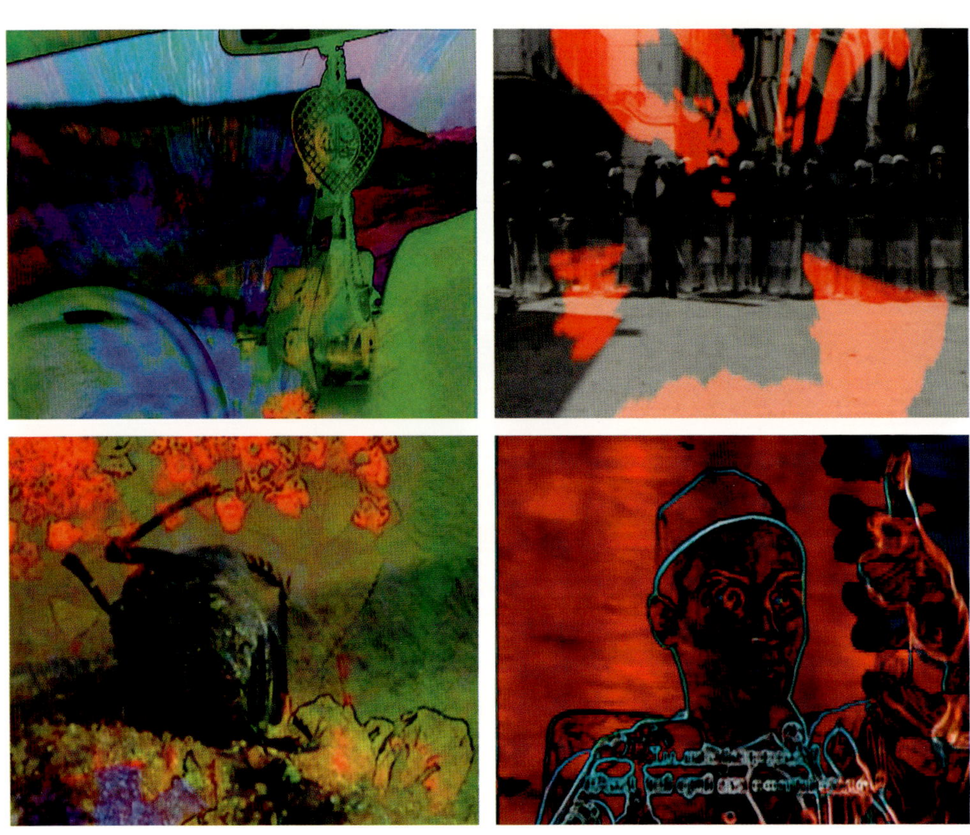

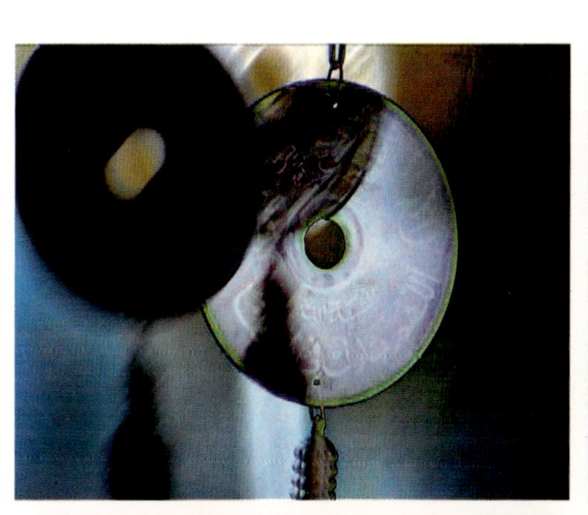

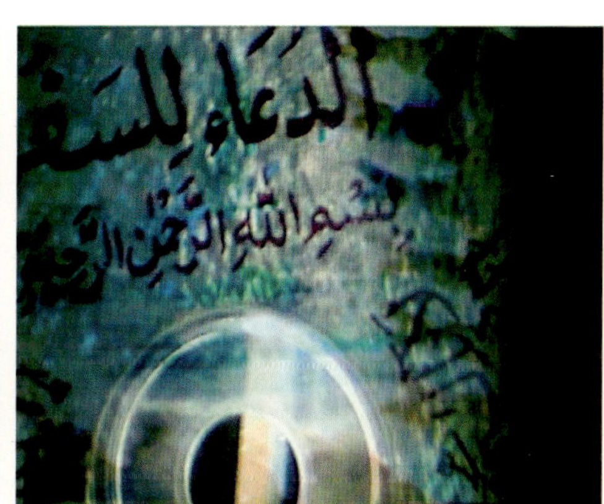
الدعاء للس
بسم الله الرحمن الرحيم

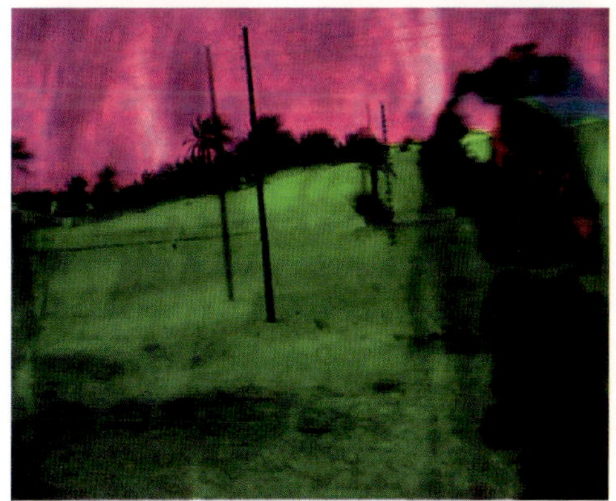

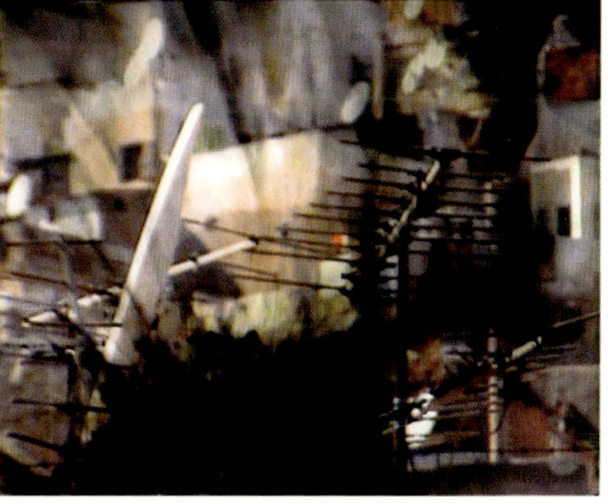

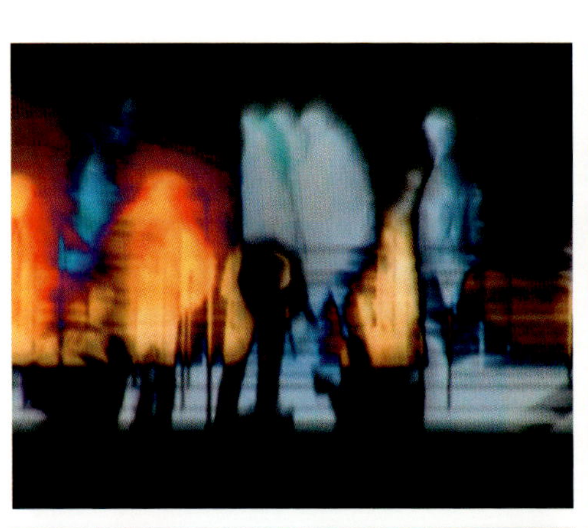
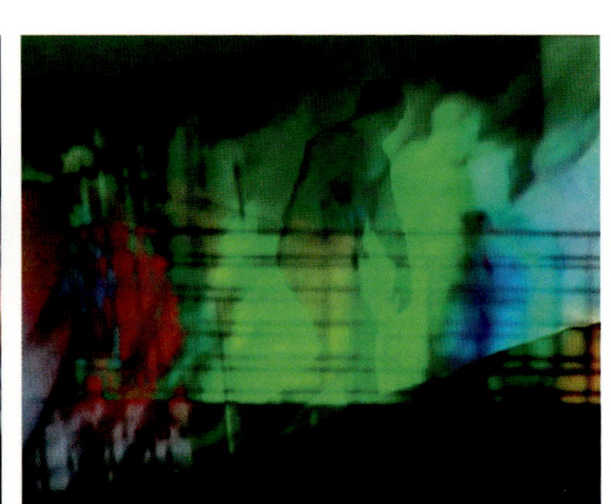
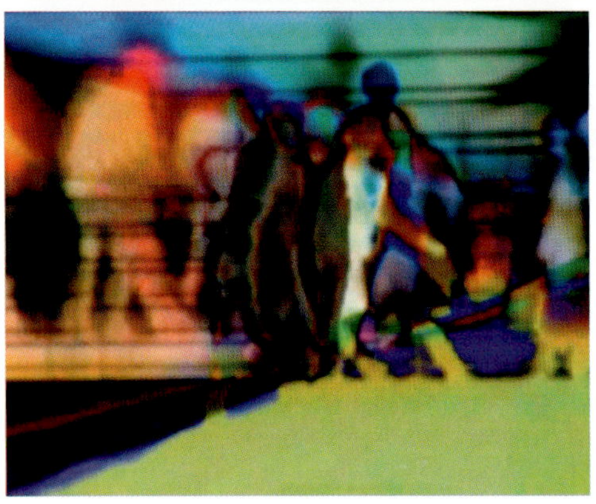
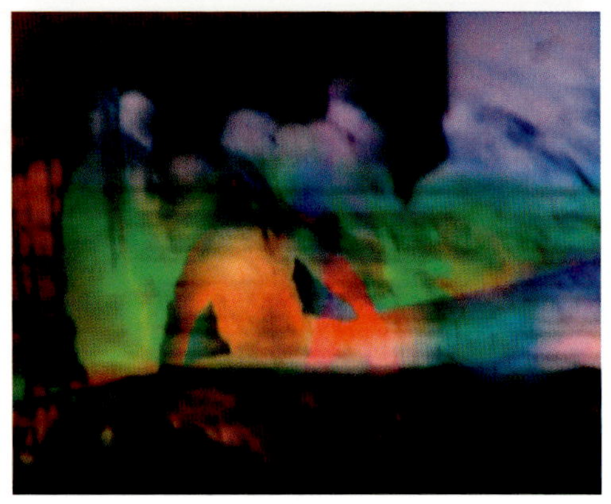

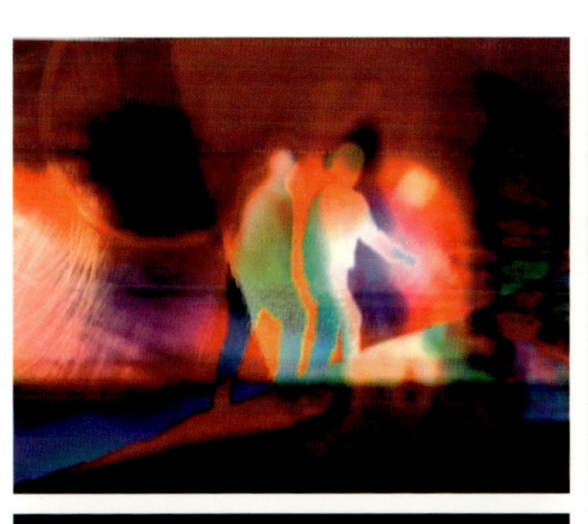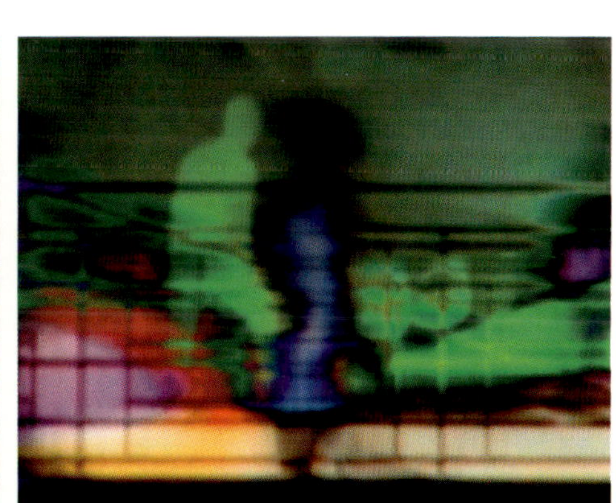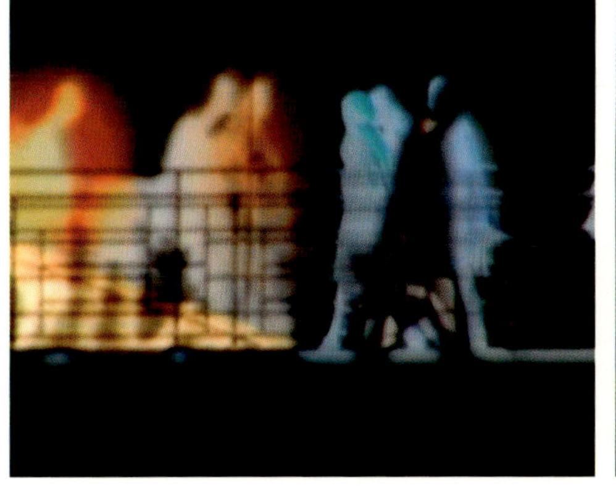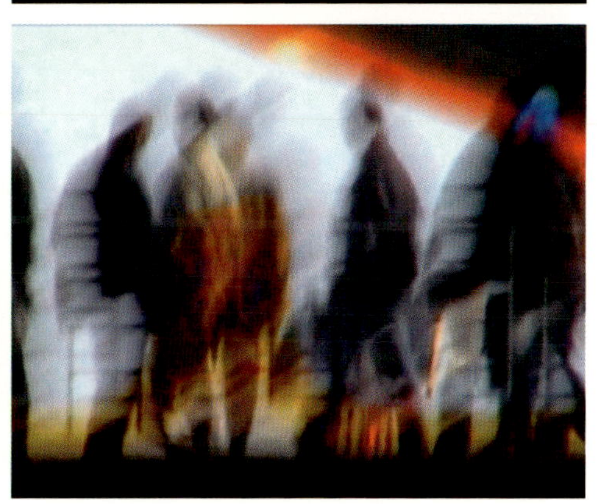

Frédéric Bruly Bouabré

Series *Connaissance
du Monde*
1981-2005
Pen and colour pencil on
cardboard
10 x 15 cm., 24 x 30 cm.
and various

"Researchers
discover also
'man'
that thinking reed."

Bruly Boaubré, catalogue of the exhibition *World Envisionned, Frédéric Bruly
Bouabré & Alighiero e Boetti*, Dia Center for the Arts, New York, United States.

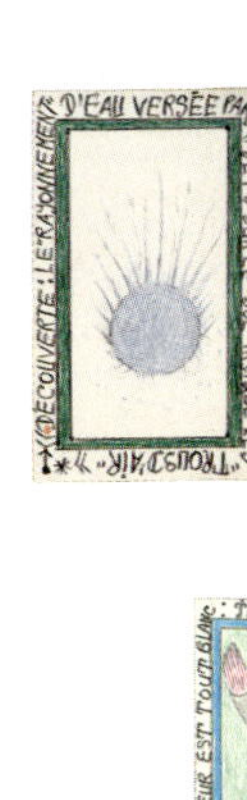
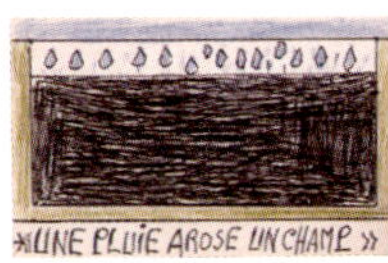
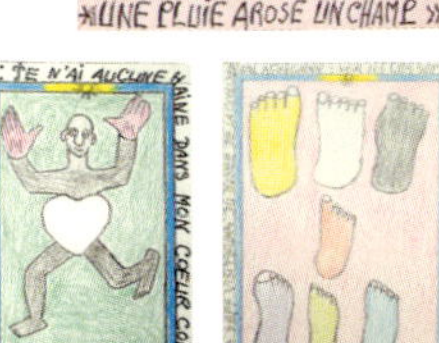
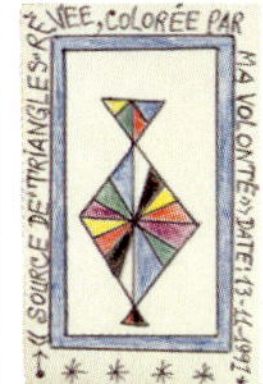
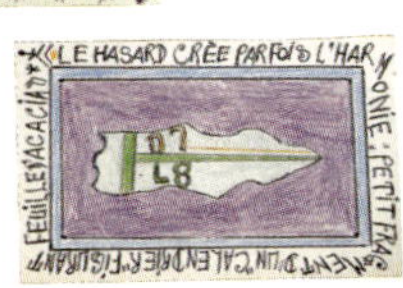
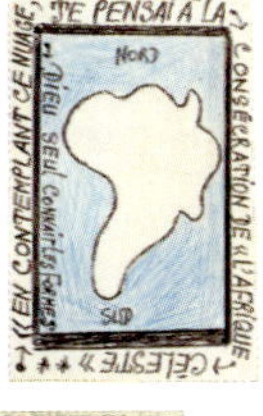
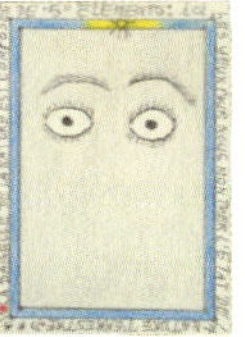
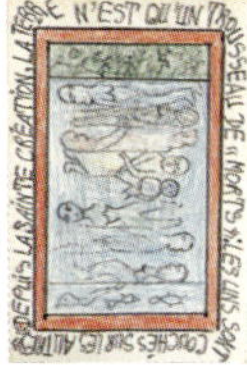
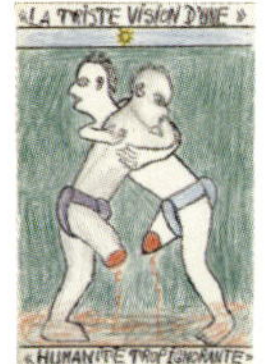
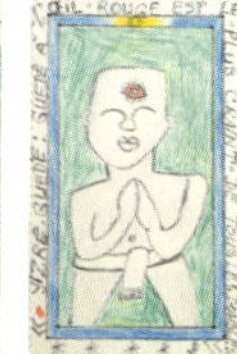
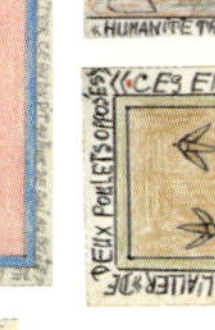
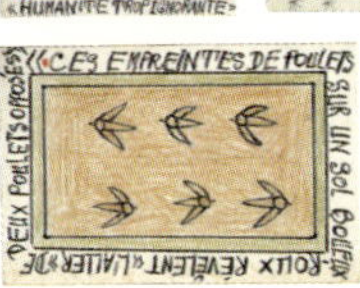
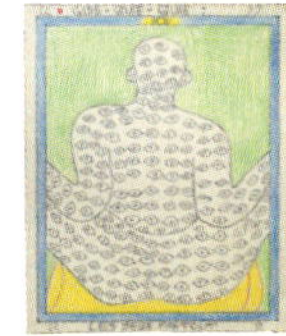
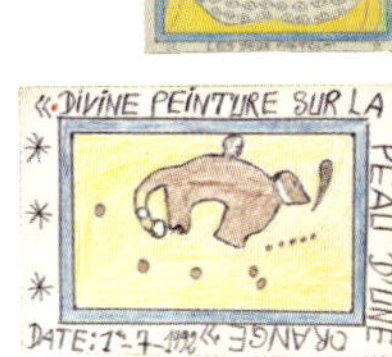
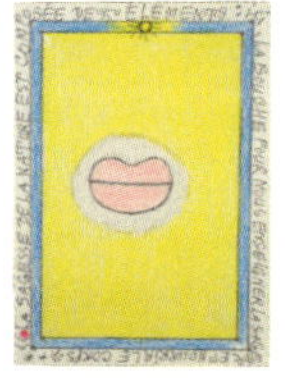
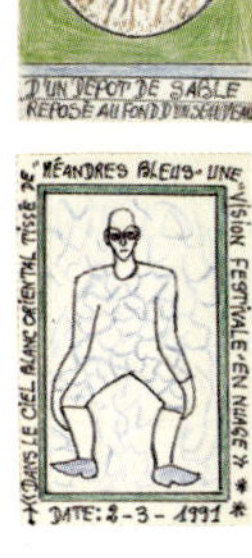
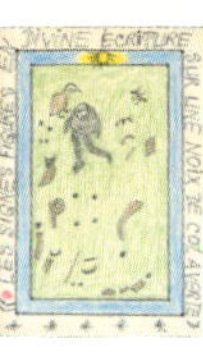

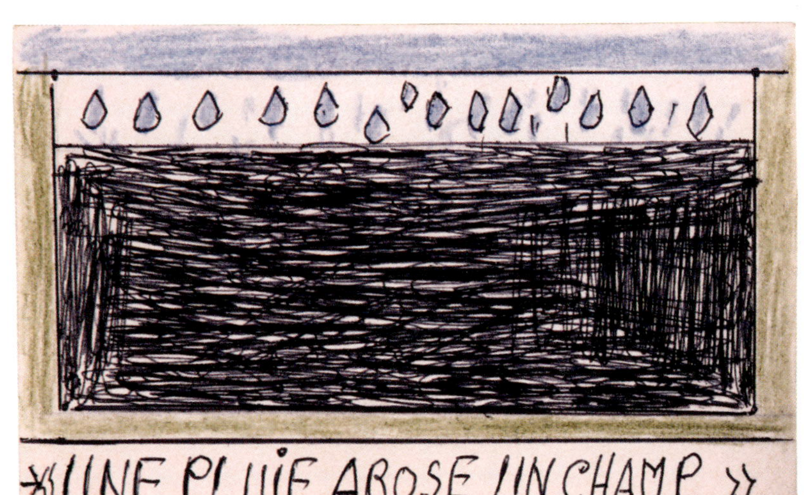

«UNE PLUIE AROSE UNCHAMP»

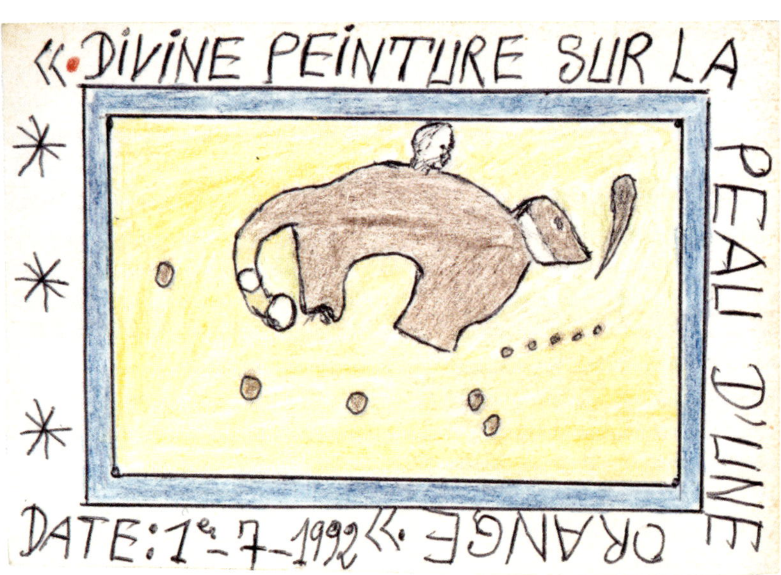

«DIVINE PEINTURE SUR LA
PEAU D'UNE
ORANGE»
DATE: 1er-7-1992

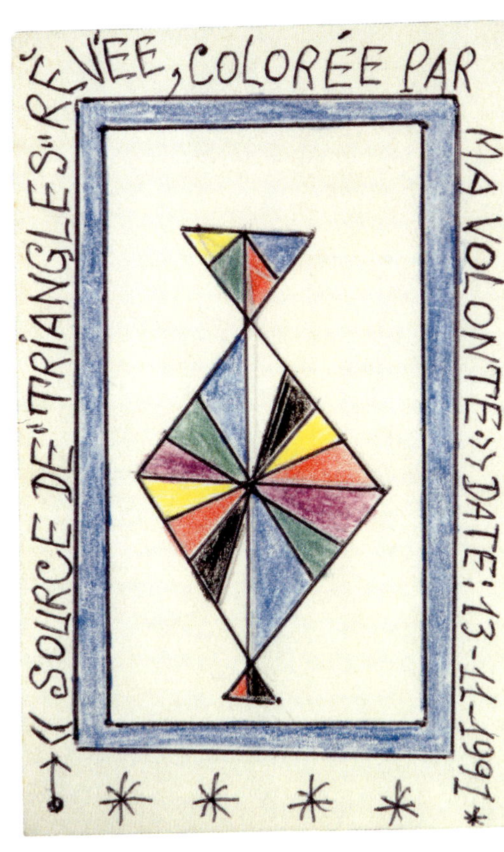

« SOURCE DE "TRIANGLES" RÊVÉE, COLORÉE PAR
MA VOLONTÉ » DATE: 13-11-1991

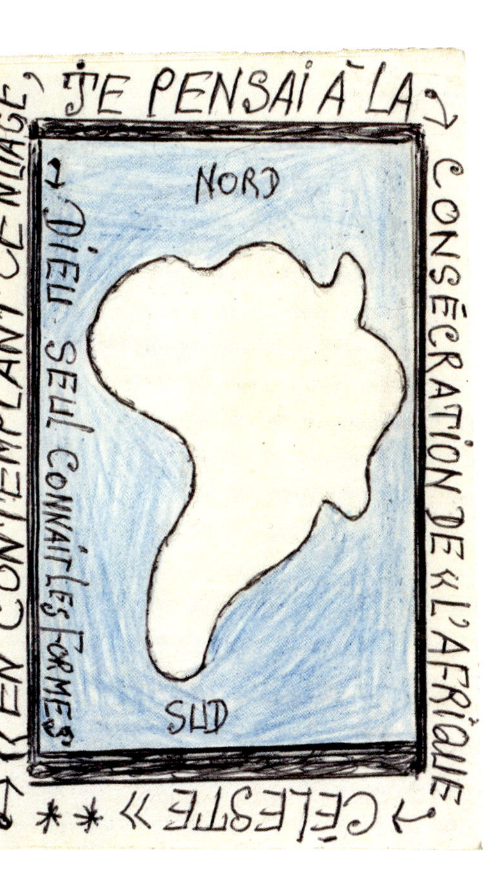

JE PENSAI À LA
EN CONTEMPLANT CE NUAGE,
CONSÉCRATION DE « L'AFRIQUE
DIEU SEUL CONNAÎT LES FORMES
NORD
SUD
CÉLESTE »

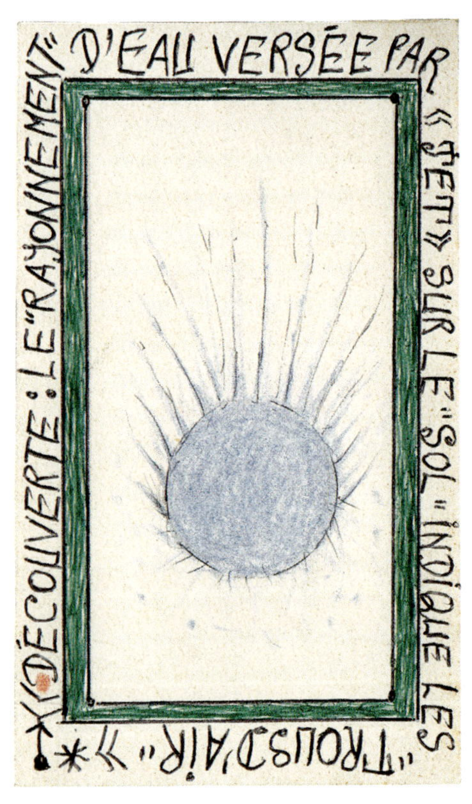
D'EAU VERSÉE PAR
« JET » SUR LE "SOL" INDIQUE LES
"TROUS D'AIR" «
« DÉCOUVERTE : LE "RAYONNEMENT"

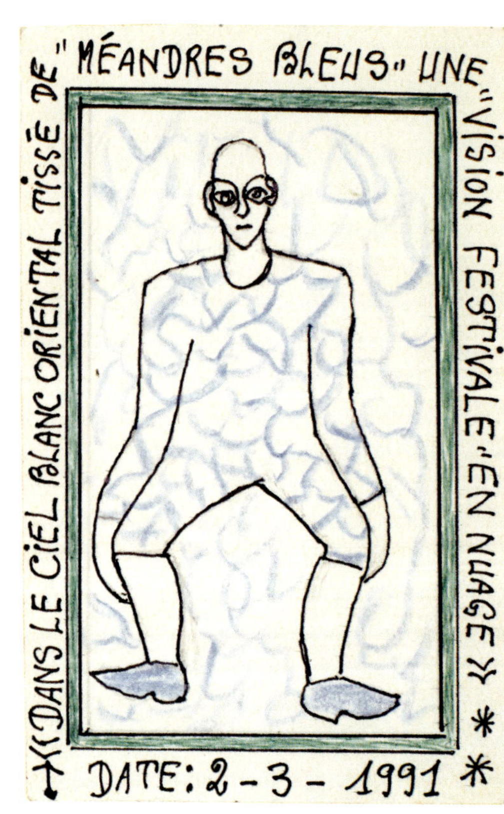
"MÉANDRES BLEUS" UNE
"VISION FESTIVALE "EN NUAGE »
DATE: 2 - 3 - 1991
« DANS LE CIEL BLANC ORIENTAL TISSÉ DE

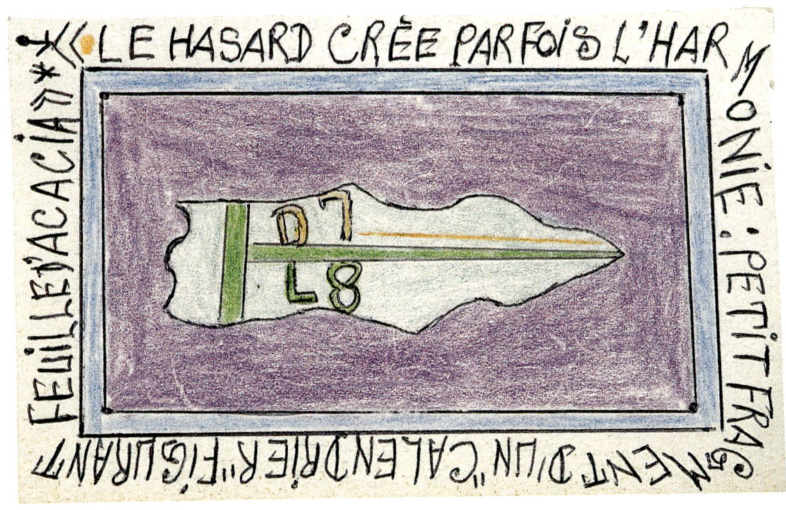

«LE HASARD CRÉE PARFOIS L'HARMONIE; PETIT FRAGMENT D'UN "CALENDRIER" FIGURANT FEUILLE D'ACACIA»
D7
L8

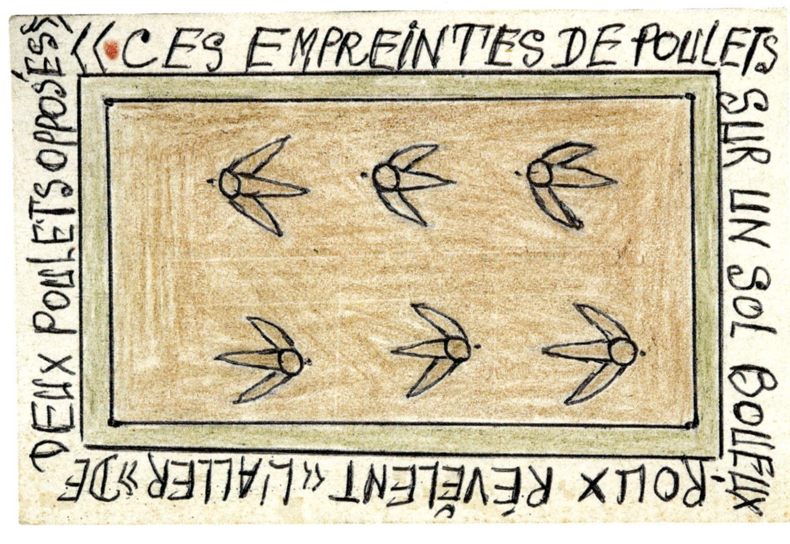

«CES EMPREINTES DE POULETS SUR UN SOL BOUEUX ROUX RÉVÈLENT "L'ALLER" DE DEUX POULETS OPPOSÉS»

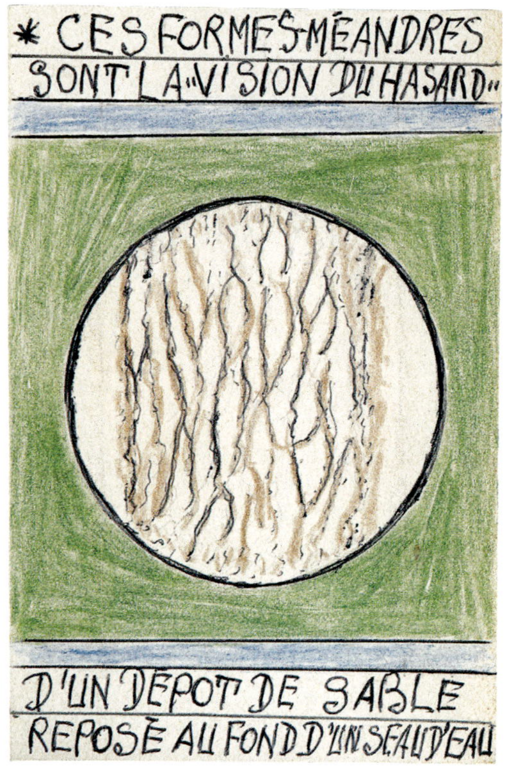
* CES FORMES-MÉANDRES
SONT LA "VISION DU HASARD"
D'UN DÉPOT DE SABLE
REPOSÉ AU FOND D'UN SEAU D'EAU

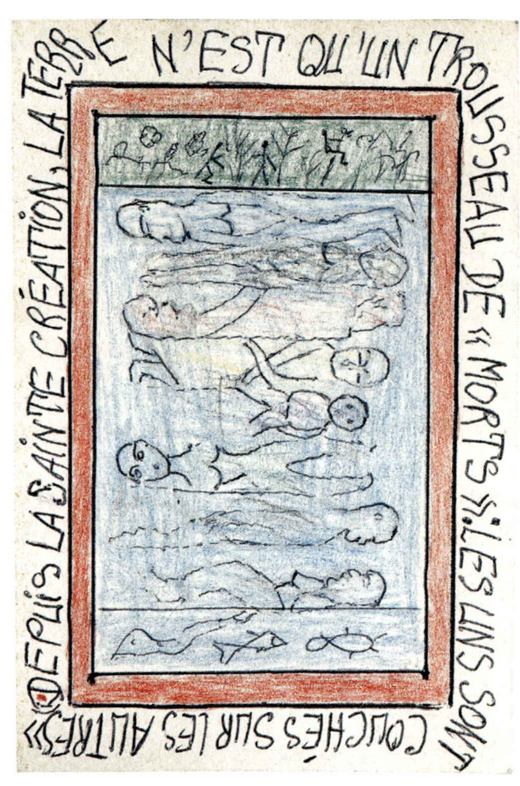
DEPUIS LA SAINTE CRÉATION, LA TERRE N'EST QU'UN TROUSSEAU DE "MORTS". LES UNS SONT COUCHÉS SUR LES AUTRES"

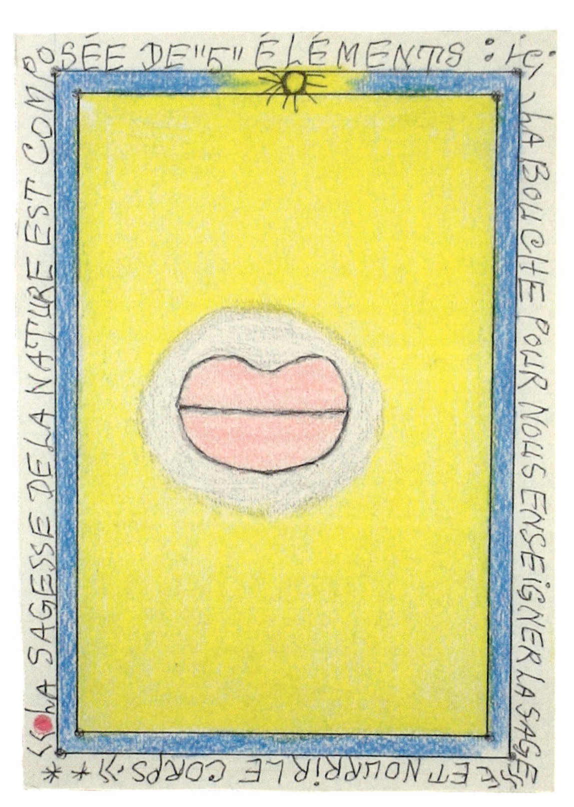
«LA SAGESSE DE LA NATURE EST COMPOSÉE DE "5" ÉLÉMENTS : ICI LA BOUCHE POUR NOUS ENSEIGNER LA SAGESSE ET NOURRIR LE CORPS.»

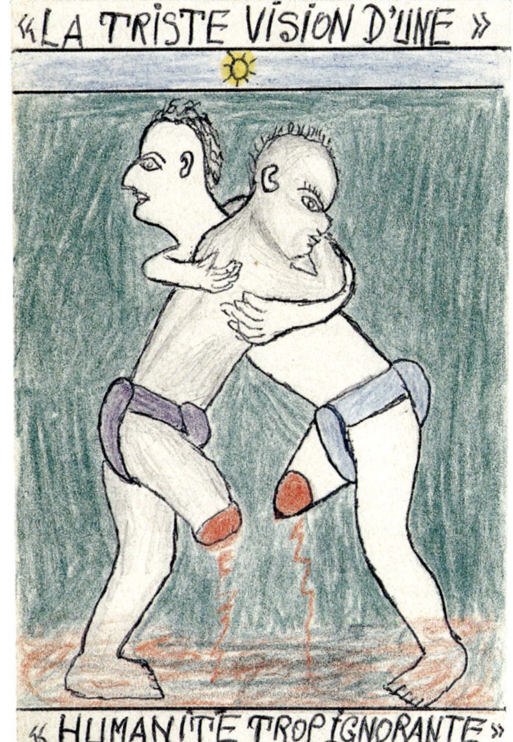
«LA TRISTE VISION D'UNE»
«HUMANITÉ TROP IGNORANTE»

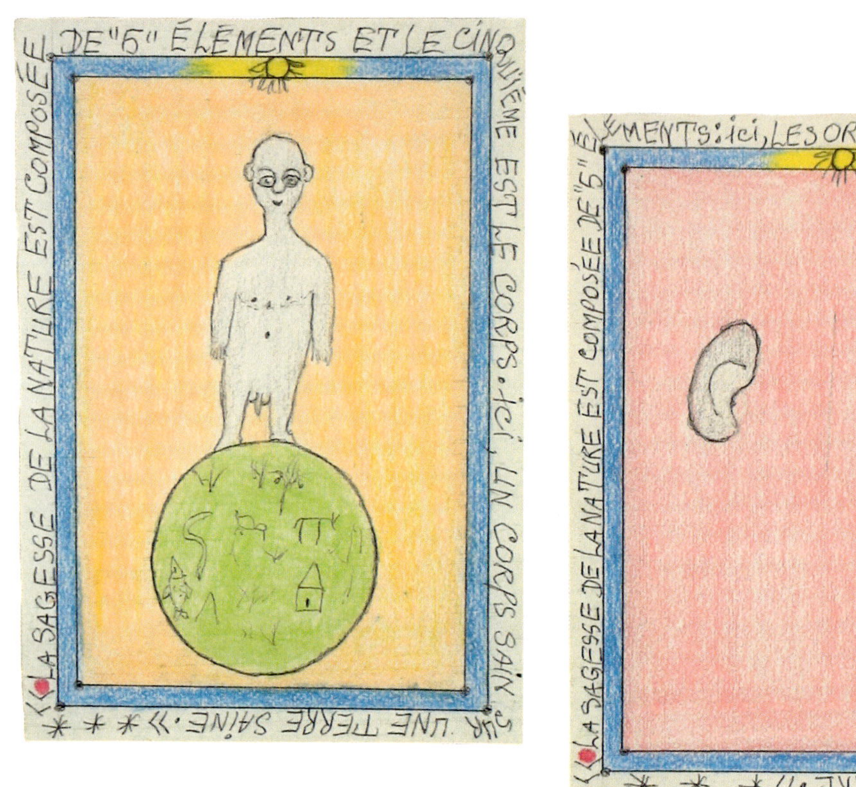

« LA SAGESSE DE LA NATURE EST COMPOSÉE DE "5" ÉLÉMENTS ET LE CINQUIÈME EST LE CORPS. ici, UN CORPS SAIN SUR UNE TERRE SAINE. »
« LA SAGESSE DE LA NATURE EST COMPOSÉE DE "5" ÉLÉMENTS: ici, LES OREILLES POUR ÉCOUTER CE QU'ON DIT AUTOUR DE SOI AU SUJET DE LA TERRE. »

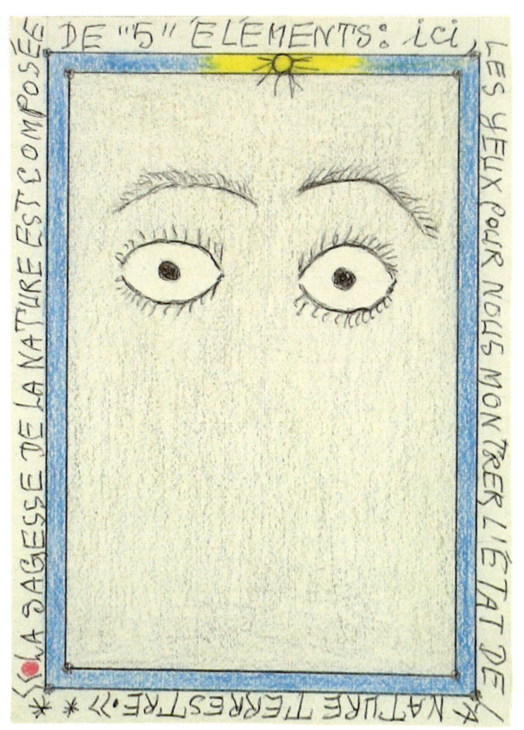
DE "5" ELEMENTS: ici
LES YEUX POUR NOUS MONTRER L'ÉTAT DE
NATURE TERRESTRE
LA SAGESSE DE LA NATURE EST COMPOSÉE

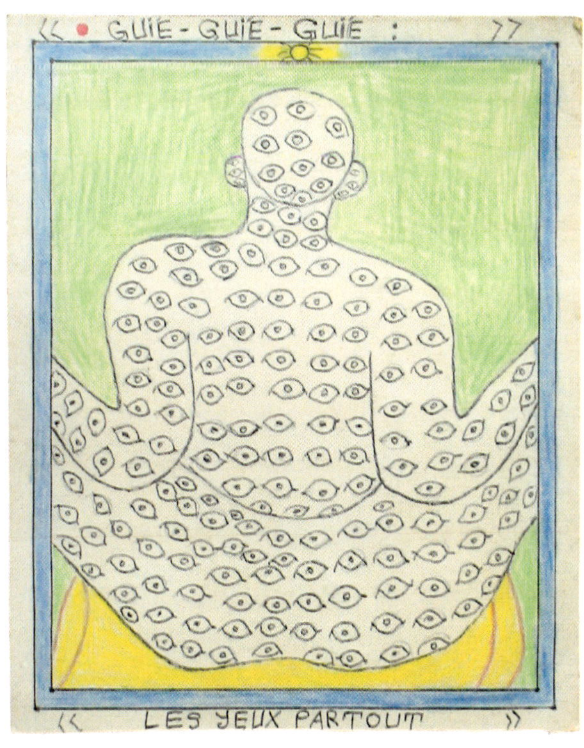
GUIE - GUIE - GUIE :
LES YEUX PARTOUT

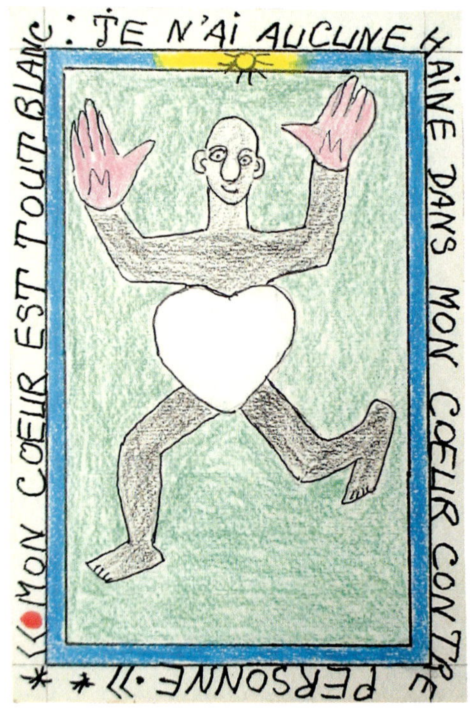
« MON CŒUR EST TOUT BLANC : JE N'AI AUCUNE HAINE DANS MON CŒUR CONTRE PERSONNE. »

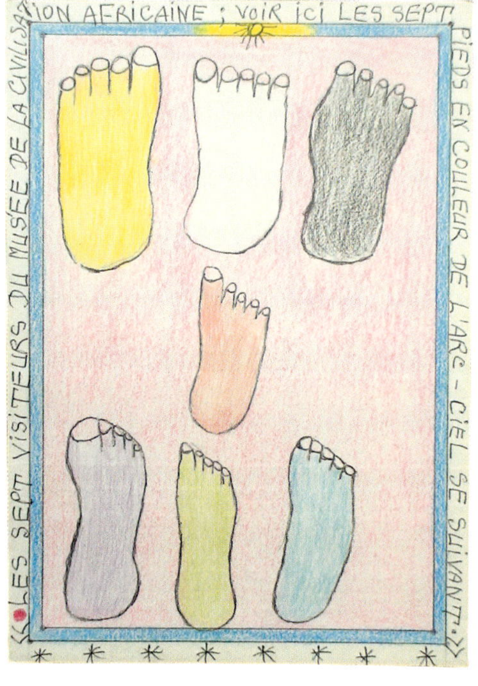
« LES SEPT VISITEURS DU MUSÉE DE LA CIVILISATION AFRICAINE ; VOIR ICI LES SEPT PIEDS EN COULEUR DE L'ARC-CIEL SE SUIVANT. »

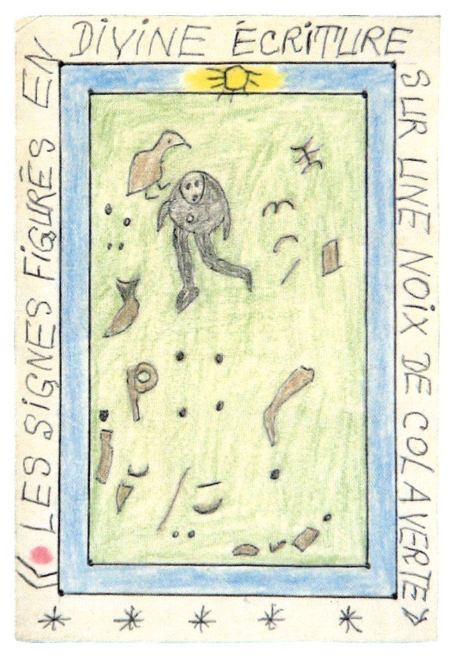

« LES SIGNES FIGURÉS EN DIVINE ÉCRITURE SUR UNE NOIX DE COLA VERTE »

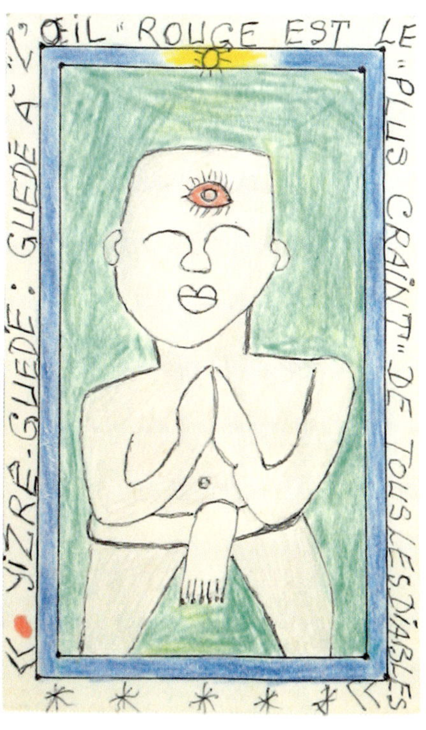

« YIZRÉ-GUEDÉ : GUEDÉ A L'ŒIL "ROUGE" EST LE "PLUS CRAINT" DE TOUS LES DIABLES »

Mbongeni Richman Buthelezi

Piano Player
2004
Melted plastic collage
120 x 60 cm.

Untitled
(People series V)
2004
Melted plastic collage
50 x 43 cm.

Jazz Musician III
2005
Melted plastic collage
200 x 250 cm.

Jazz Musician IV
2005
Melted plastic collage
200 x 250 cm.

Untitled
(People series I)
2004
Melted plastic collage
55 x 42 cm.

Untitled
(People series VI)
2004
Melted plastic collage
55 x 42 cm.

Untitled
(People series II)
2004
Melted plastic collage
50 x 43 cm.

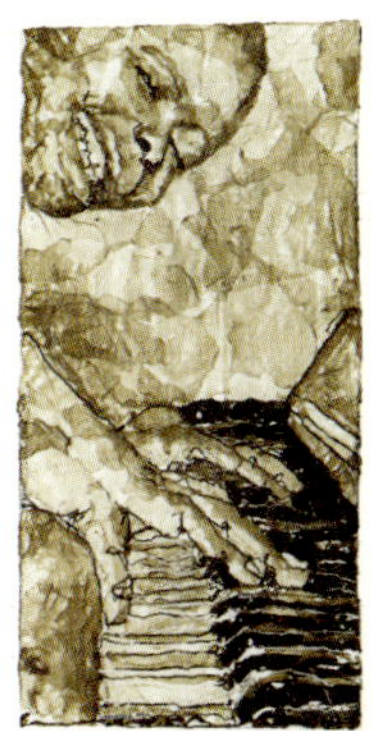
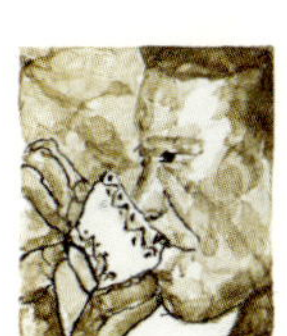
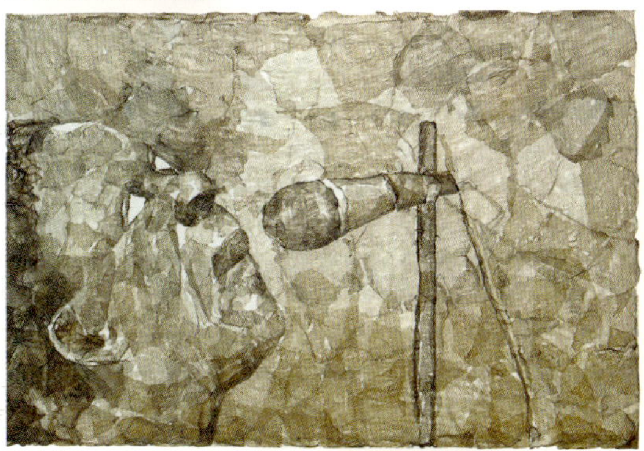
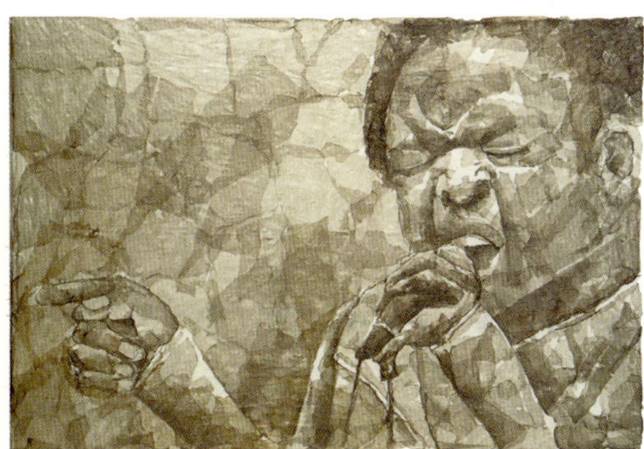
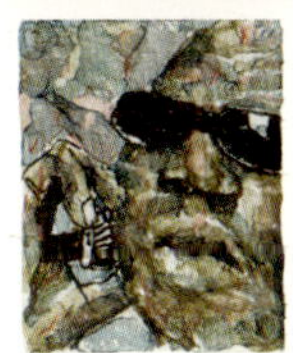
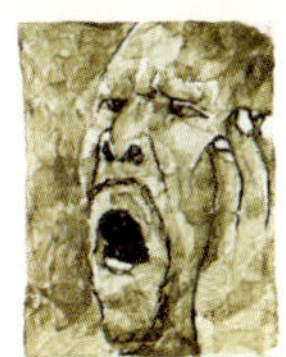
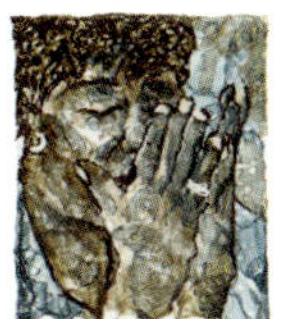

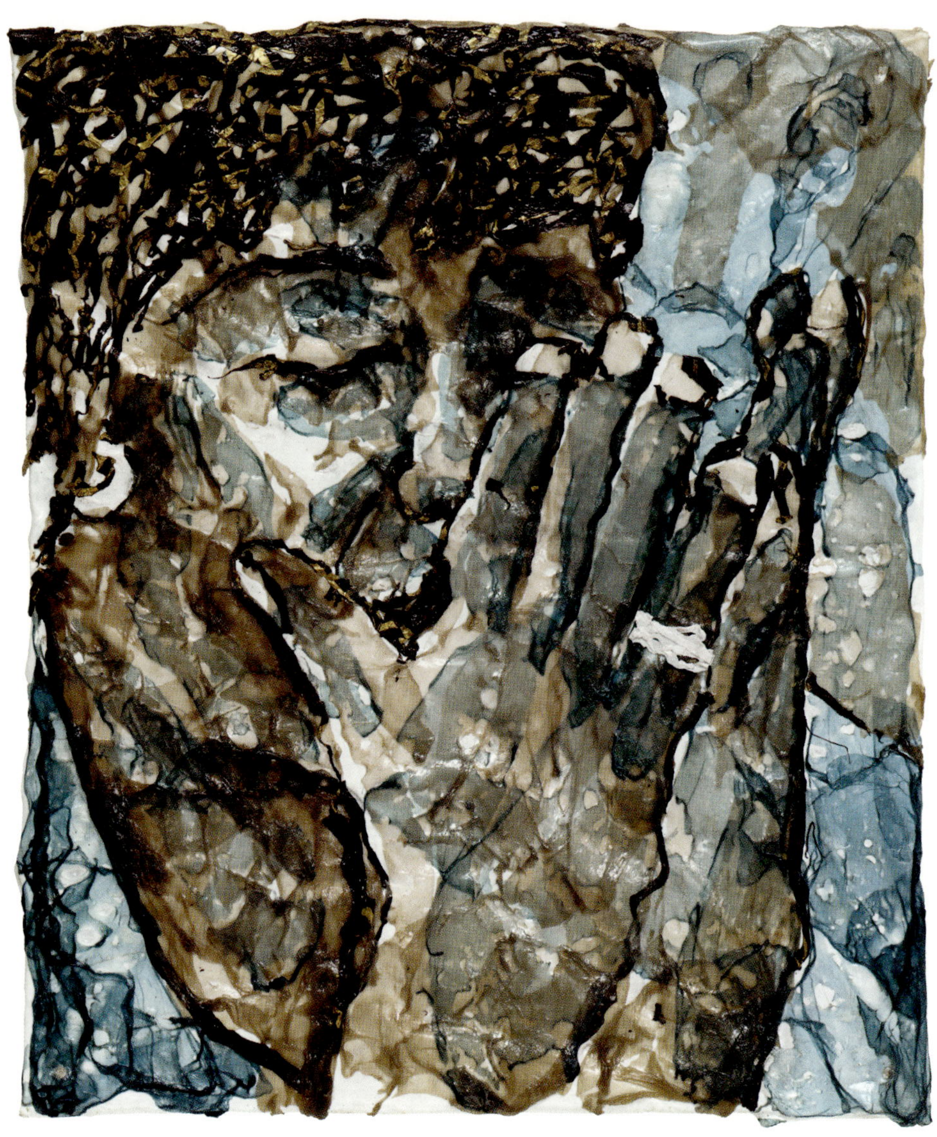

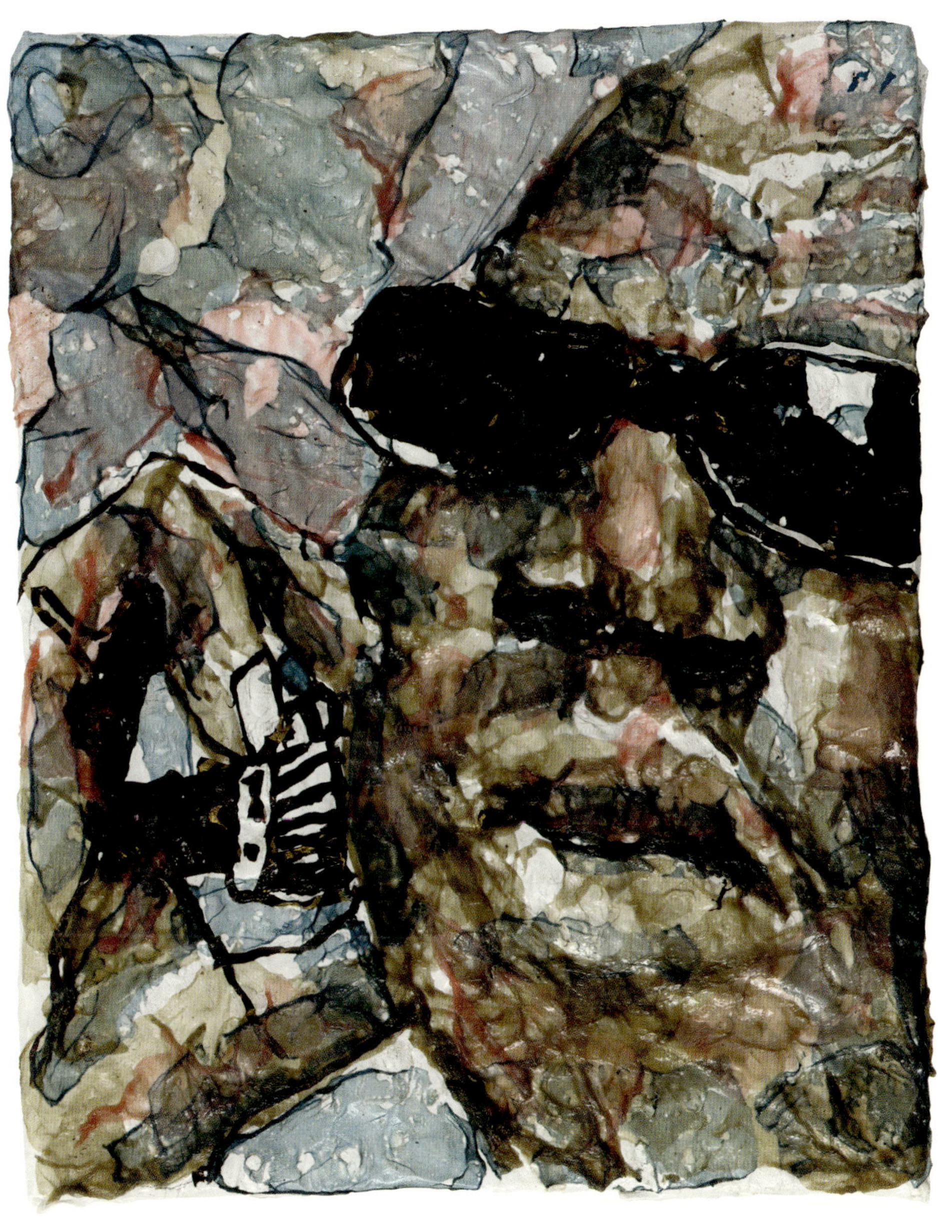

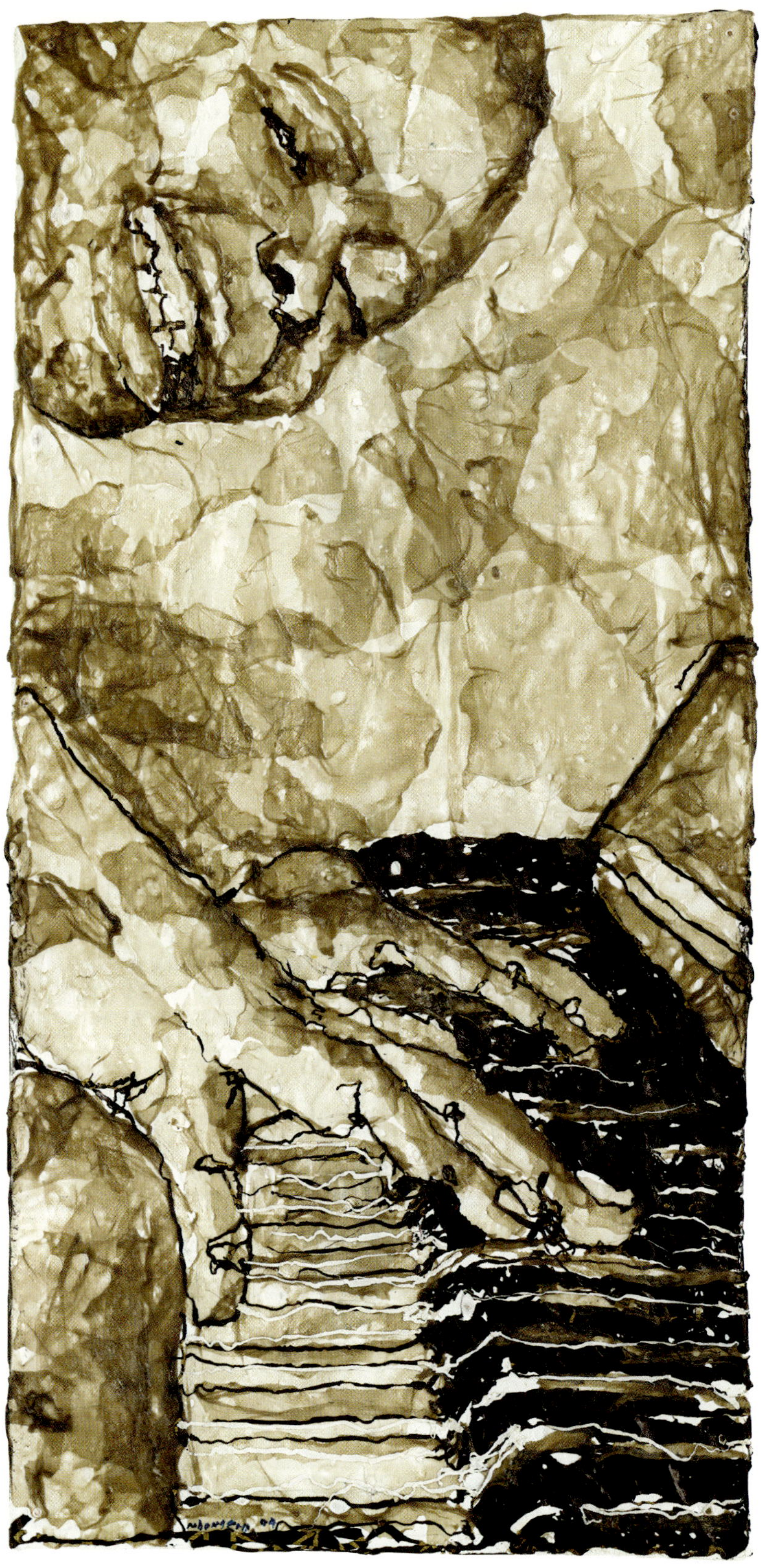

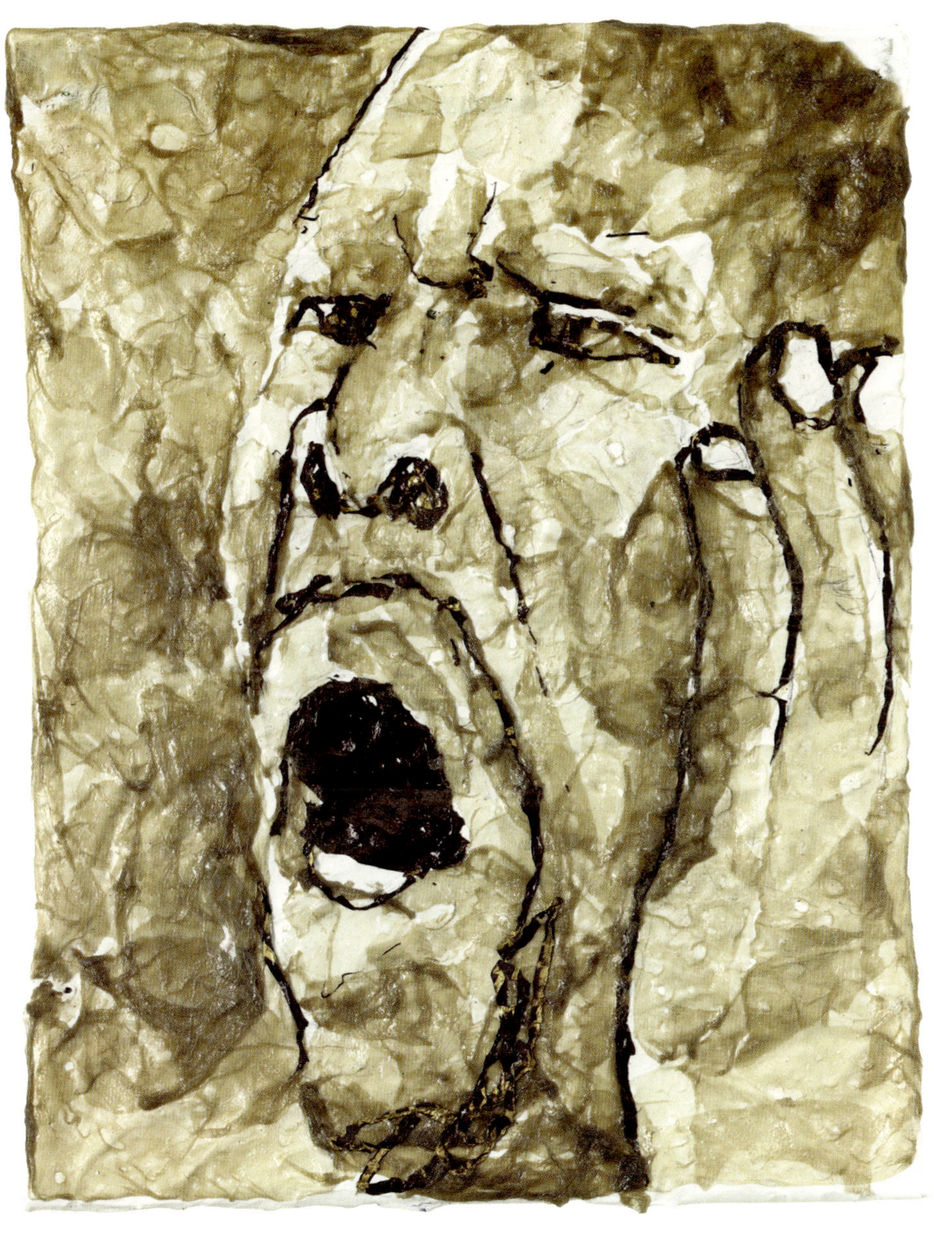

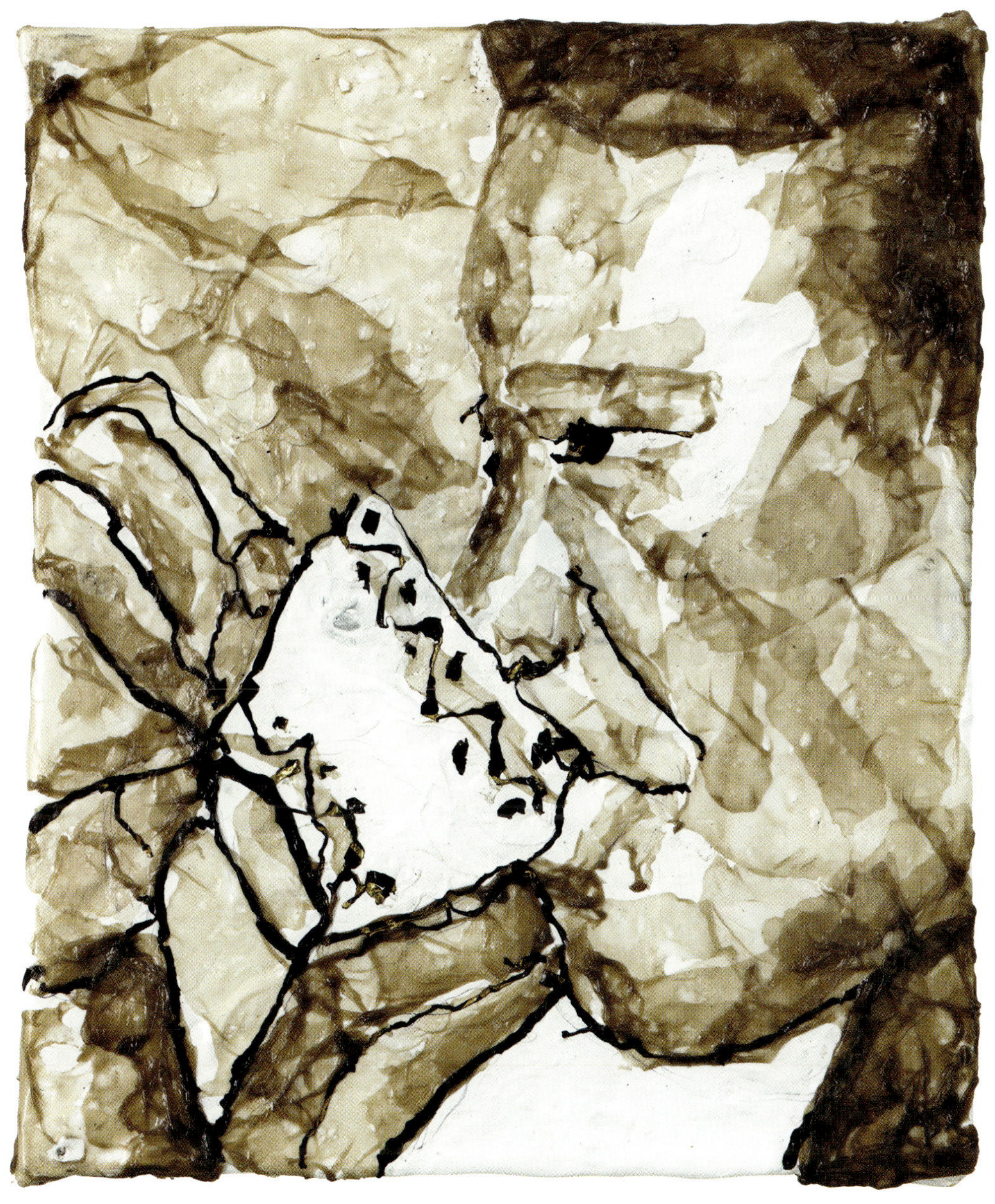

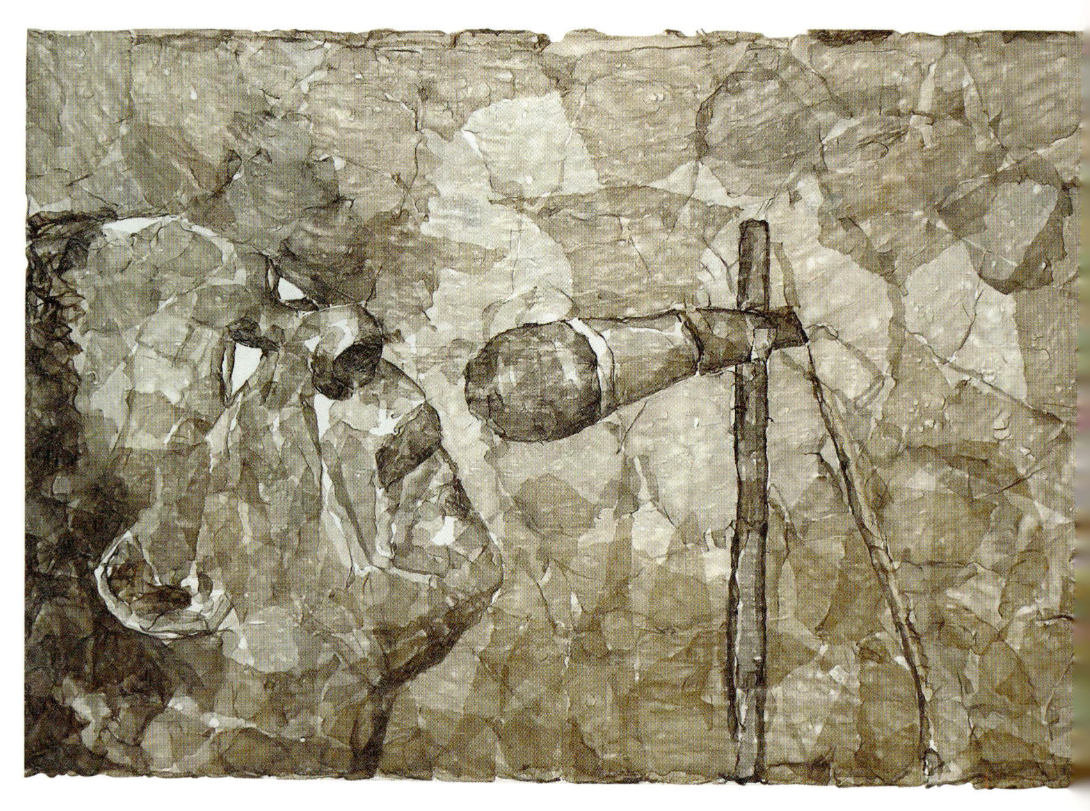

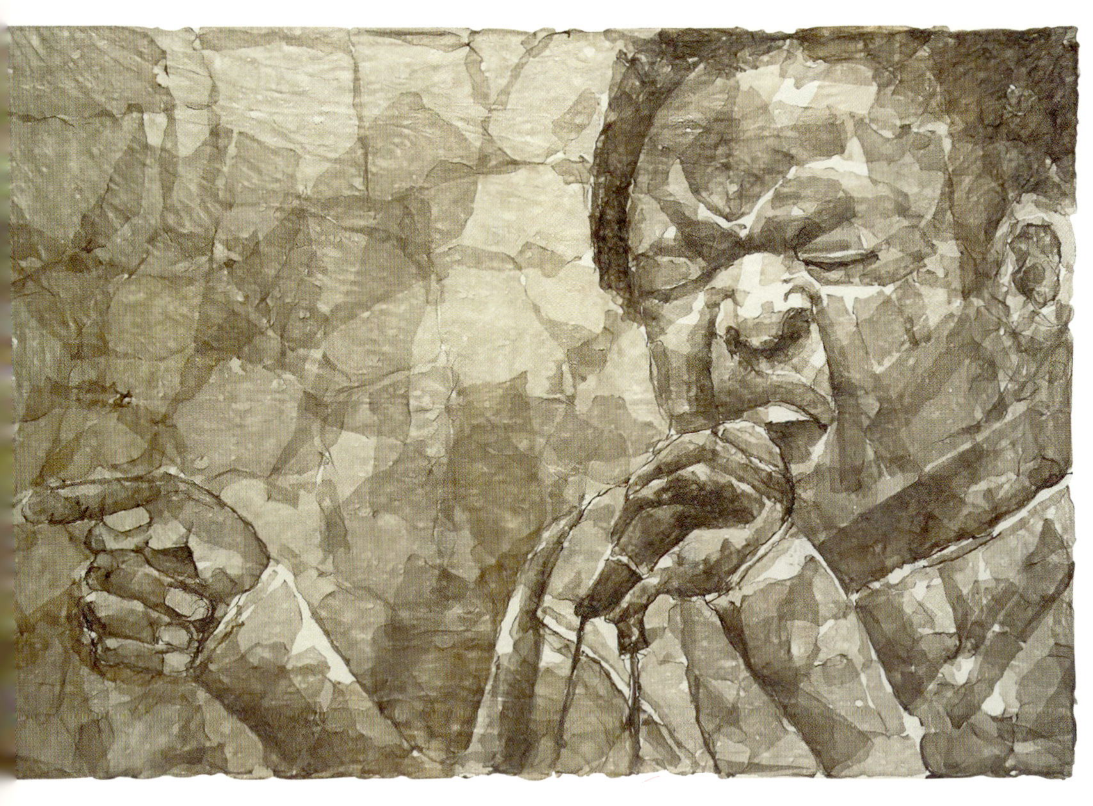

Soly Cissé

Untitled
2005
Acrylic on photographic
paper
78 works, 23 x 32 cm.
each one

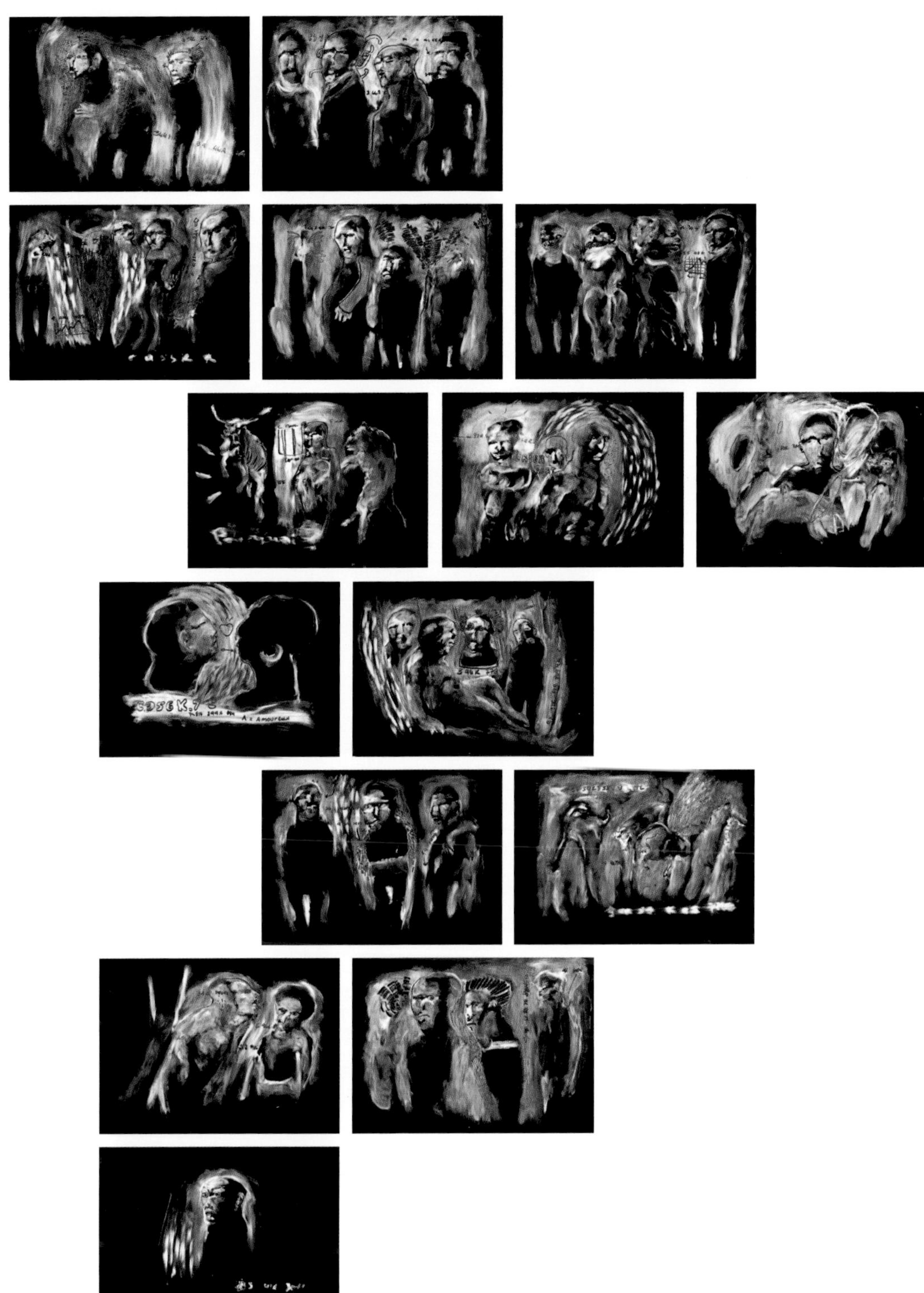

One day, I went to the Canal Plus office in Dakar to pay the digital television bill. In the foyer I noticed a mosaic of television screens, each one broadcasting a different channel, and I was suddenly struck by the way that western civilisation is invading Africa.

Unlike the images that we are bombarded with, I have taken a different road, using the mosaic of television screens as my inspiration for the appearance (the shape), the way the modules are arranged, to highlight the genuinely important things in the images we see: the human aspect, human beings subjected to the pressure imposed by the capitalist systems of the world.

In this work, each module represents a television screen, each screen a portion of image, a real situation, a news item, human beings as opposed to the material world... which is why there are no nice houses and no expensive cars. I want to place the emphasis on human beings, which the visual media world (television, photography, new technologies) uses as actors. Actors as synonymous with performance, comedy... So the viewers receive the images passively and I act as a filter, discarding the details of the image that don't interest me and presenting human beings in their most natural state. In other words, I demonstrate the ecosystem (linked elements).

I chose black and white because I don't present images in colour and because the stark contrast between black and white is meant to symbolise human races, the most ignored race and the most respected race, although they walk hand in hand and value each other. In the future I hope to explore this concept of black and white further, which for me are two extremes that people tend to place in opposition when in fact they complement each other.

The arrangement of the modules provokes a confrontation between the various images presented, demanding close attention from the viewer. This positioning is determined by the modules, there has to be communication between the images, and, as in the beginning, the television is in black and white.

As far as organic material is concerned, there are no differences between men. I believe there are two races, the fair-skinned race and the less fair-skinned race. It is the negative way of defining both races that affects the human perception of this contrast. As for pigmentation, I don't believe in the existence of a red, yellow or coloured race. These are ill-fitting labels, rashly imposed for the purpose of division, but also for greater domination of the planet.

Soly Cissé

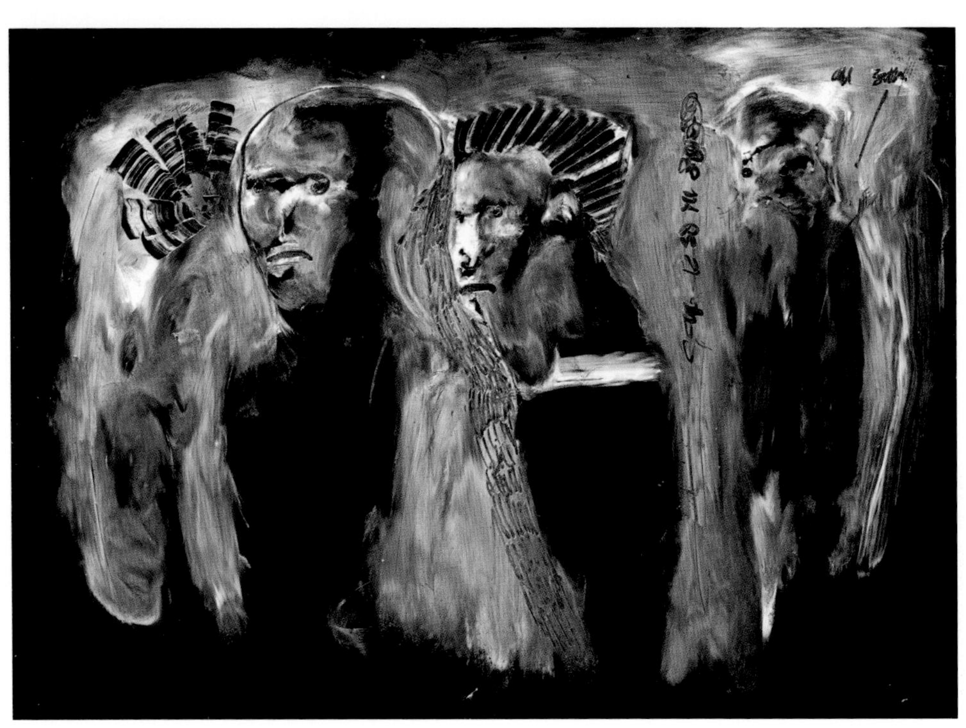

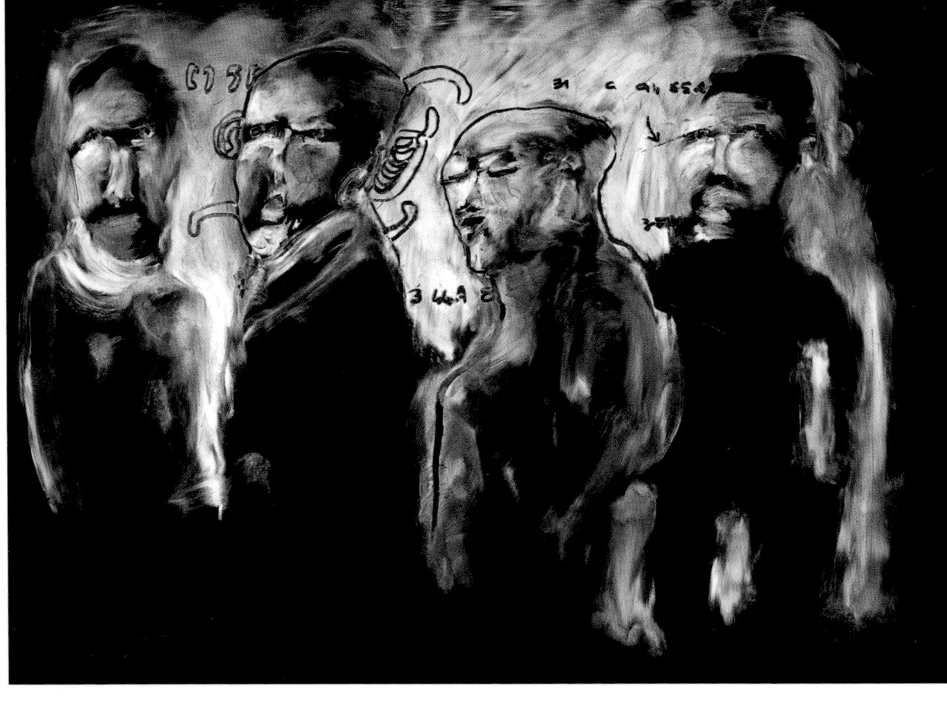

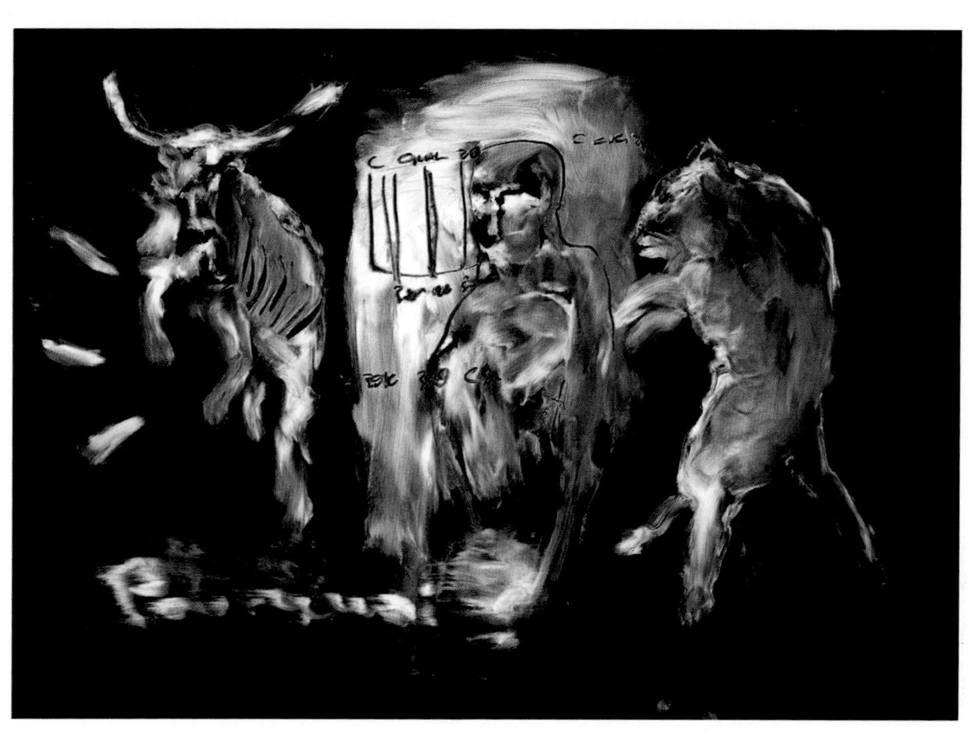

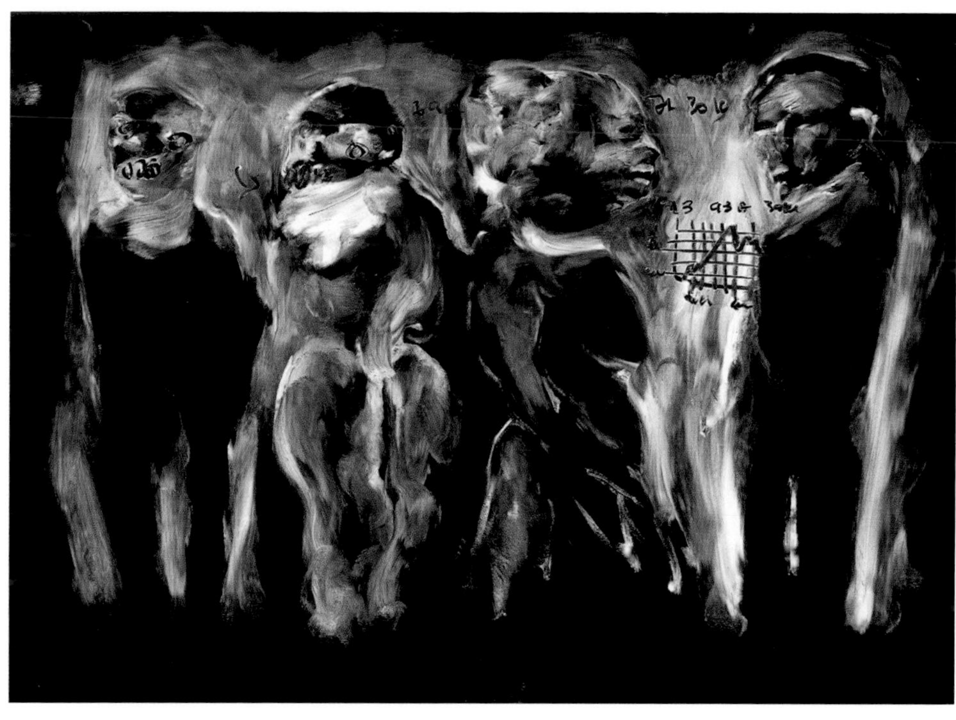

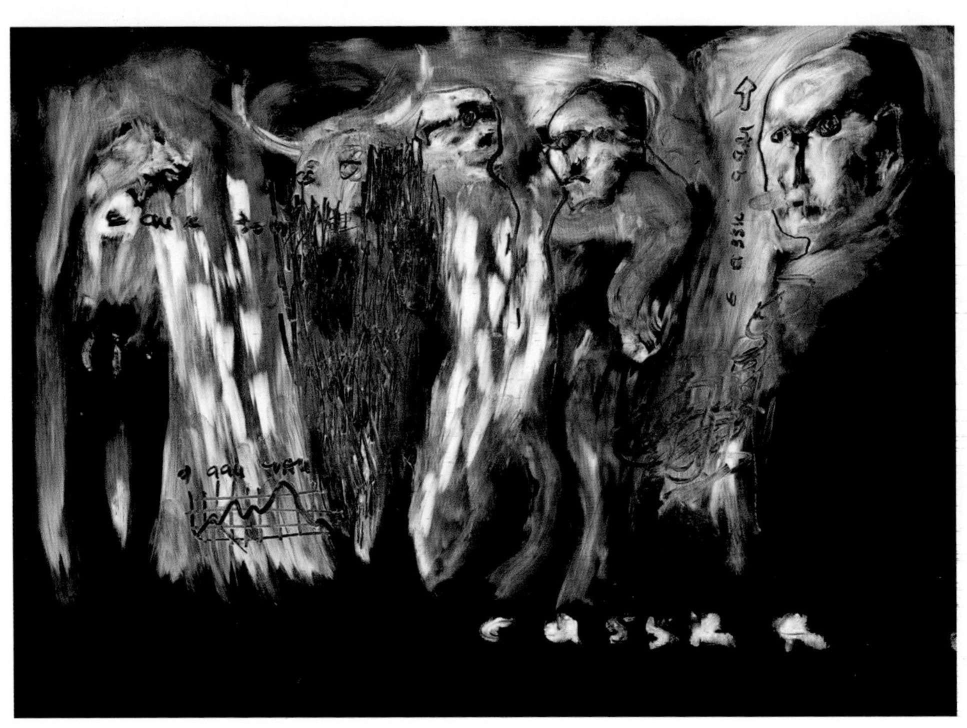

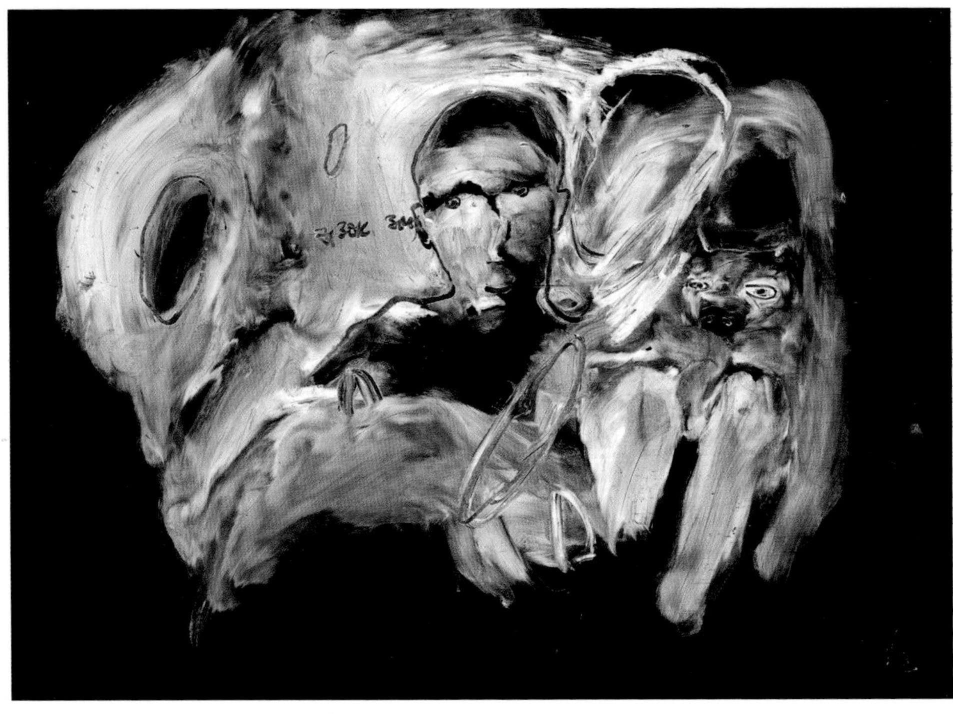

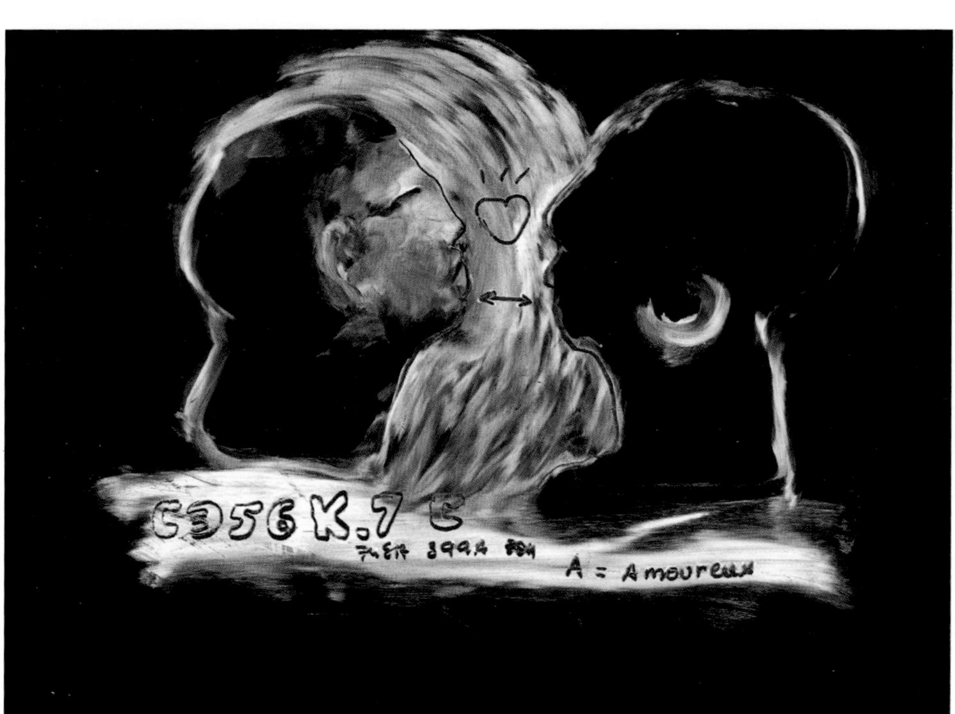
CD56K.7 C
A = Amoureux

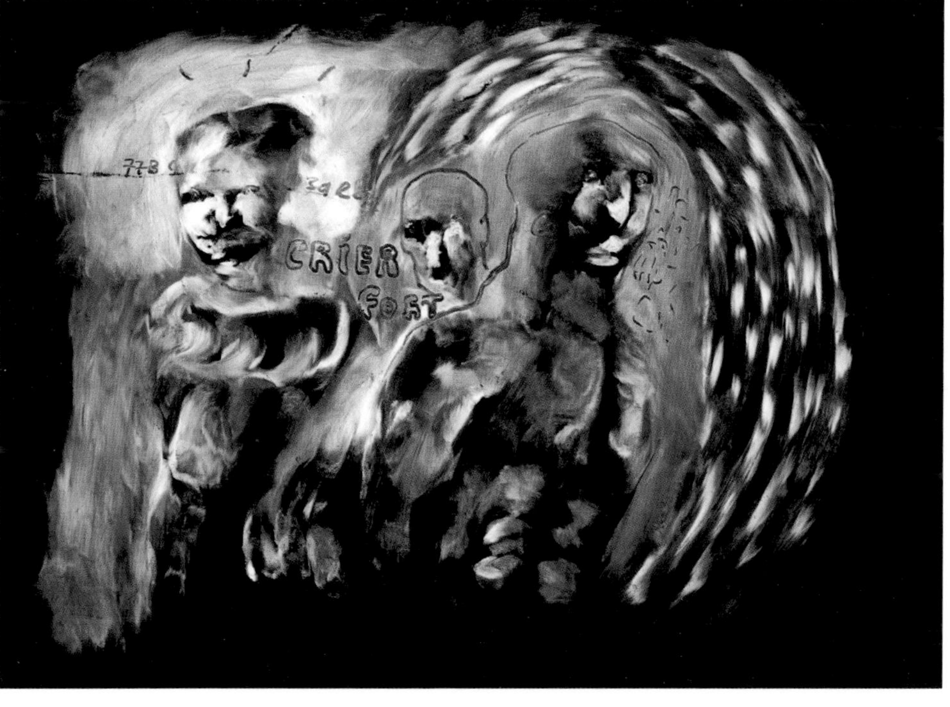
CRIER
FORT

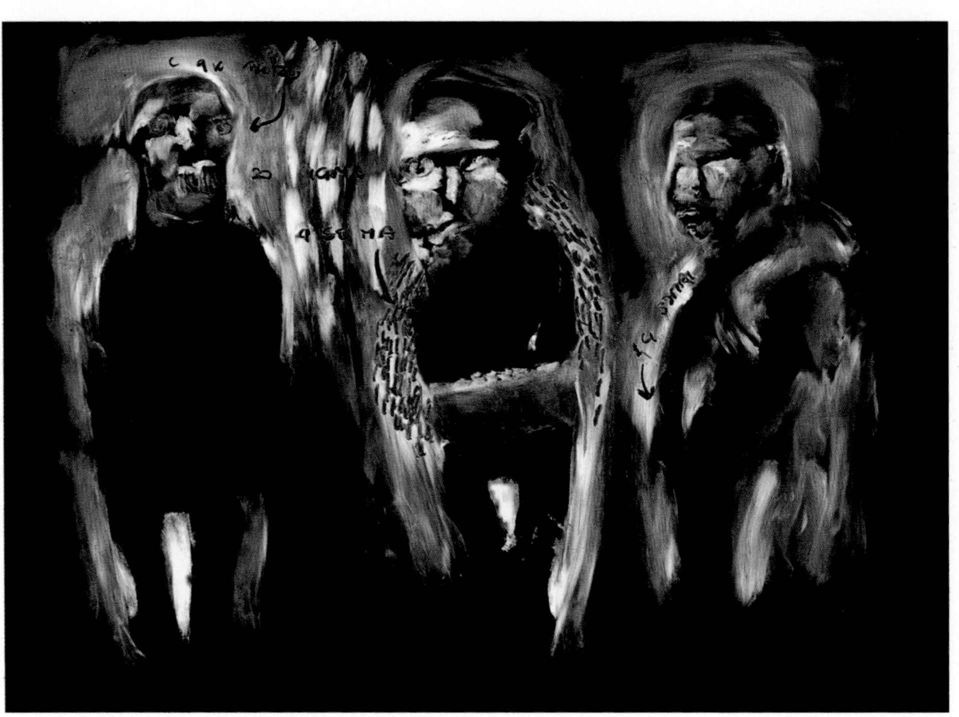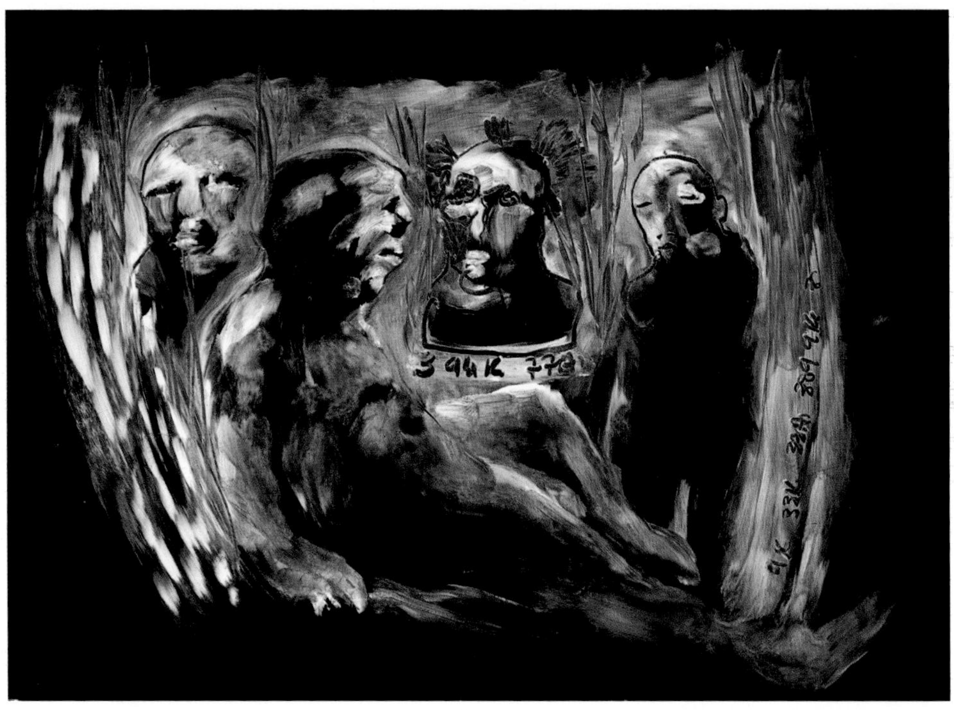

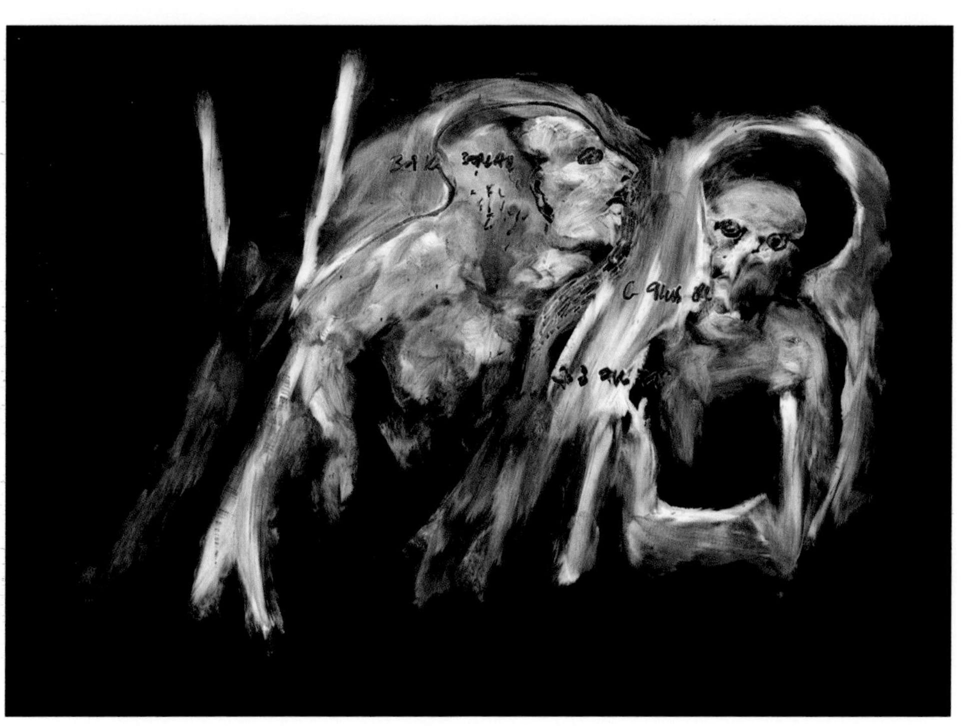

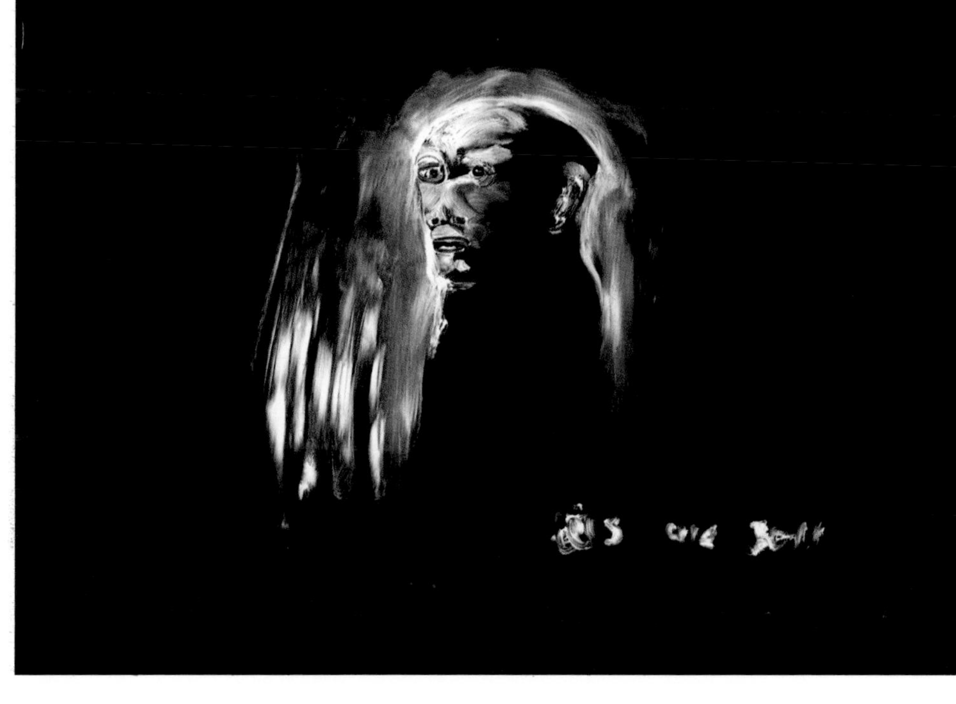

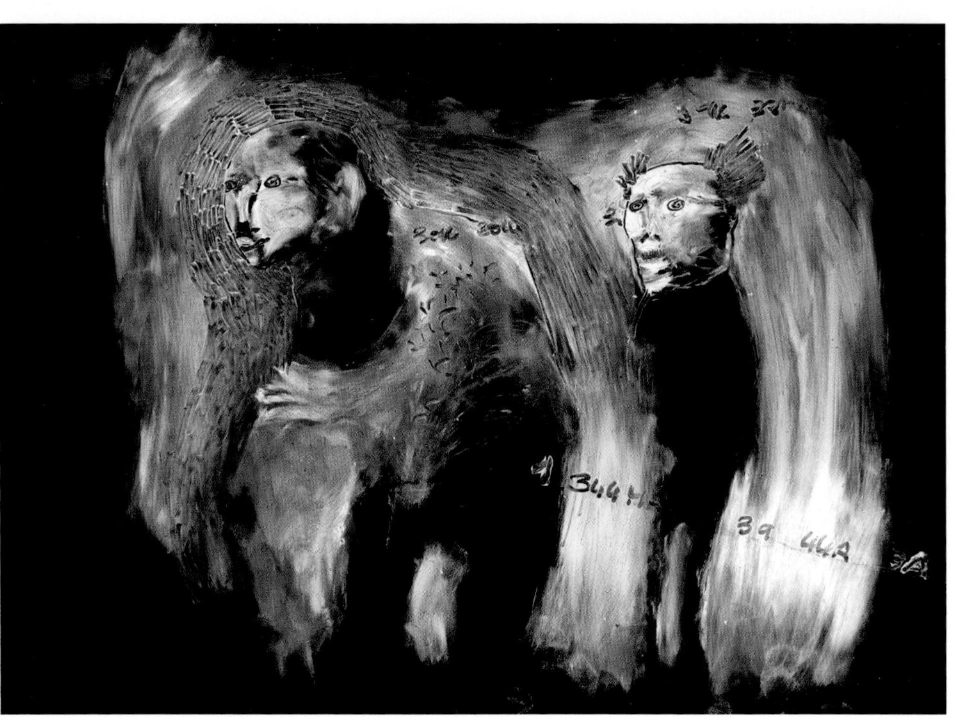

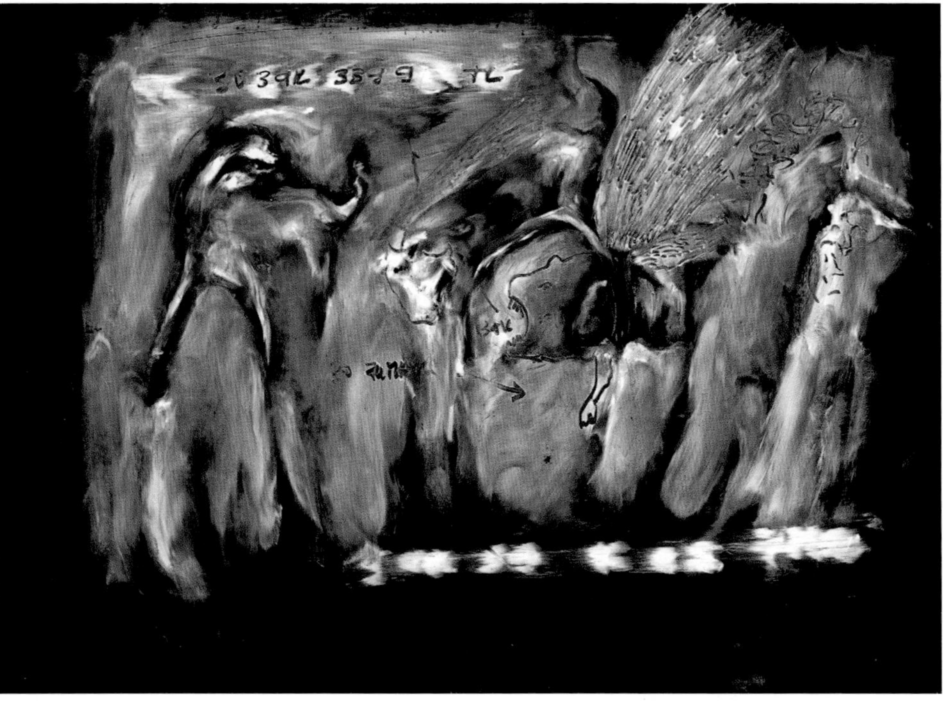

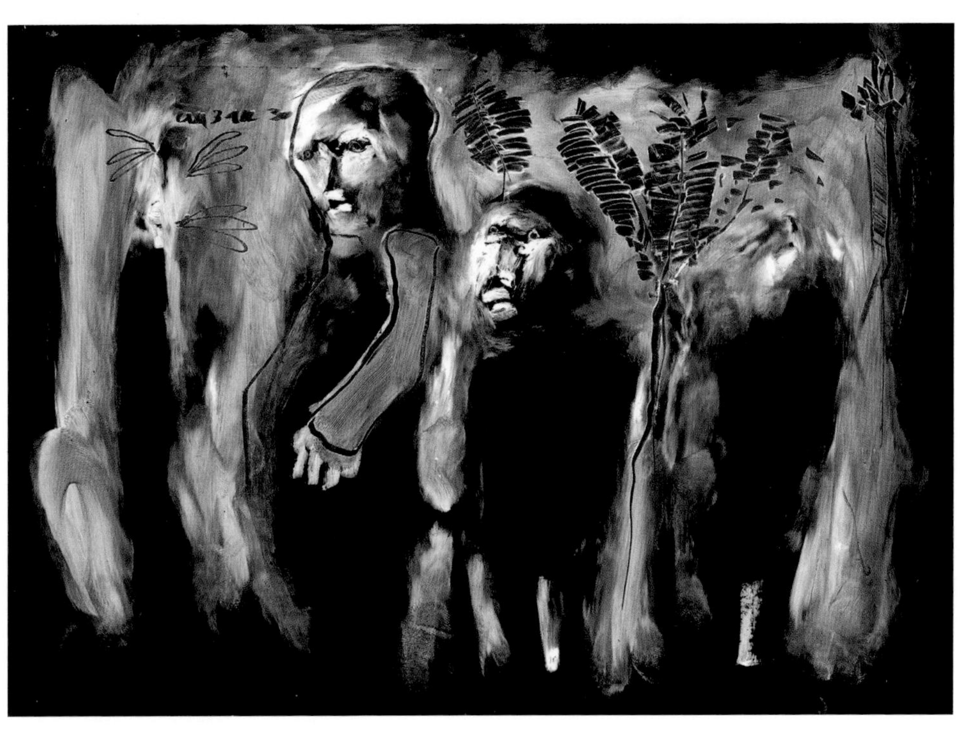

Viyé Diba

Messe nue
2001-2002
Installation, mixed media
380 x 350 x 700 cm.

Messe nue is a performance installation and forms part of the *Ere Pré-Pygmée 2003-2006* (*Pre-Pygmy Era 2003-2006*) file developed as a result of a debate on the Democratic Republic of Congo chaired by Madeleine Moukamabano for the programme *Débat Africain*, broadcast by RFI (Radio France Internationale) in August 2003. I use the term "file", borrowed from the business field, to describe those of my art projects that deal with all the aspects of an issue. The text by Sylvie le Gall is an excellent introduction to *Ere pré-pigmée* and leaves me little to add about the project. I shall simply highlight what I consider to be the decisive factors for me as an artist. *Messe nue* creates an atmosphere whose epicentre is the Church. It is not in any way my intention to discredit an institution which, as a believer, I respect. It is merely that the Church is a framework of human experience that is interesting from the aesthetic point of view. A place with human bodies littering the ground to talk about Rwanda, but also an anonymous place, somewhere near Gbadolite, defined exclusively by a cross, and where darkness is the only garment. Everywhere, human bodies in life like situations, a favourite notion amongst phenomenologies.

Messe nue (Naked Mass)

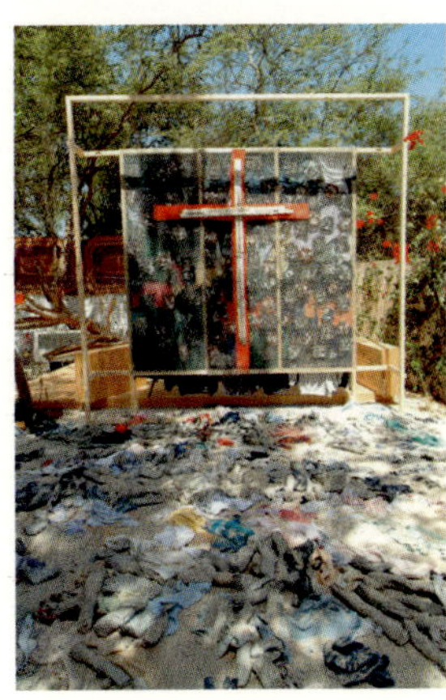

Bodies as objects on the ground, anxious faces behind a screen, protected by a cross. What a scenario! A bright light that gradually fades into total darkness, a darkness penetrated by religious music with words in a local language, and vice versa. Here, nakedness is a language: both when provoked, as in Rwanda – where those engaging in genocide also steal the clothing of those they execute – and when the result of poverty, the human body is always there. This is a story of anxiety and despair. The aesthetic is based on mutating states: the state of light that becomes half-light, and then suddenly the aesthetic of black on black invading the space, generating a chain of mental images in our minds. An experience not only to be viewed but to be had and shared.

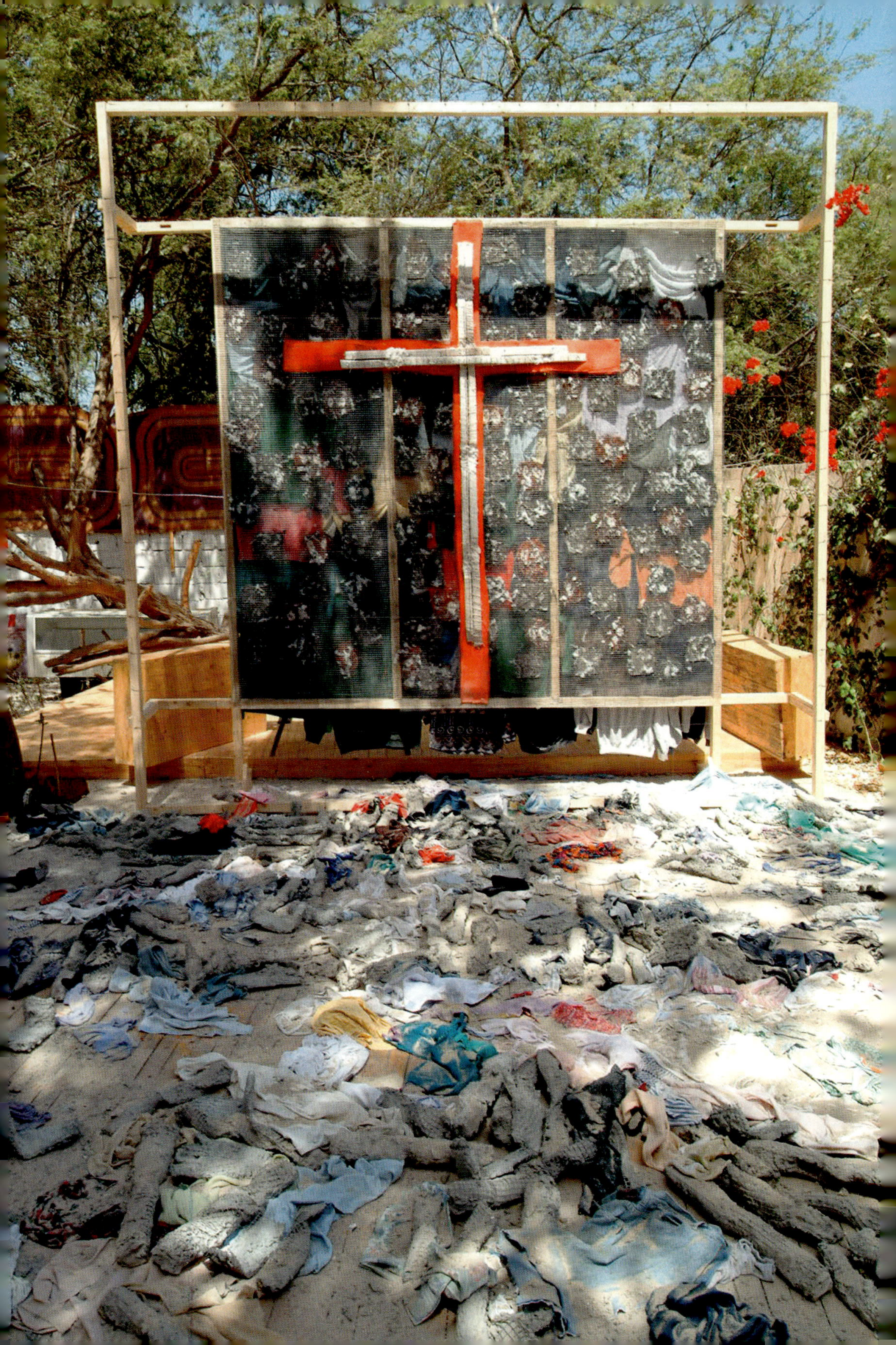

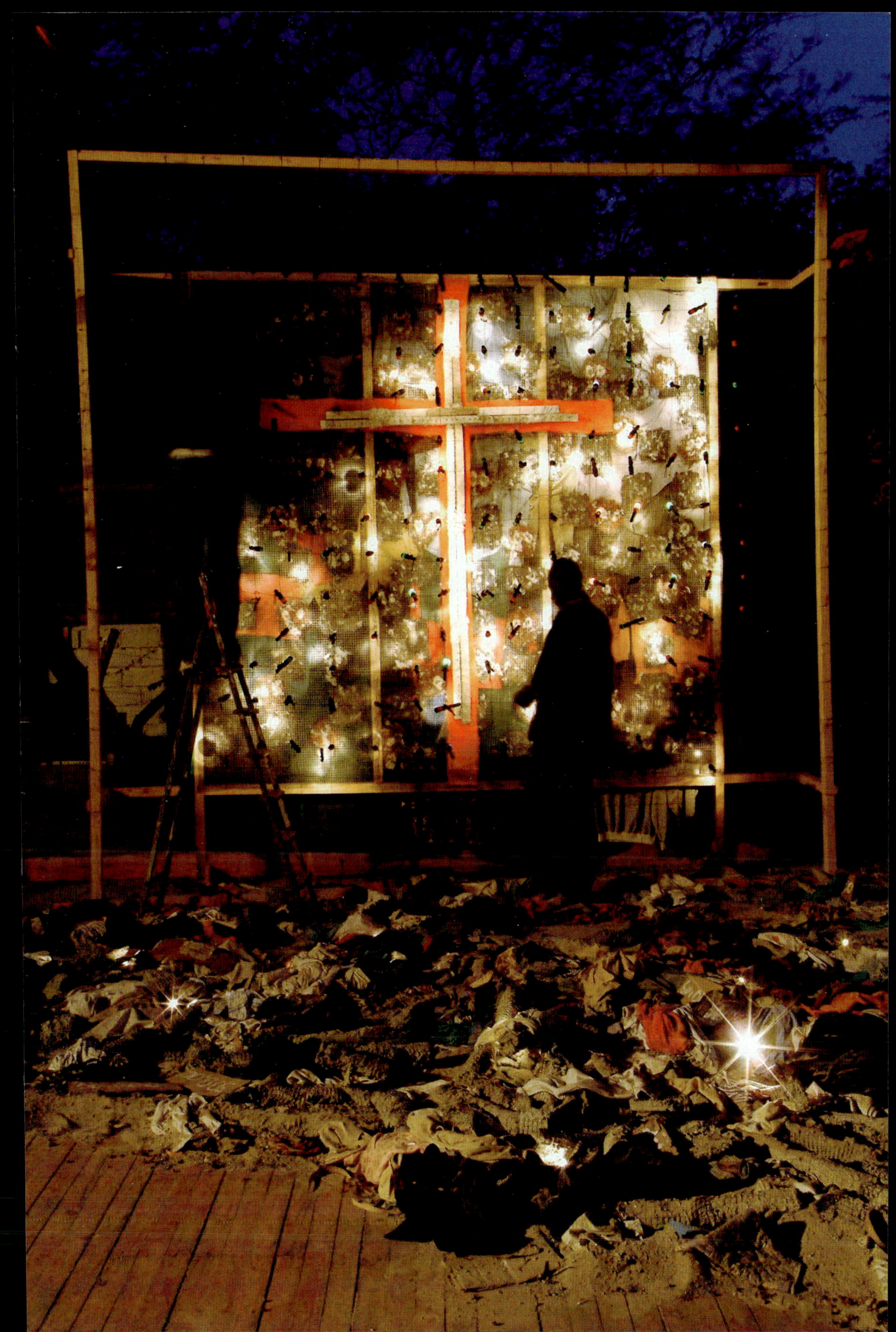

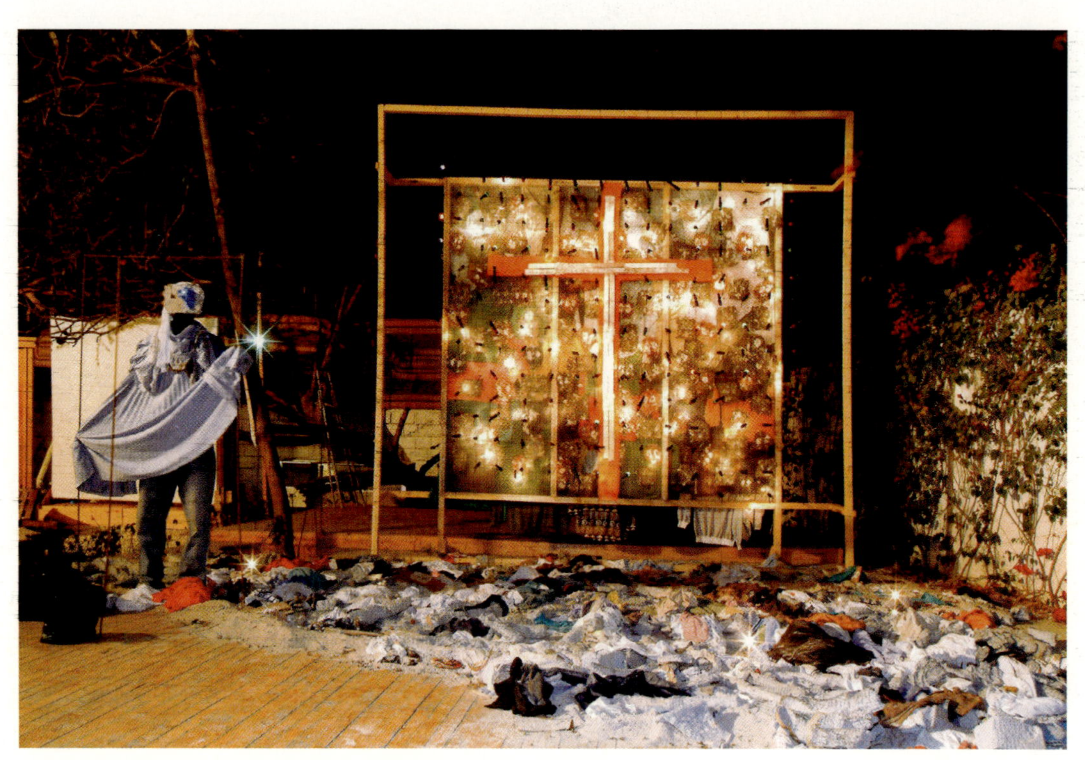

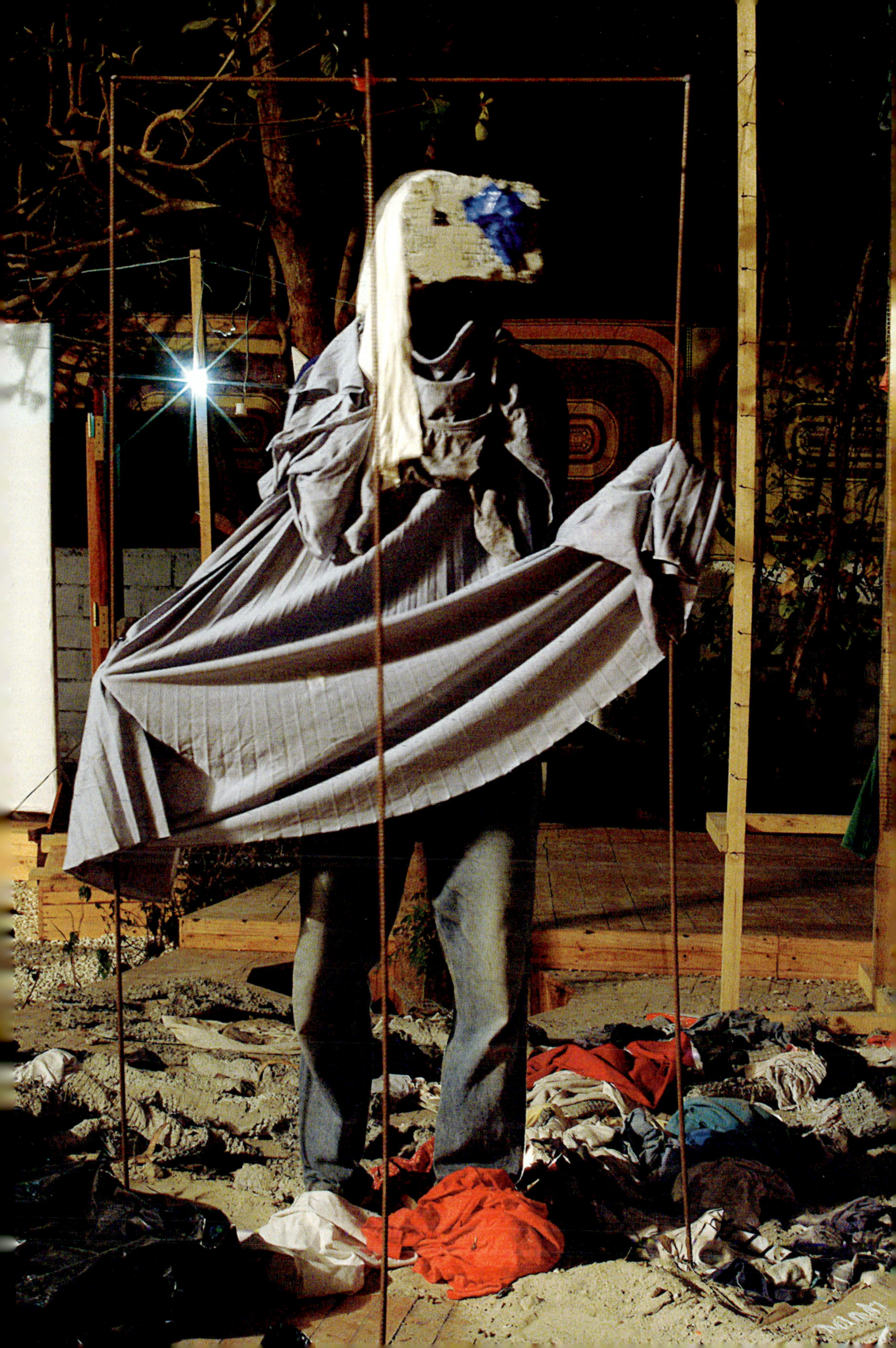

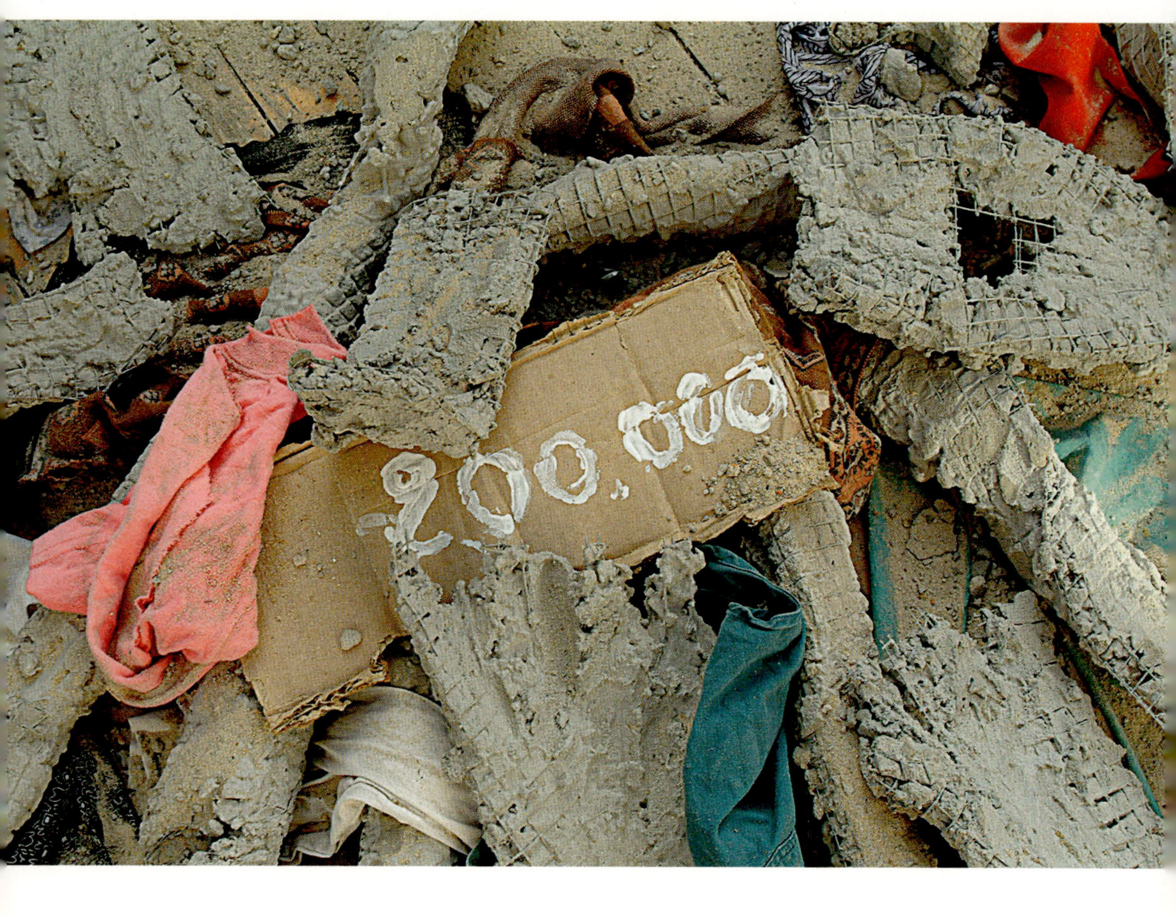

200,000

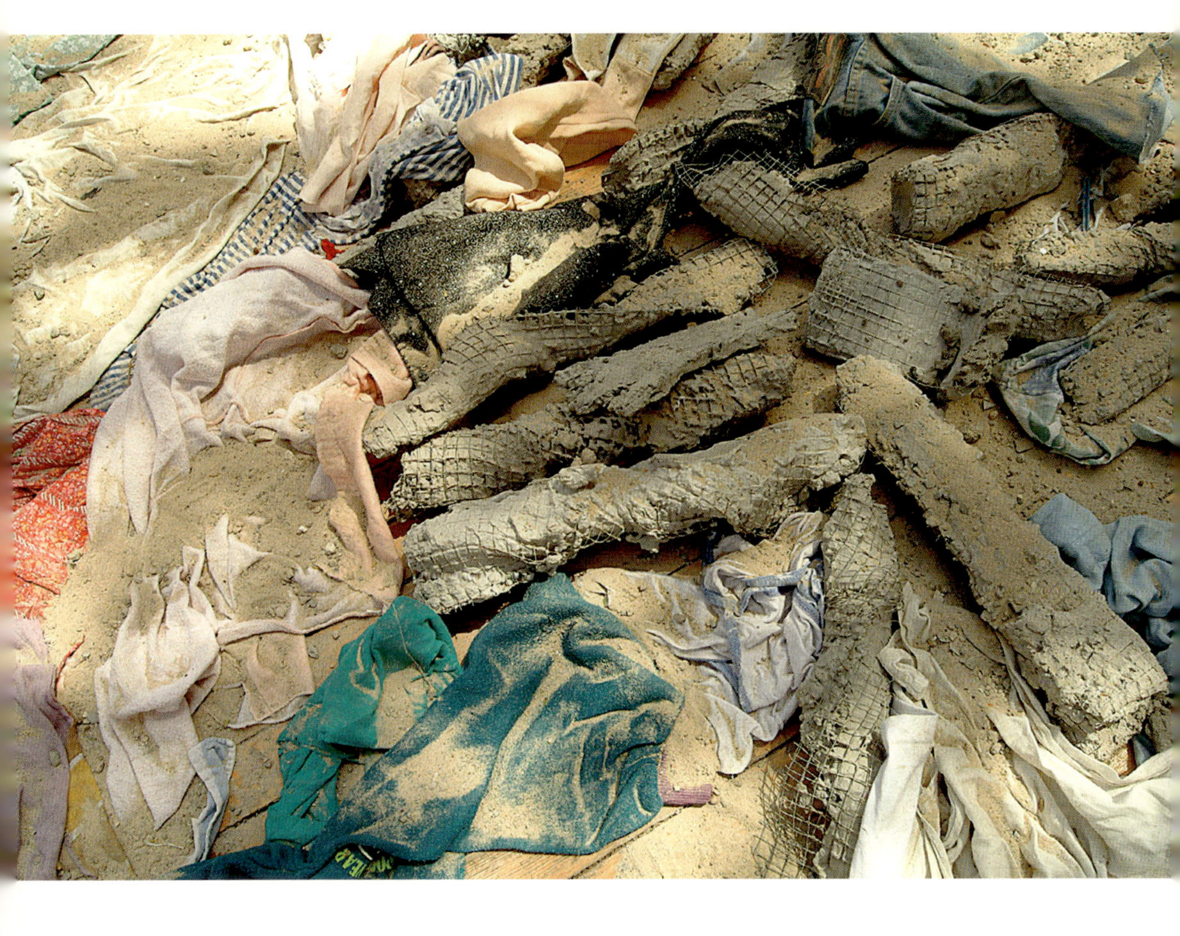

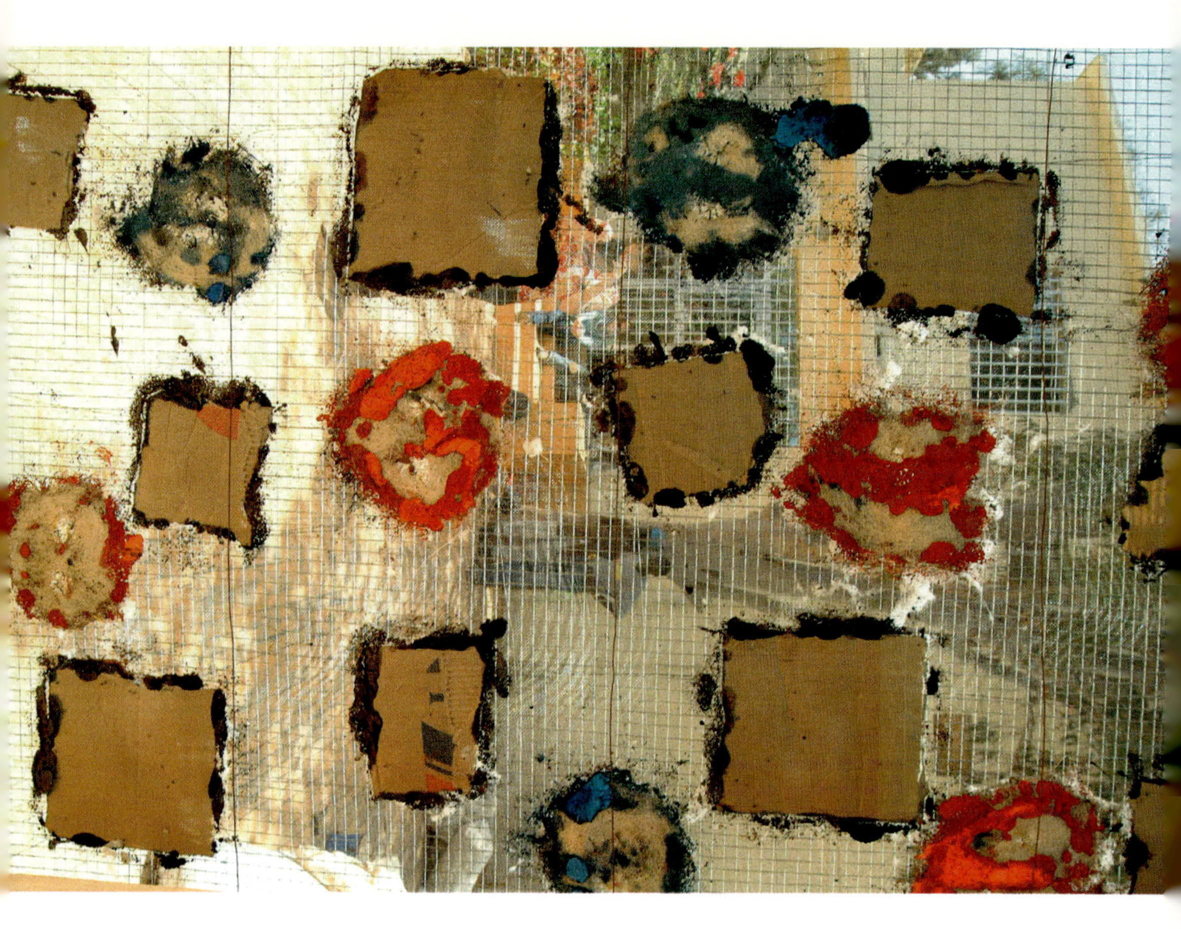

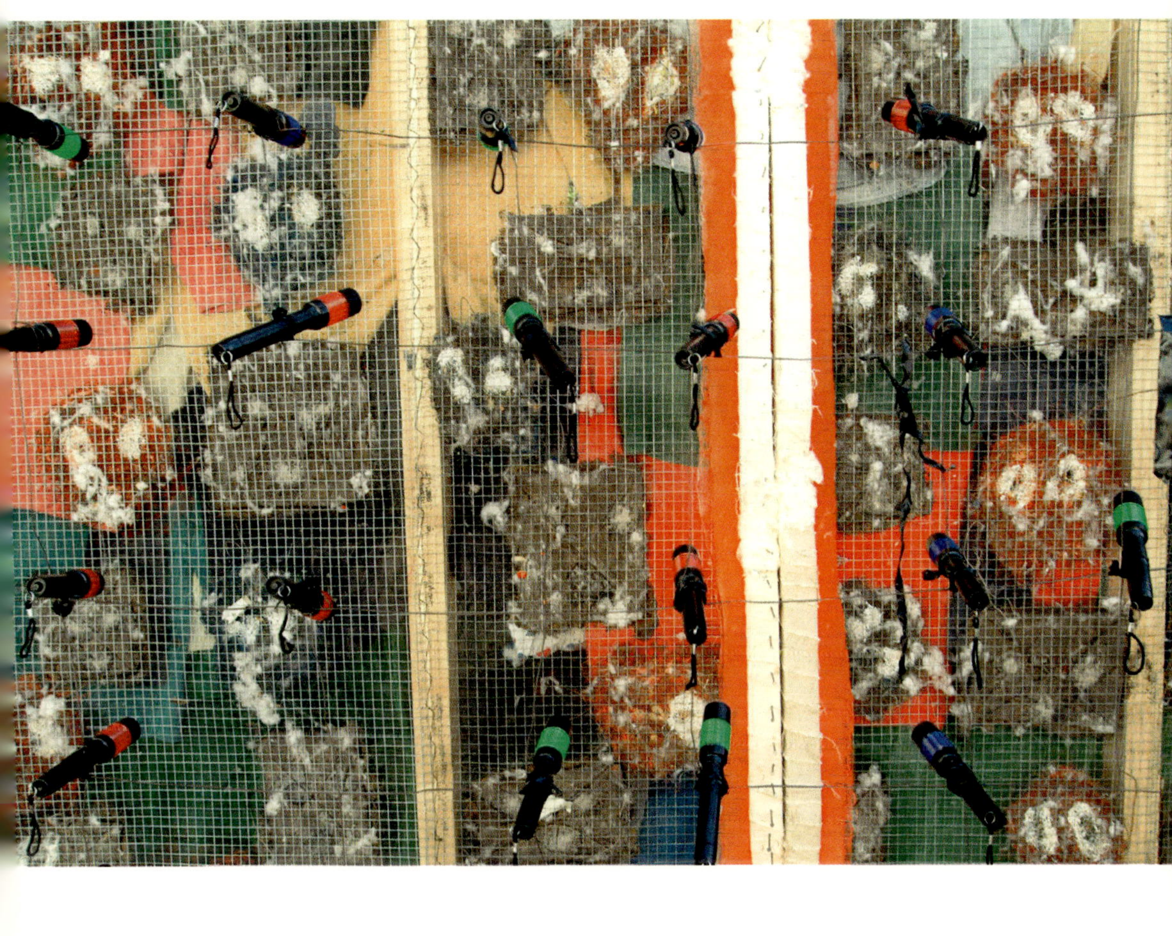

Modou Dieng

Arrow
2005
Mixed media and
collage on panel
120 x 300 cm.

Charlie Parker
2005
Mixed media and
collage on panel
Diptych: 182 x 484 cm.

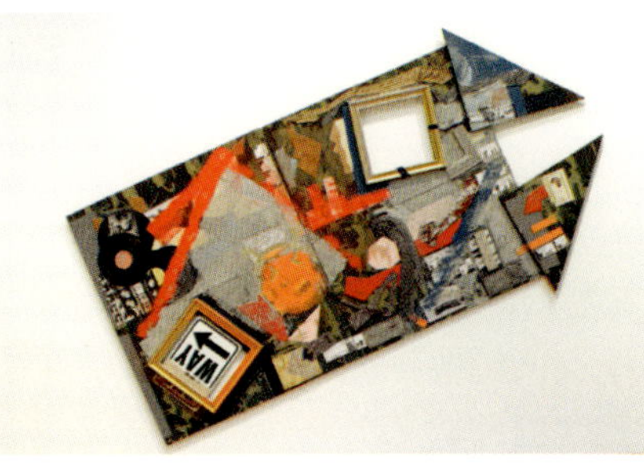

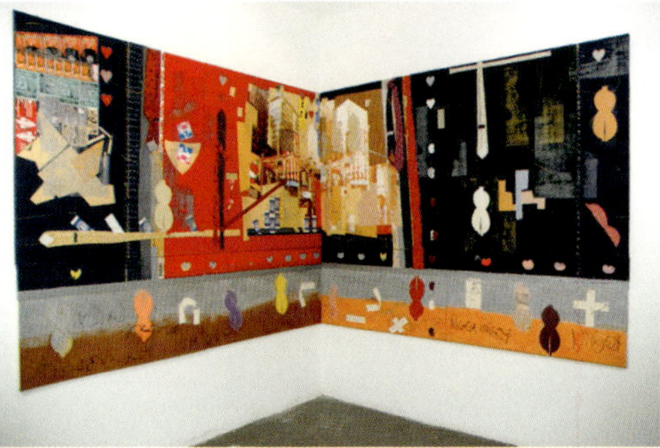

For a visual artist, I suppose that even more difficult than pursuing one's artistic practice is attempting to sum it up. When asked to describe my work, what it is about, my responses are usually vague. I will typically say:

I paint, I make paintings that explore urban identity and urban culture, drawing from the modern aesthetic of black culture. I use photographs that I either take myself or that I appropriate. I make collages with materials that speak to me or sensitise me. My paintings are constructions; reference is made to architecture, because cities are built environments.

I approach each piece as if it were a painting, even if I paint very little and rarely use oils or acrylics. I do, however, use inks—bronze, silver and gold—to evoke the hierarchies and value systems that these colours impose.

There are staples and other metals; while serving as references to ancient cultures these are presented in their modern, functional incarnations as signifiers of contemporary life. I additionally integrate everyday objects with which we are associated in one way or another.

Why do I paint? Being of African origin, having received a modern, western education, I find myself as an artist whose every option is double; I am squarely situated between two societies, two cultures, two perceptions. My work is an attempt to force a merger, rather than relegate one of these options to the margins.

The product is a cross-cultural collage, in which the social aligns itself with and becomes accomplice to the philosophical, where practice meets theory. Here one finds both traces of the object's history and, at the same time, the object in all its agency, actively determining its own history.

There is juxtaposition between my social and racial history and my means of apprehending the tradition of painting, which might also be found among such artists as Robert Rauchenberg, Jean-Michel Basquiat and Raymond Saunders.

My work is additionally the product of a rereading of various modern movements and schools of thought, performed in a postmodern context. It is for this reason that the notion and process of assemblage is integral to my work. My pieces establish associations between various elements of differing origin, as well as various stereotypes and techniques which often contradict one another.

The use of traditional techniques from painting, printmaking, collage and photography are instruments that serve to forge a personal aesthetic language whose depths I explore in moving from full to empty, from compact to transparent.

In brief, painting for me is an activity that engages my individuality as a black man in the History of Art.

Modou Dieng

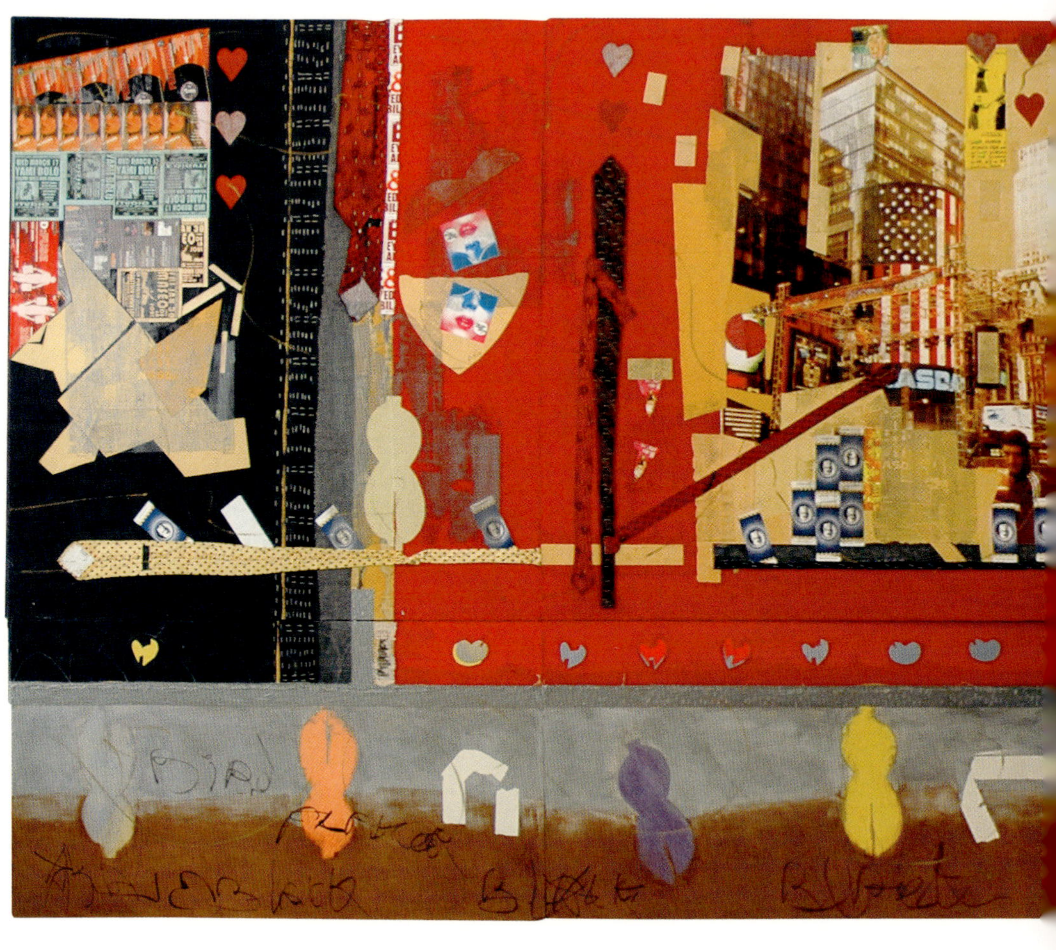

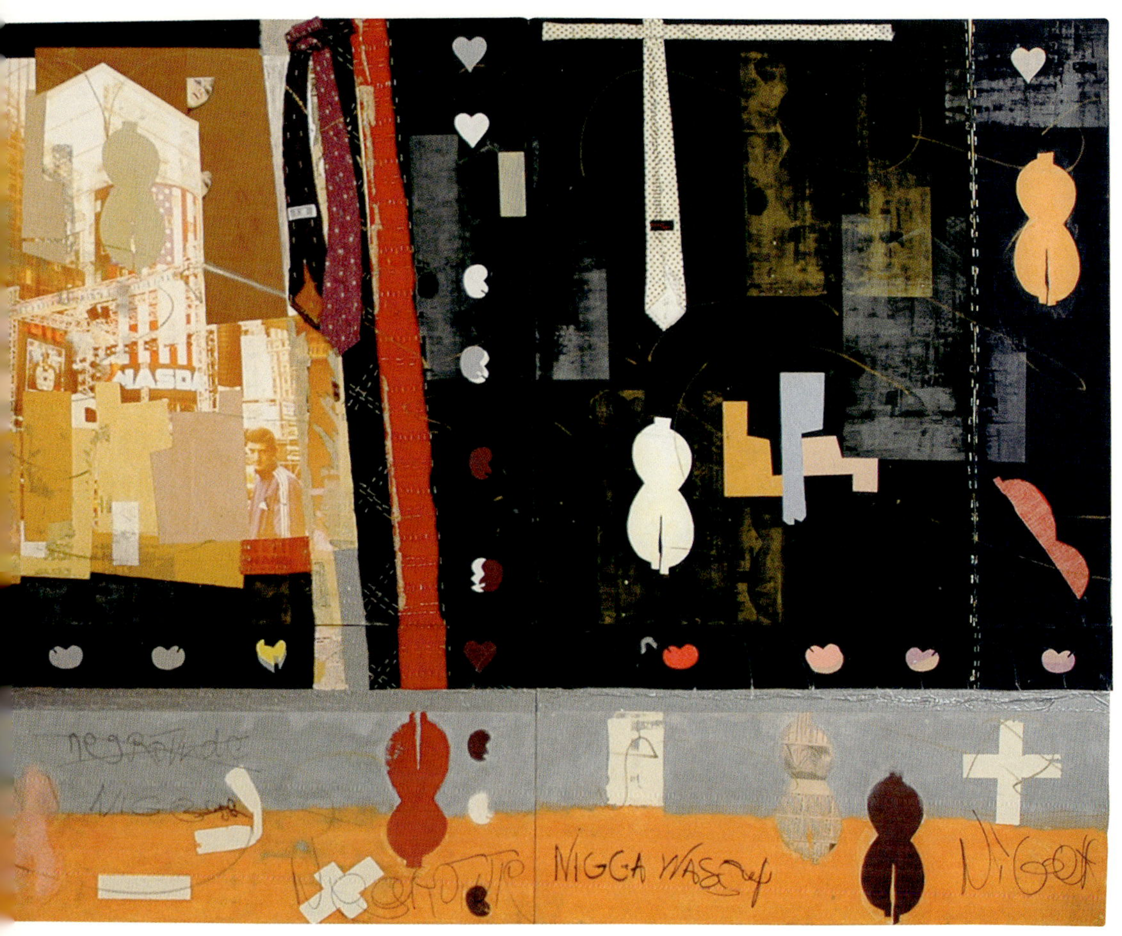

negrohido
NIGGA WASSup
NiGGA
NASDA

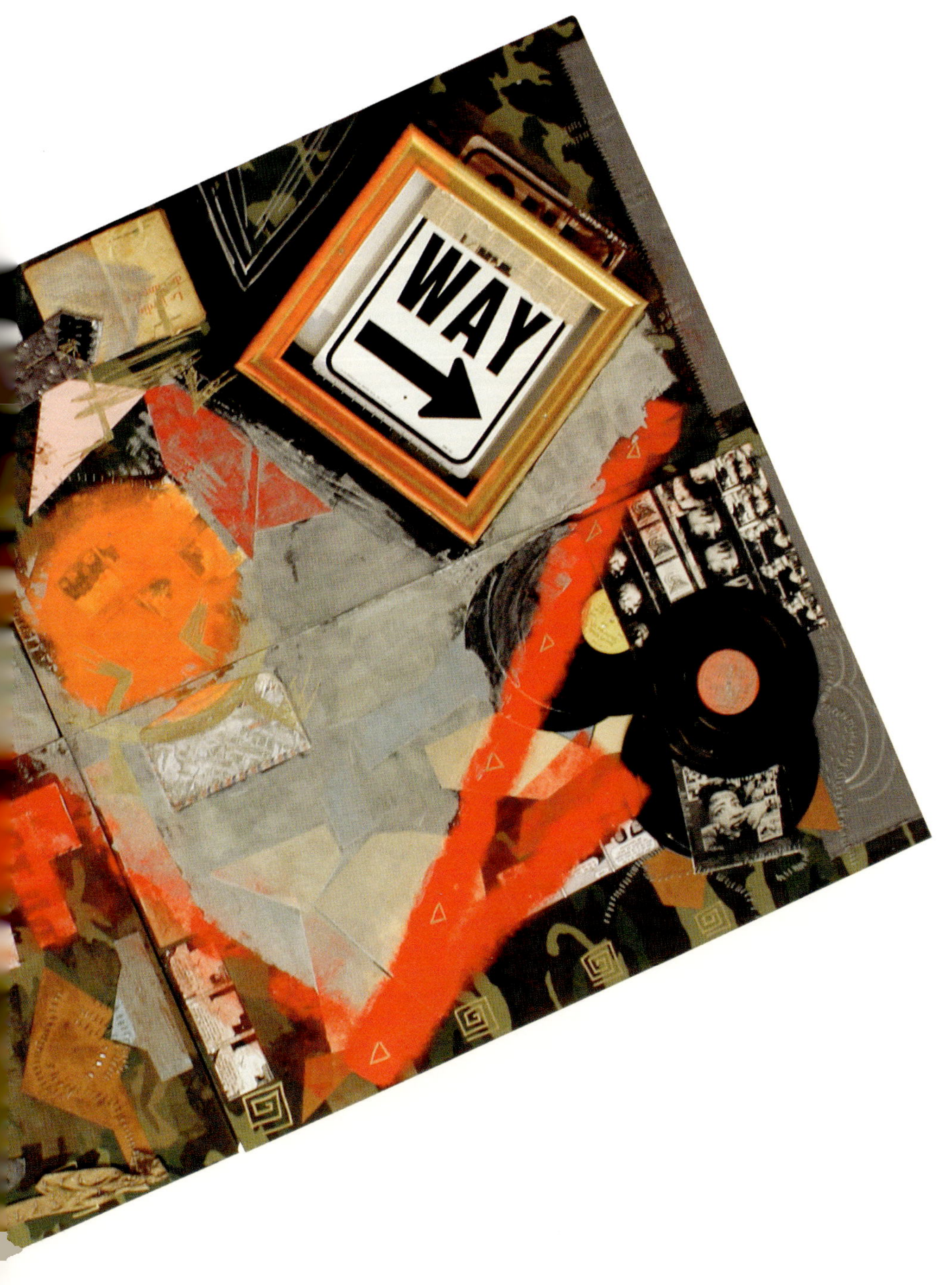

WAY

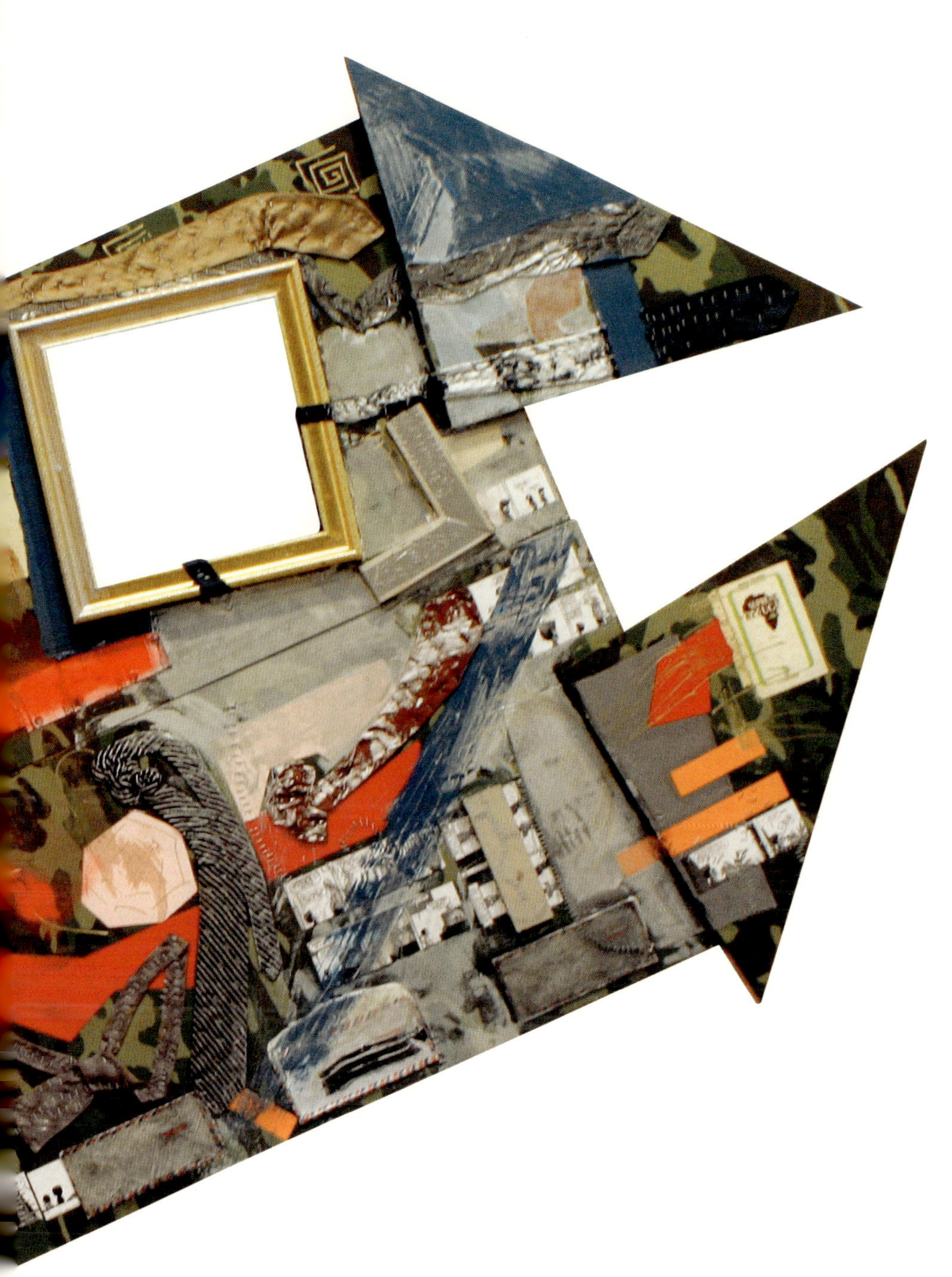

Moustapha Dimé

La Grande Danse
1995
Sculpture, 11 units,
wood and metal
300 x 200 cm. approx.

"I firmly believe that, in terms of one's ancestors, each person is the synthesis
of all his or her previous generations. I am convinced of it. I carry the legacy
of my first ancestor."

Interview wirh Moustapha Dimé conducted by Daniel Sotiaux on 25 March
1996 (Gorée), published in the catalogue for the Moustapha Dimé exhibition
held at the City Hall in Paris in 1999.

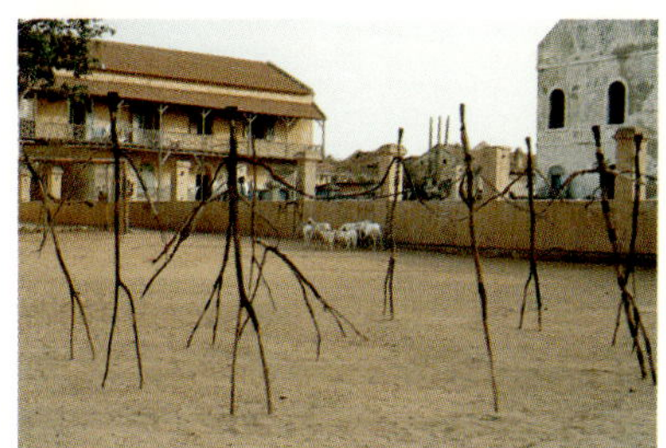

"Nowadays, artists have to get back to the essence: MAN.
MAN is the foundation, the starting point and the end.
MAN… I try to put myself in the position of someone trying to be successful
in life."

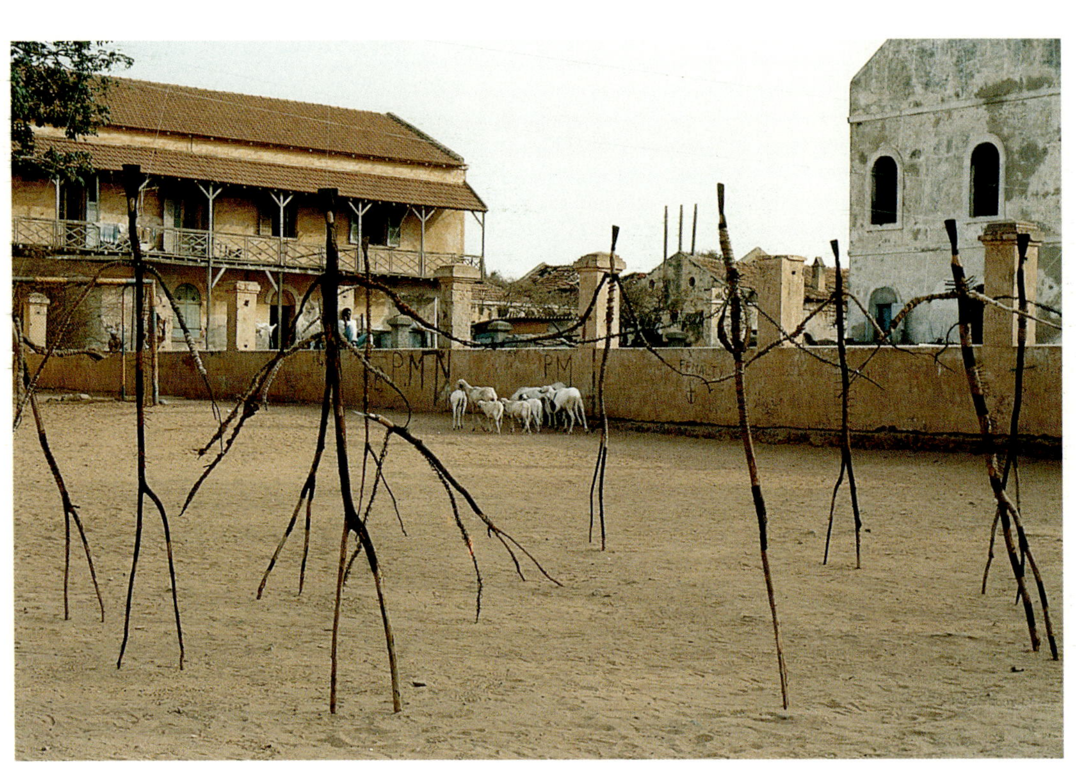

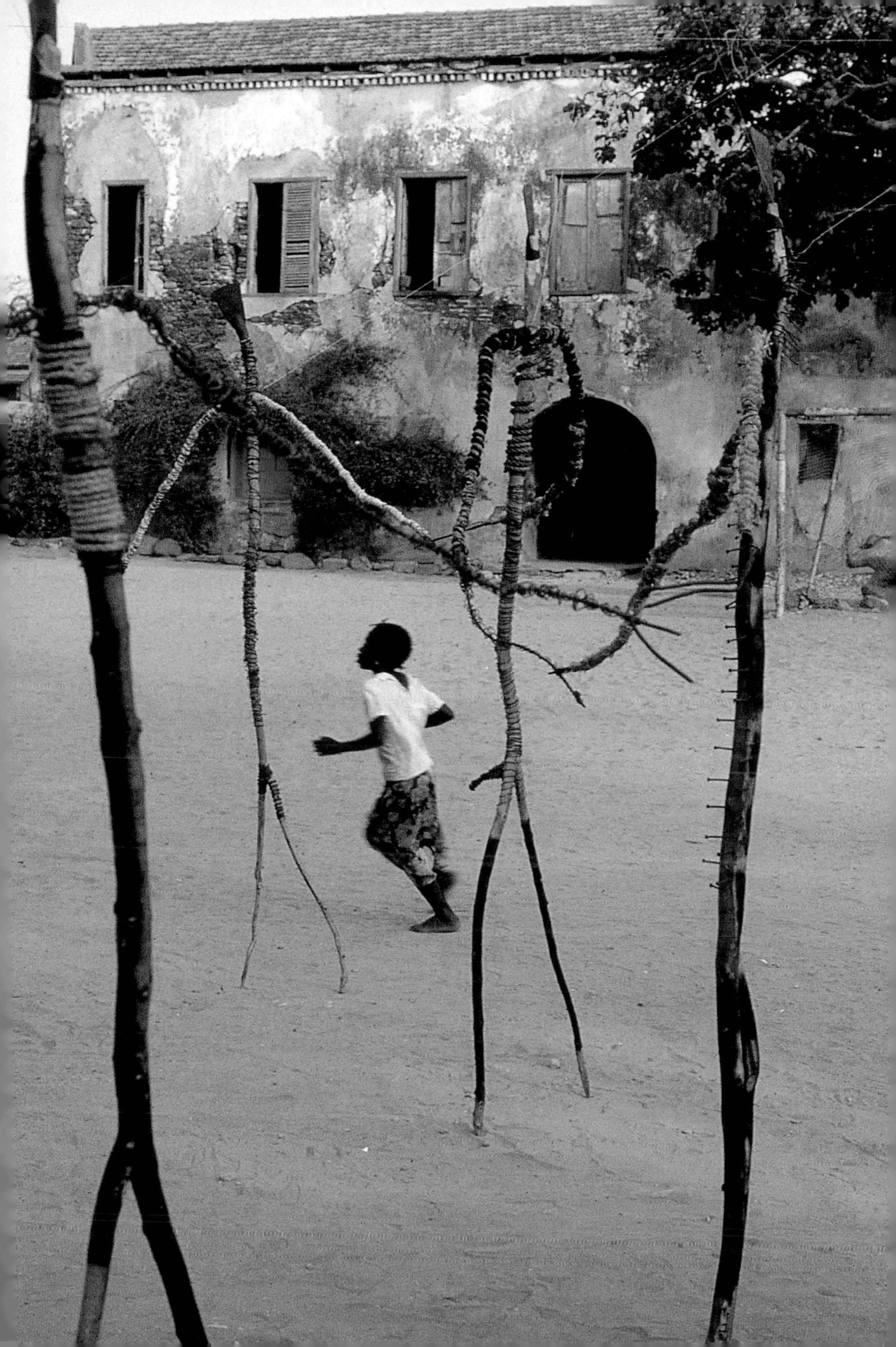

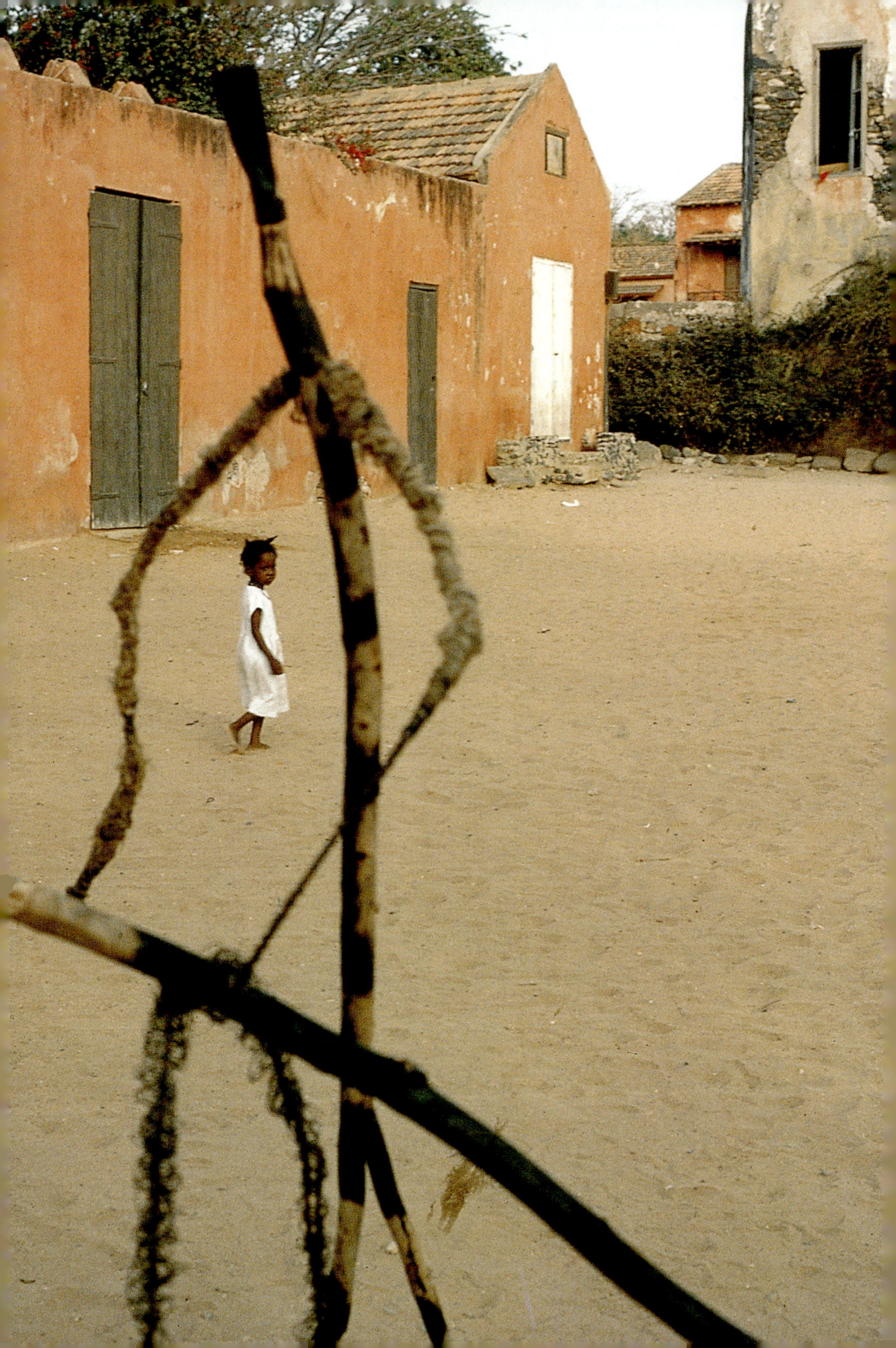

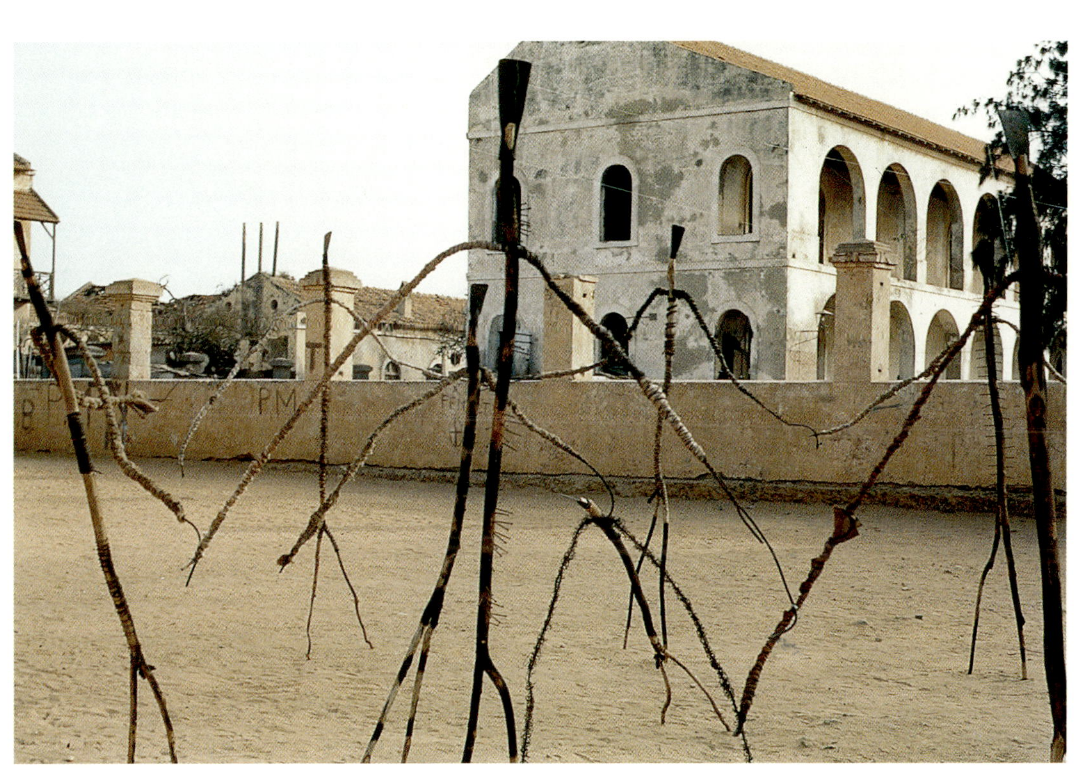

Touhami Ennadre

New York 9/11
2001
Black/white
photography
Triptych: 150 x 120 cm.
each one

Corps de nuit
2005
Black/white
photography
Diptych: 150 x 120 cm.
each panel

Corps de nuit
2005
Black/white
photography
Diptych: 150 x 120 cm.
each panel

Under New York
2003-2004
Black/white
photography
Diptych: 150 x 120 cm.
each panel

Under New York
2003-2004
Black/white
photography
Diptych: 150 x 120 cm.
each panel

"When I take a photograph, I don't allow myself to be photographed by my subject. Instead of just being content with reproducing reality, I erase it so as not fall into the trap of the image but rather let my own imagination reveal reality."

"The aim of my work is to highlight the essence; it is never explanatory. My photos depend on the light with which I surround my subject, who never poses. I shoot on the move and don't use the viewfinder. There are no intermediaries between my gaze and my subject. I am my own viewfinder. How can you take a photograph

From a conversation with François Aubral.

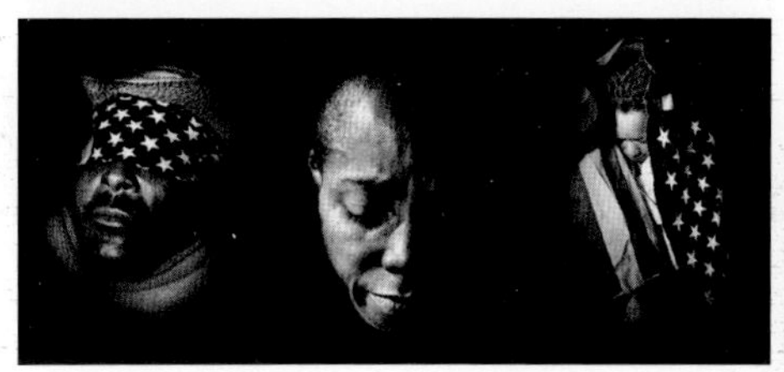

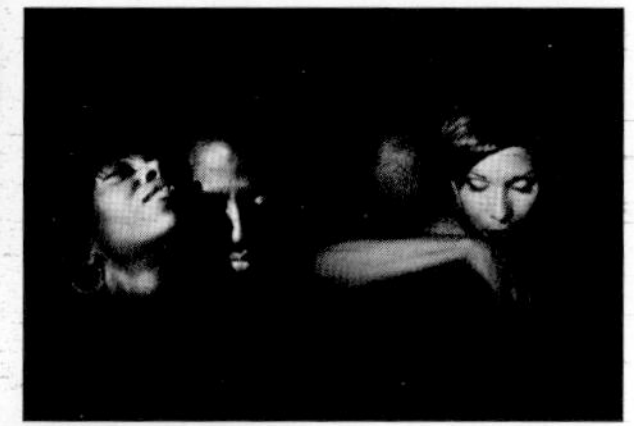

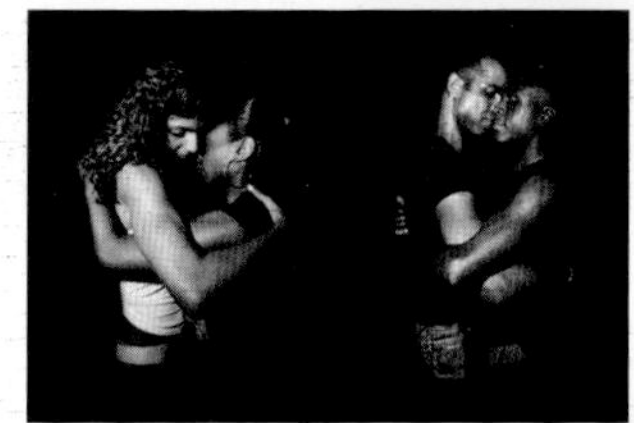

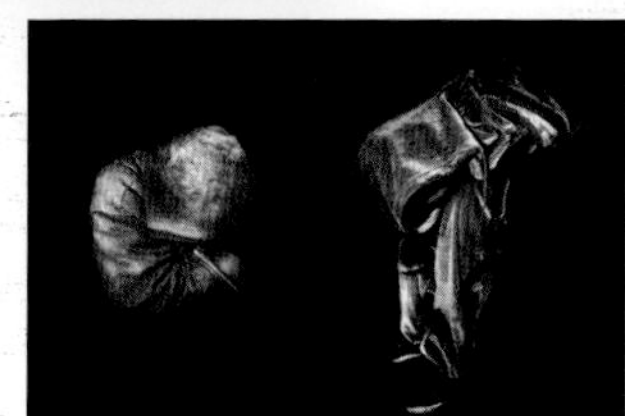

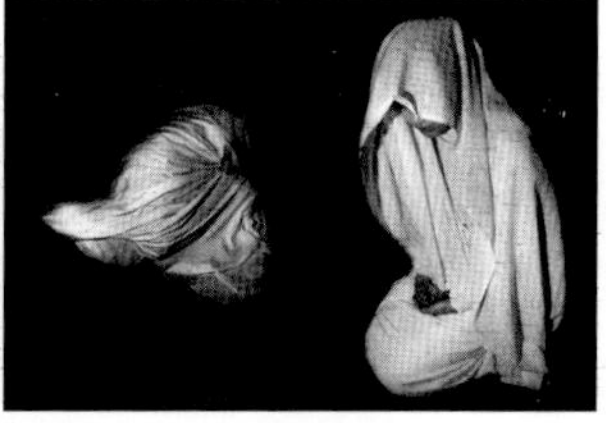

while squinting and peeping through a keyhole? For me, the camera is not a rifle with a telescopic sight. Being present, looking at someone directly, is a way of not falling into voyeurism. Afterwards, it takes me between twelve and fiveteen hours to develop each negative. My presence is absolute, I illuminate, darken, whiten, draw masks. I always try to find the black that illuminates, that provides meaning to the drama. I have nothing in common with photographers who run to the processing lab as soon as they've got a decent negative. Light is the action that leads to the deepest black."

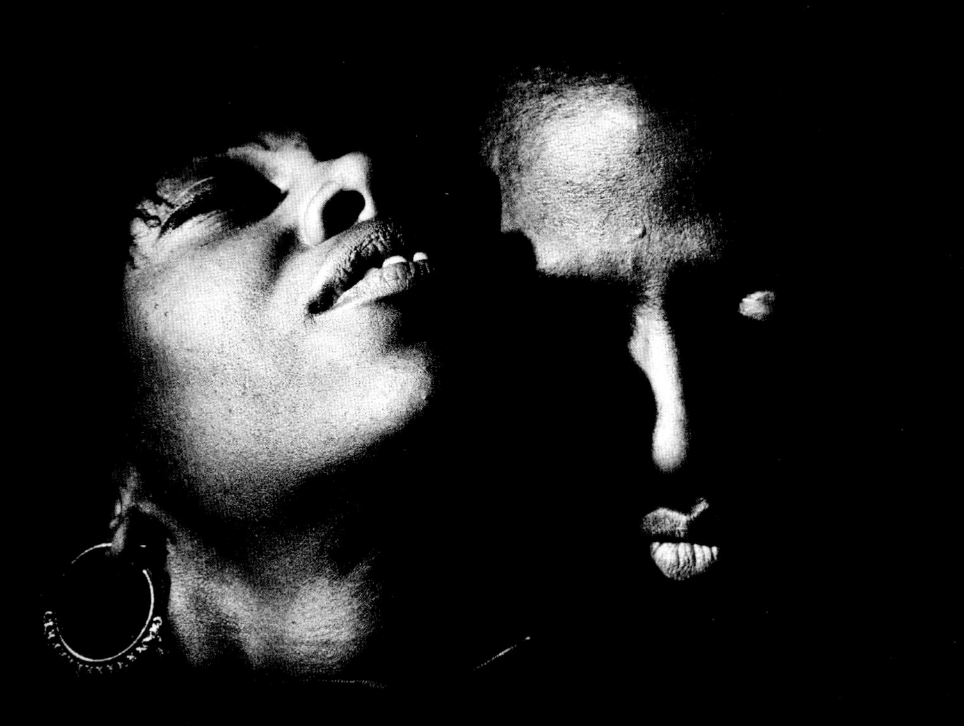

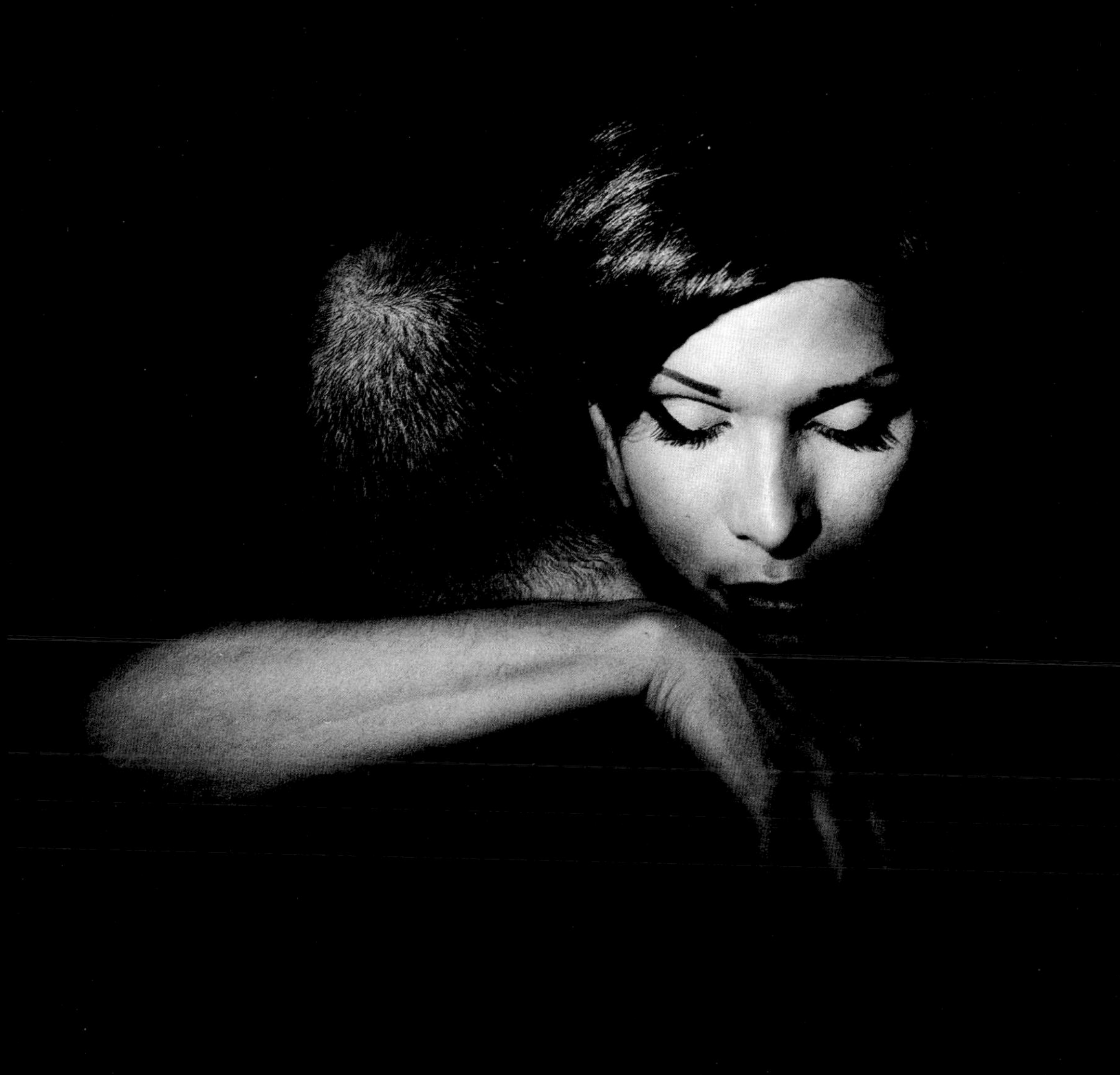

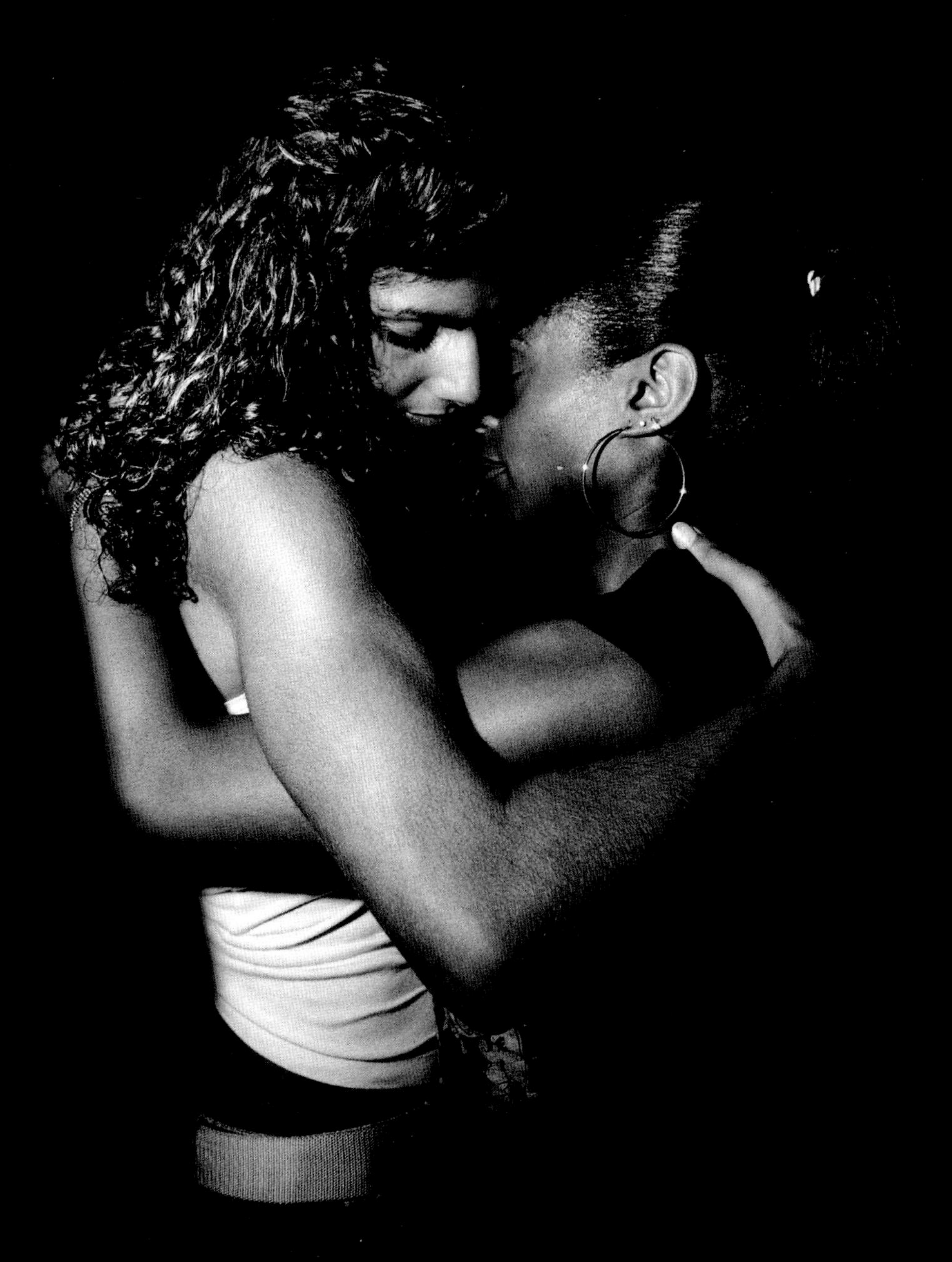

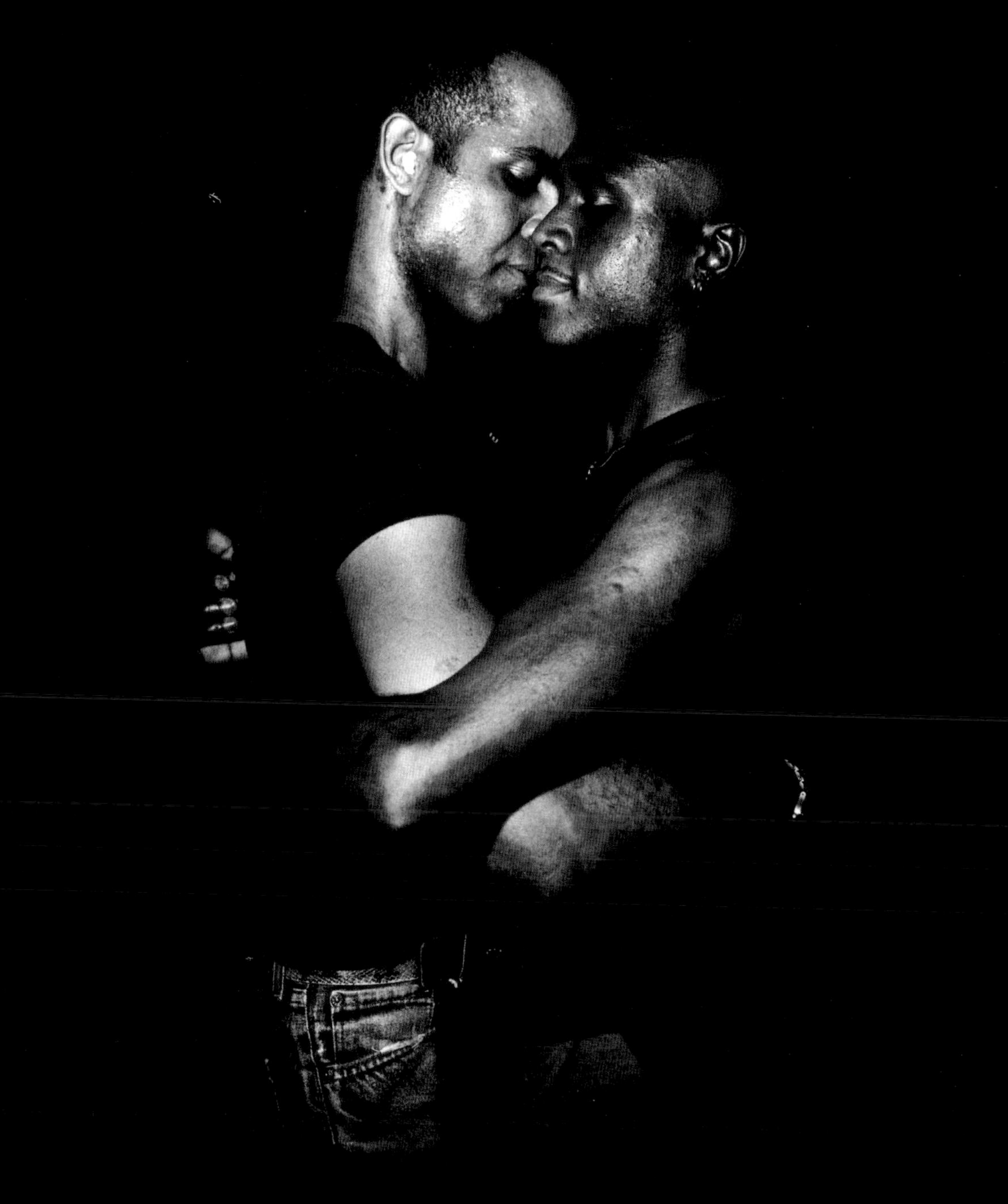

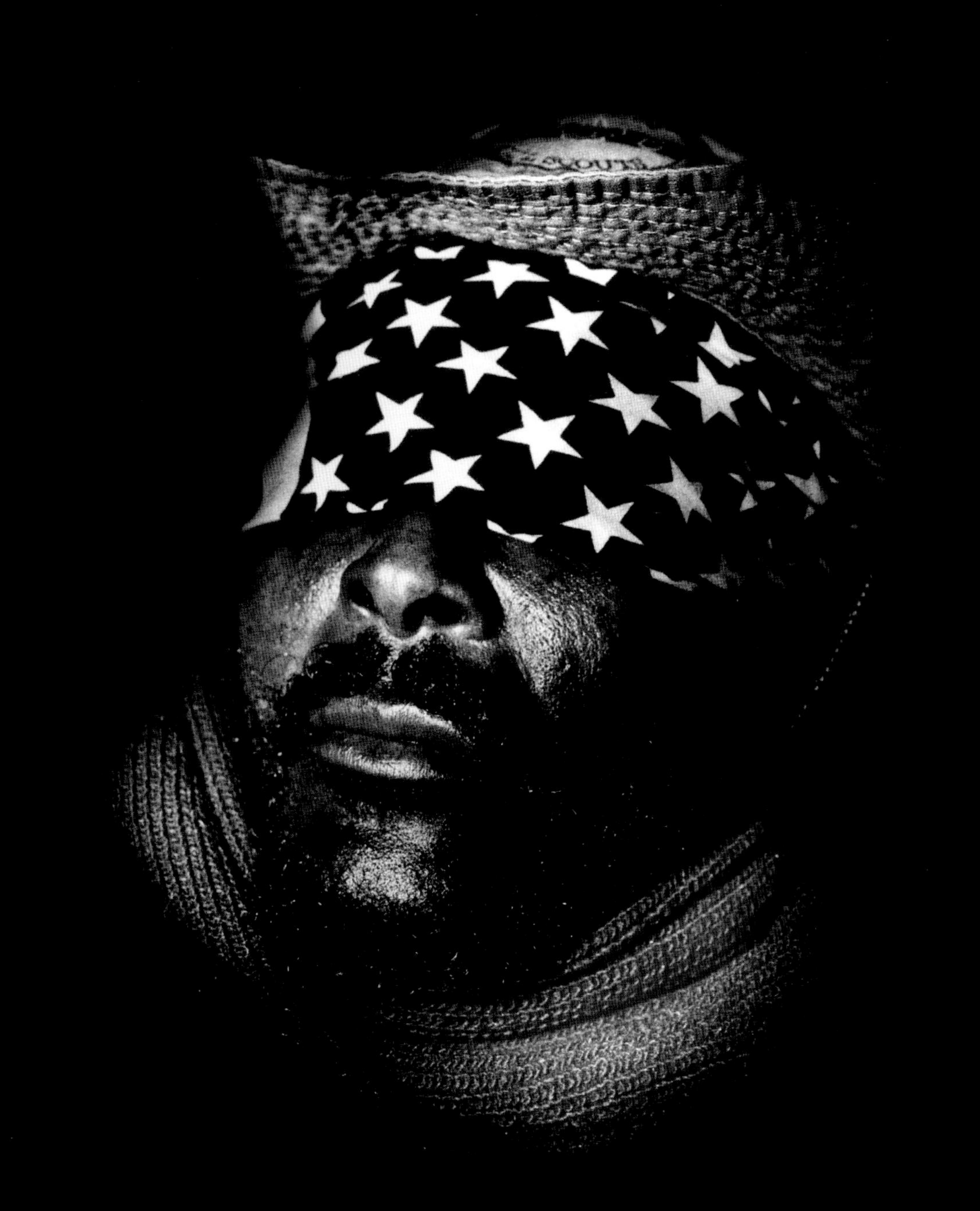

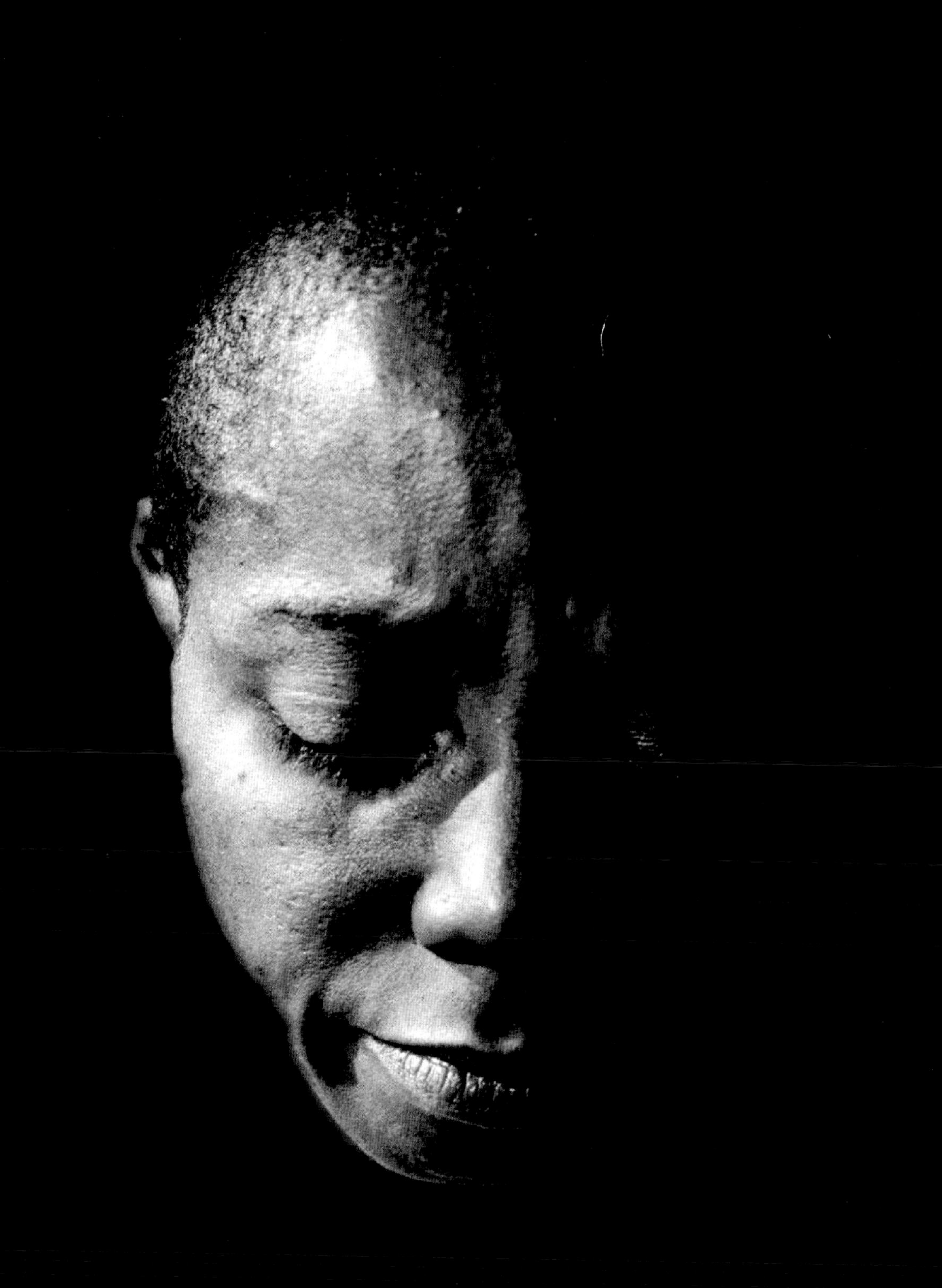

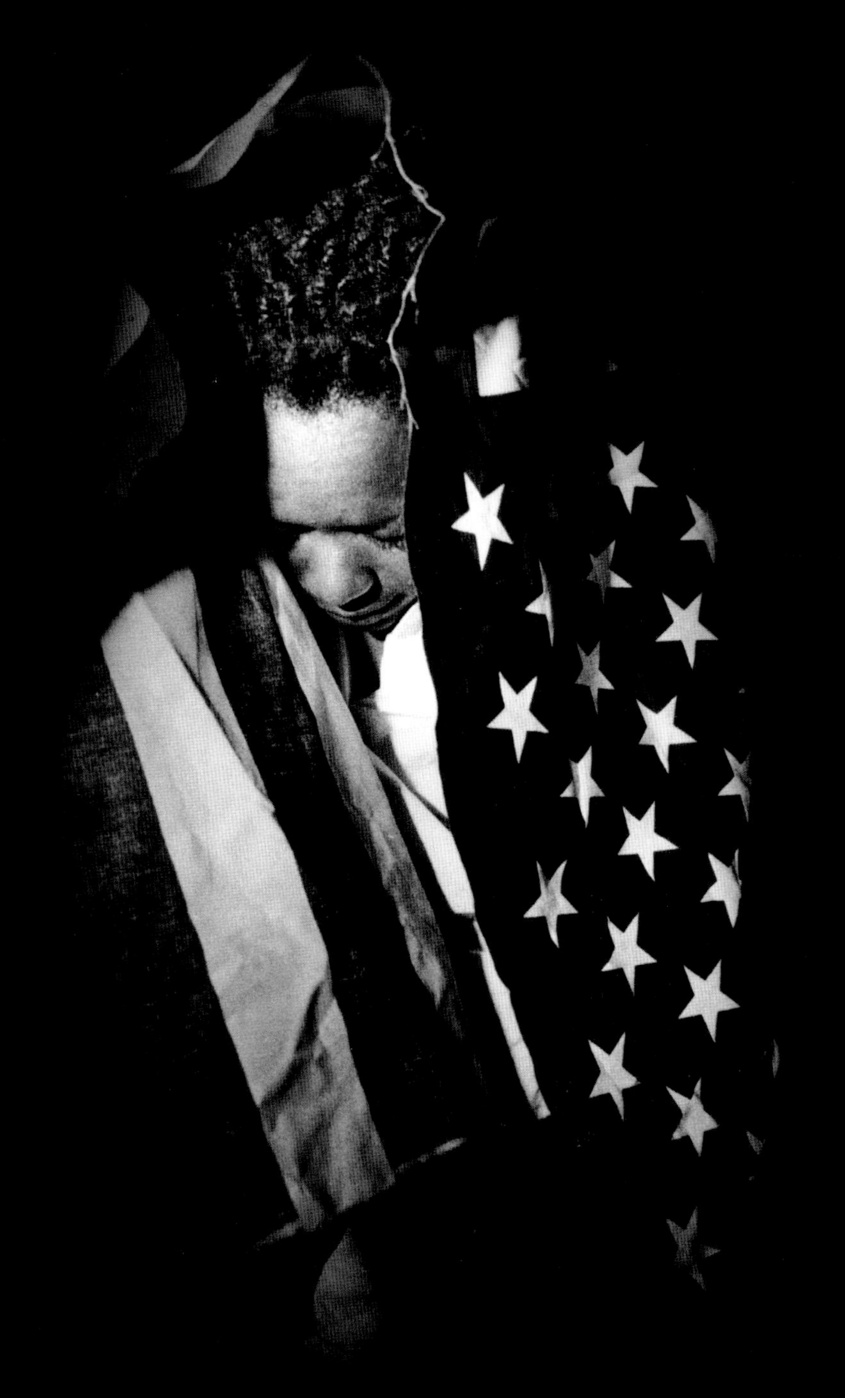

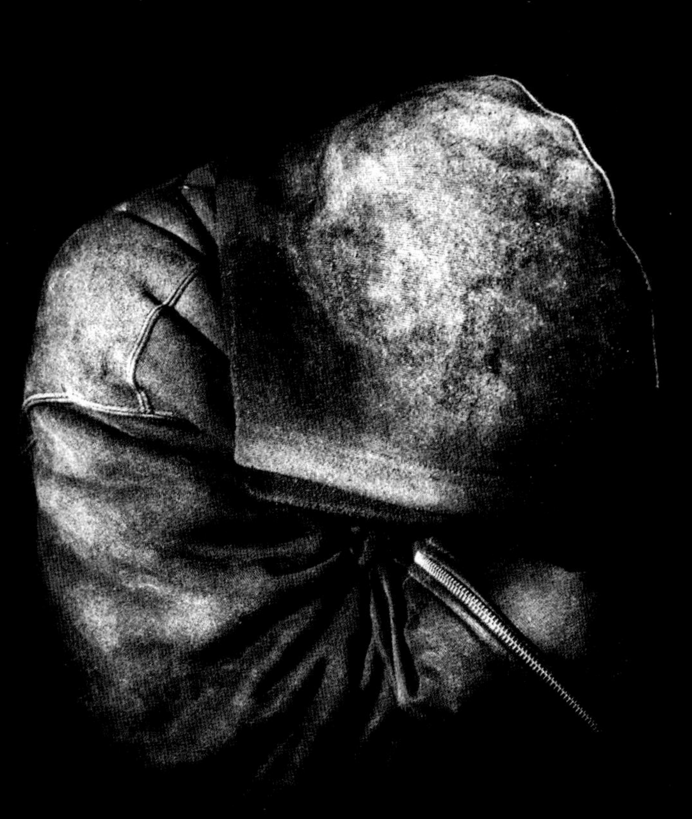

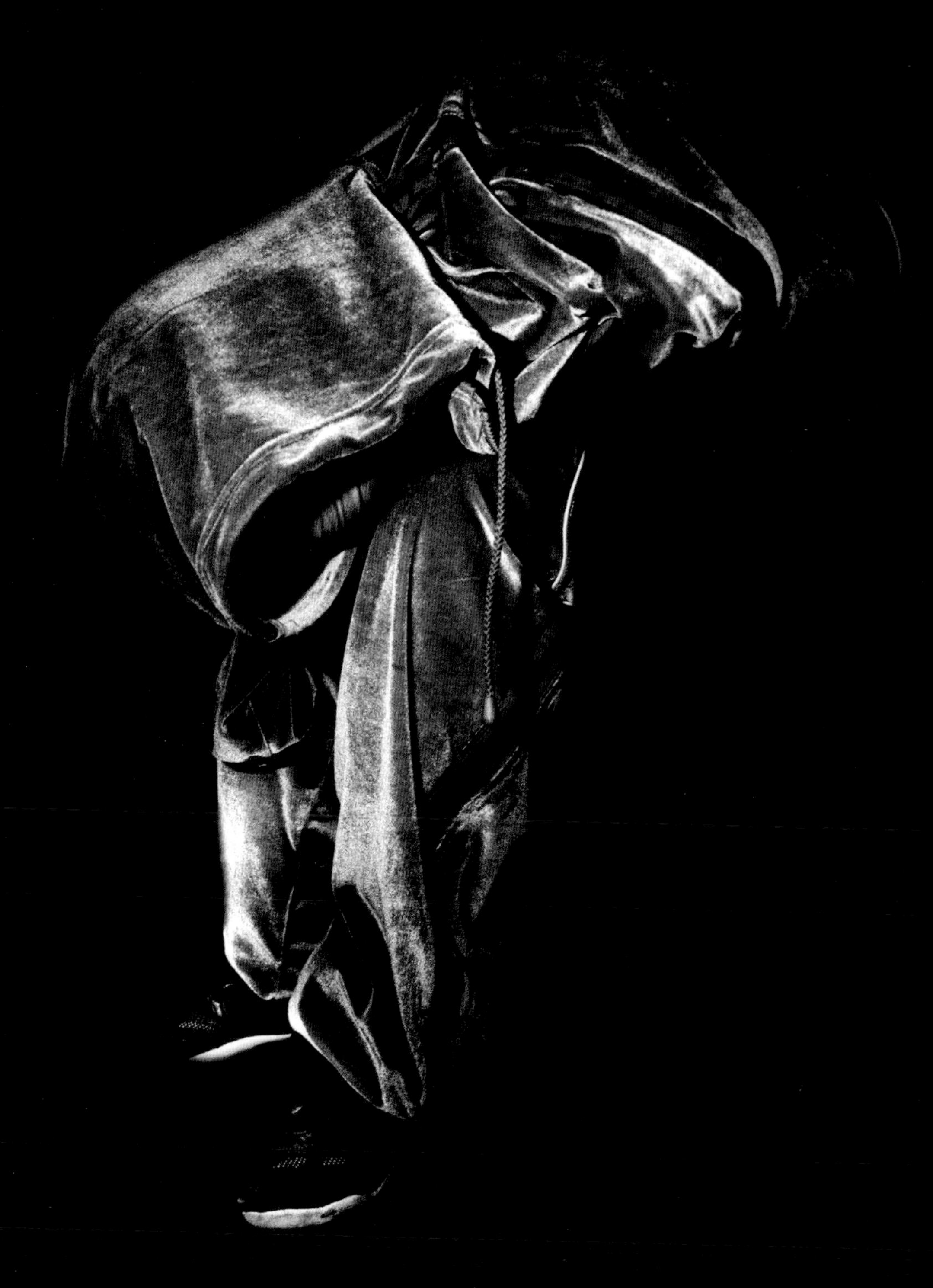

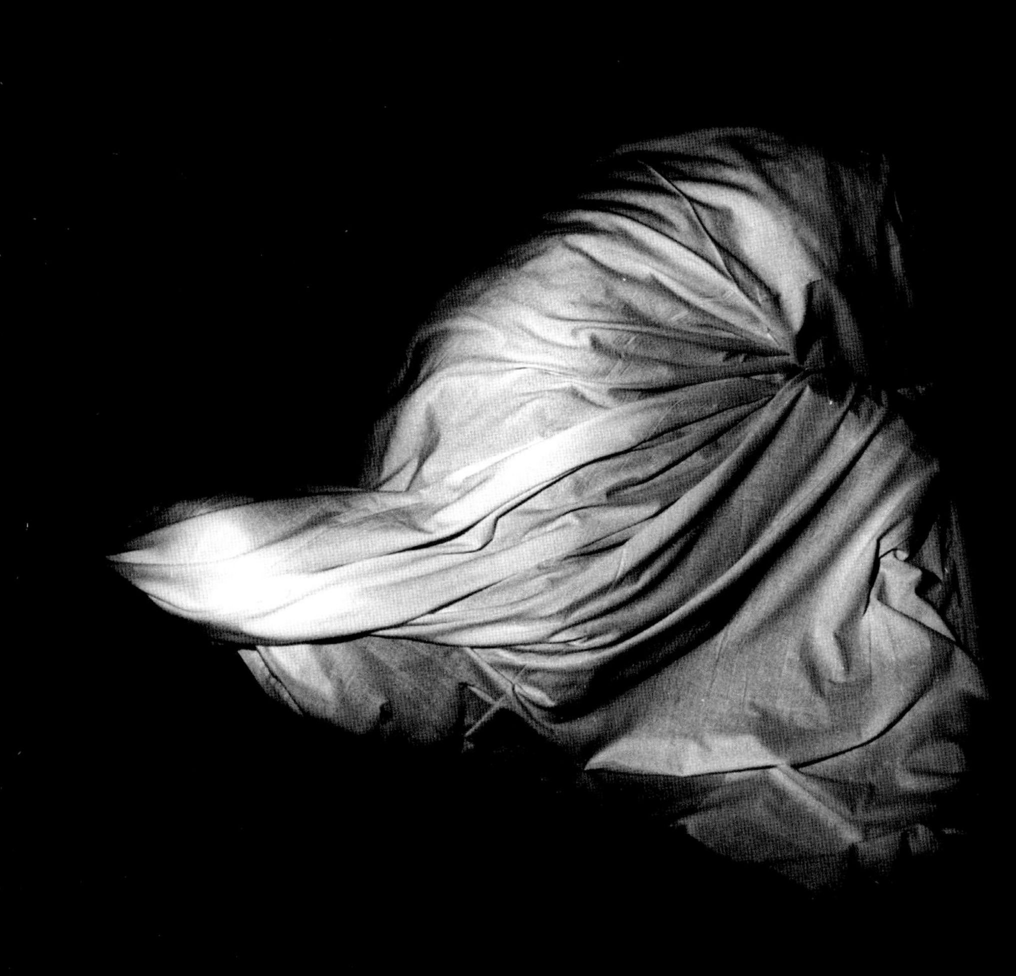

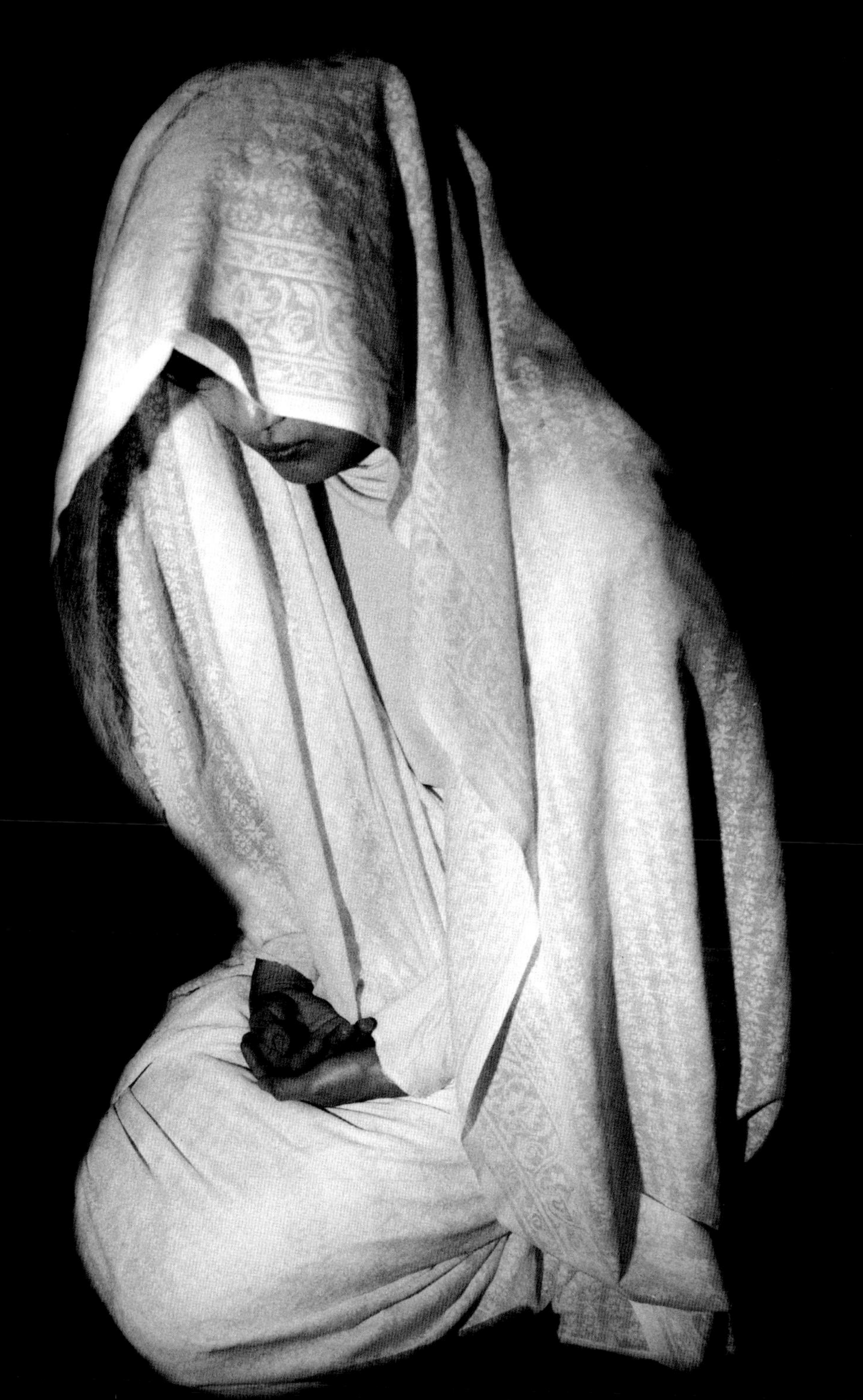

Frances Goodman

Voice of Reason
2000
Audio installation
25' 19"
Variable dimensions

This work examines the fine line that exists where daily routines become obsessions, when they cease to be acceptable practices and become an embarrassment
to society. The work looks specifically at people's fears of germs and how these
phobias and neuroses are often a reaction to the physical structures of society
today, where there is a distinct lack of personal space.

The piece is made up of 7 tracks played on a loop. The subject matter of the sepa-
rate tracks includes: eating meals with other people, kissing other people, hair,
sleeping in other people's beds, pimples, shoes and being sick.

Voice of Reason

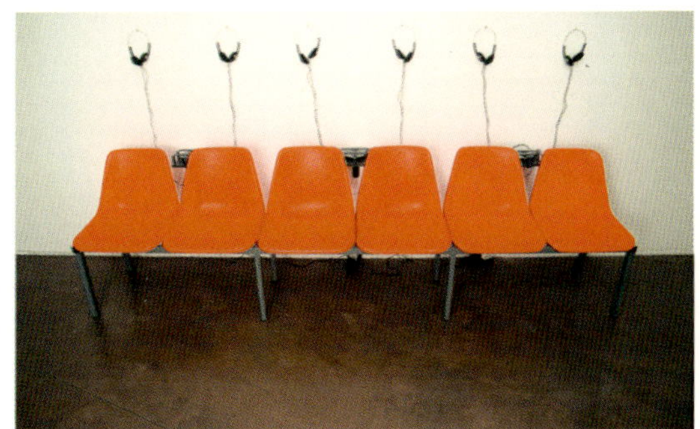

"After working with a number of media I eventually found that words and language had the uncanny ability to unnerve and get under people's skin in a way that visual images and modes could not. Words function in a similar way to my (aesthetic) concerns: on the surface they seem simple and clear, and yet they are often full of innuendoes and subtexts. They seem to have a dark underbelly. This is because they do not hold a sacred position in society, which often seems the case with many art forms. They are the raw matter of life, the building blocks of relationships and social interactions"

Frances Goodman in a conversation with James Sey, Artthrob Reviews, August 2004.

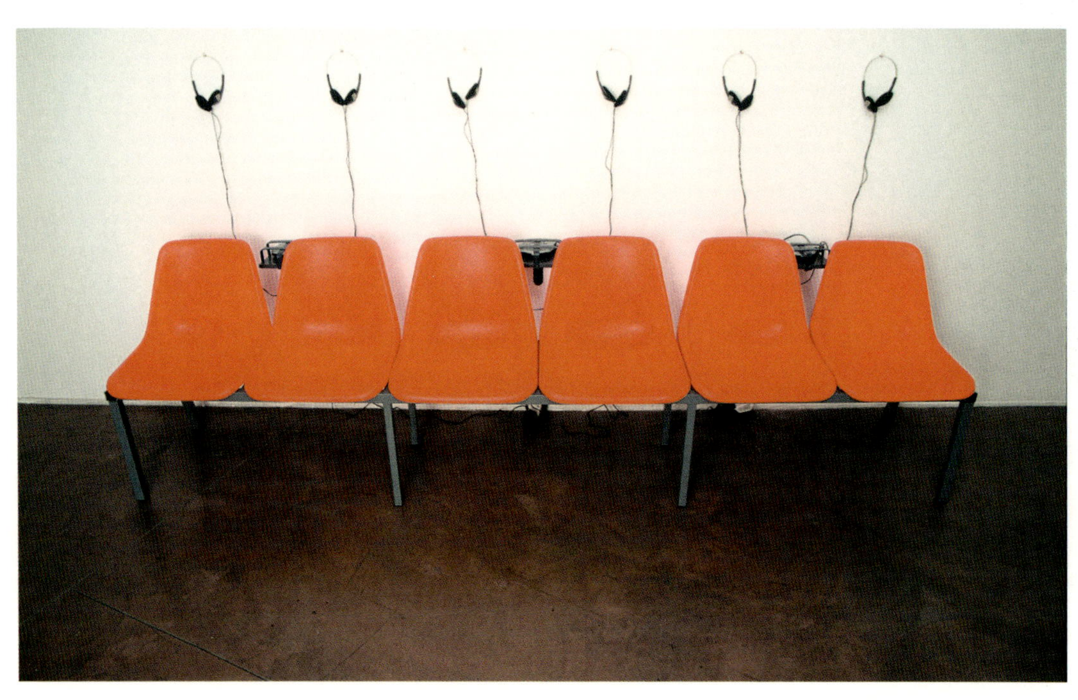

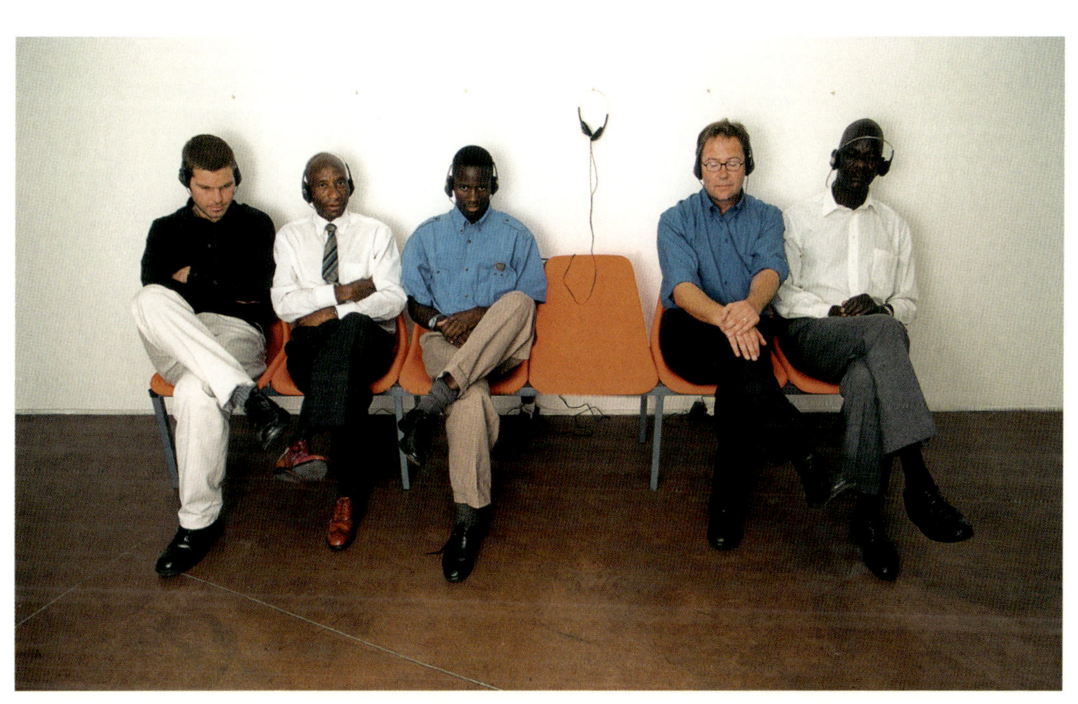

Romuald Hazoumé

Homme à terme
2004
Colour photography
76 x 50,6 cm.

Panne sèche,
2004
Colour photography
76 x 50,6 cm.

Bidon Armé
2004
Colour photography
76 x 50,6 cm.

Peut-être
2004
Colour photography
76 x 50,6 cm.

Sans Risque
2004
Colour photography
76 x 50,6 cm.

Avion de terre
2004
Colour photography
76 x 50,6 cm.

BB
2004
Colour photography
76 x 50,6 cm.

Transport en commun
2004
Colour photography
80 x 120 cm.

Guerrier
2004
Black/white
photography
50,6 x 76 cm.

Tyson
2004
Black/white
photography
108 x 72 cm.

Pièce montée
2005
55 gasoline cans
390 x 446 x 50 cm.

Laisser nous vivre
2004
Black/white
photography
50,6 x 76 cm.

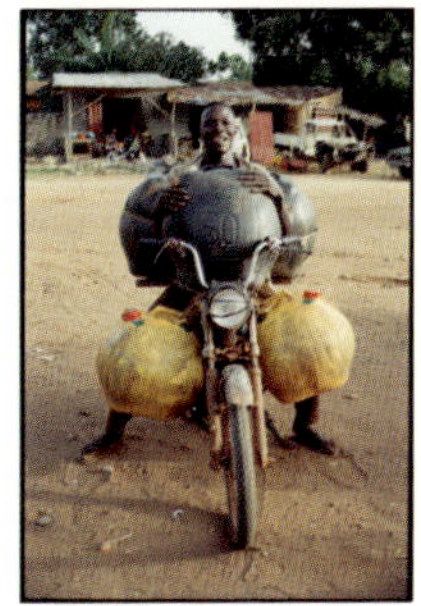
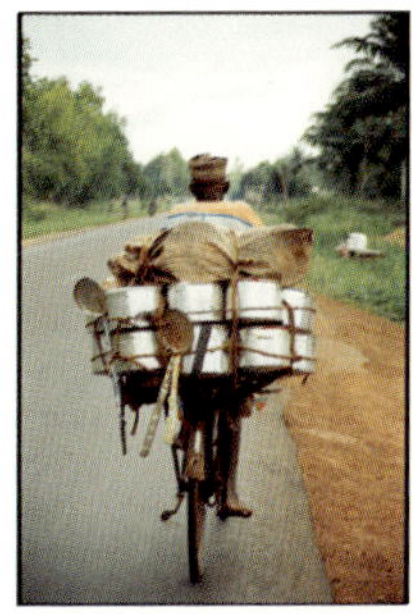
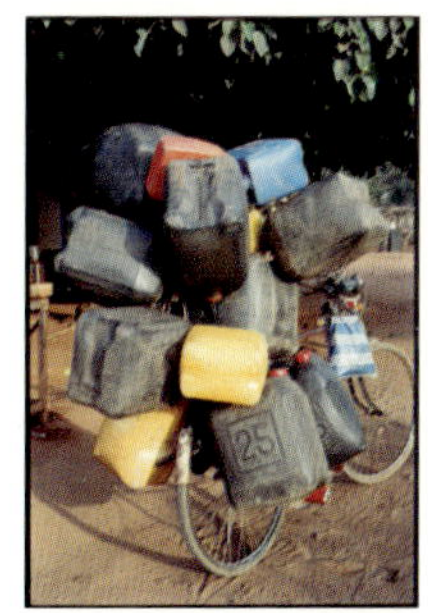
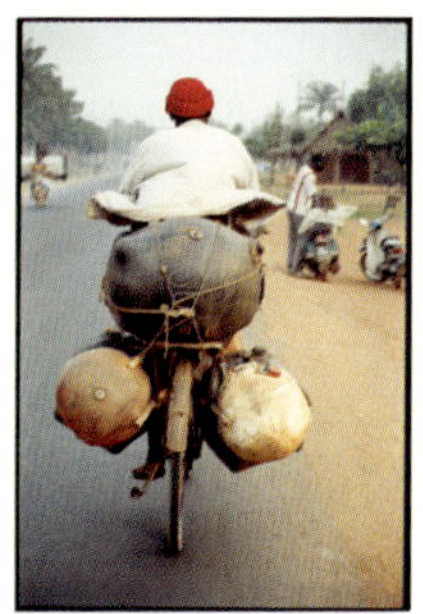
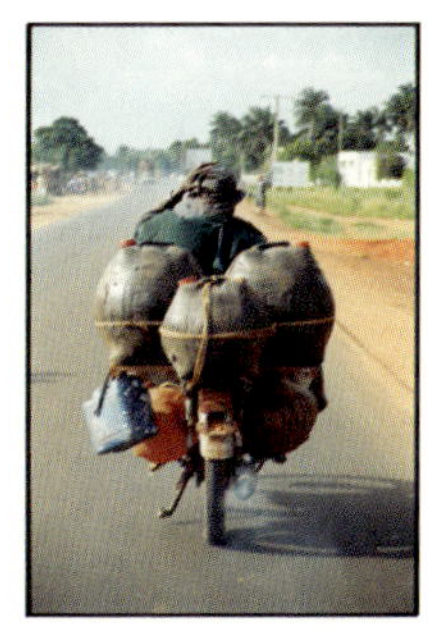
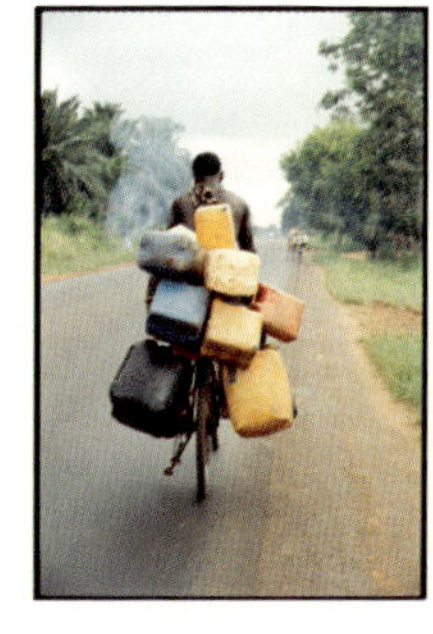
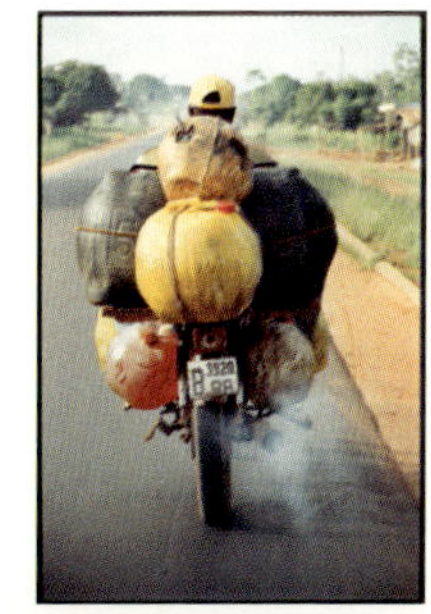
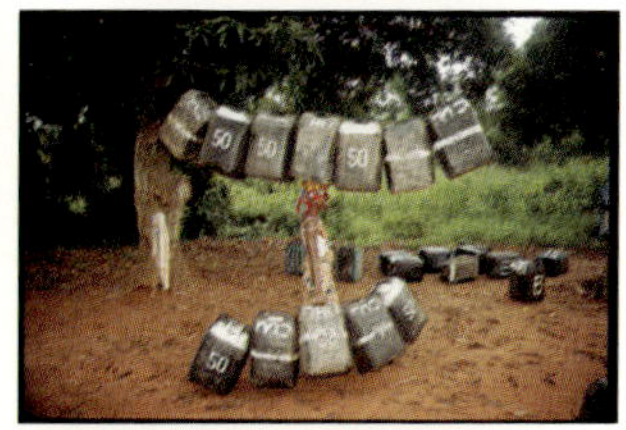
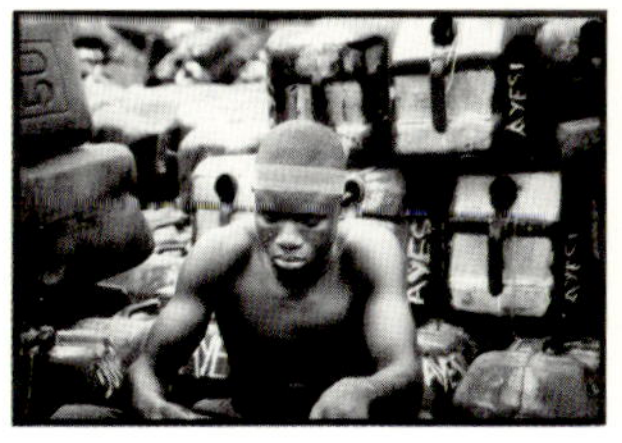
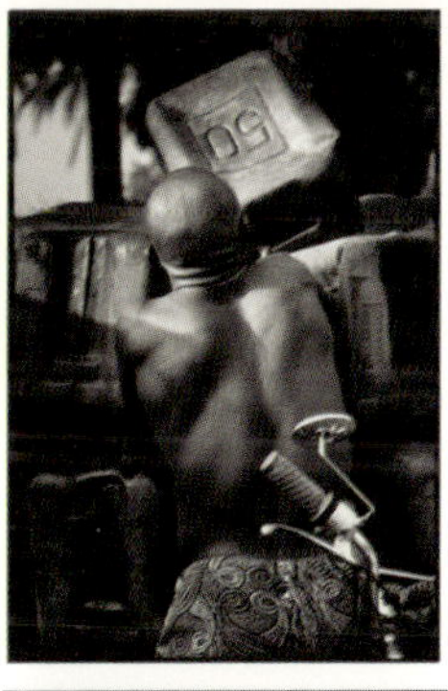
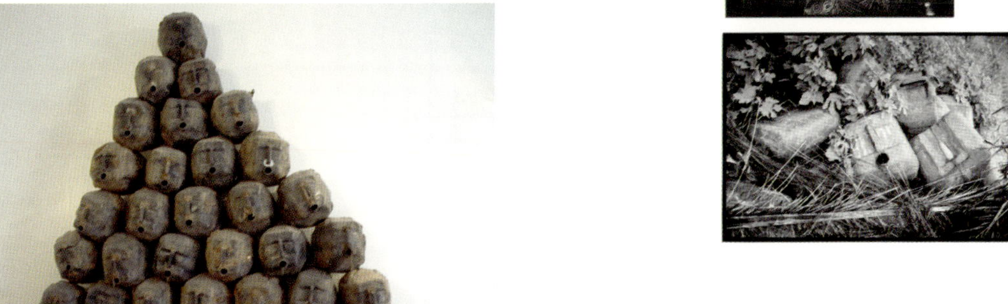

A representation of Africa today. A cake with a piece for everyone. Africans take the first bite, and the greediest ones are those at the top of the pyramid.

It's also a failed marriage, like the failed independence that reflects the situation of Africa today: it's a rich continent but where do all the riches go?

La Pièce Montée (Celebration Cake)

At the bottom all that remains is a few crumbs. On closer inspection, the cans, patched and patched again, look like men and women suffering. Part of the work was made by children as their little hands fit the nuts and bolts through can spouts.

Romuald Hazoumé

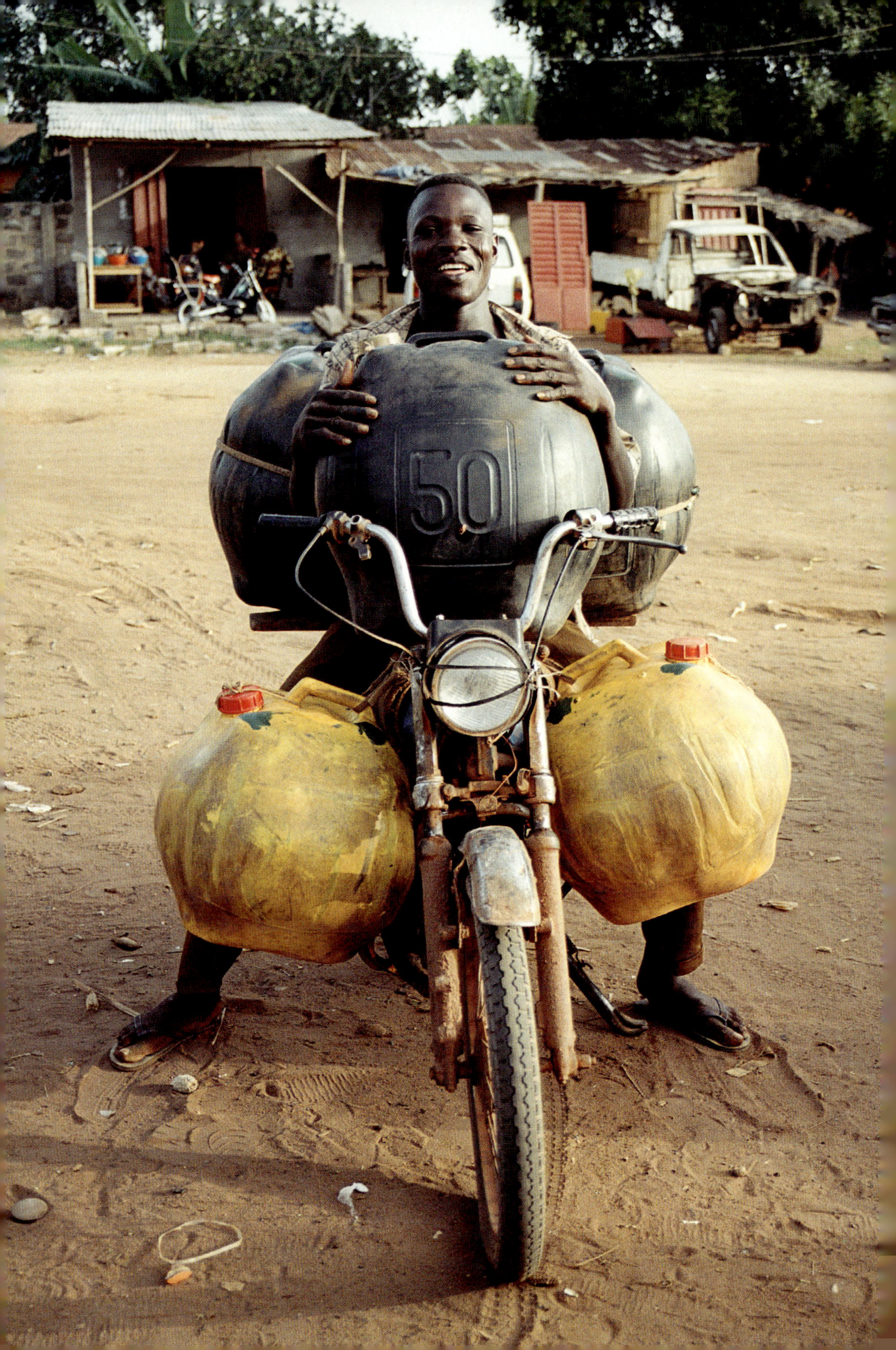

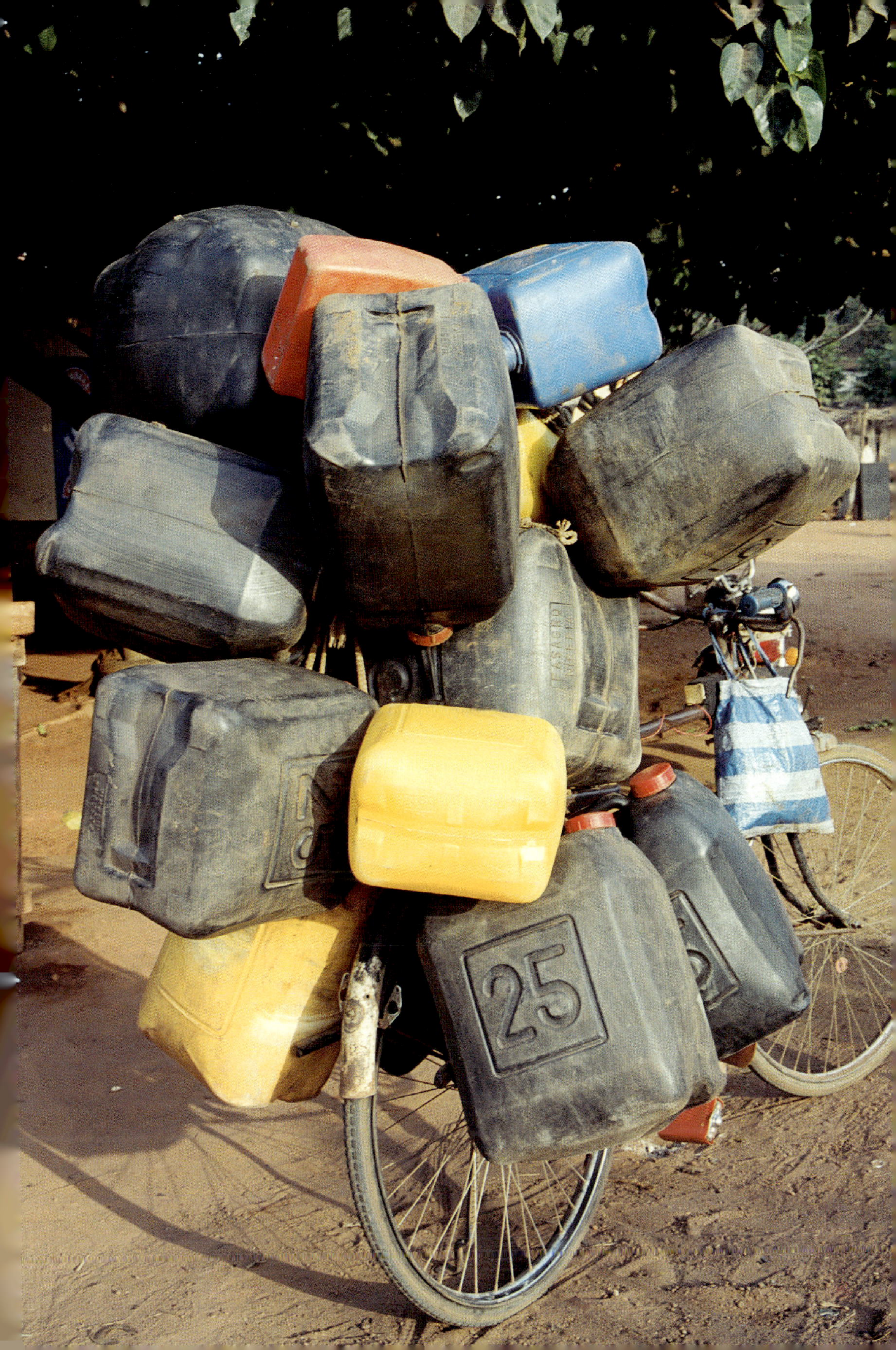

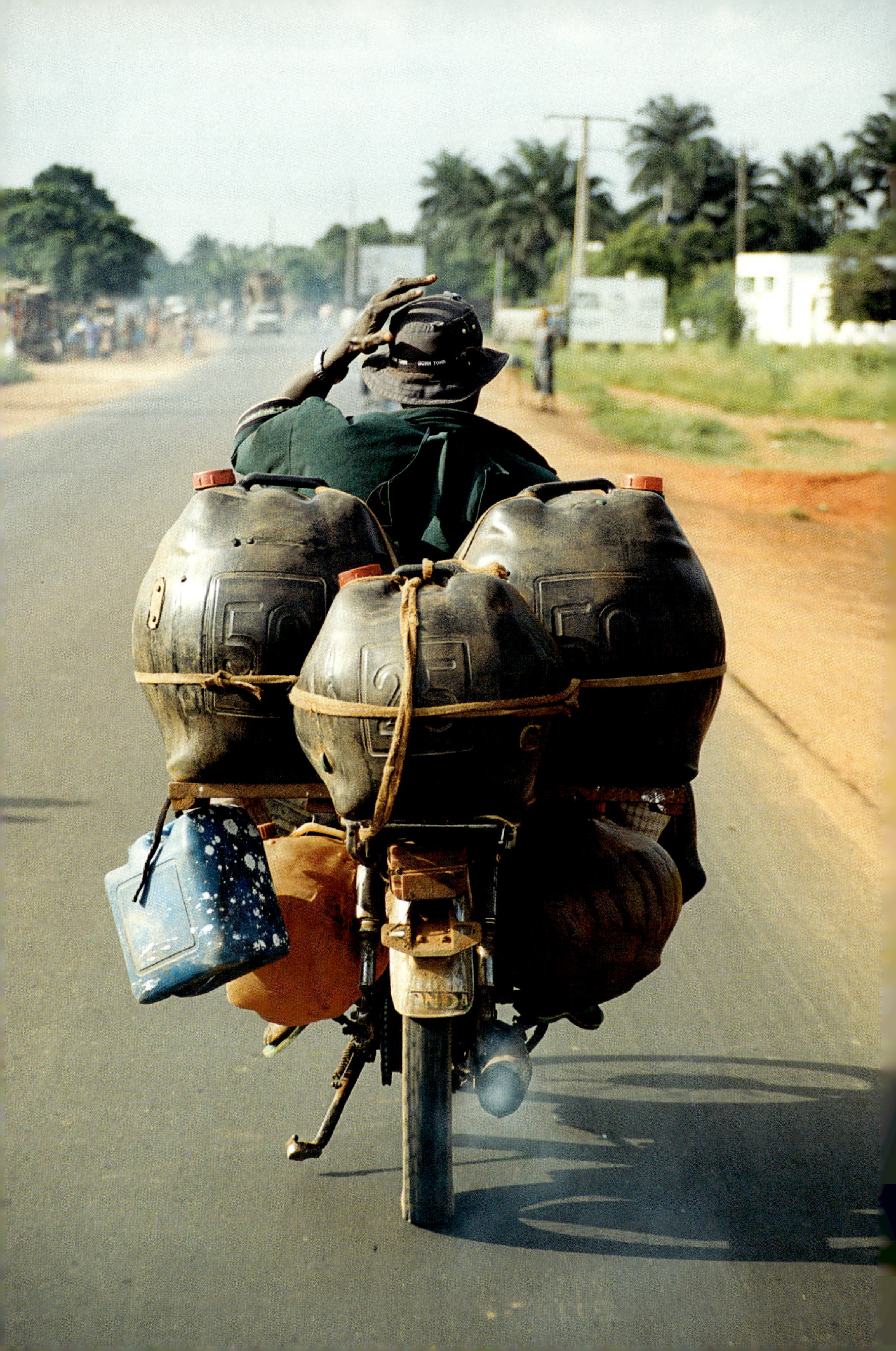

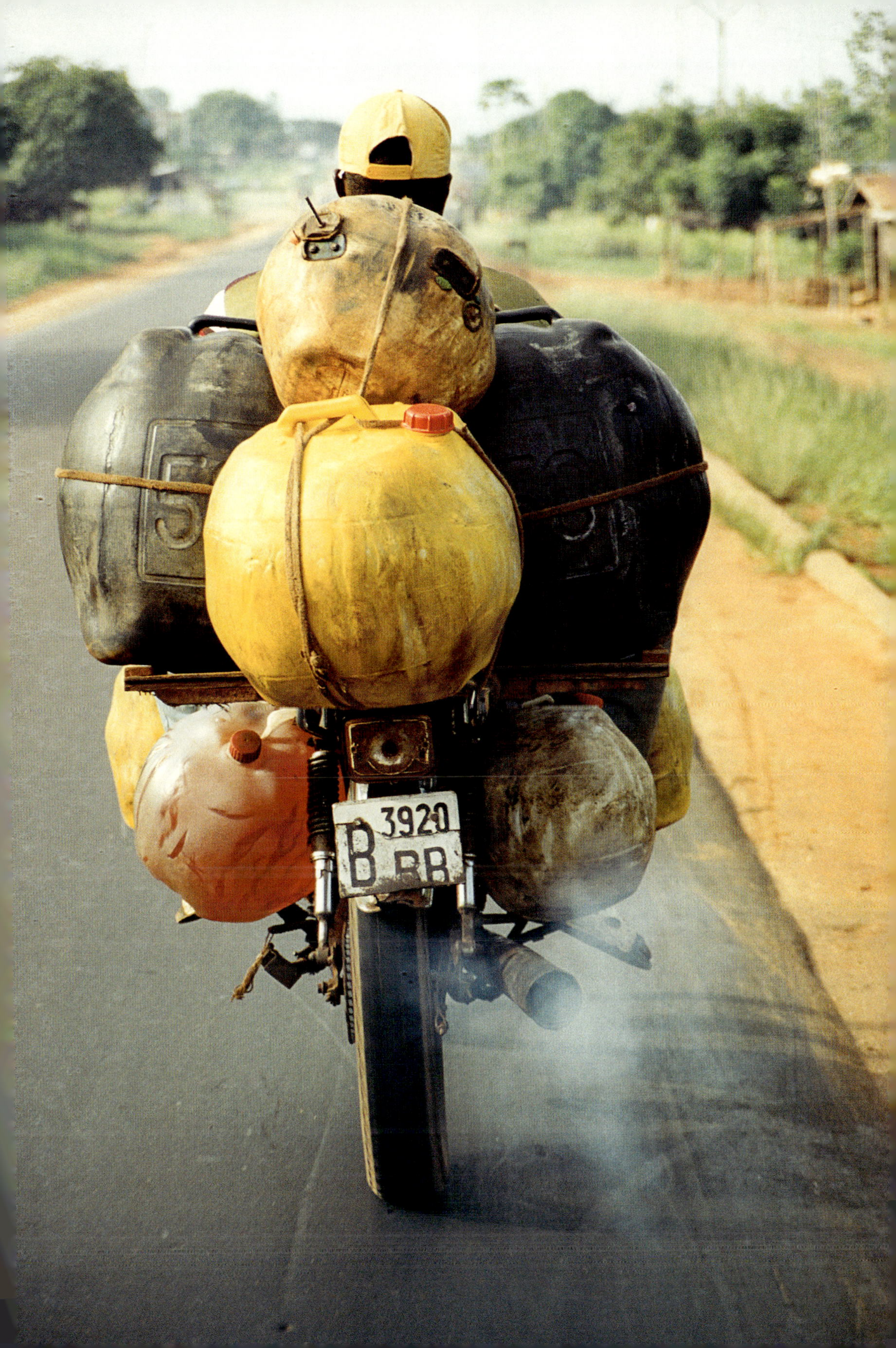

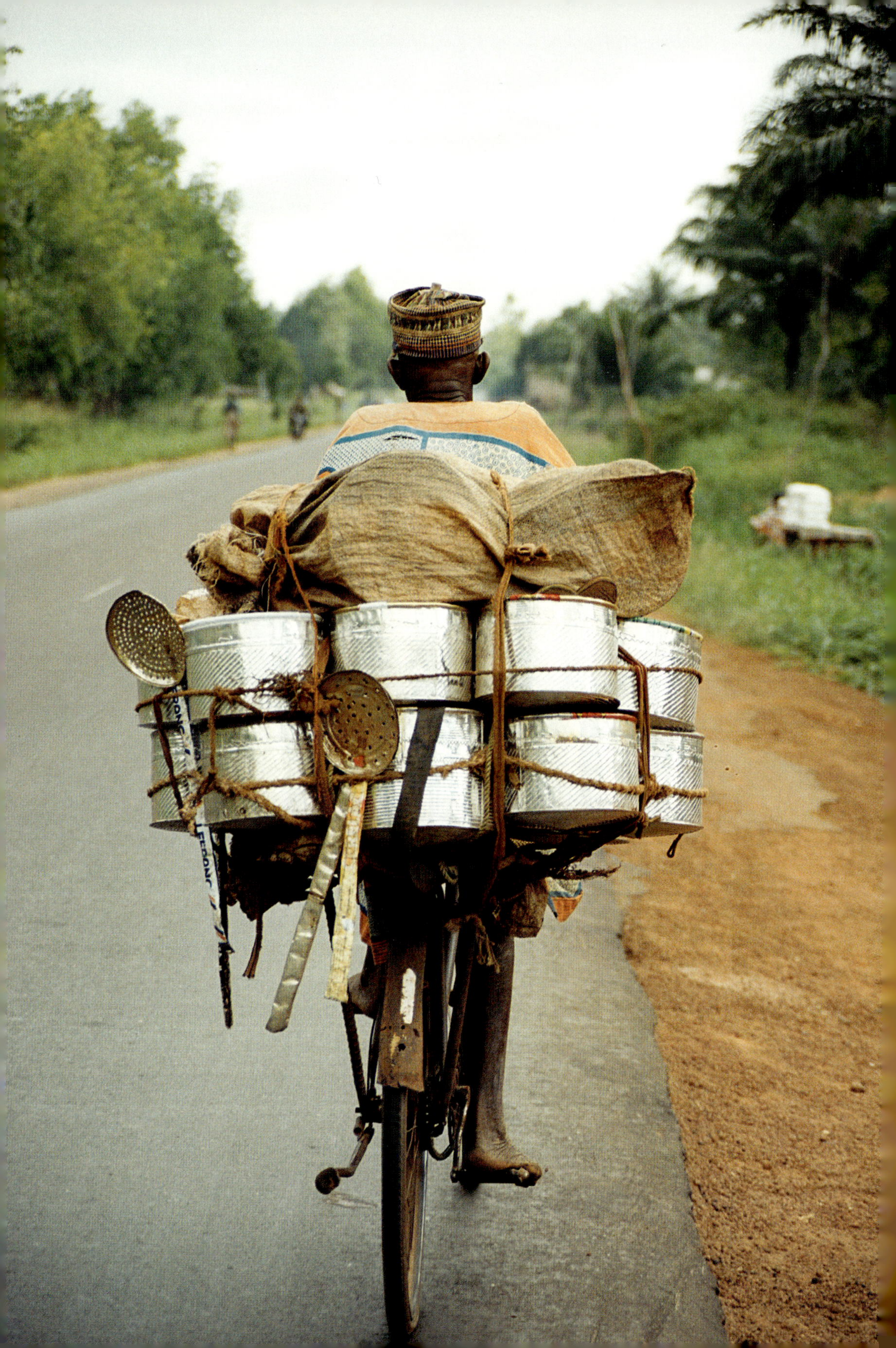

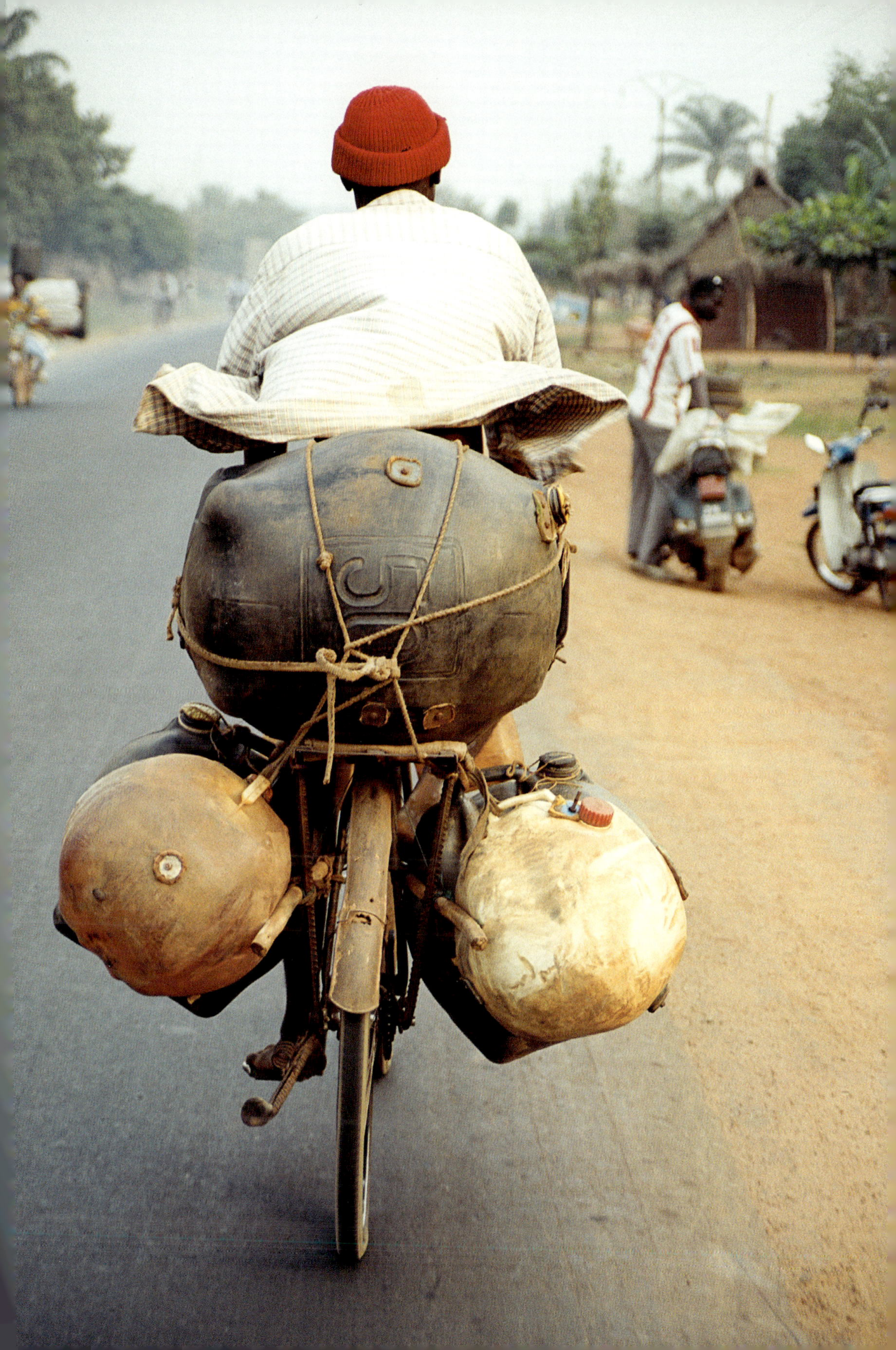

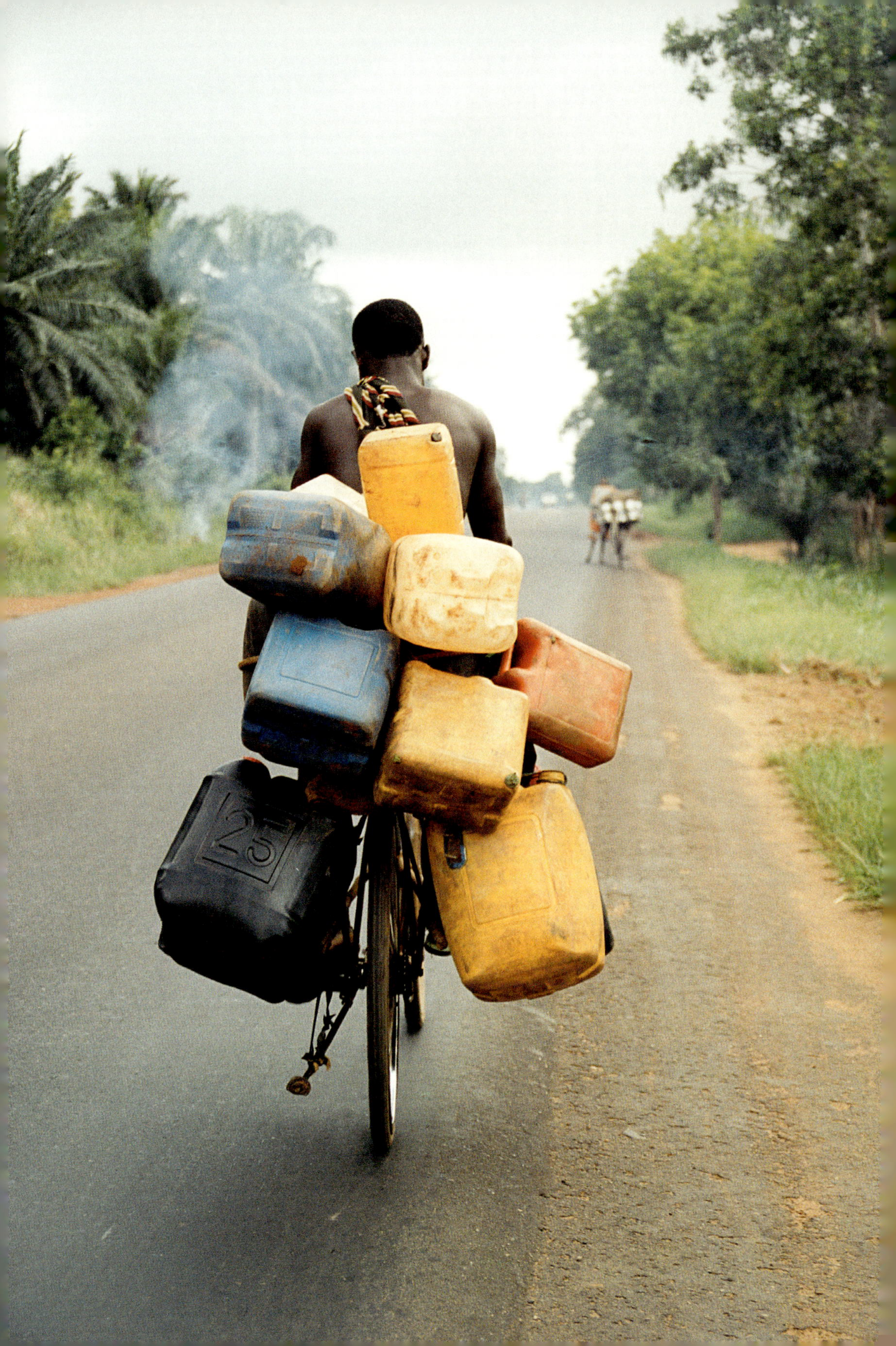

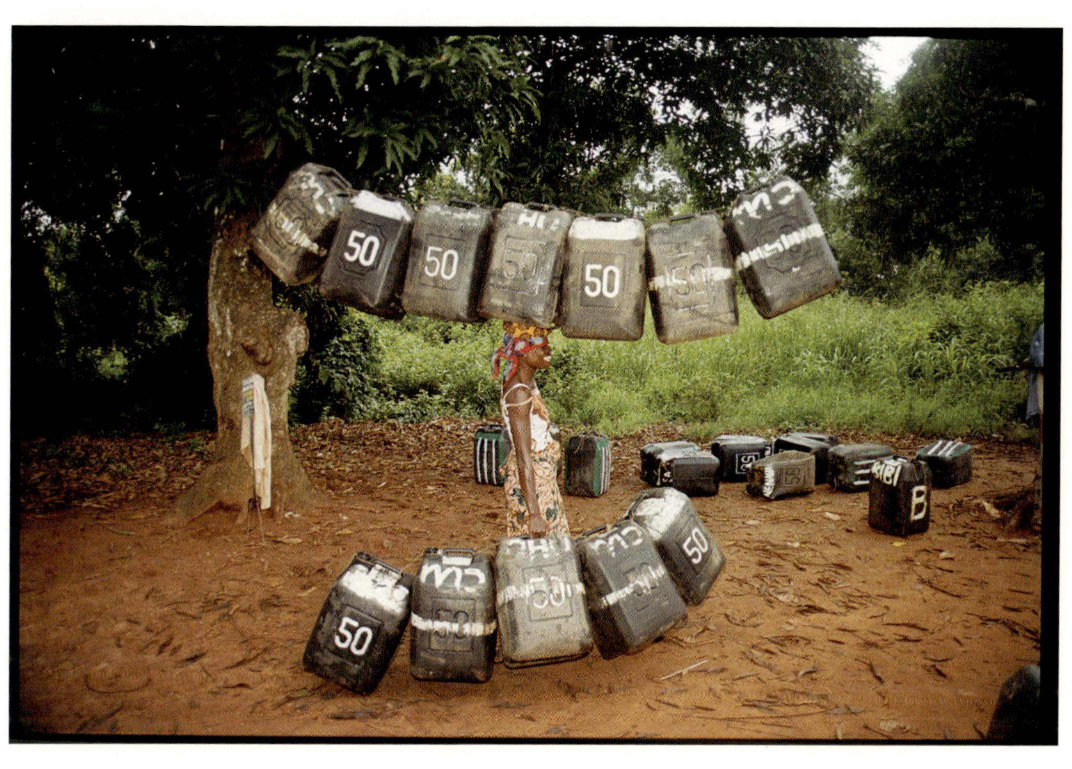

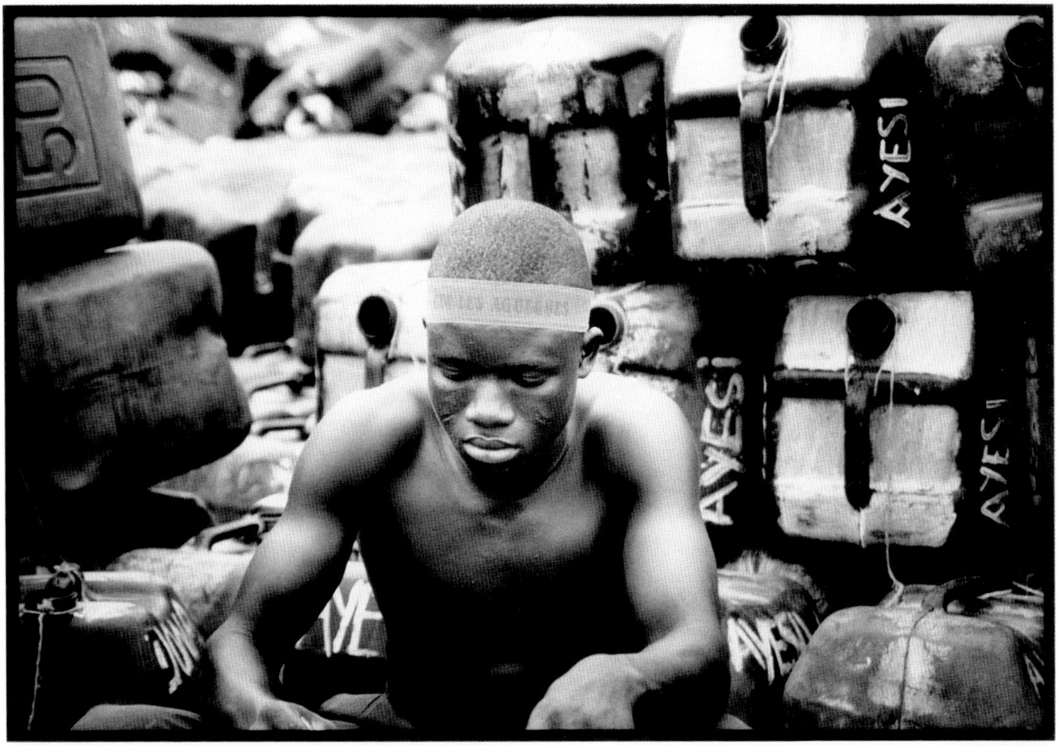

50
AYESI
AYESI
AYESI
AYESI
AYESI
AYESI

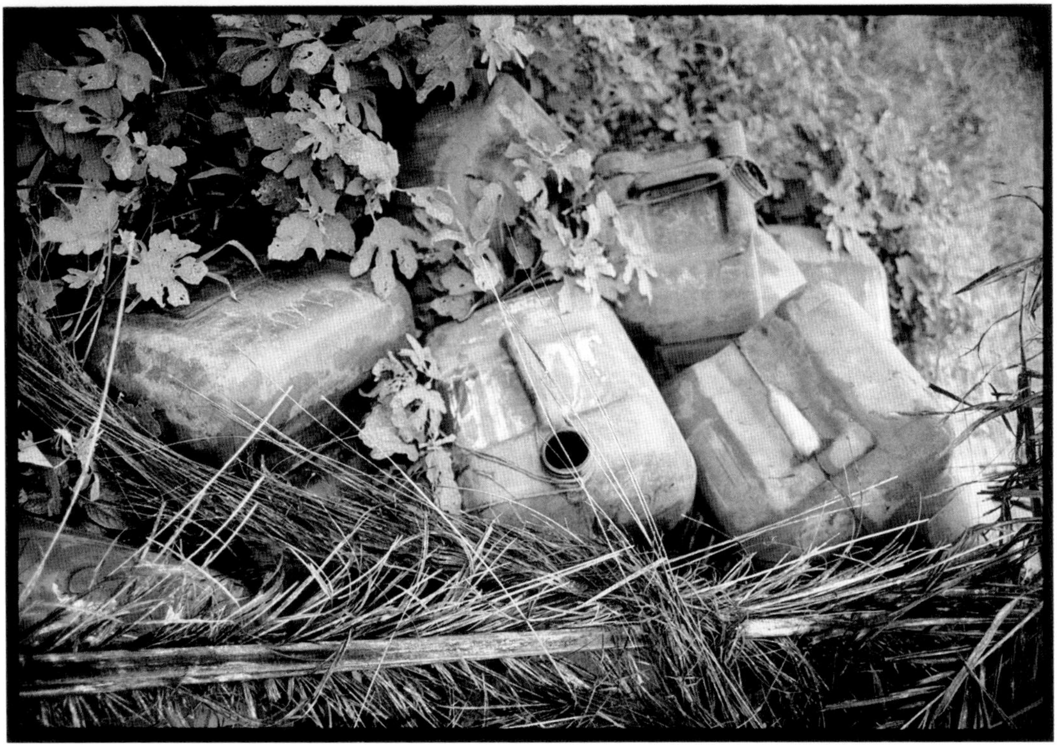

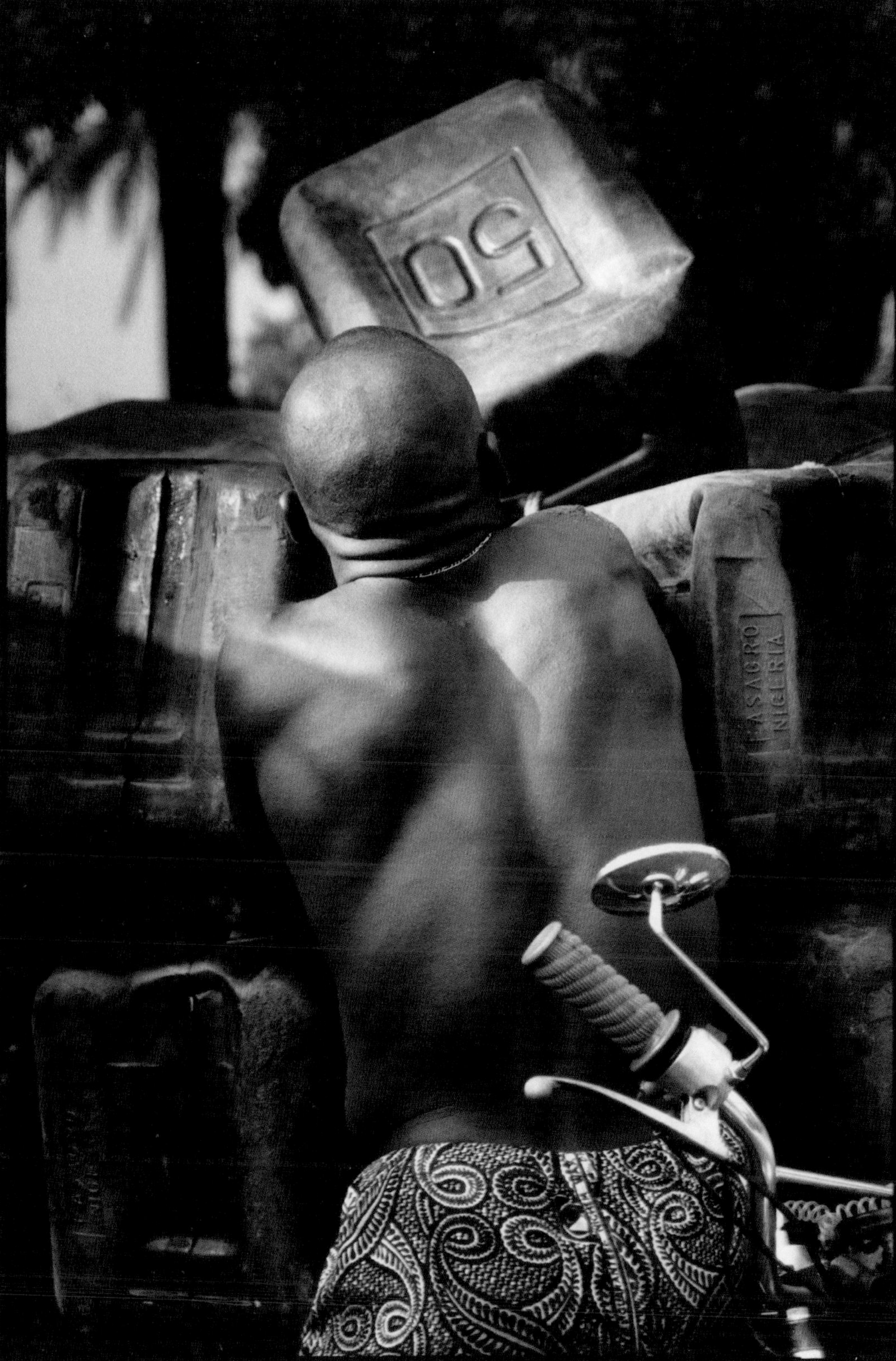
50
ASAGRO
NIGERIA

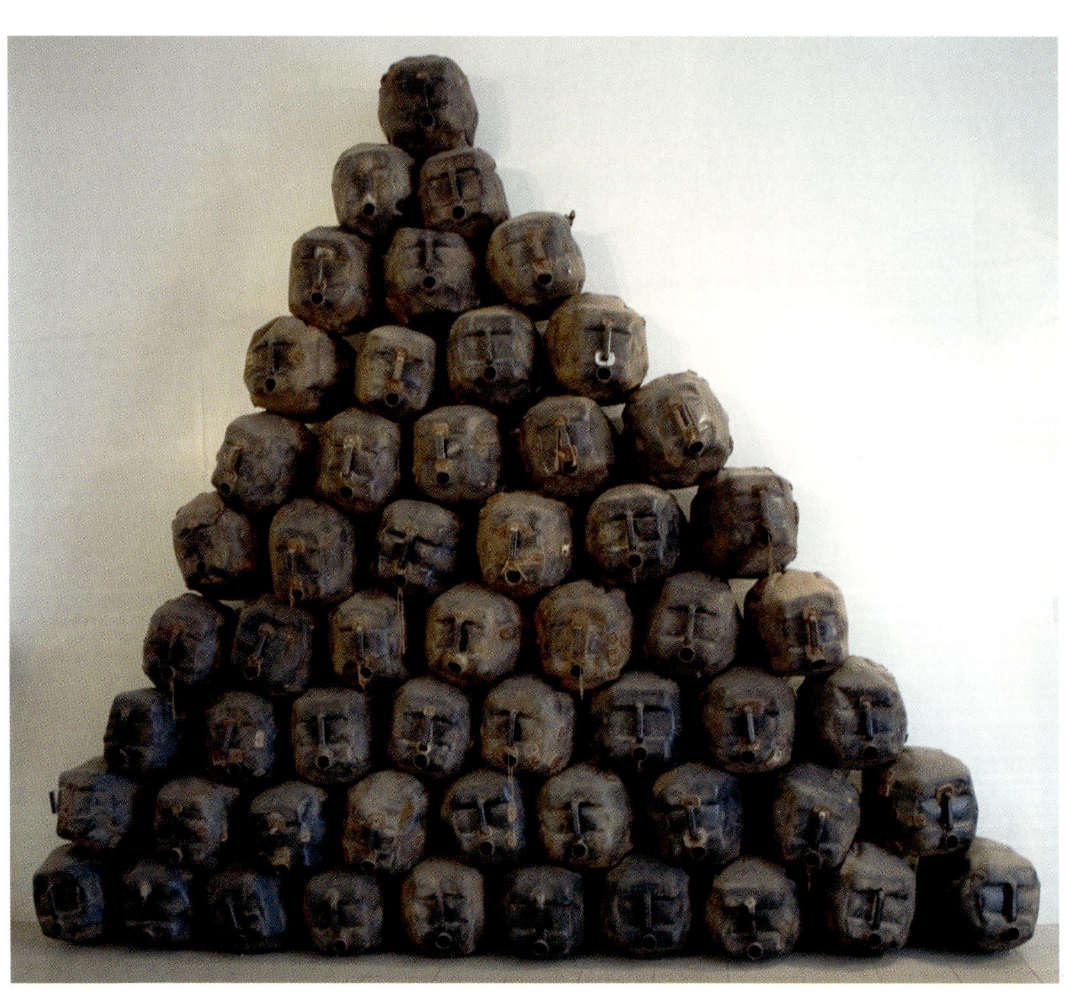

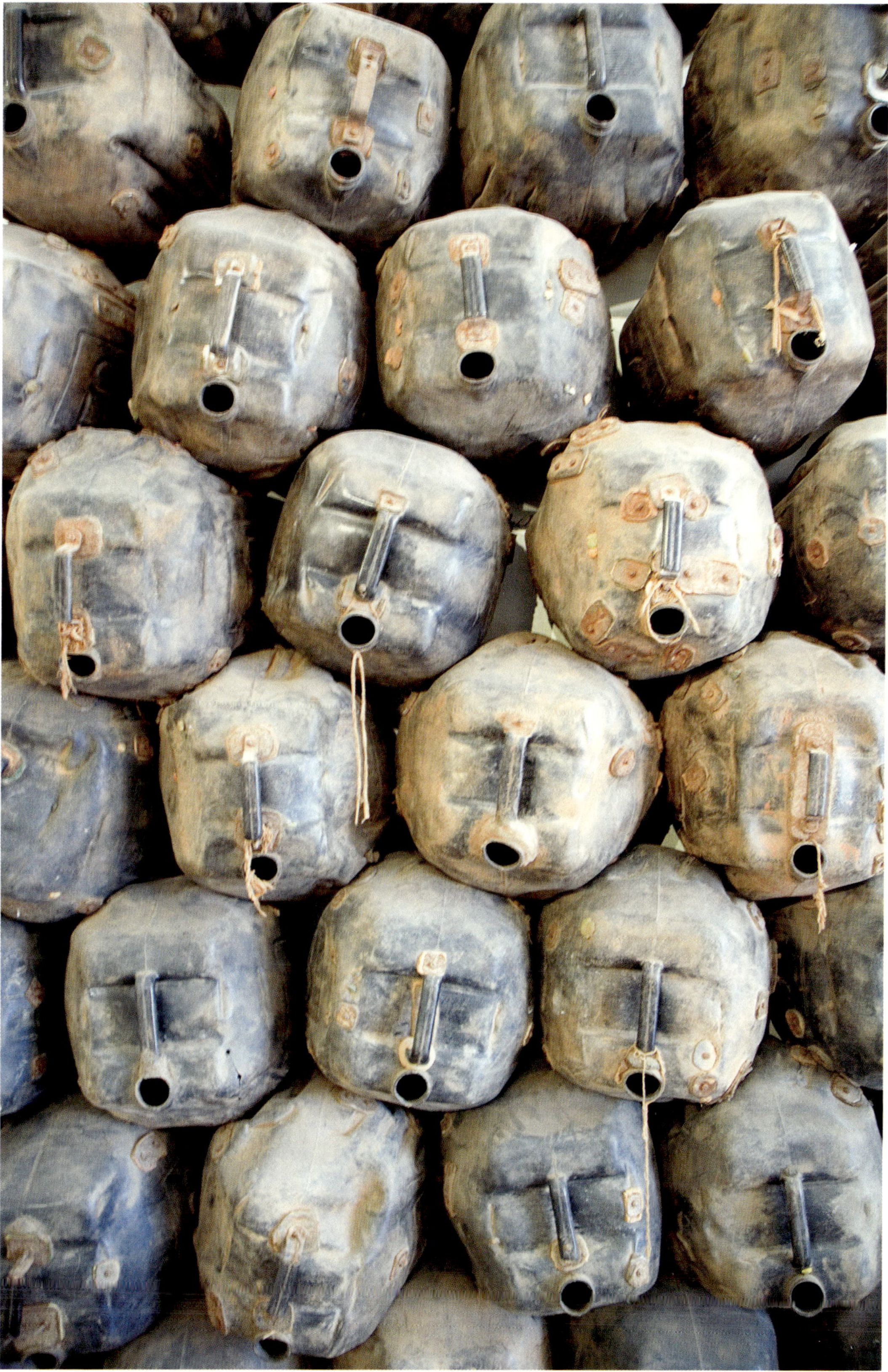

William Kentridge

Ubu Tells the Truth
1997
Video projection
8'

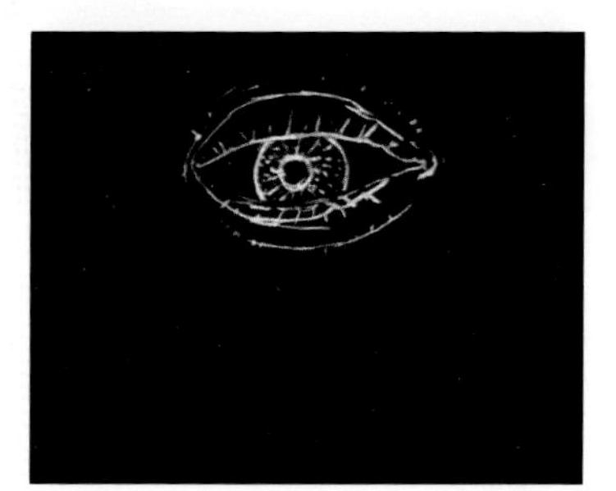

"I hate the idea that my work has a clear, moral high ground from which it judges and surveys. To put it blandly, my work is about a process of drawing that tries to find a way through the space between what we know and what we see.

The drawings attempt to map things which normally one just talks about. For example, if you have a notion of two rooms, one full of secrets, the other an empty room of truths – how can you draw these two spaces? We have a certain sense of ourselves that derives from our surface, our skin. So much of the history of western art consists of representations of the surface, yet there's this whole other side of us, our interior. We hope that the engineering inside us will work, day after day, year after year."

William Kentridge in conversation with Carolyn Christov-Bakargiev. Catalogue of the exhibition *William Kentridge*, Palais des Beaux-Arts, Bruxelles, 1998.

" I was working on a series of etchings based on Jarry's Ubu (for an exhibition marking the centenary of the first production of Ubu Roi on stage in Paris). These etchings invoved a drawing of a naked man in front of a blackboard. On the blackboard were chalk drawings of Jarry's Ubu with his pointed head and belly spiral. After the etchings were done, I wanted to animate the chalk Jarryesque drawings and then thought that if these were animated, so should the figure in front be. I then asked a choreographer friend if she wanted to do a piece using a dancer in front of a screen, in which a schematic line-drawing of Ubu would be moving. Thus the Ubu project was begun...

At this time too, the first hearing of the Truth Commission began and it rapidly became clear that if we were looking for found texts we had an avalanche of remarkable material arriving every day. Even as I started the process of convincing the participants in the different projects that it made sense to combine them, it became clear that in some ways the contradictory projects – sober documental material and wild burlesque – could make sense together. The material from the Truth Commission could give a gravitas and grounding to Ubu (which was always in danger of becoming merely amusing). At the same time the wildness and openness of Jarry's conception could give us a way of approaching the documentary material in a new manner and so enable us all to hear the evidence afresh."

Ubu tells the truth
Notes by director William Kentridge (in Jane Taylor Ubu and the Truth Commission, University of Capetown Press, 1998, reproduced in Carolyn Christov-Bakargiev, op. cit.)

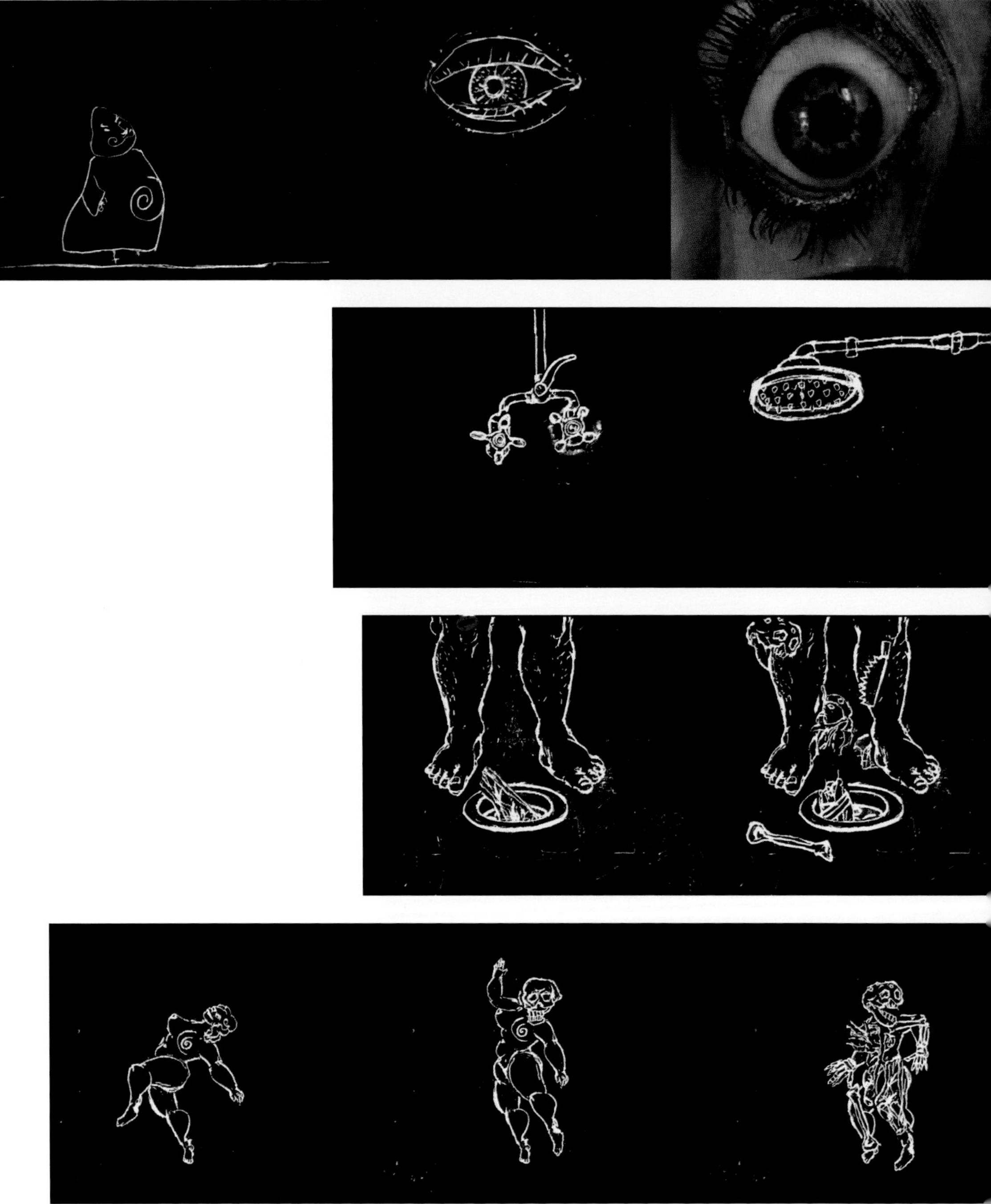

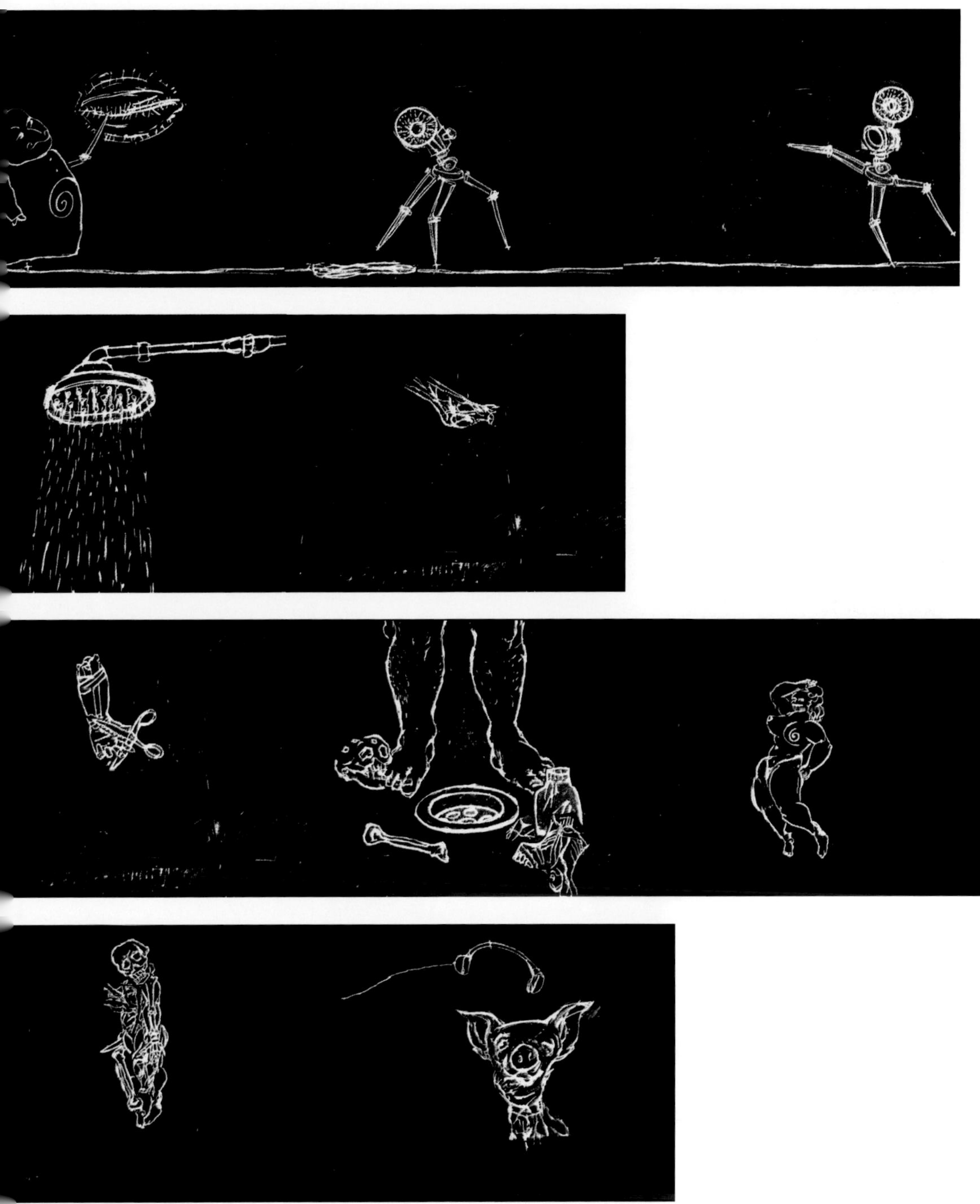

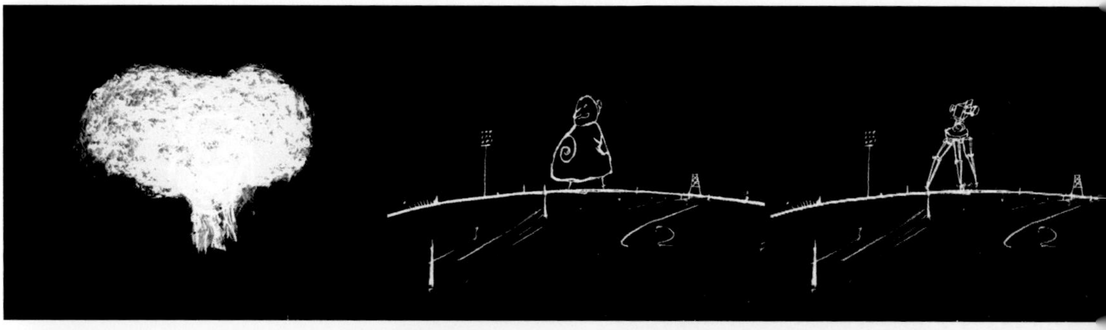

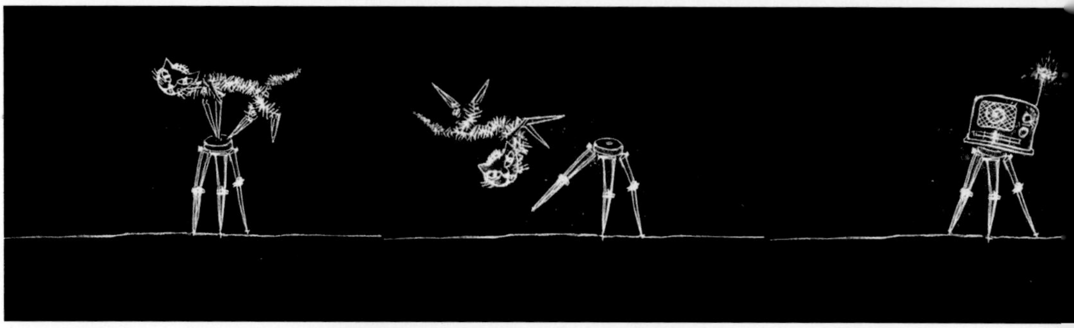

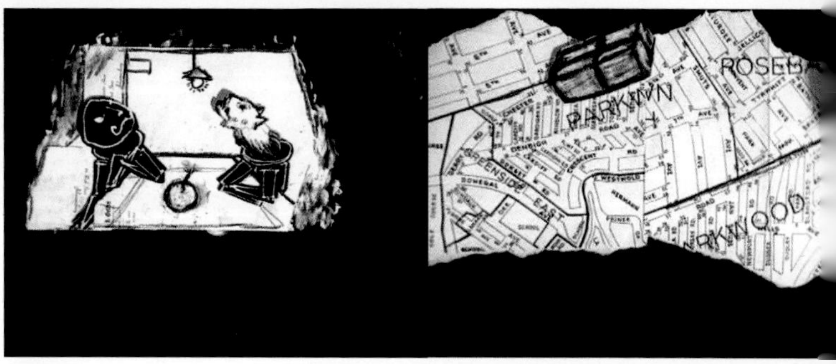

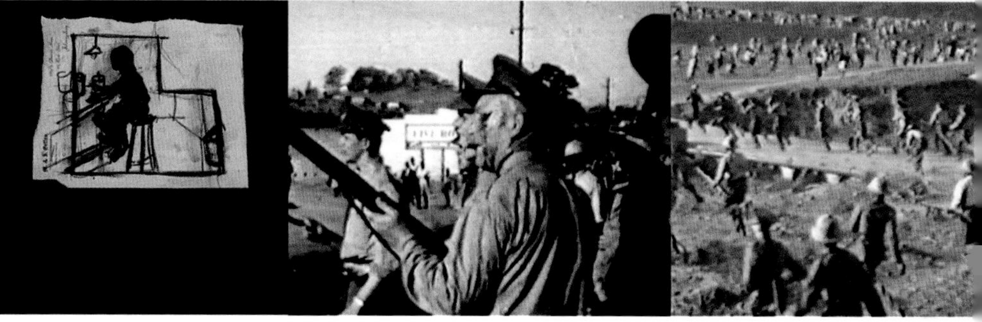

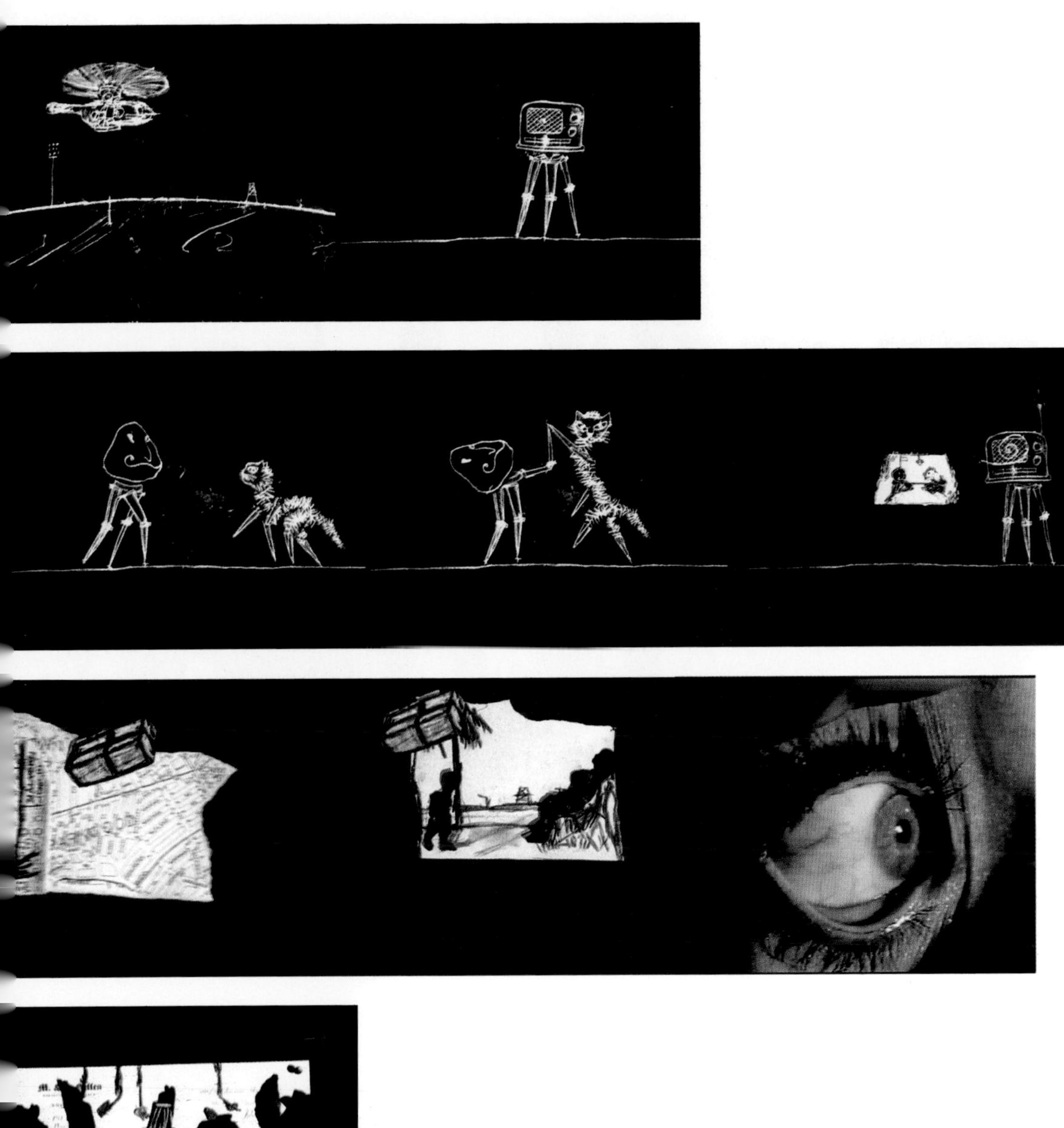

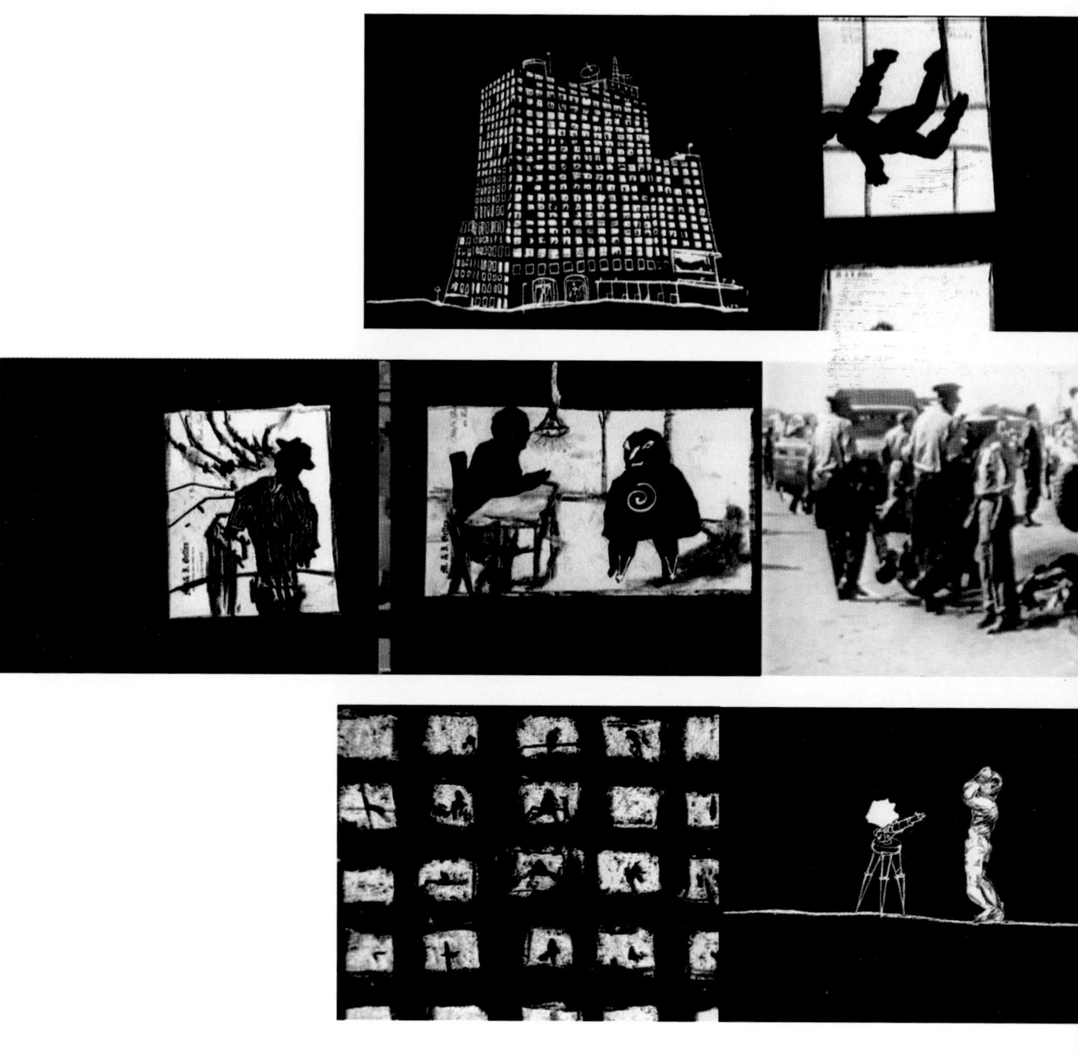

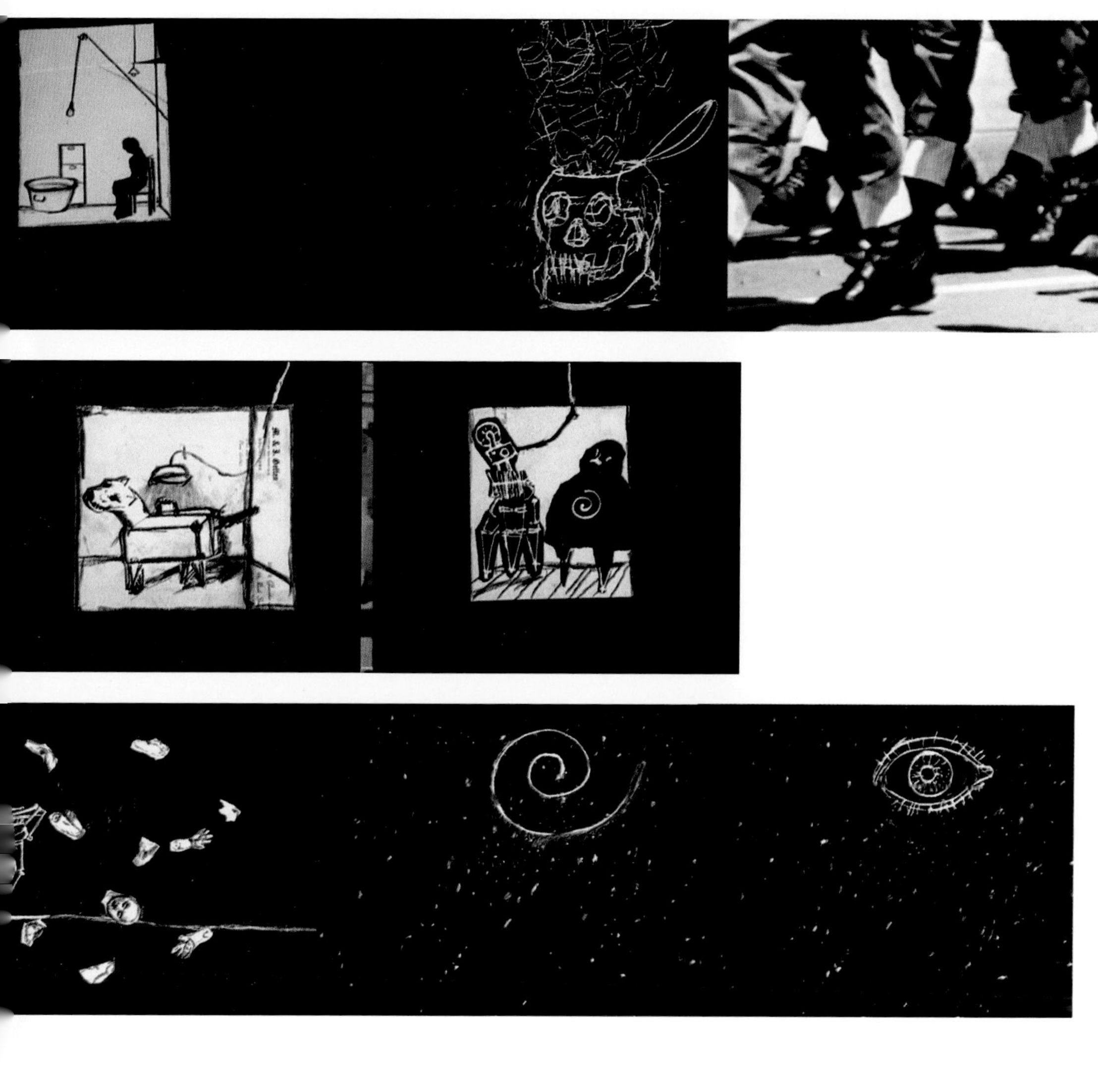

Bodys Isek Kingelez

Work for U.N.-50th Ann
1995
Paper, cardboard,
polystyrene and plastic
91 x 74 x 53 cm.

Sports internationaux
1998
Paper, cardboard,
alluminium and plastic
90 x 85 x 25 cm.

Bodystand
1997
Plywood, paper
and cardboard
100 x 150 x 150 cm.

"Art is a rare product, requiring great thought and even greater imagination. Art is privileged wisdom, a force of individual renewal that promotes a better future for everyone".

From a conversation between the artist and André Magnin.

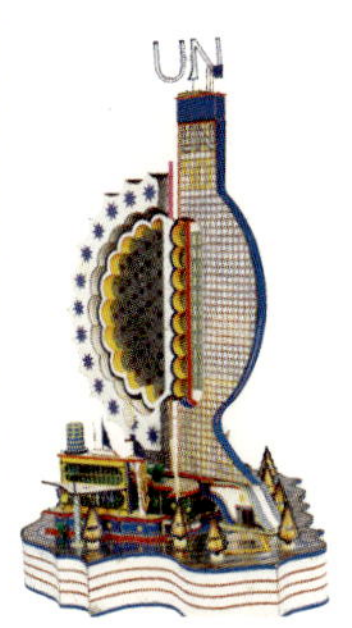

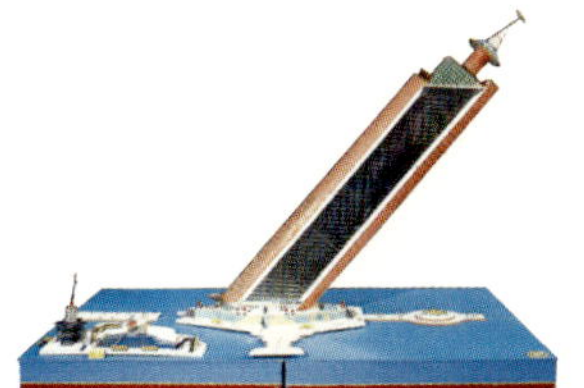

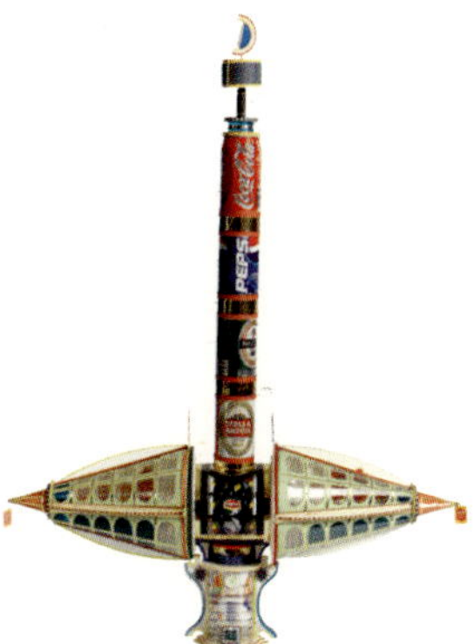

"I wanted to place my art at the disposal of the community that is being reborn to create a new world, because earthly pleasures depend on the people who inhabit the earth."

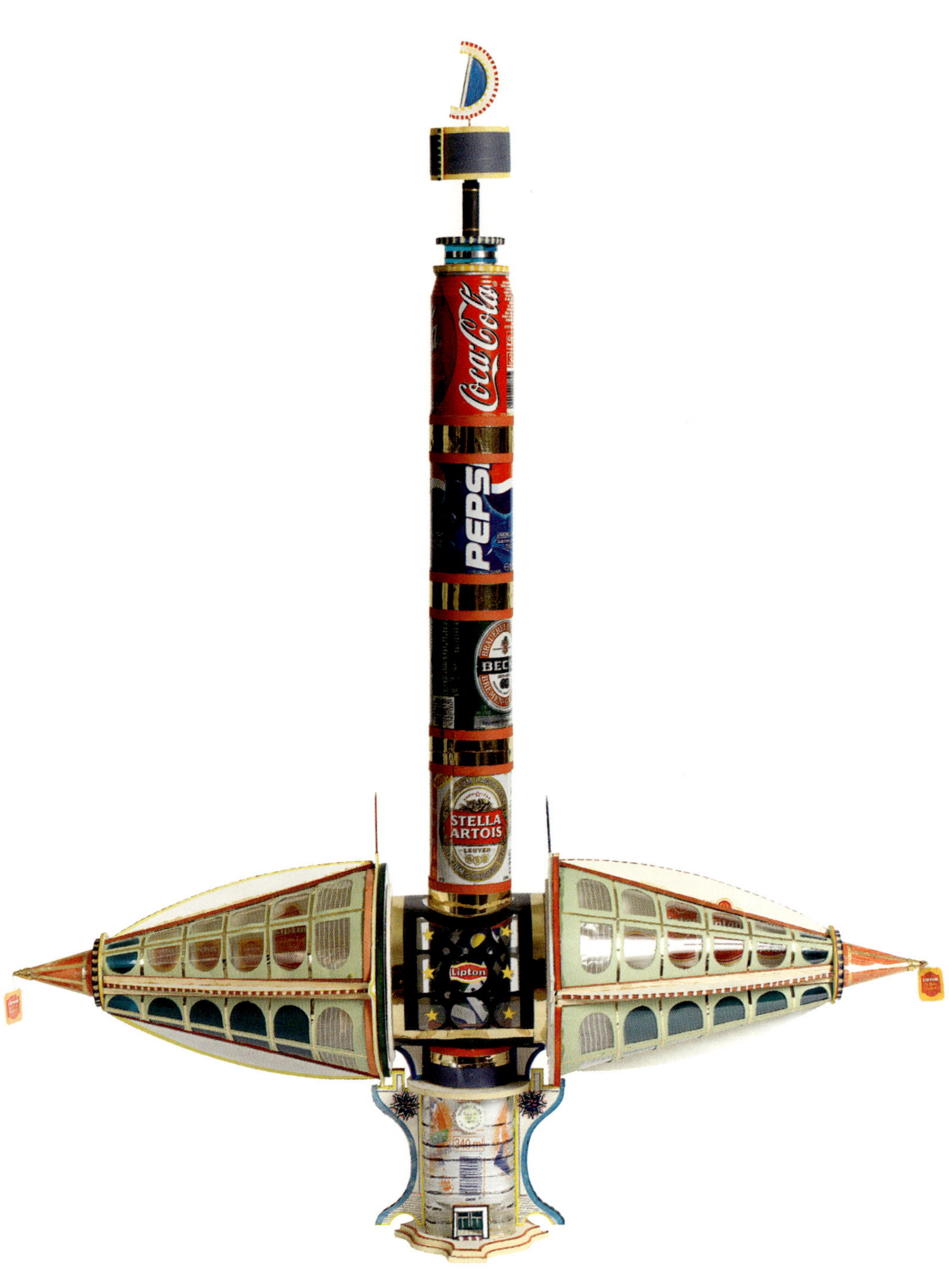

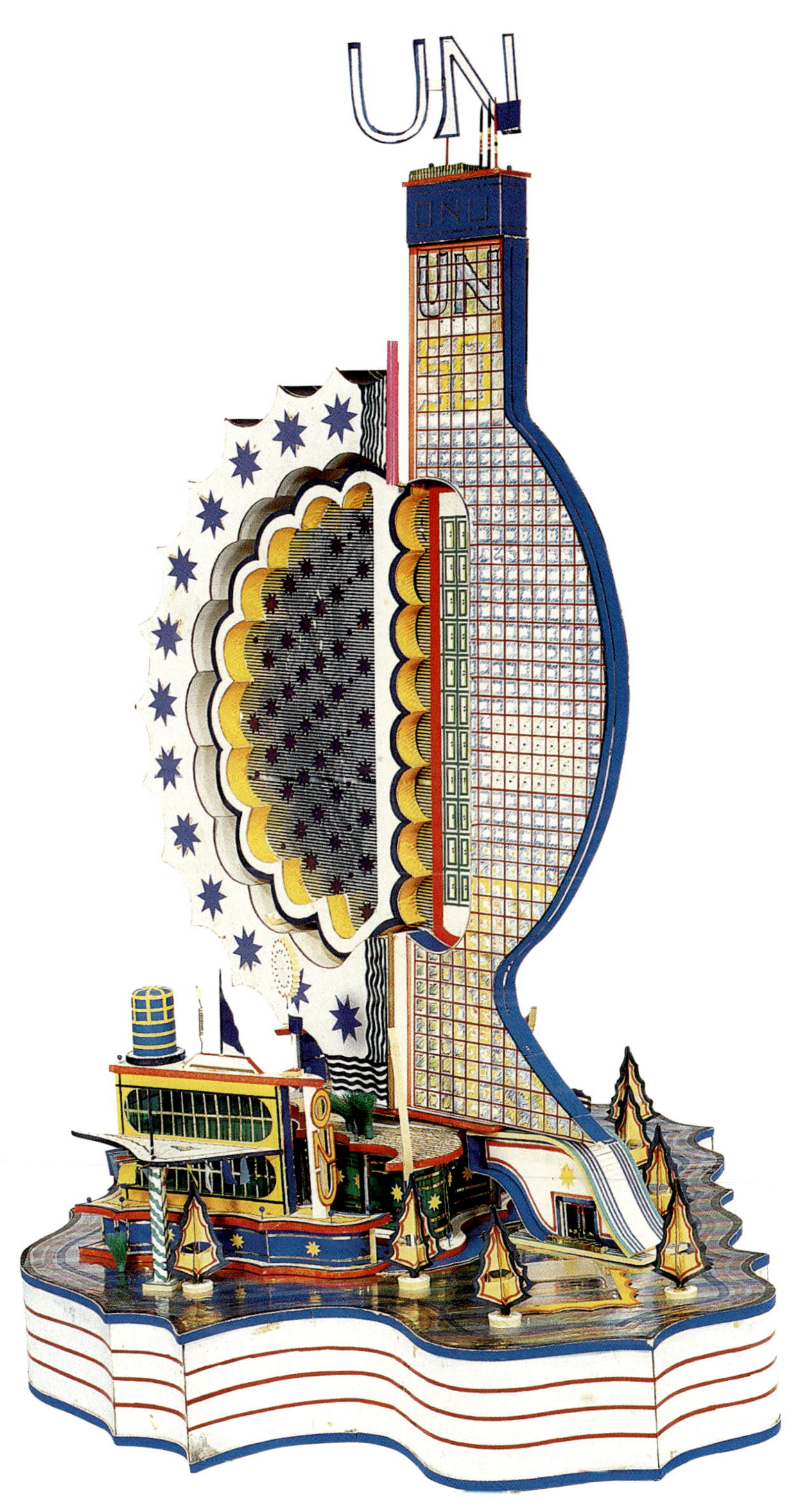

UN
ONU
UNO
50
ONU

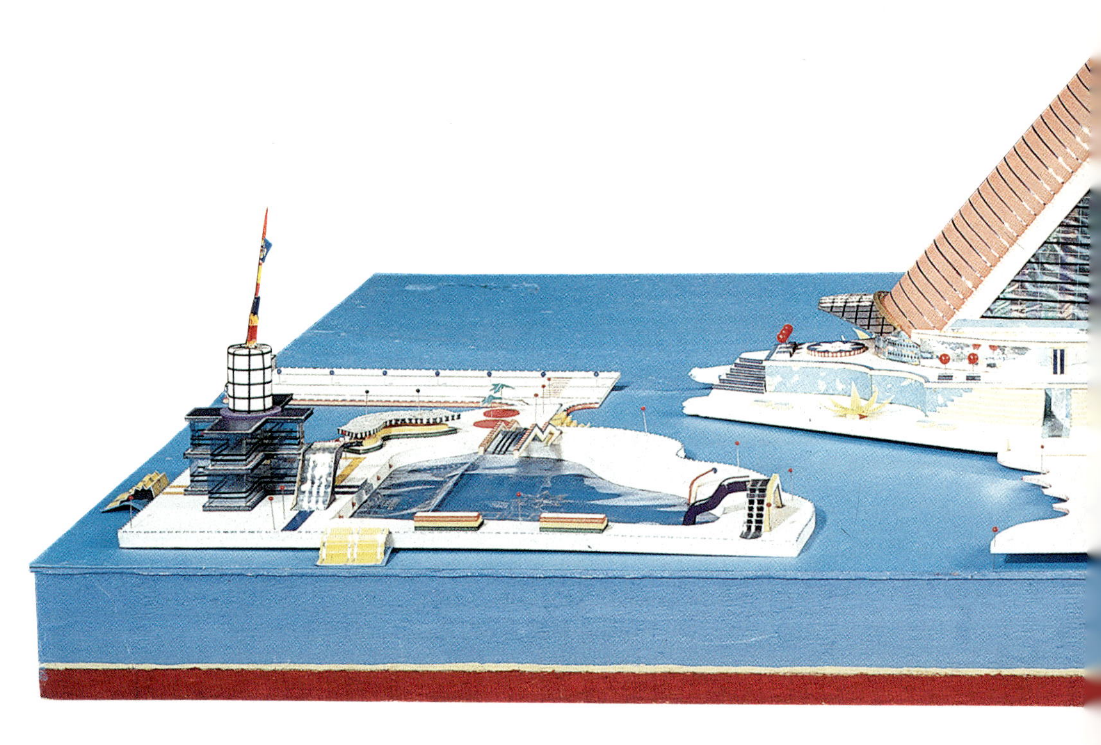

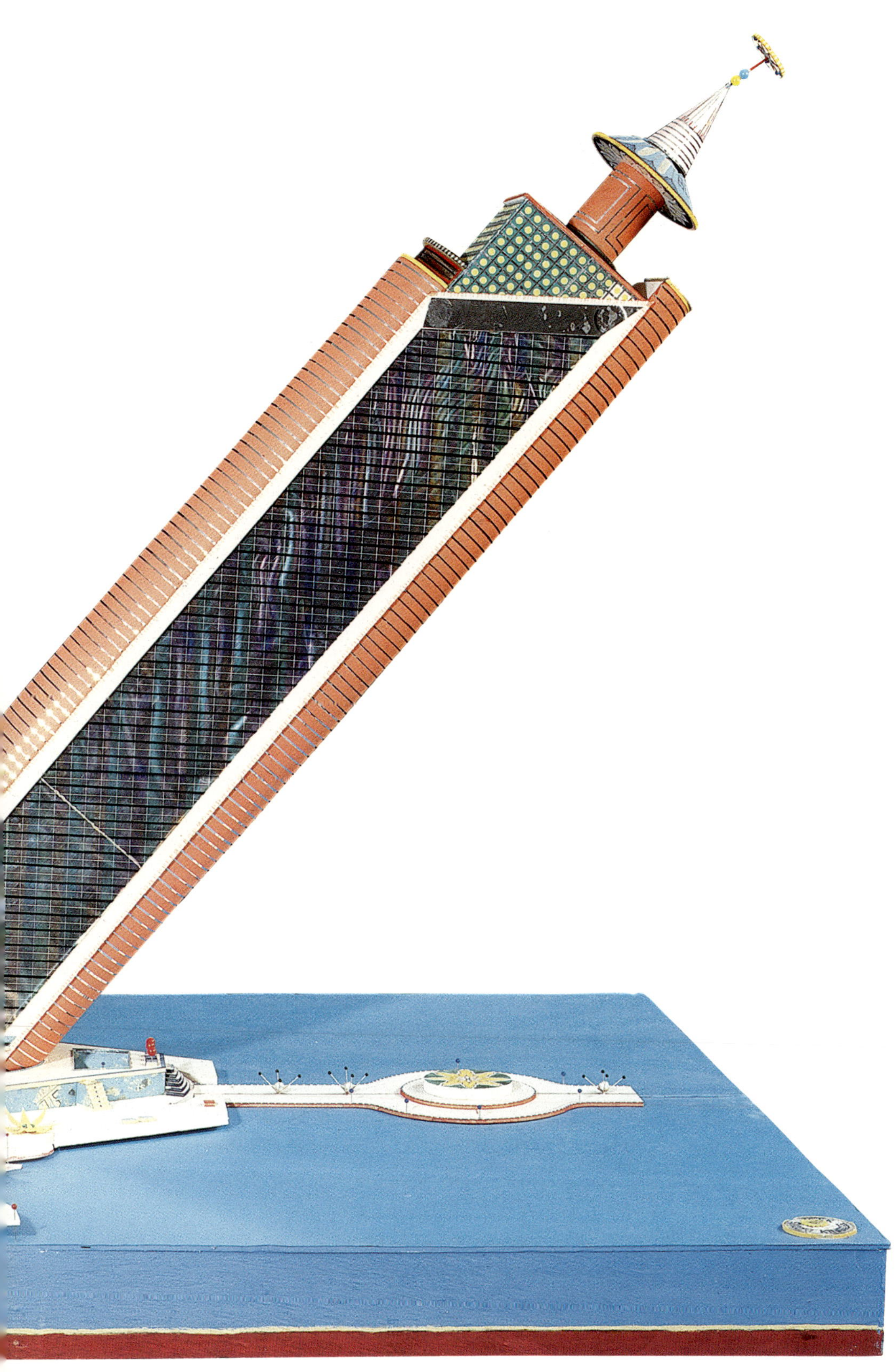

Abdoulaye Konaté

Hommage aux arbitres
2006
Textile
440 x 460 cm.

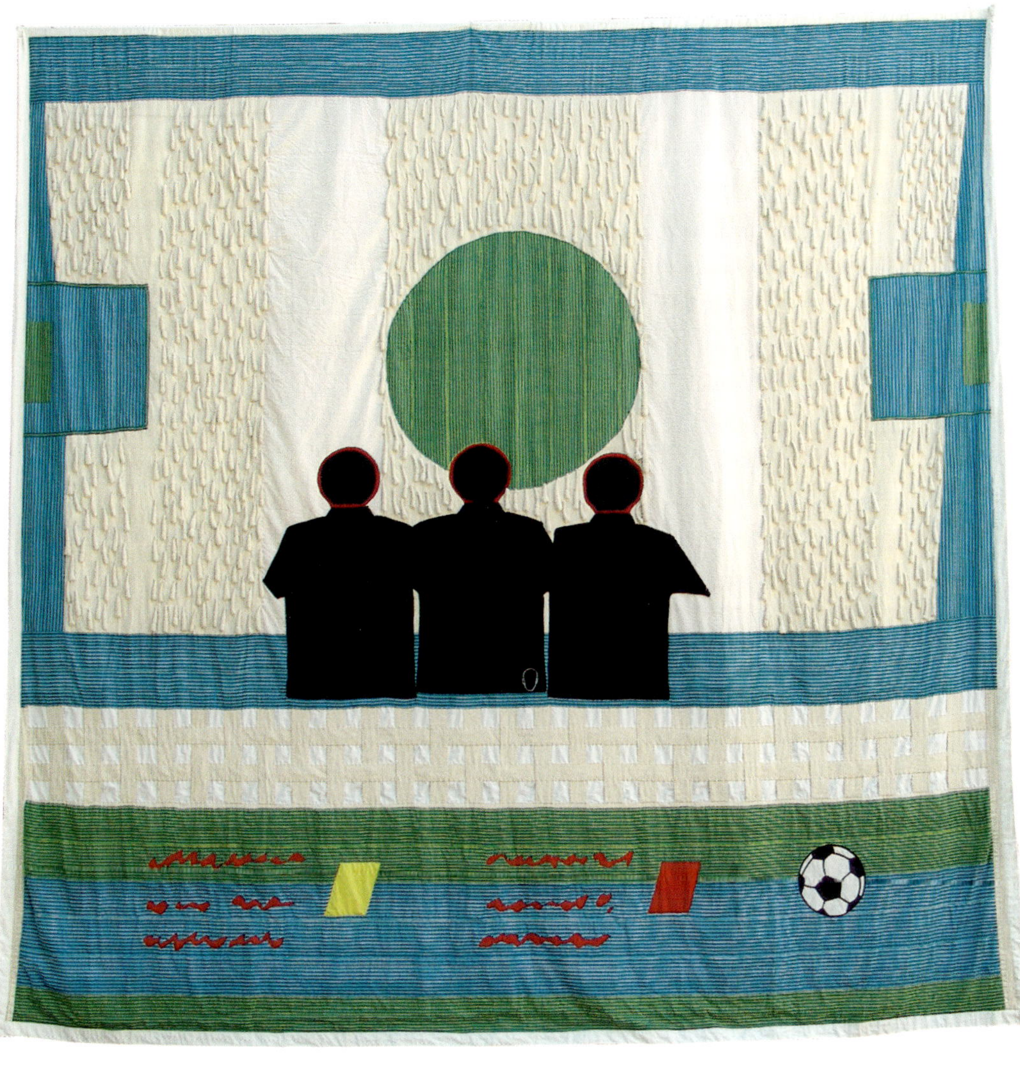

Moshekwa Langa

Estrangement
2006
Acrylic, spray paint
(enamel) and oil stick
on paper
140 x 100 cm.

Socialite
2006
Acrylic and transparent
lacquer on paper
140 x 100 cm.

Golddigger
2006
Acrylic, oil stick and
transparent lacquer
on paper
140 x 100 cm.

Index: Fool on the Hill
2005
Indian ink and acrylic
on paper
140 x 100 cm.

Trump Card-The Joker
2006
Acrylic, spray paint
(enamel) and oil stick
on paper
140 x 100 cm.

That Landscape
2002-2005
Acrylic, collage, spray
paint (enamel), oil
pastels, Indian ink
on paper
140 x 100 cm.

Windows
2004-2006
Mixed media on
refuse bags
230 x 250 cm.

Where do I begin
2001
Video projection
4' 30"

The Limits
2004-2006
Mixed media on
refuse bags
203 x 160 cm.

The Islands
2003-2006
Mixed media on
refuse bags
208 x 198 cm.

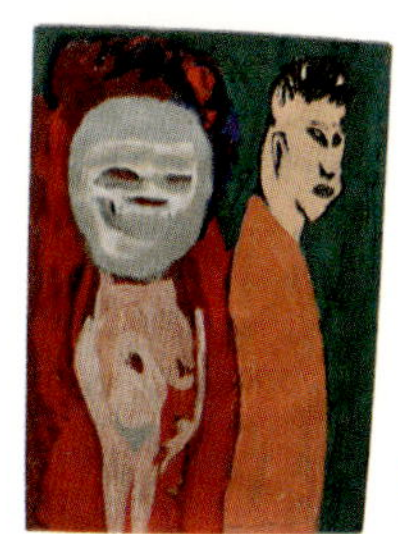
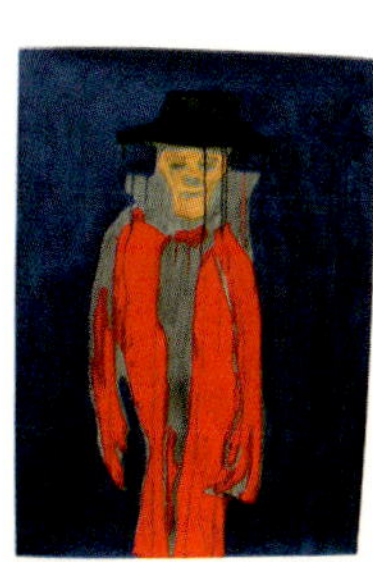
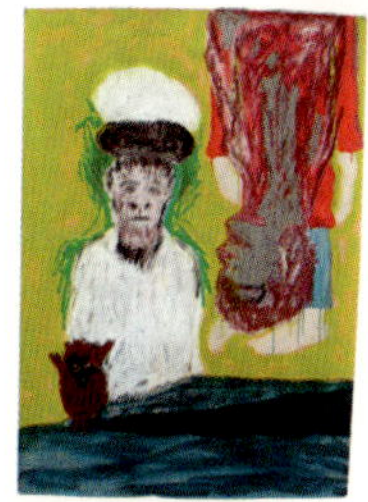
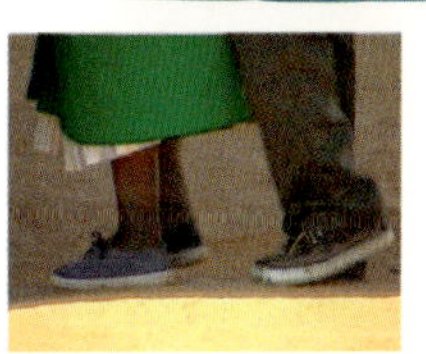
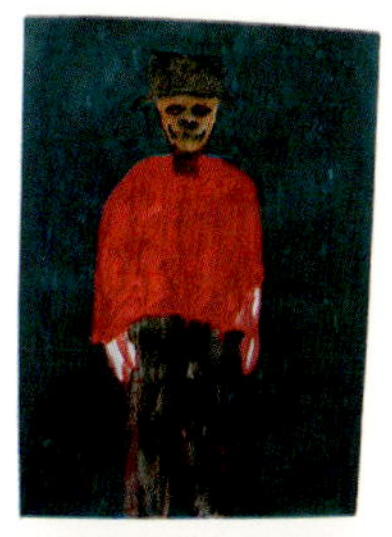
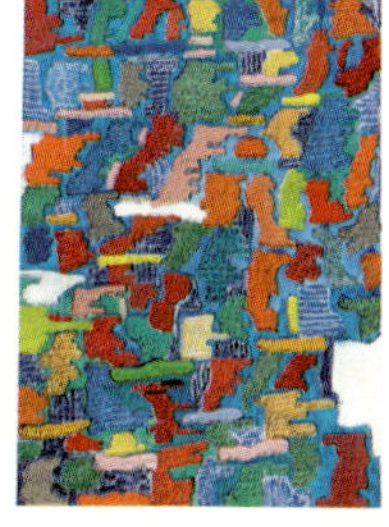
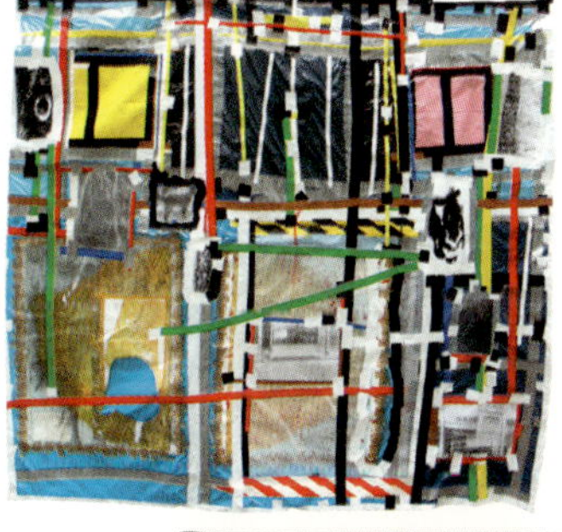
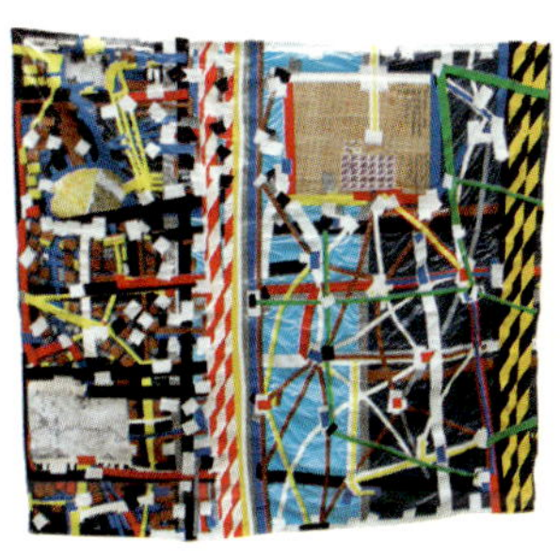
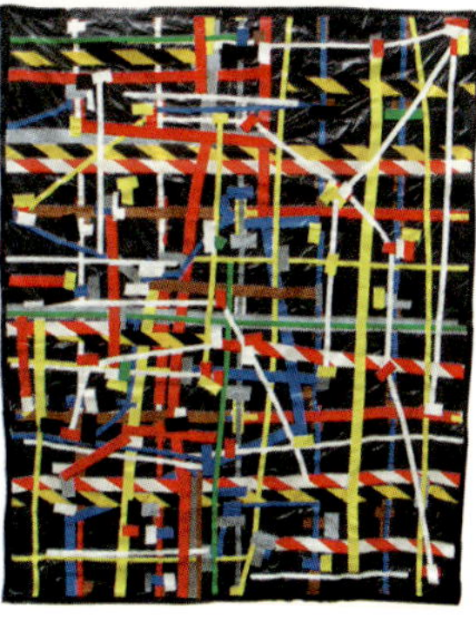

There are drawings and collages, the drawings are on paper, and the collages are on plastic bags. The drawings stem from a longer series of projects that I have been working on in the last few years, initially mapping my immediate environments and using the motivations from my reflections on the sociological dimensions therein, looking at apartheid, forced cohabitation and forced segregation, education, and a general narrowing of a sphere of life.

Initially the maps used were official documents that were erased and then redrawn to make new documents and a new sense of place. The works that I have prepared here stem from that project. The new works adopt a similar approach but the mapping ideal has been expanded to include more private elements, reflections of a new home, a new place. This means that there is a mental lapse of what was there, and a slight negation of what is here. In this way I see my new drawings as a marriage of two ideas and ideals. They are maps that show neither a starting point of departure nor an end point.

Also parallel to the maps are a series of figurative paintings that to my mind are a kind of portrait of the same individual in different states, in different areas. There is a drawing that combines elements of Dutch and South African landscapes, and there is a memory map made up of text and names of peoples and places, a map that recounts various time frames, but a map without a visible legend or scientific objectivity.

Moshekwa Langa

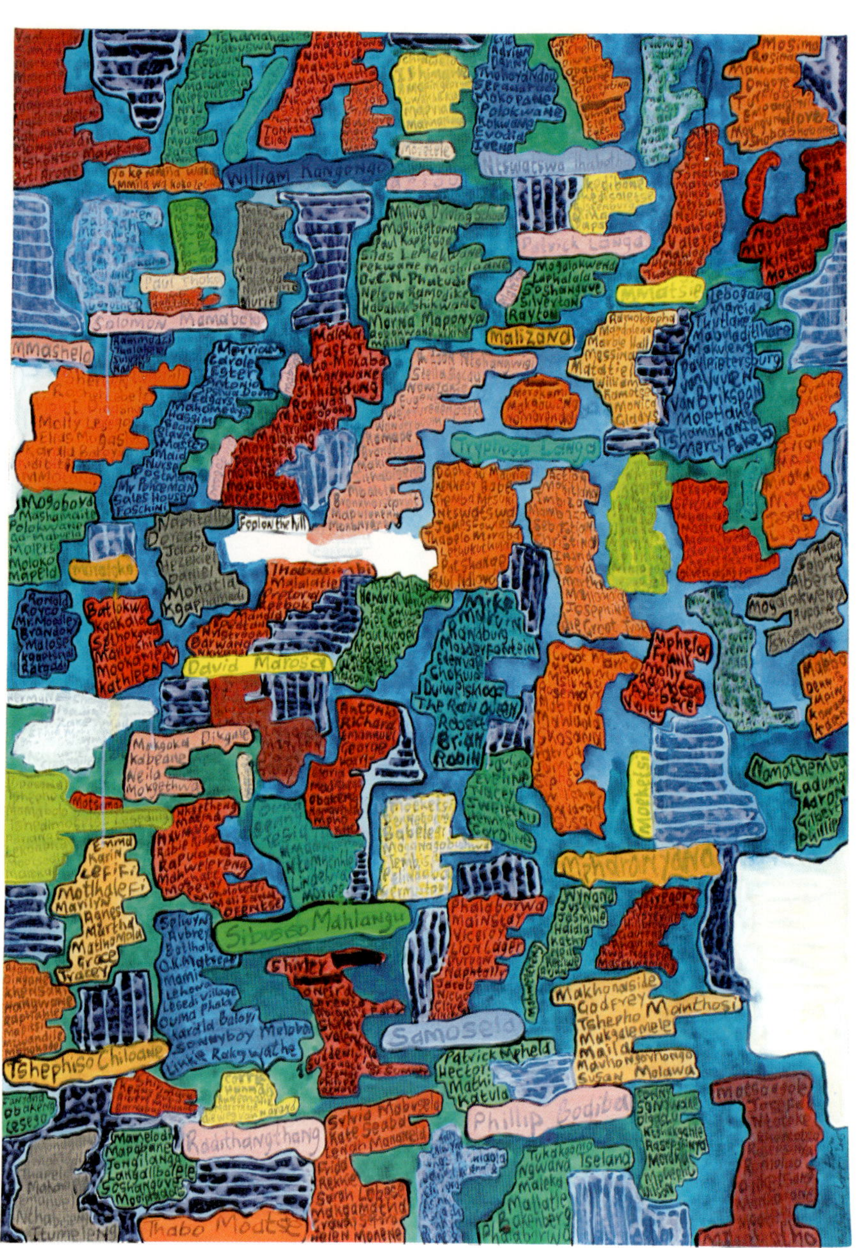

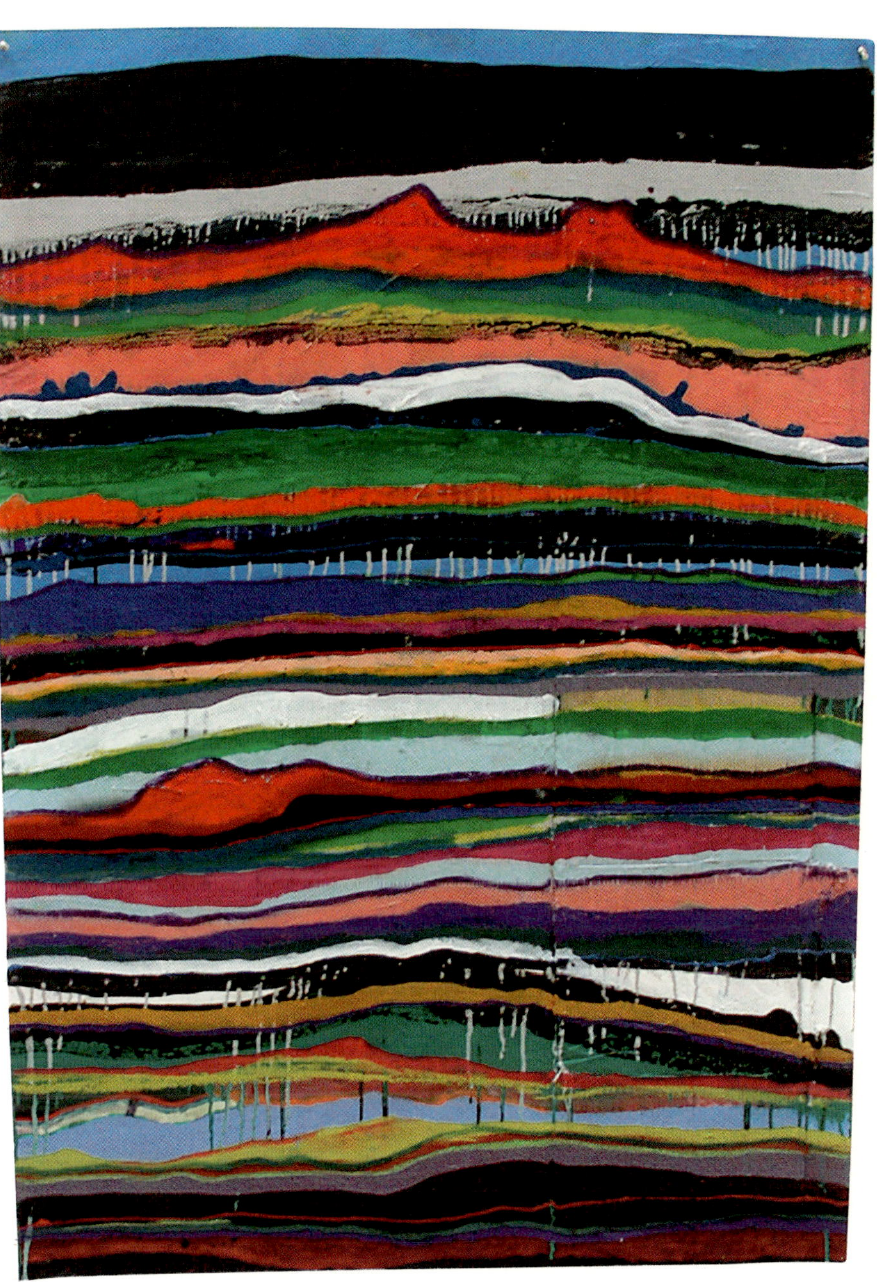

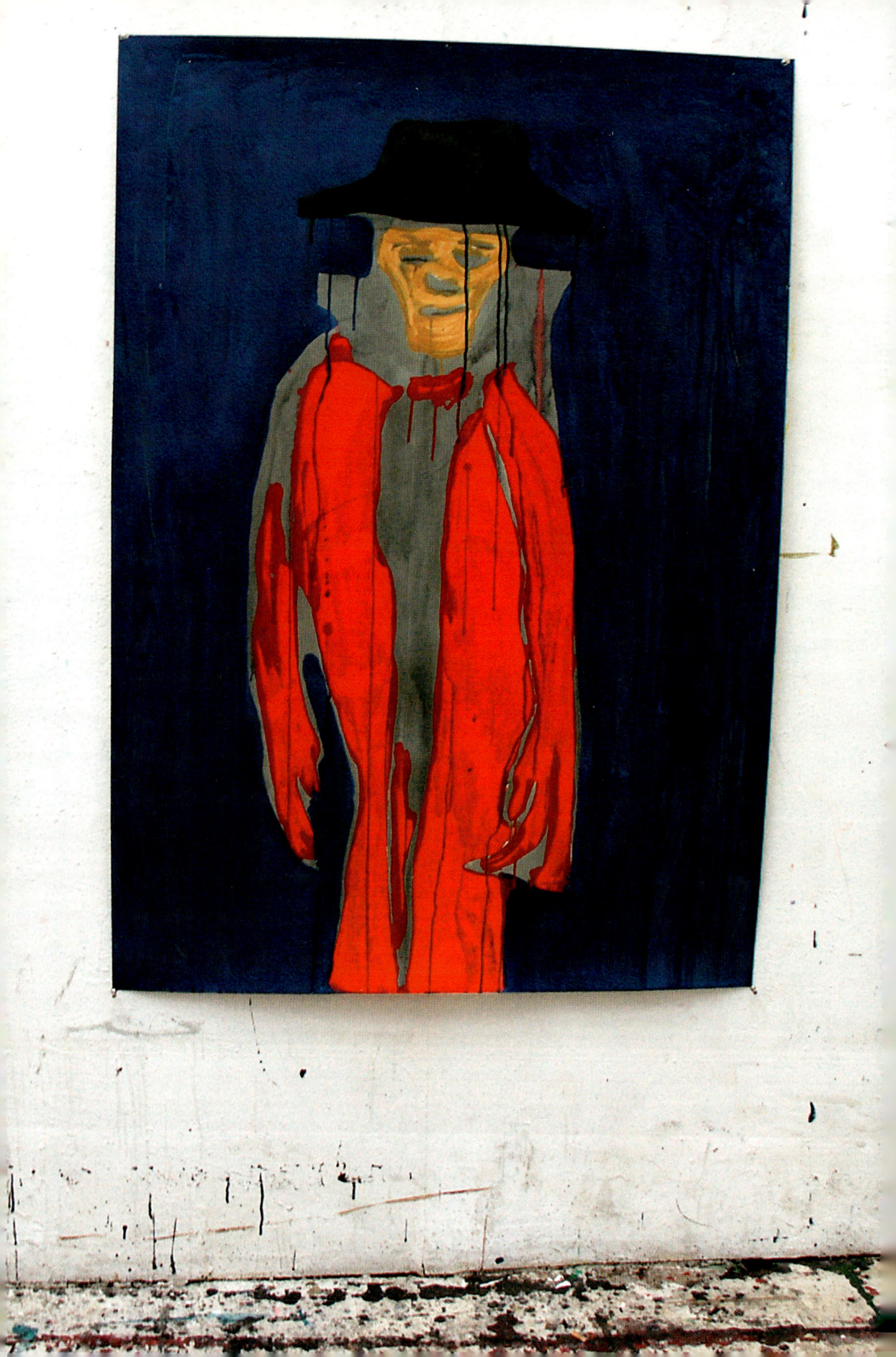

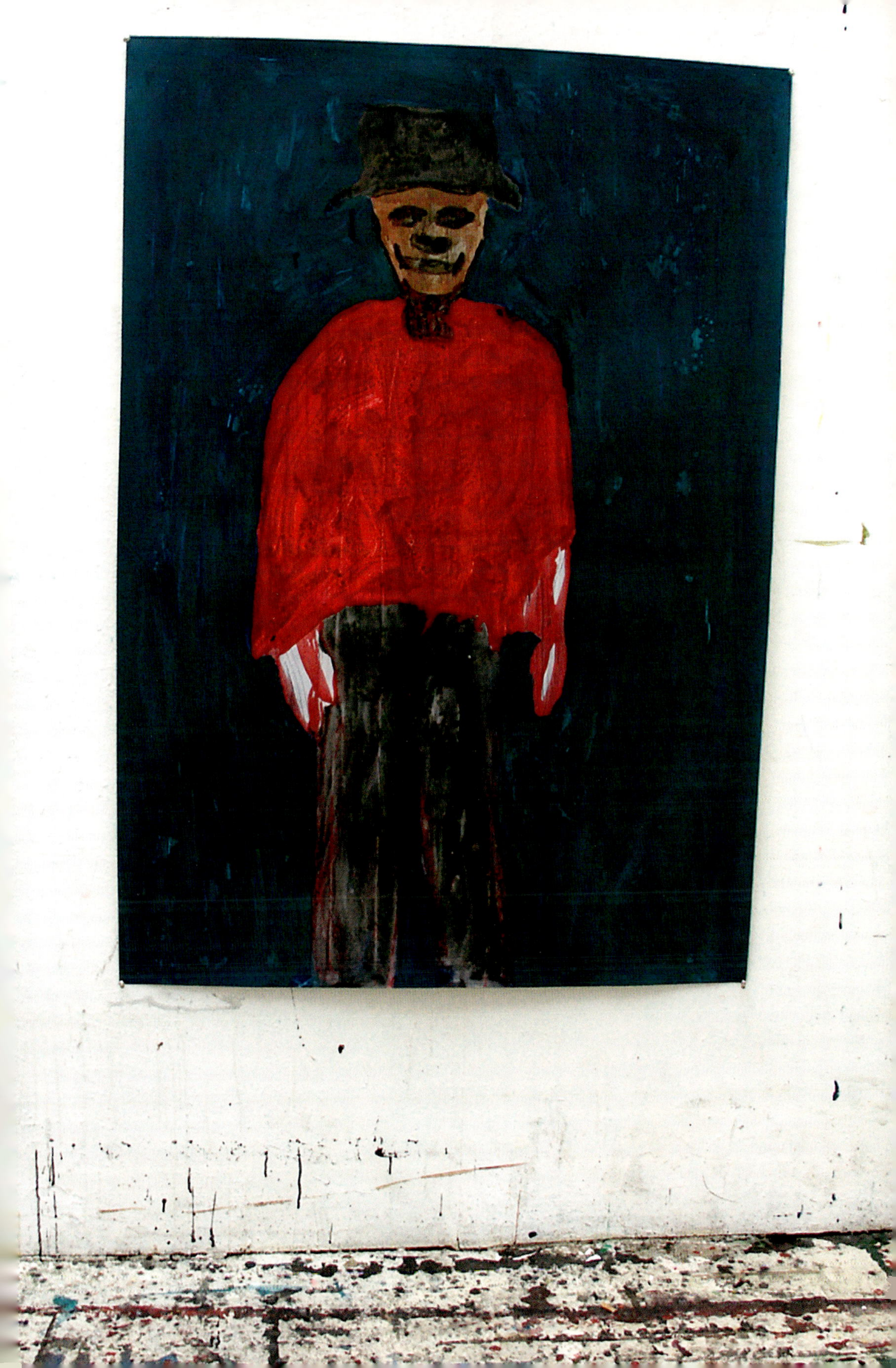

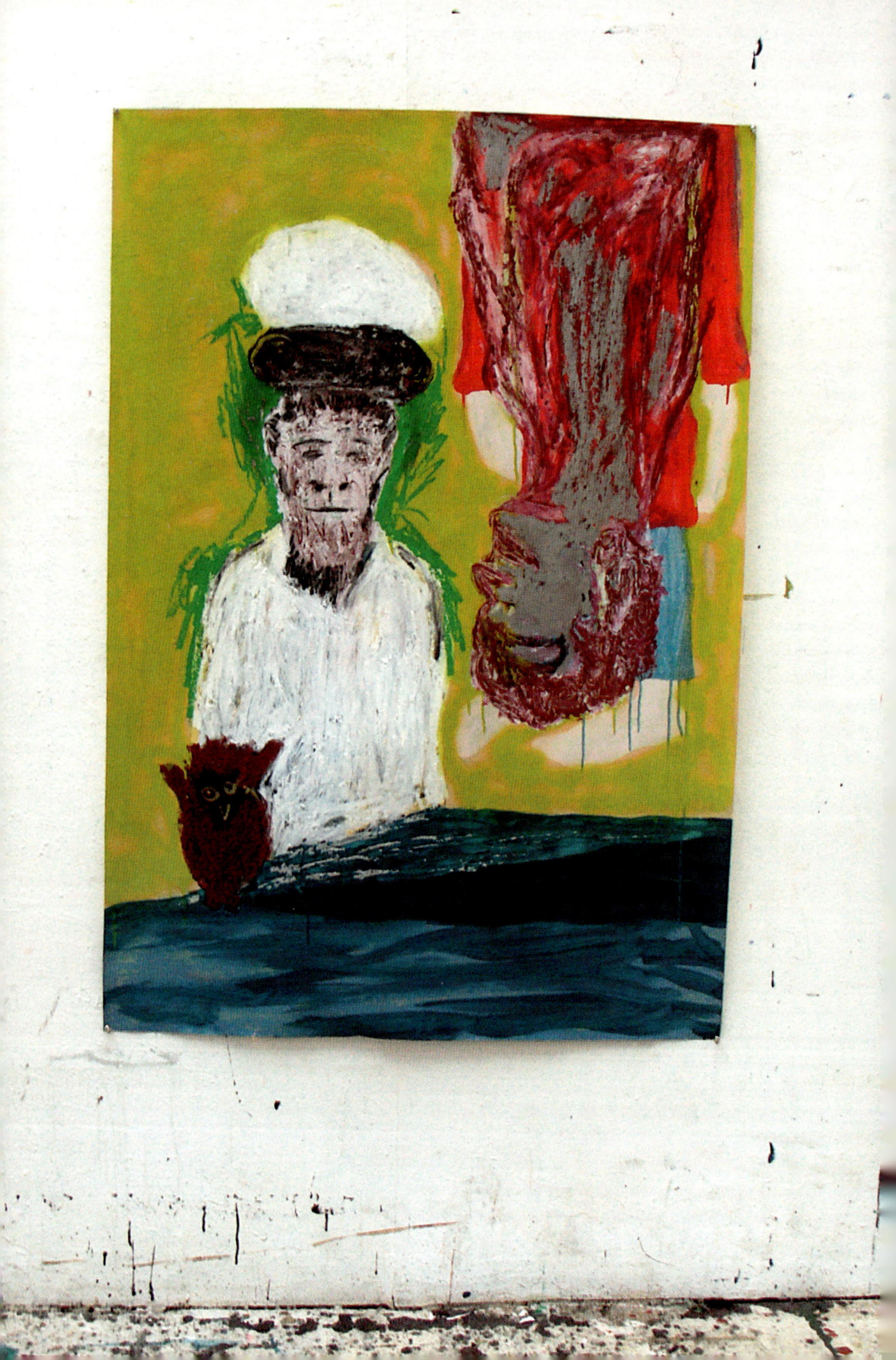

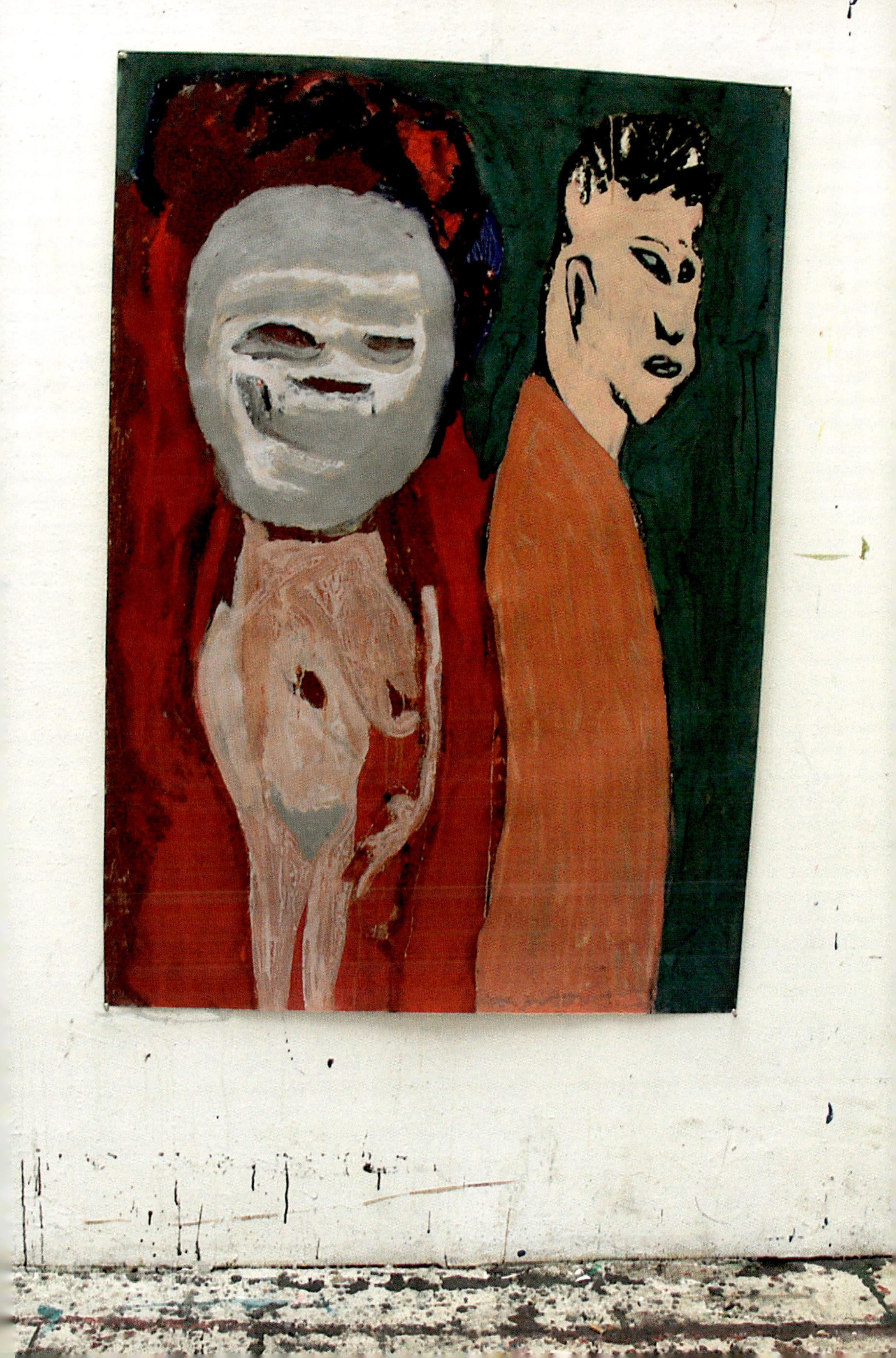

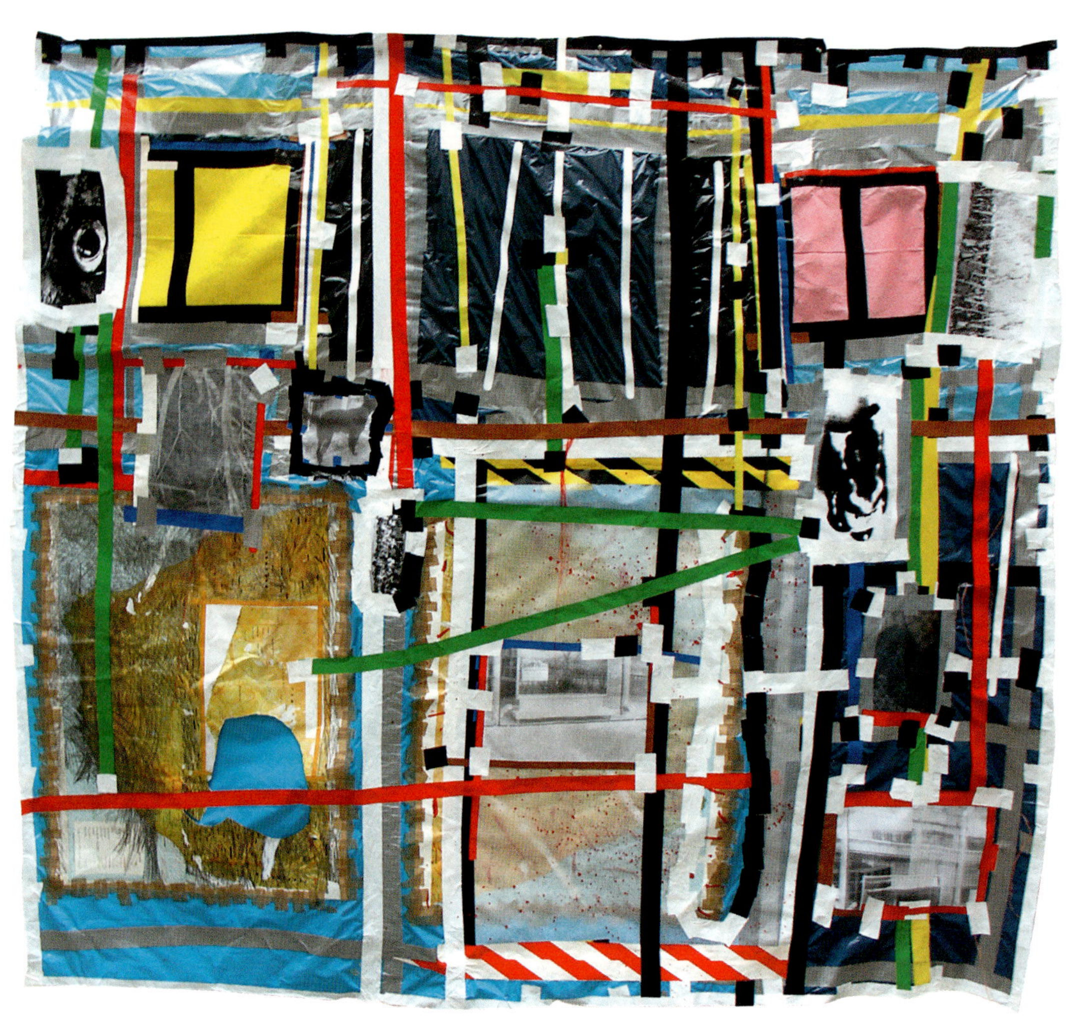

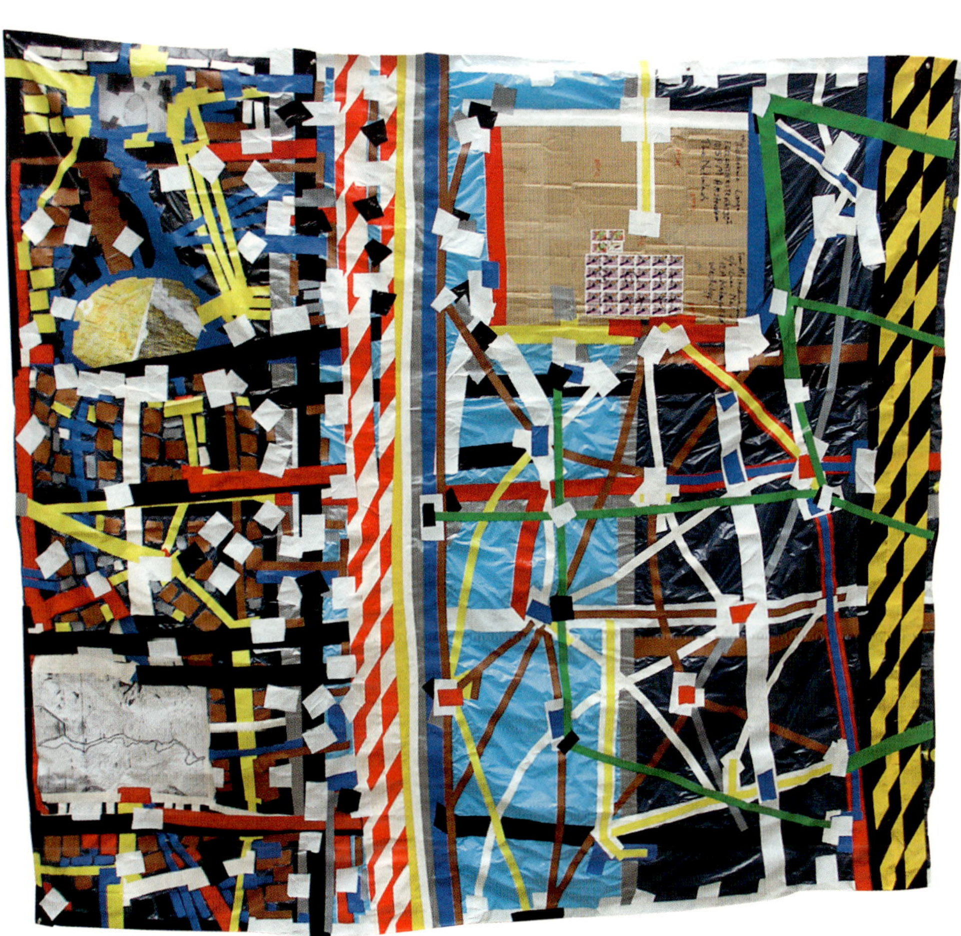

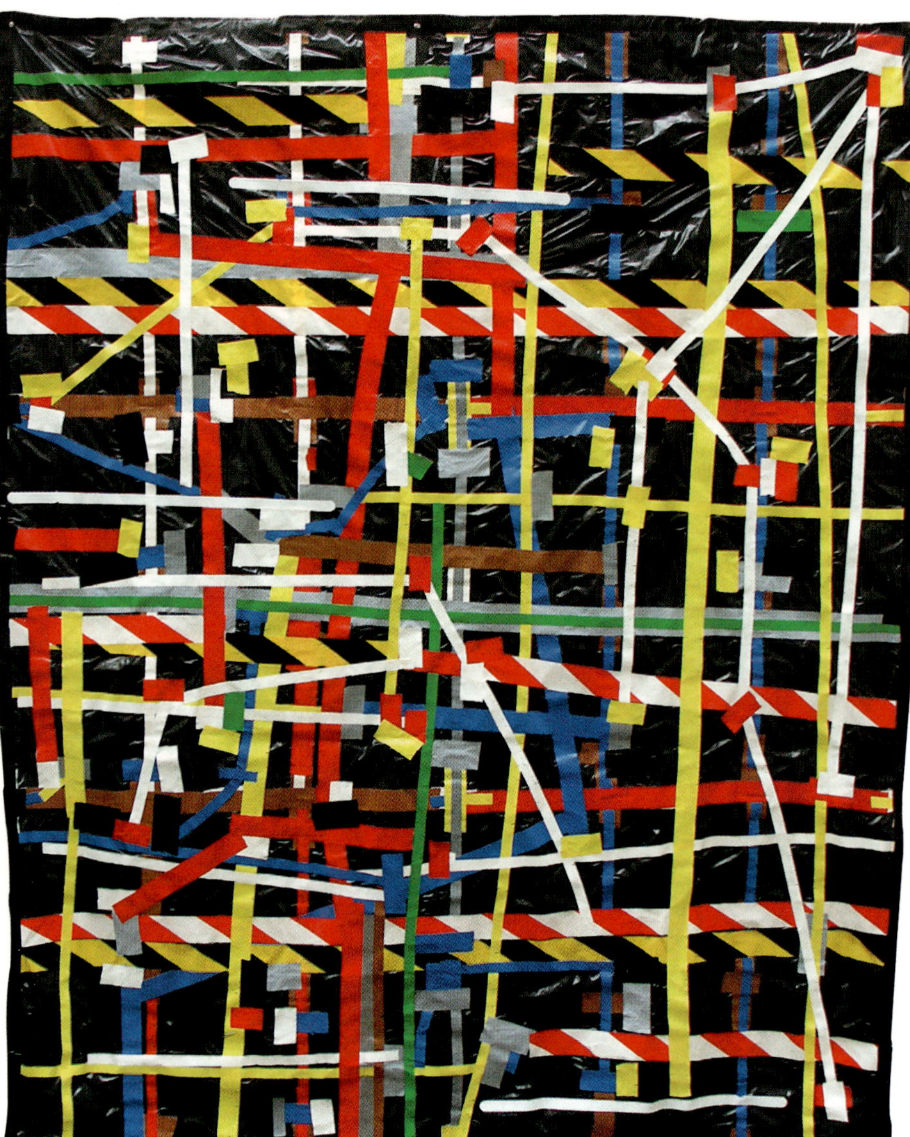

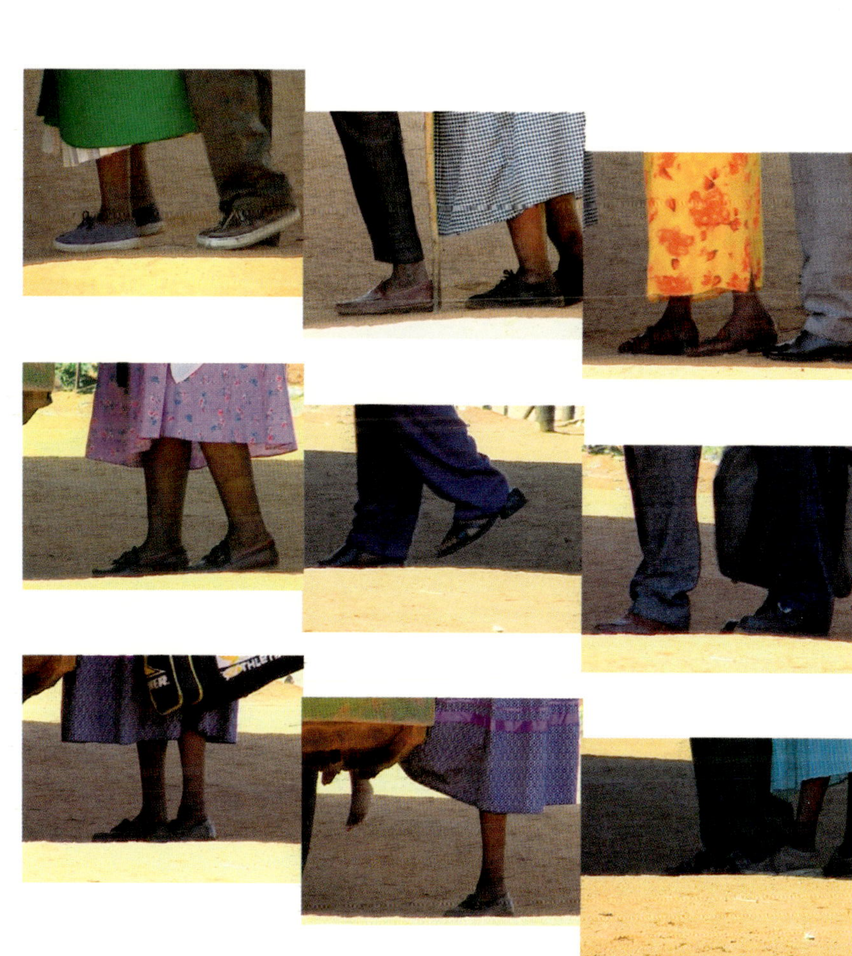

Otobong Nkanga

Delta Stories:
Landscape II
2005-2006
Lacquer, pen, ink and
acrylic on paper
70 x 49,5 cm.

Delta Stories:
Landscape I
2005-2006
Lacquer, pen, ink and
acrylic on paper
70 x 49,5 cm.

Delta Stories:
Collapsed Projects
2005-2006
Ink and acrylic on paper
32 x 24 cm.

Delta Stories:
Crying Blood
2005-2006
Acrylic on paper
13 x 24 cm.

Delta Stories:
No Vacancy for Locals
2005-2006
Acrylic on paper
36,5 x 23 cm.

Delta Stories:
Disposable Waste
2005-2006
Silver adhesive tape and
acrylic on paper
19x25 cm.

Delta Stories: Gift to the
next Generation
2005-2006
Acrylic on paper
32 x 15 cm.

Delta Stories:
Blind folded history
lesson
2005-2006
Acrylic on paper
32 x 24 cm.

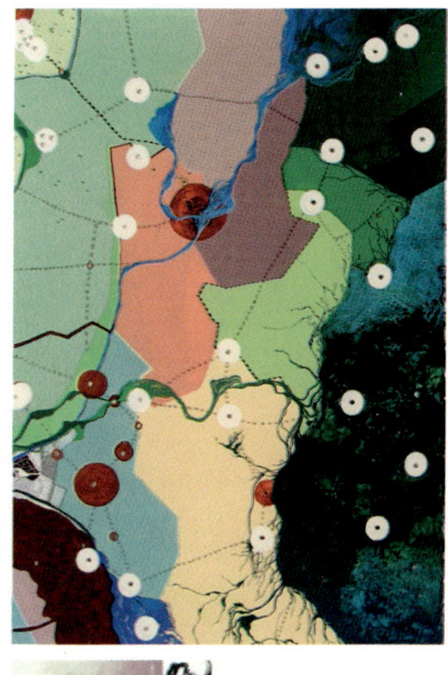
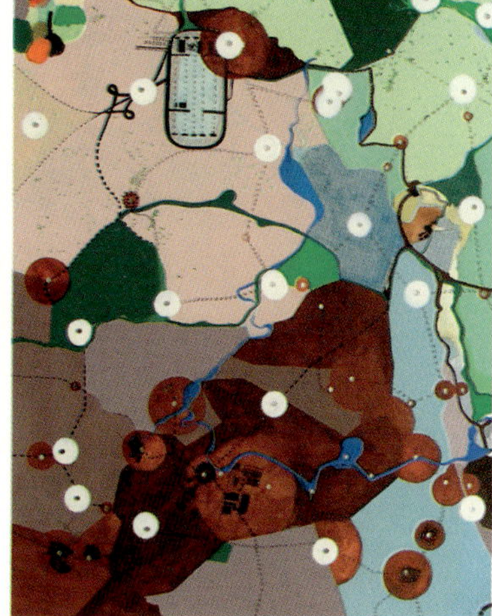
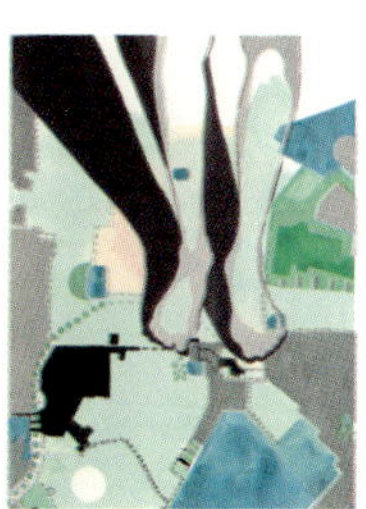
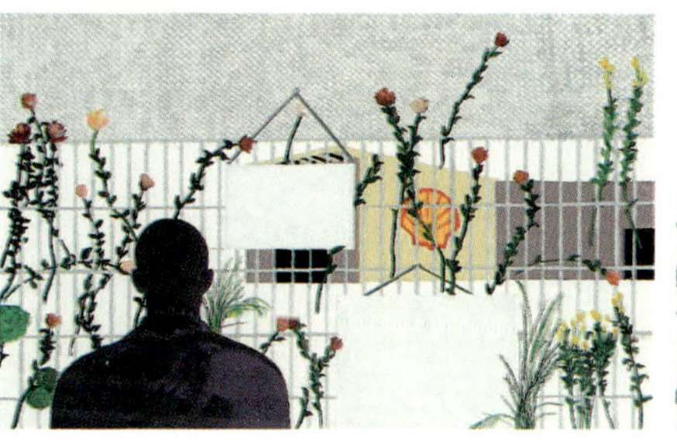
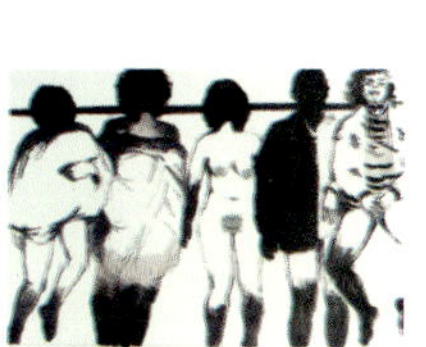
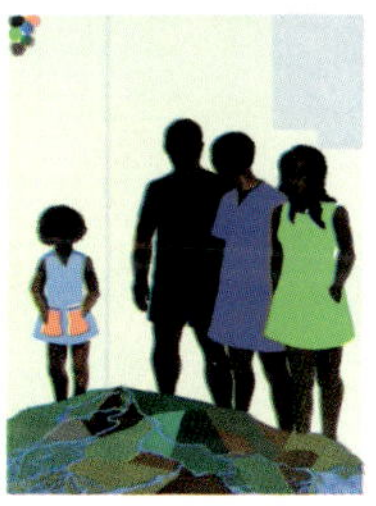
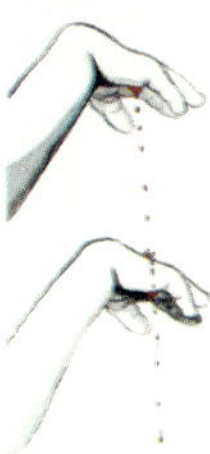

Delta Stories is a series of drawings which are narrated in fragments, putting emphasis on gestures, memories, disillusionment, fears, hope and the absurdity of human beings and their environment.

Landscapes in their slow process of change provided an important starting point. Deltas are spaces where the signs of change are evident, leaving traces, deposits and transforming the landscape.

The drawings *Delta Stories: Landscapes I –IV* portray an aerial view of an imaginary landscape going through a metamorphosis which gradually overflows with water and at a later stage with a spillage of crude oil. These drawings indicate a two-way state of mutation in the delta zone: geological, and the course of development inflicted by mankind.

Delta Stories

The stories are told through juxtaposing images, and the titles of the drawings provide another insight into the narrative.

One of the changing landscapes I am interested in is the oil-rich delta region in Nigeria, which has undergone ecological, political and social changes resulting in conflicts, violence and ecological damage. The writer and activist Ken Saro Wiwa turned the focus on this area and publicised hitherto unknown stories about the people.

Otobong Nkanga

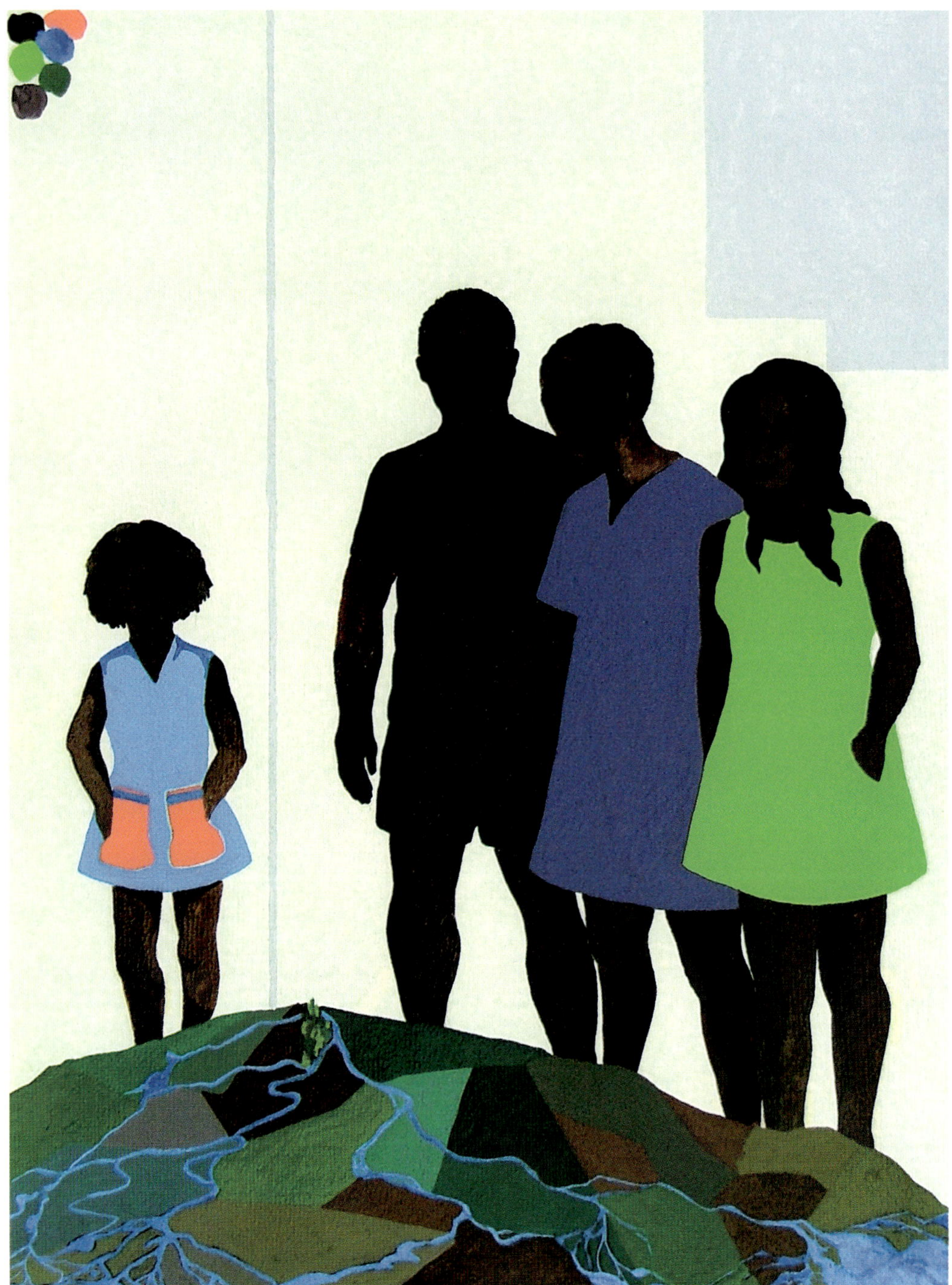

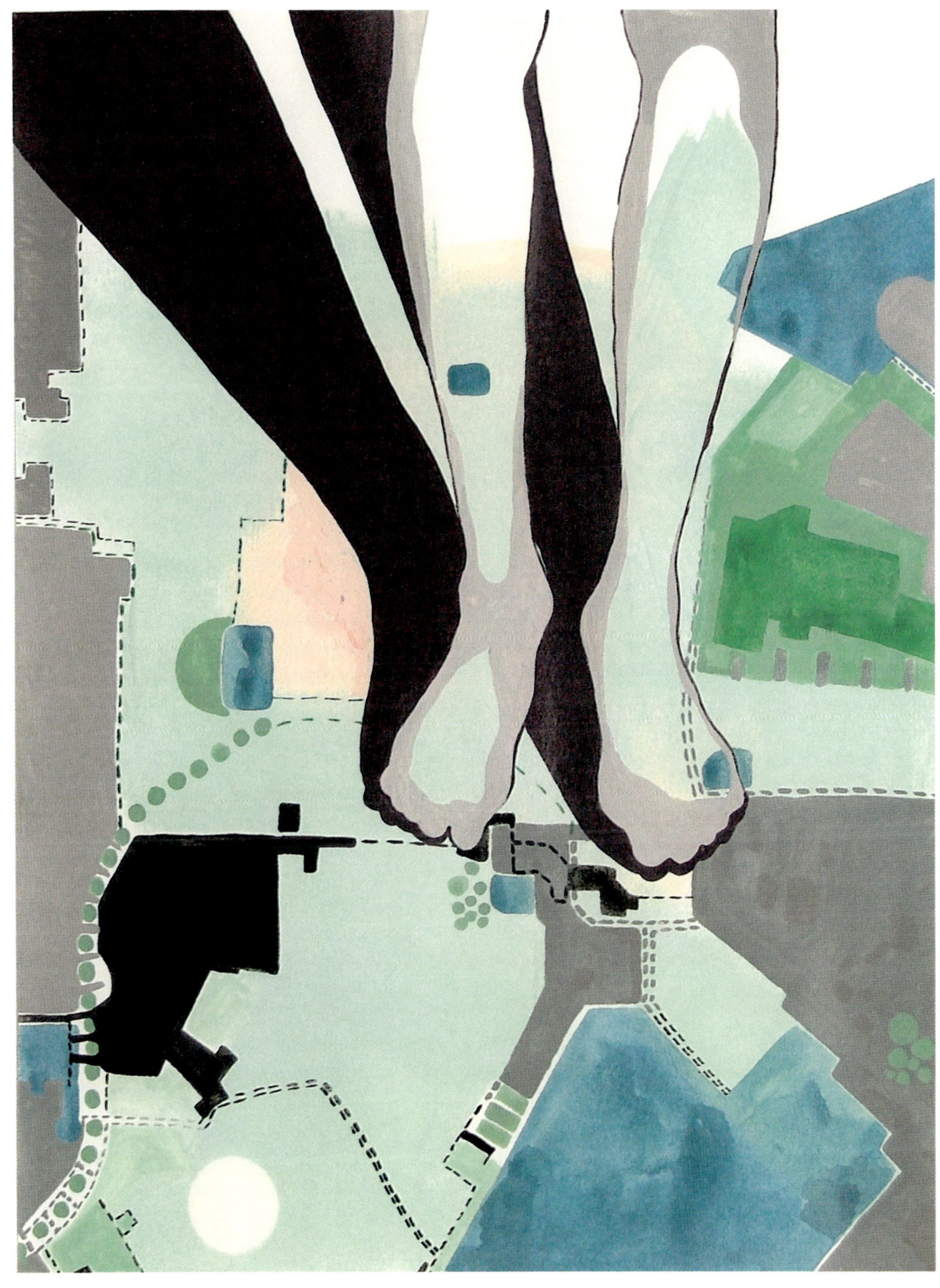

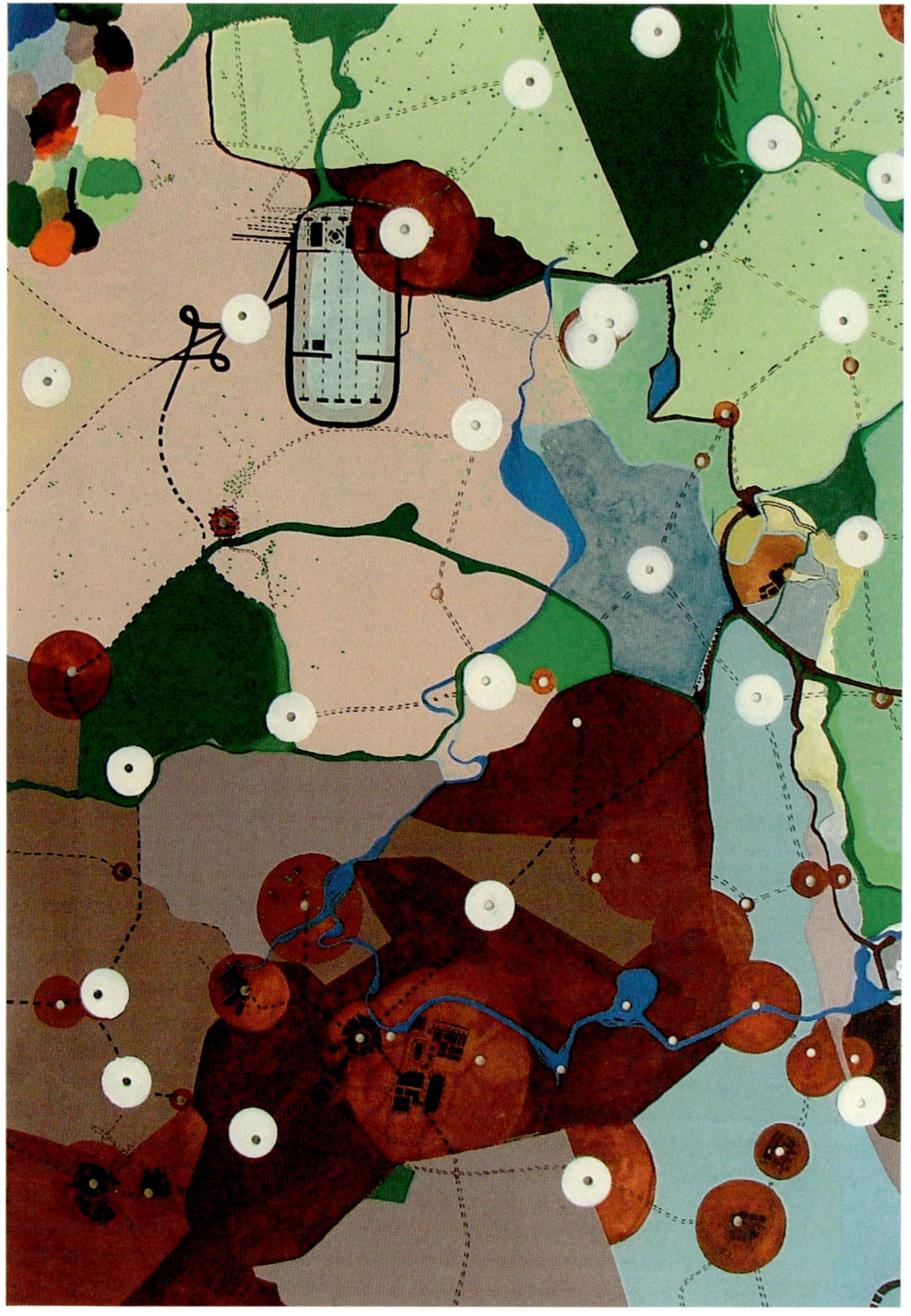

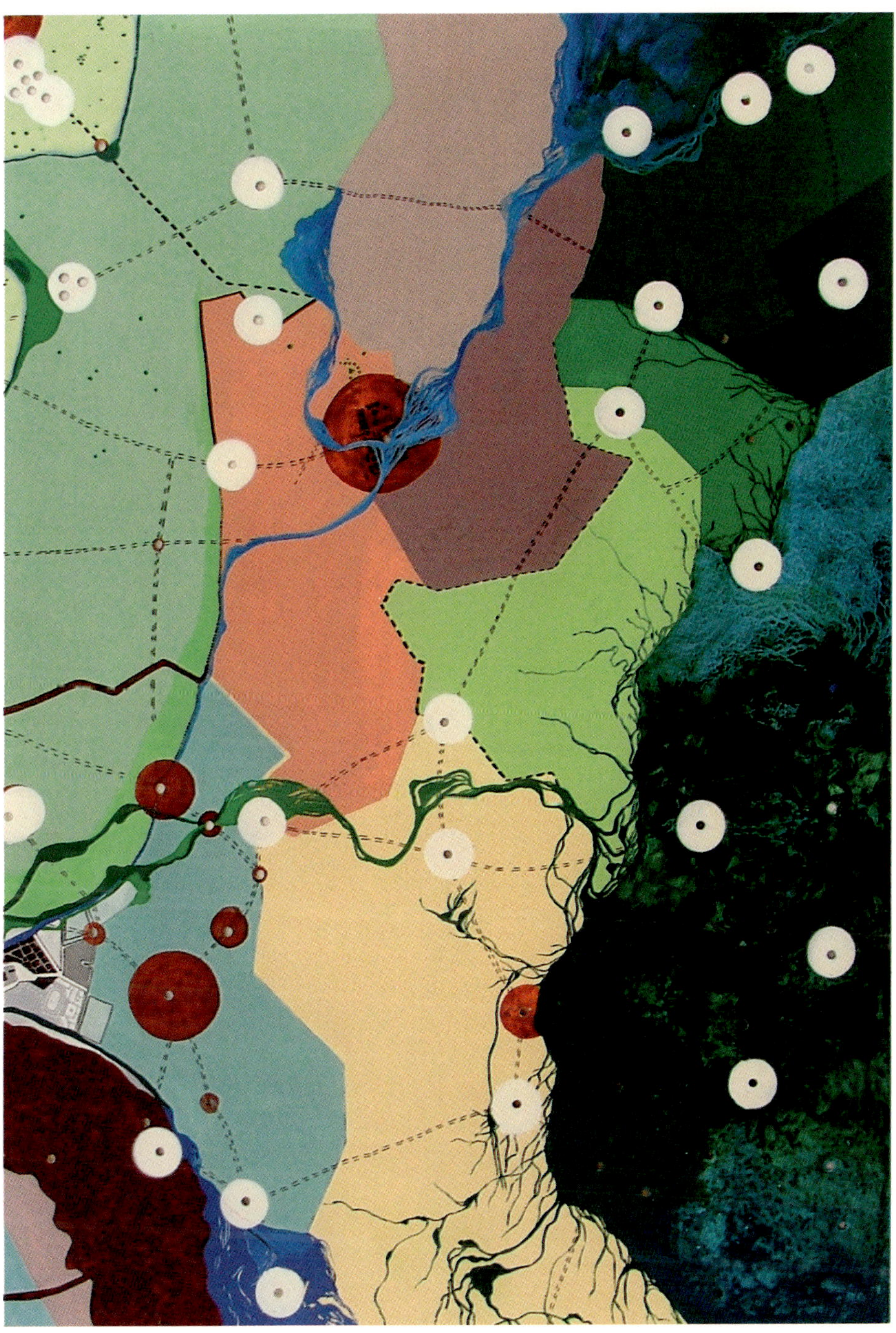

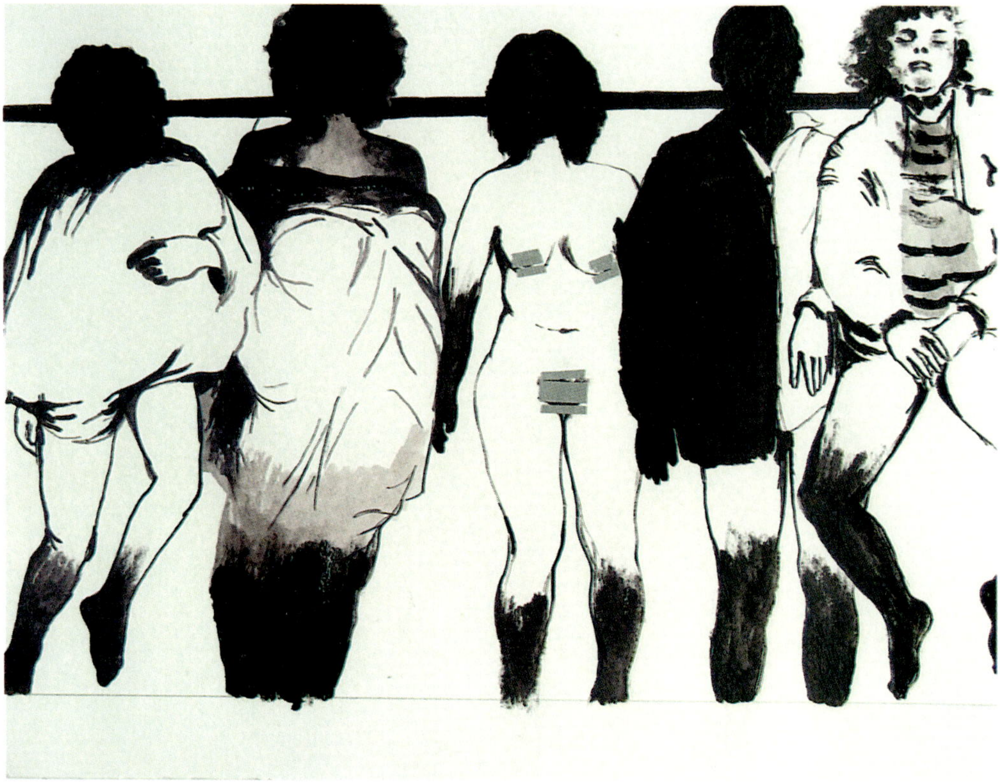

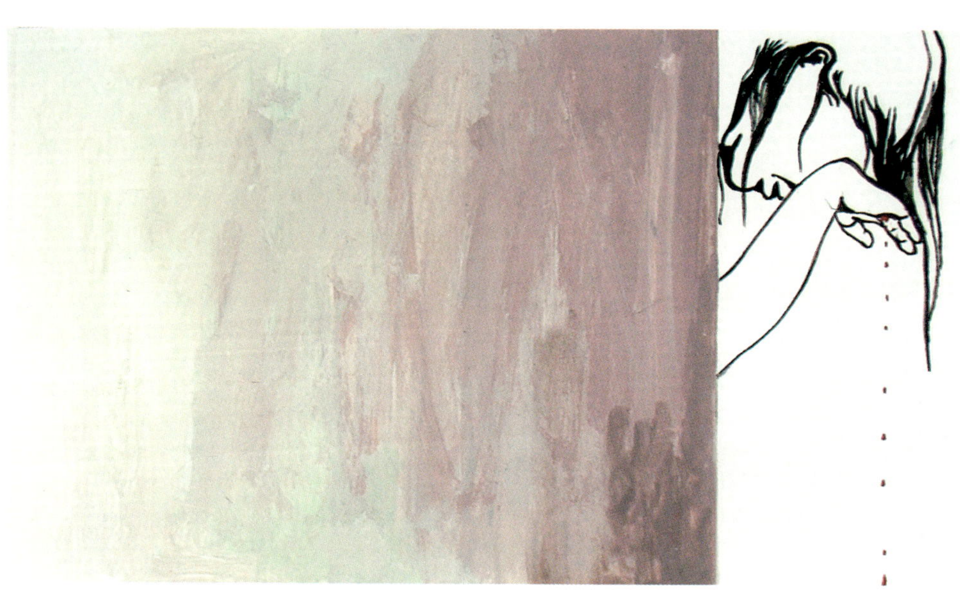

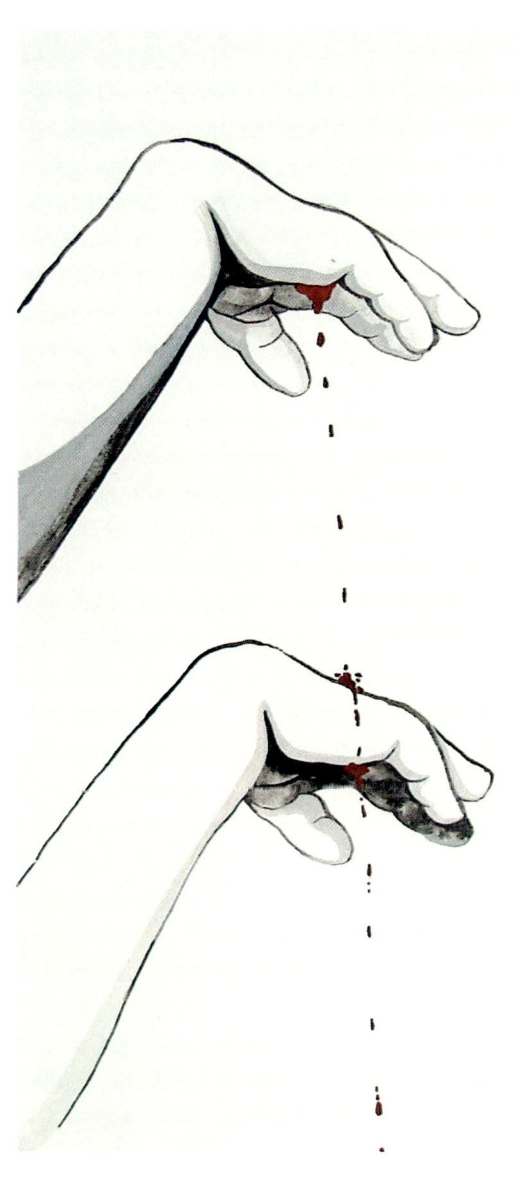

Marie Blanche Ouedraogo

Series *Recette et Mythe*
2005
Mixed media on
cardboard
7 works, 84 cm.
diameter each

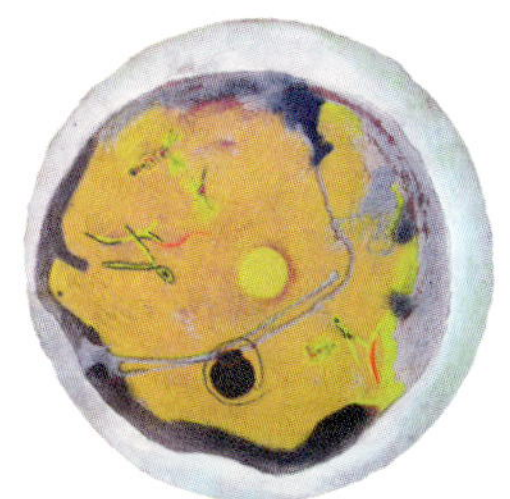
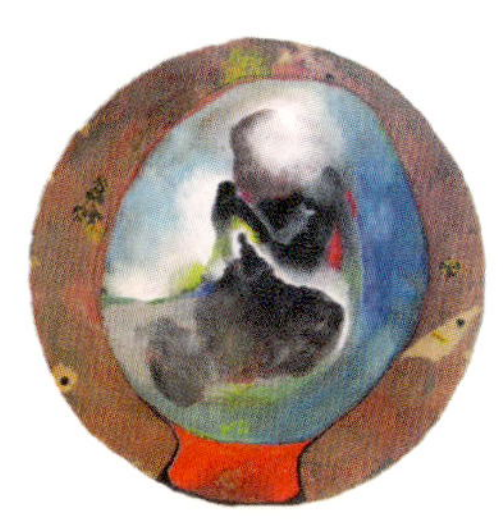
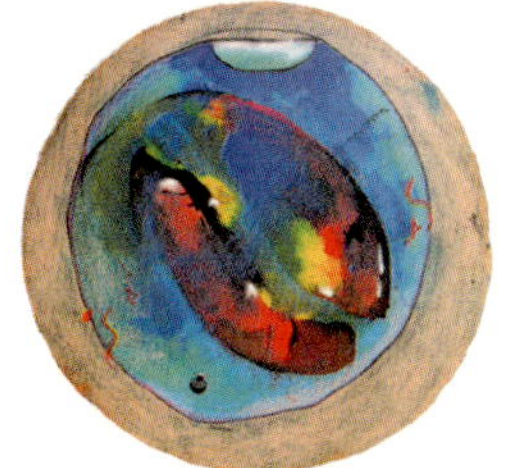
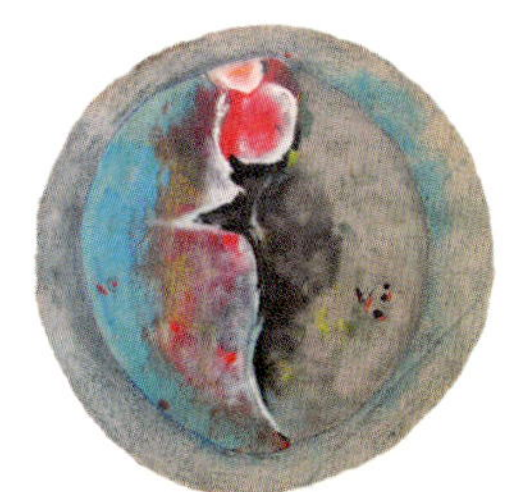
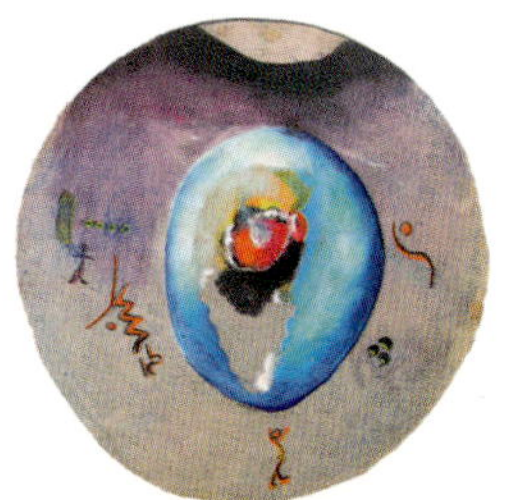
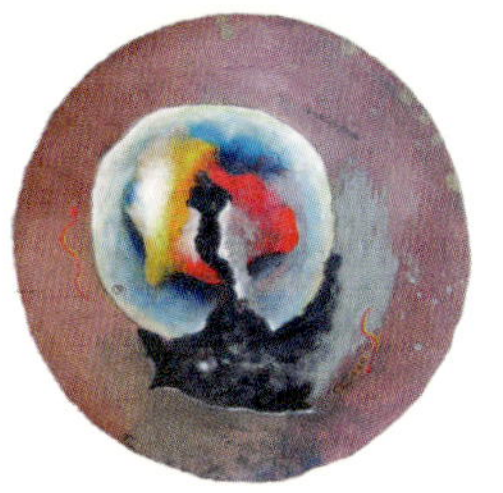
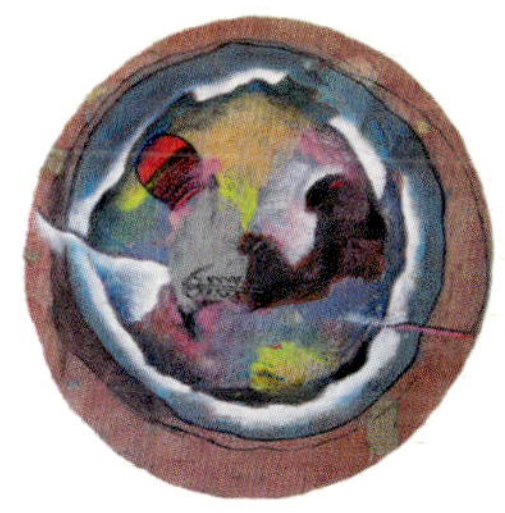

Based on the concept of the circle,
We have extracted the following symbols:
The globe, the earth, the *canari**, @, which suggest the history of creation;
Icons present in both tradition and modernity, universal symbols that can be found in
all civilisations, present and past.

The similarities with the circle have led me to create a uniform group of elements,
all in one.
Particles that denote a presence, a life.
Within this roundness, like the round belly of a woman that produces life, the origin,
the beginning of life, a birth.
In this unique universe divisions are formed; that is where life unfolds.

My work comprises a series of eight
round objects, all with their own originality,
Made up of several colours, they are the sum of all colours, the beginning
and the end.
The myth that is born with a story of globalisation brings together eight to support
the rest, to improve distribution.
A uniform series that denotes a diversified uniqueness.

Conservation of one's originality;
Immersion in a web of cultures and societies,
The need to recognise
The intrinsic value of peoples and civilisations
In the face of a mutating world,
In a kitchen with a single recipe
The rebirth of communism.

** Clay Pot*

Recipe and Myth

Technical description, *Recipe and Myth*

Round cardboard, ash, red earth, pigment, a mixture of acrylic paint and oil paint, collages around the edges.

I have chosen the circle deliberately to represent my vision of roundness, the symbolic nature of roundness, and to deal with the issues of globalisation, diversity, tradition and modernity yet to be defined;

Ash, from which rise new births and which is the colour of miscegenation,
Red or bronze-coloured earth, the colour of our life, replete with substances for life, where everything is possible.

Around the edges, collages to define the numerous links that serve to close wounds.

An assortment of acrylic paints, the world is prepared like a kitchen recipe; the question is, how to eat it? There in lies the myth.

Marie Blanche Ouedraogo

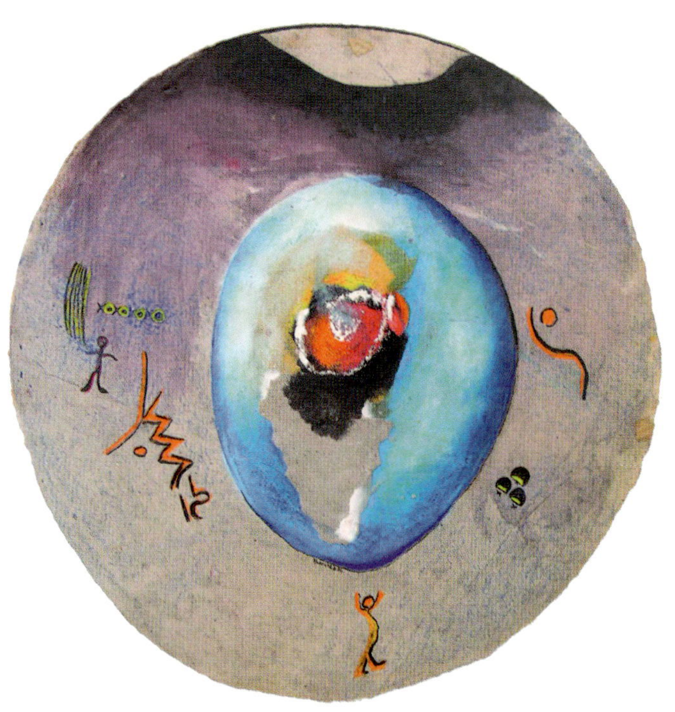

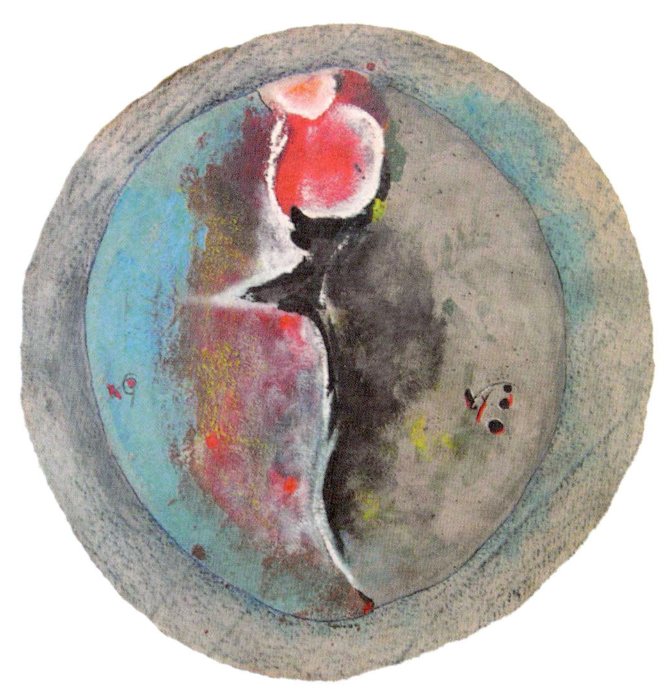

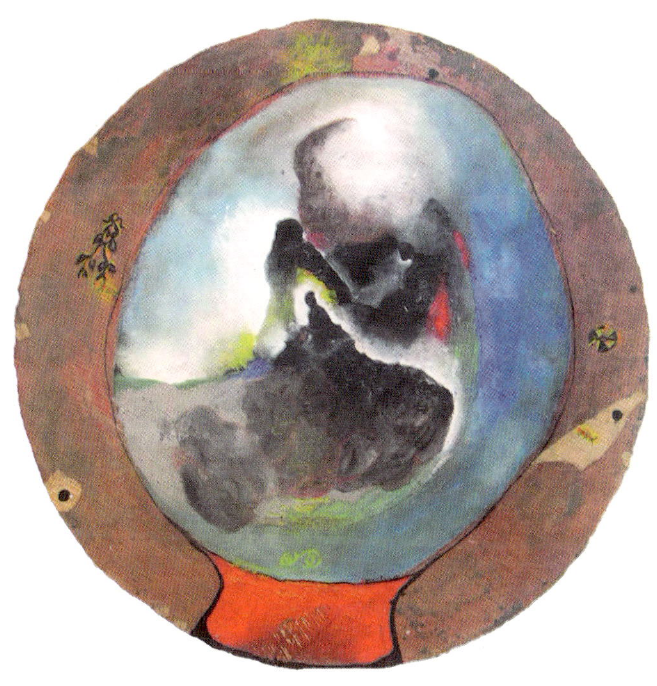

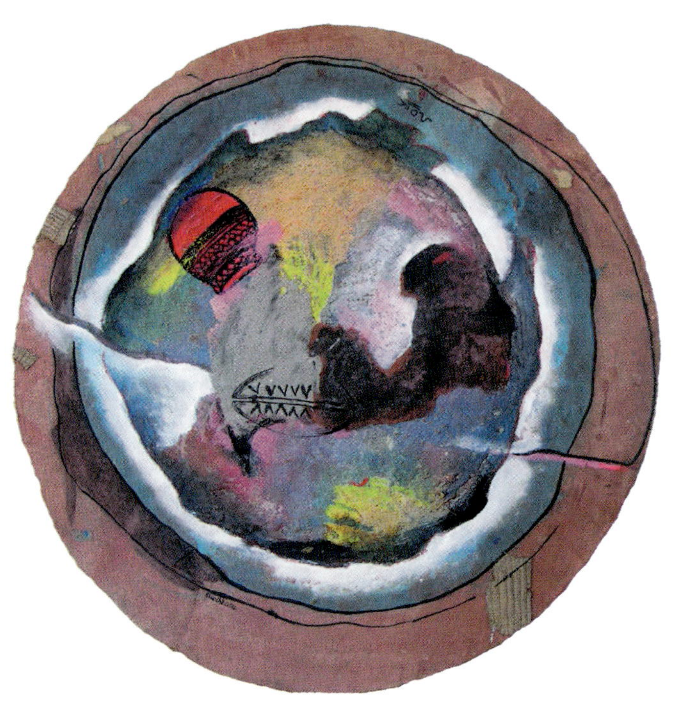

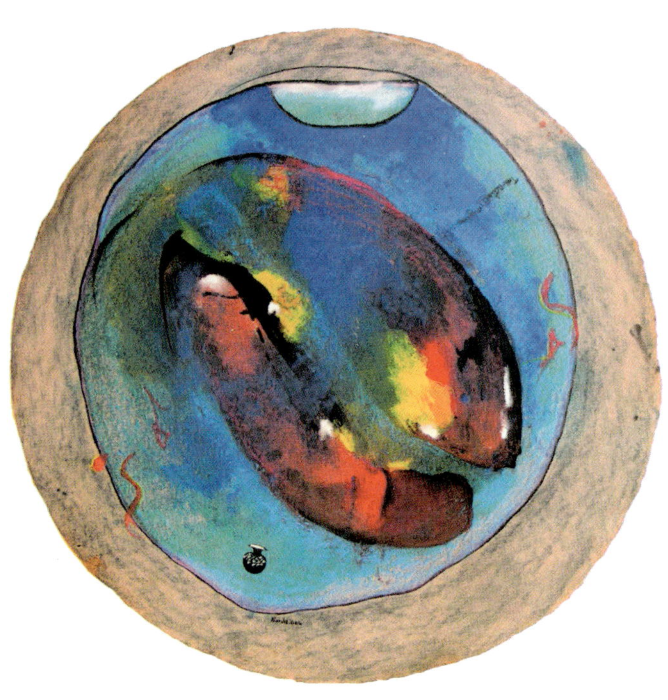

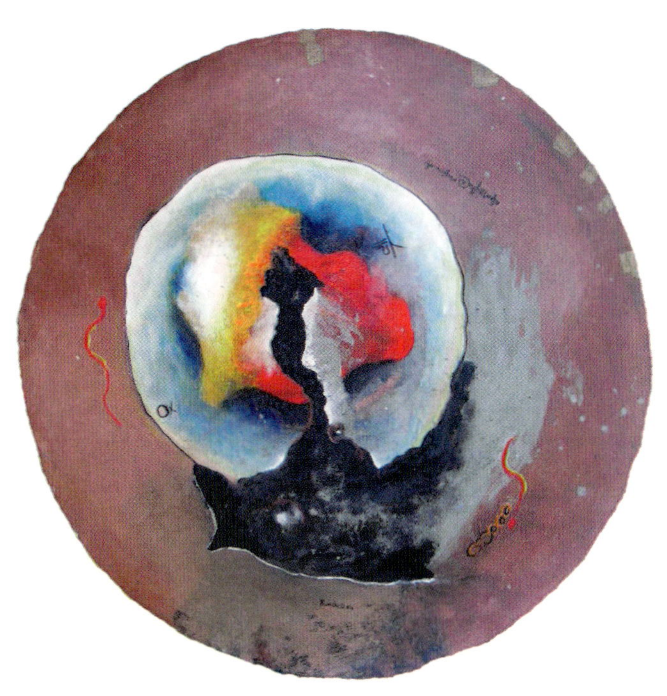

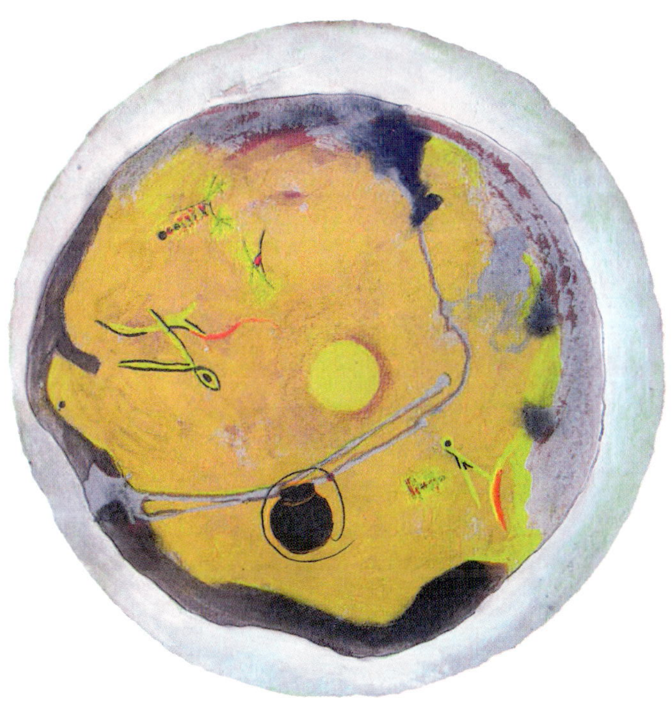

Miguel Petchovsky

West Side Story
2004
Oil on canvas
Diptych: 150 x 290 cm.

Modernism
2005
Oil on canvas
Diptych: 100 x 240 cm.

The Ejaculation of God
2005
Oil on canvas
140 x 140 cm.

The artistic approach of cultural and multi-layered concepts, associated with broader contemporary practices, gives rise to complex constructions comprising different hierarchies and invites various interpretations of its risky search for new meanings and creative syntaxes. Limits fade away according to the experimentation, flowing to the edges of what may be contemporary artistic reasoning where idiomatic experiments may indicate the possibility of intervention along with boundaries of representation and its interchanges. Wherever the contamination of different experiments is allowed, the space between the juxtaposition of simultaneous versions and narratives generates unpredictable chain reactions, God/Evil, Space/Time, Us/The Other, etc.

Under construction

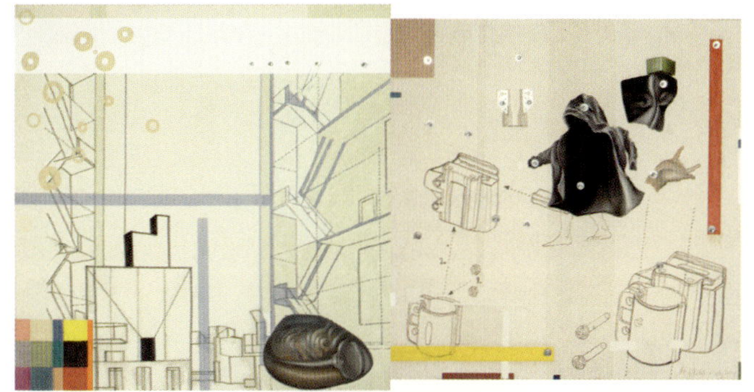

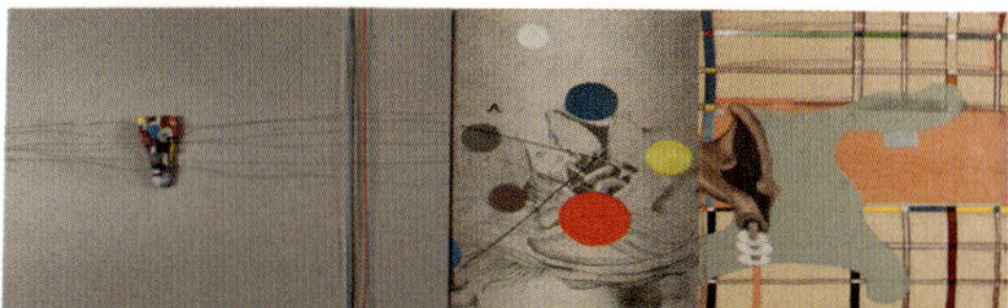

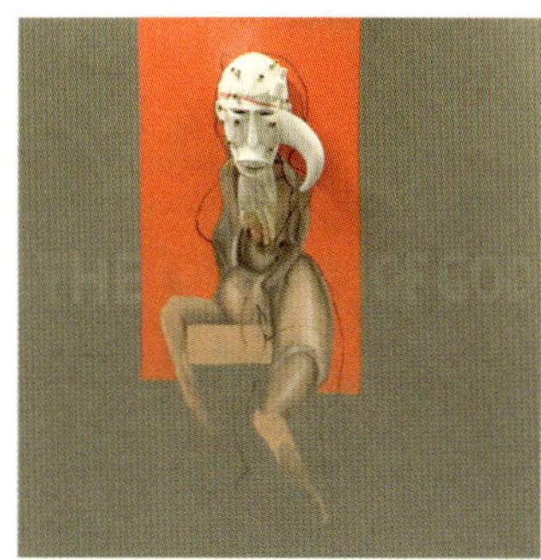

The works in *Under Construction, Modernism, The Ejaculation of God*, and *The West Side Story* - are visual exercises of concepts well established within a framework of western meta-narratives that are currently being scrutinised in transitional societies in Africa, reminding us that History remains to be fully revealed and needs to be deconstructed and redefined in the act of articulating artistic practice within individual experiences of confrontation.

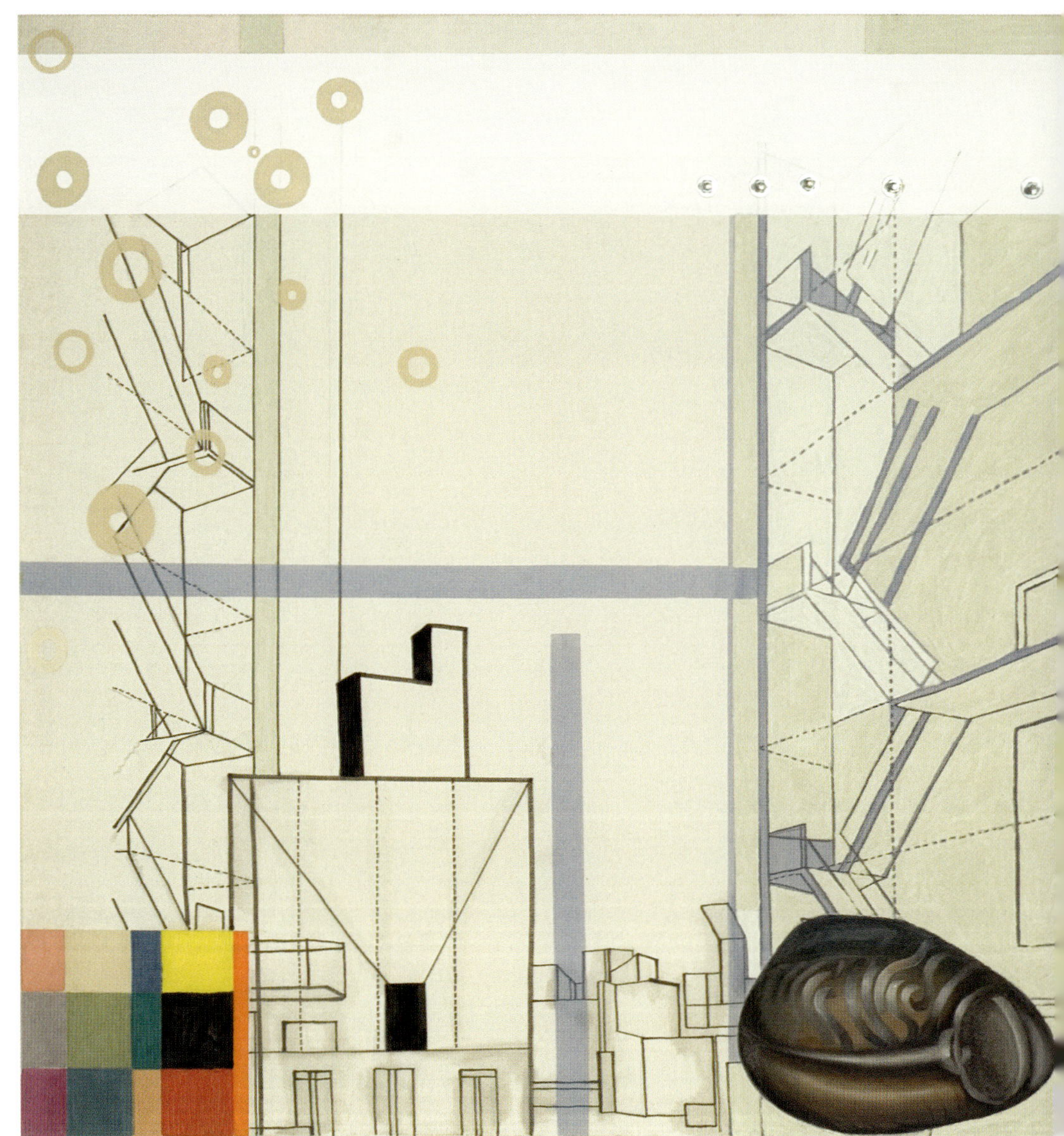

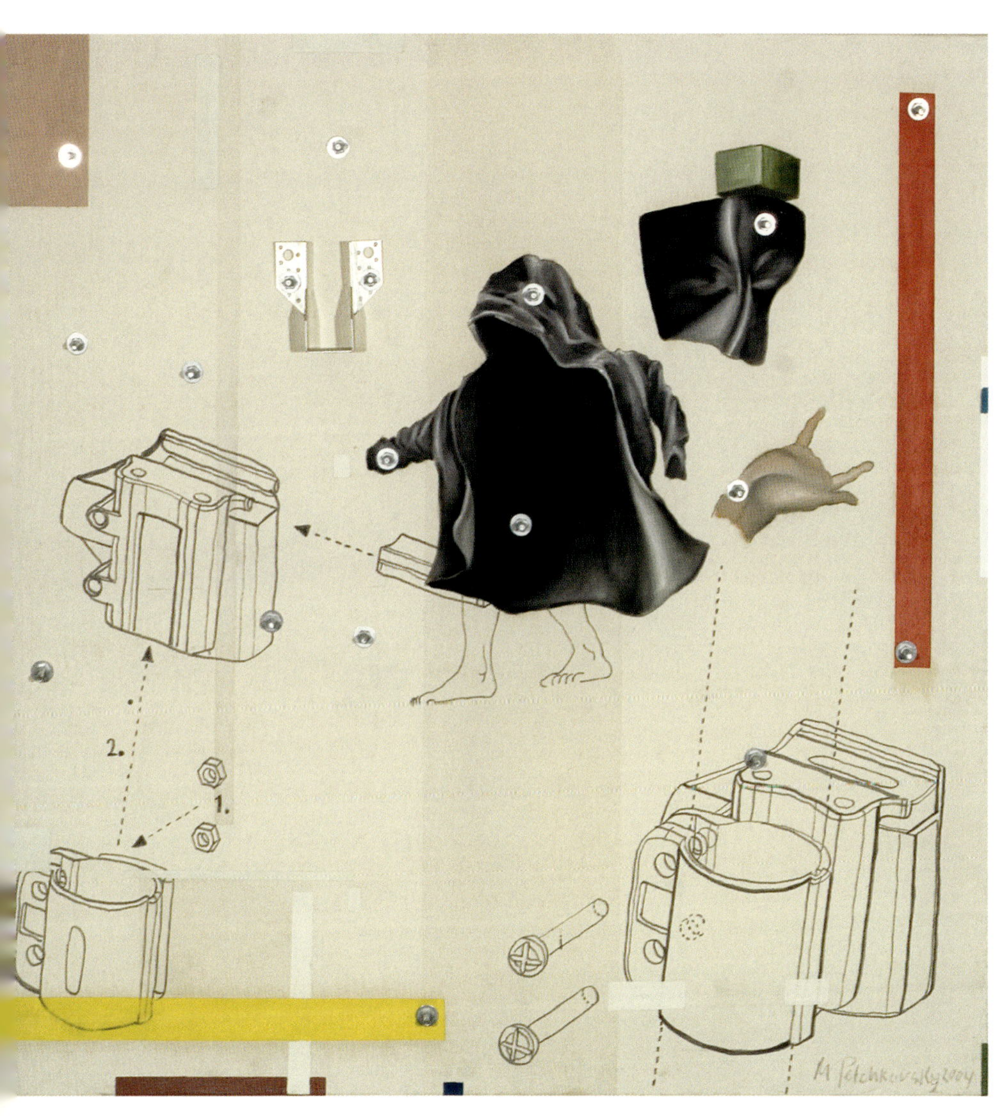

2.
1.
M. Petchkovsky 2004

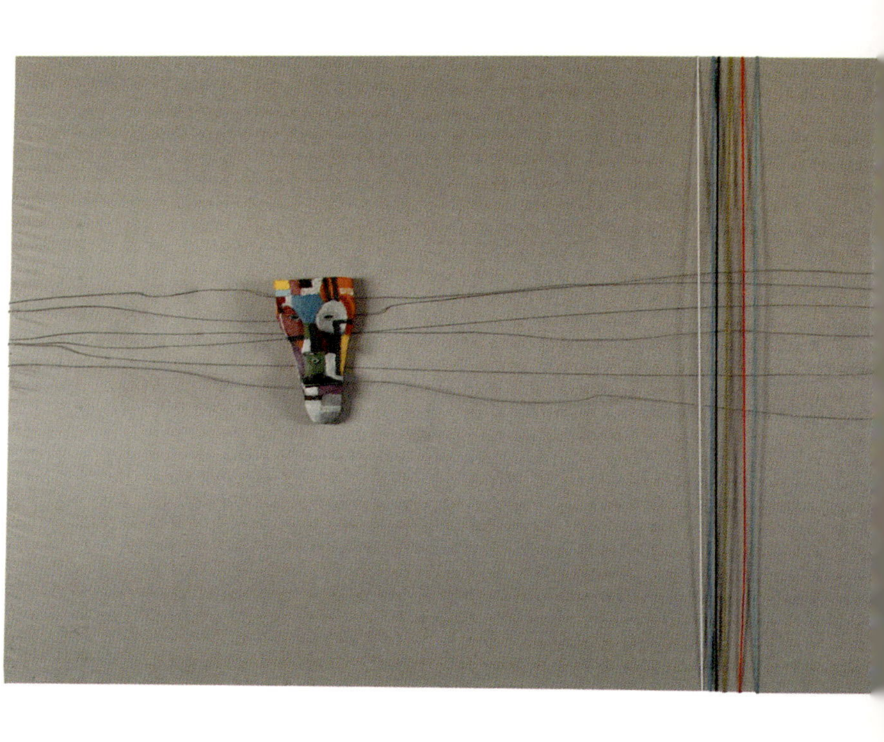

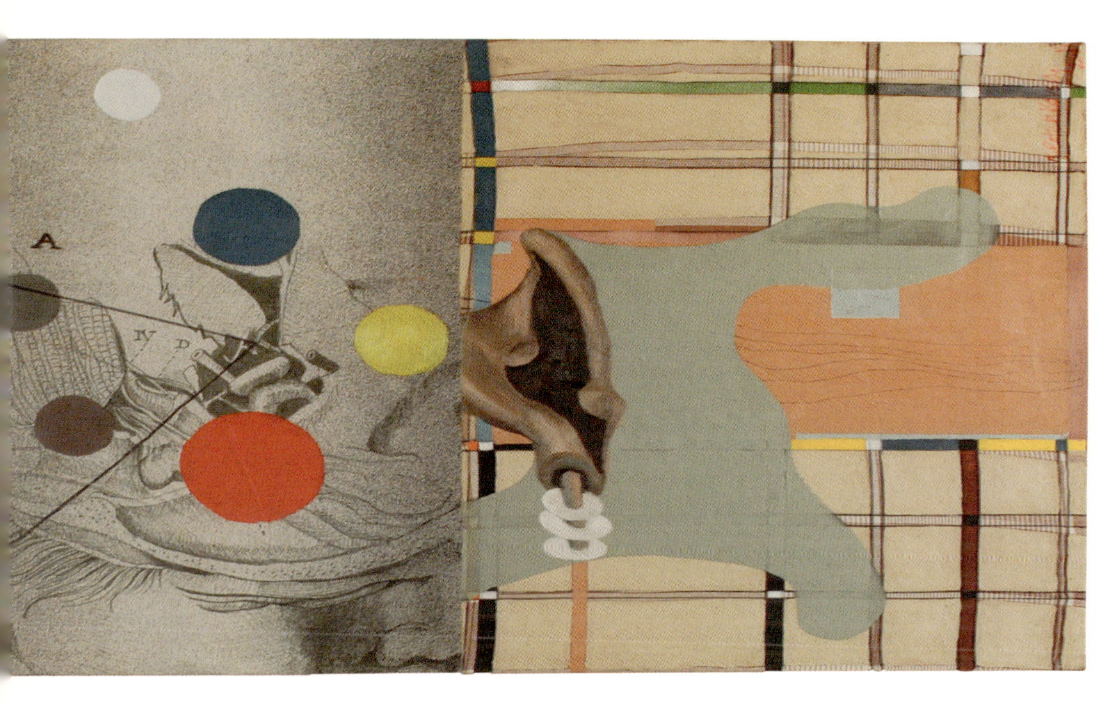

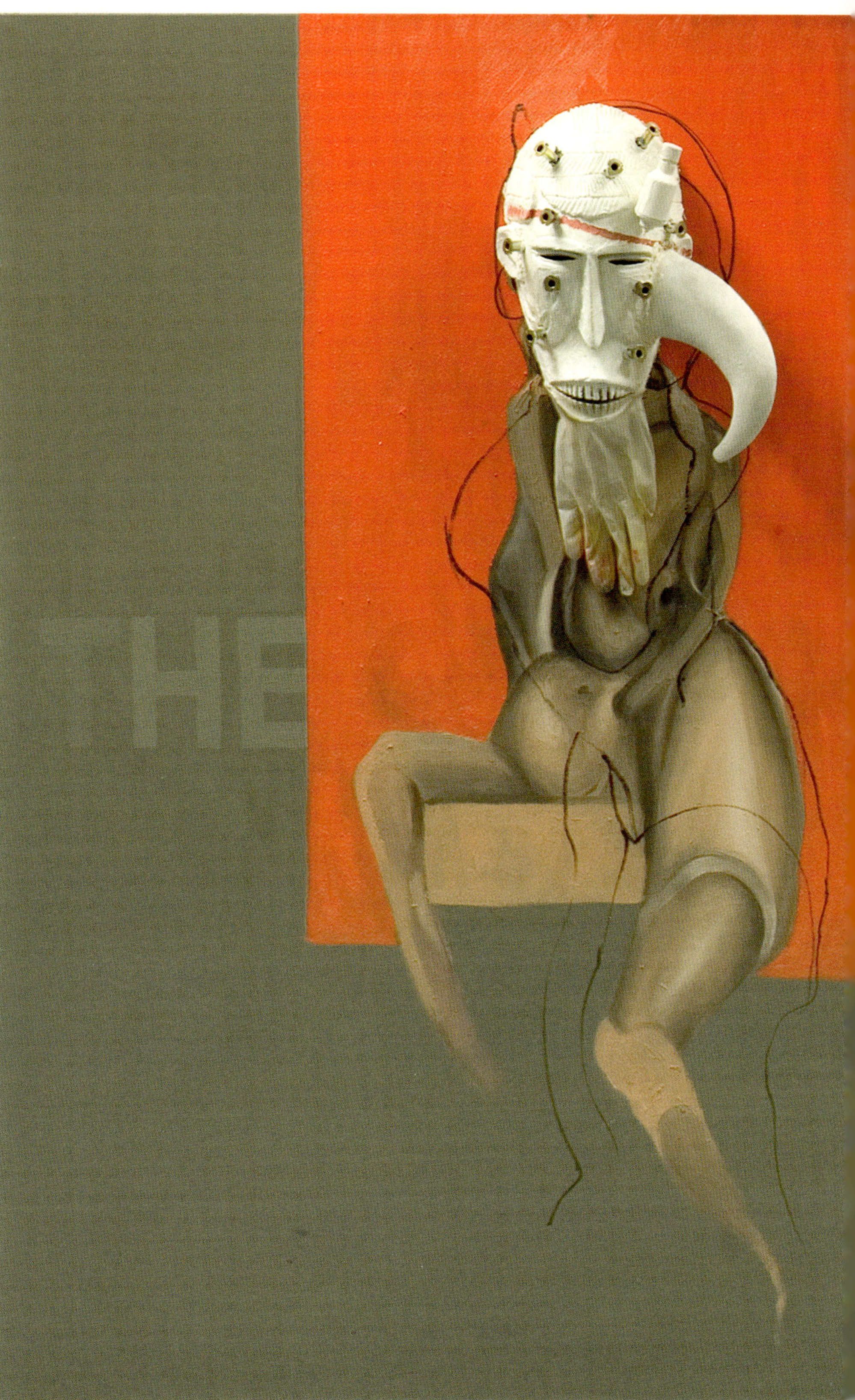
THE

Chéri Samba

Ultimatum
1999
Acrylic on canvas
195 x 138 cm.

*Le Commun des
politiciens*
2004
Acrylic on canvas, glitter
and collage
182 x 135,5 cm.

Une peinture à défendre
1993
Oil on canvas and glitter
129 x 193 cm.

Le monde à l'envers
2000
Acrylic on canvas, glitter
and *collage*
131 x 189 cm.

Lutte contre l'insalubrité
1998
Acrylic on canvas and
collage
130 x 195 cm.

"…I use what's in my environment and it pervades my art. But I don't want to have any limits, and I'm not interested in being categorised. Whatever an artist's background and roots, he has to be understood all over the world. You're born in one place but you don't only speak about that place. I want the artist to be considered as such. Art is constantly evolving and I have no particular definition."

In conversation with André Magnin, "Je ne vois pas de mal à me chanter moi-même" (I don't see any harm in singing my own praises), from the catalogue published by the Fondation Cartier pour l'art contemporain, Paris, 2004.

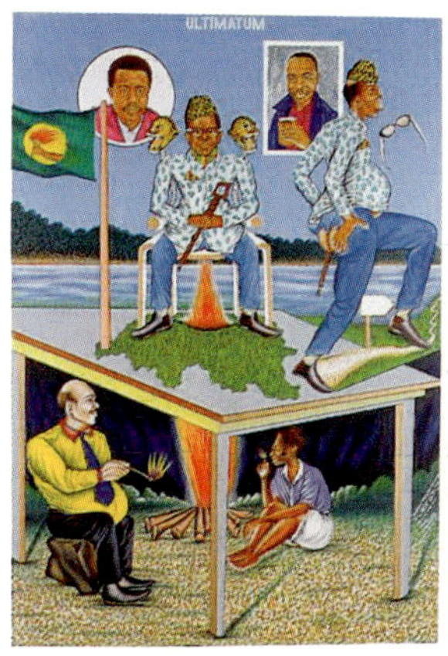

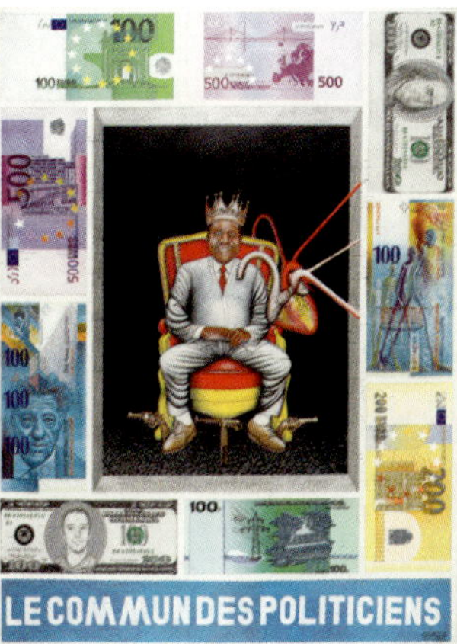

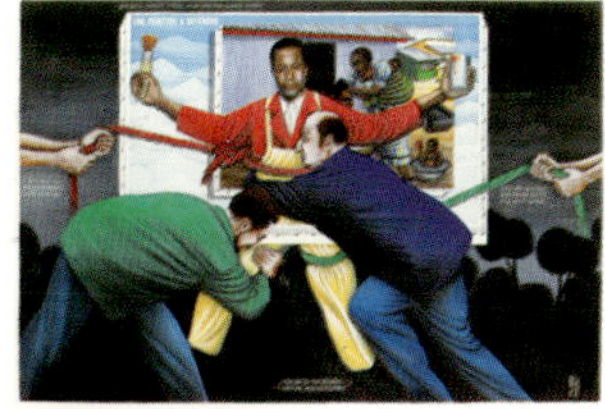

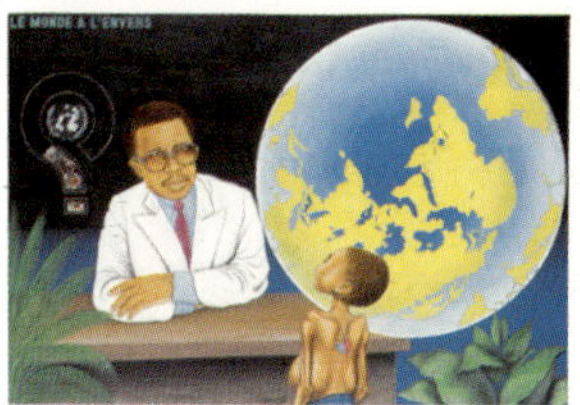

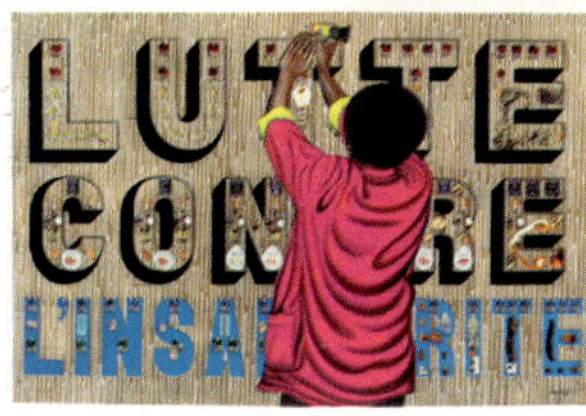

"Painting is the best way I've found to convey my thoughts, my messages, our culture and our civilisation. I labelled my painting "popular", but does art really need to be labelled? I realise that it was misinterpreted. I prefer to say that art must be free, and even that it should be looked at rather than talked about."

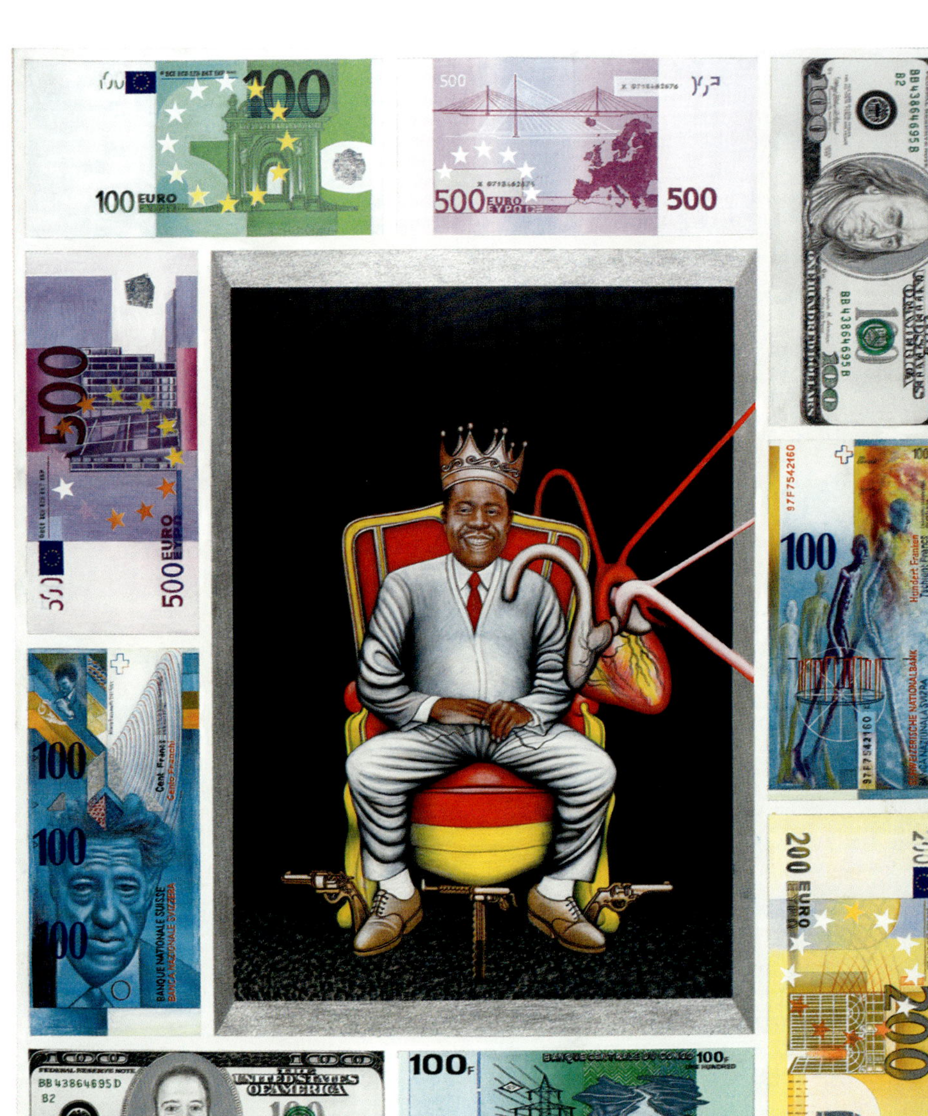
100
100 EURO
500
500 EURO 500
100
BANQUE NATIONALE SUISSE
UNITED STATES OF AMERICA
ONE HUNDRED DOLLARS
100
100F
100F
BANQUE CENTRALE DU CONGO
100
SCHWEIZERISCHE NATIONALBANK
200
200 EURO
LE COMMUN DES POLITICIENS

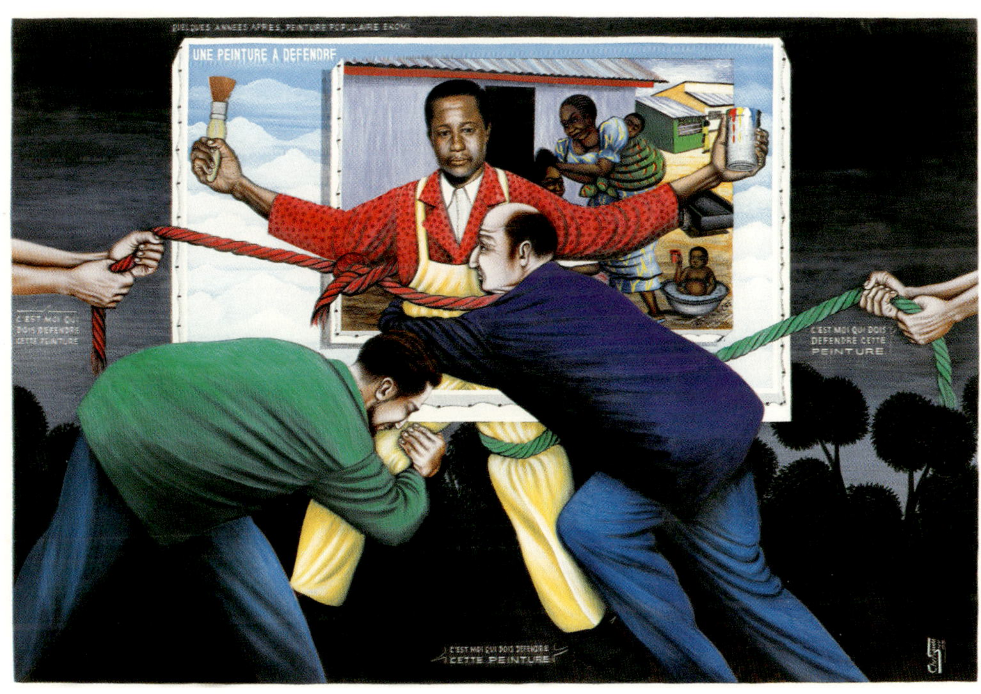

QUELQUES ANNÉES APRÈS, PEINTURE POPULAIRE EKOMI
UNE PEINTURE A DEFENDRE
C'EST MOI QUI DOIS DEFENDRE CETTE PEINTURE
C'EST MOI QUI DOIS DEFENDRE CETTE PEINTURE
C'EST MOI QUI DOIS DEFENDRE CETTE PEINTURE

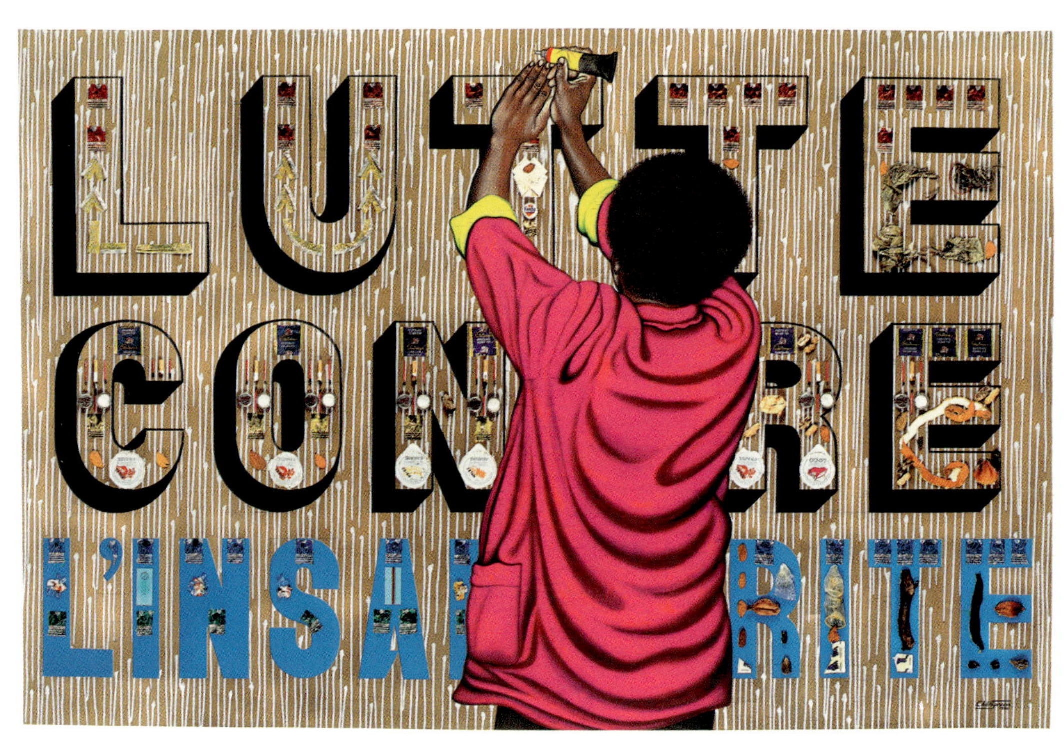

LUTTE
CONTRE
L'INSALUBRITE

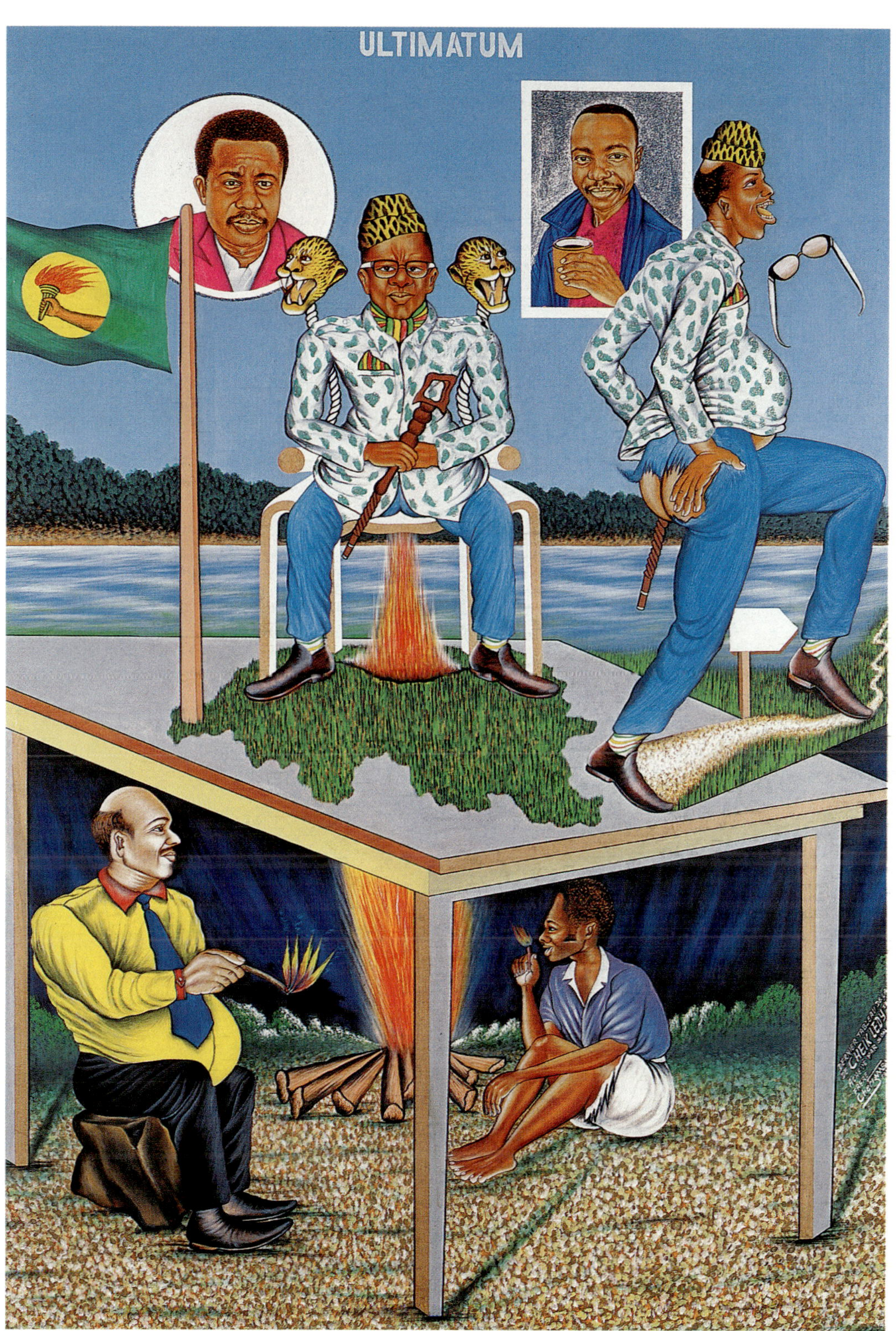

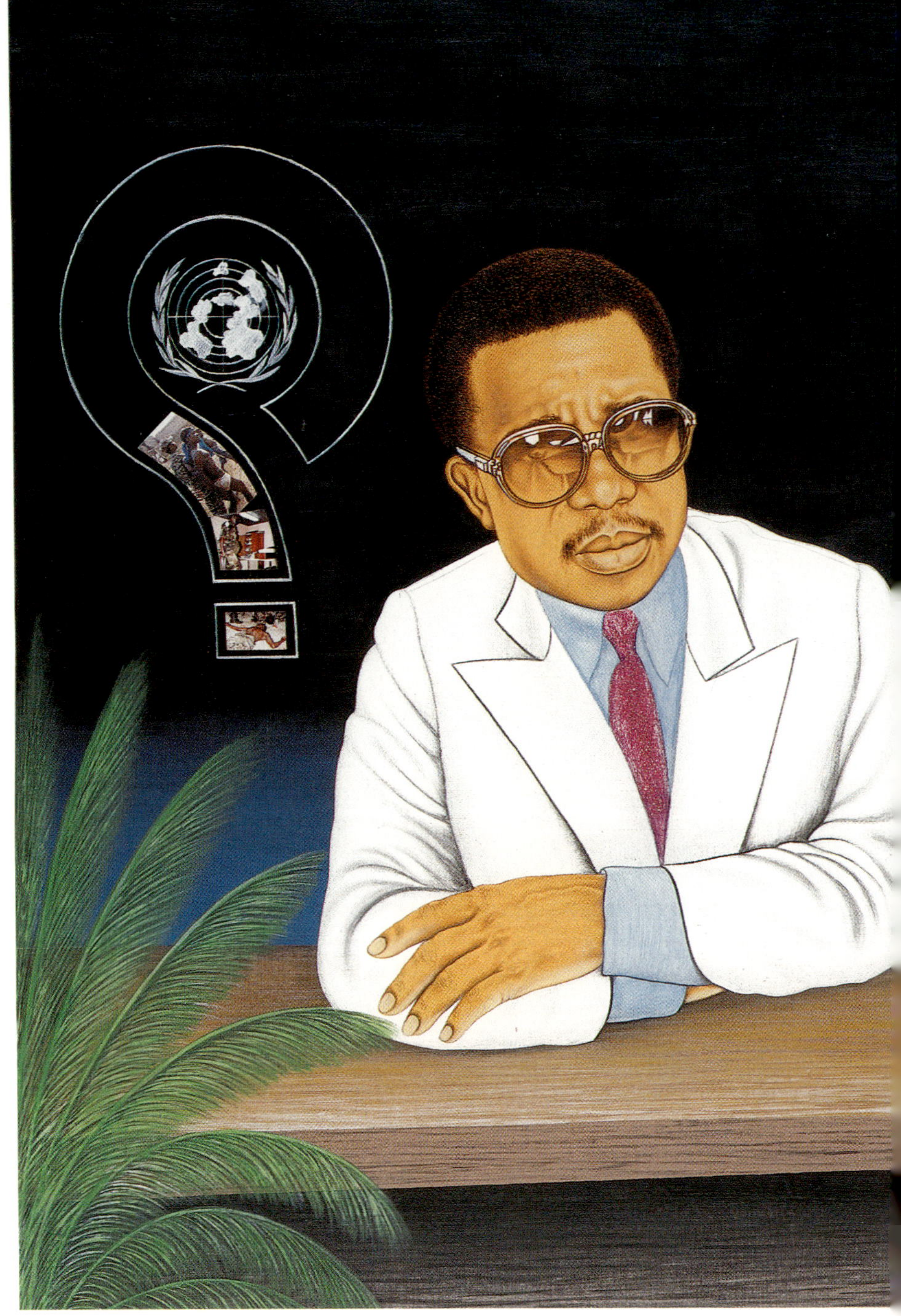

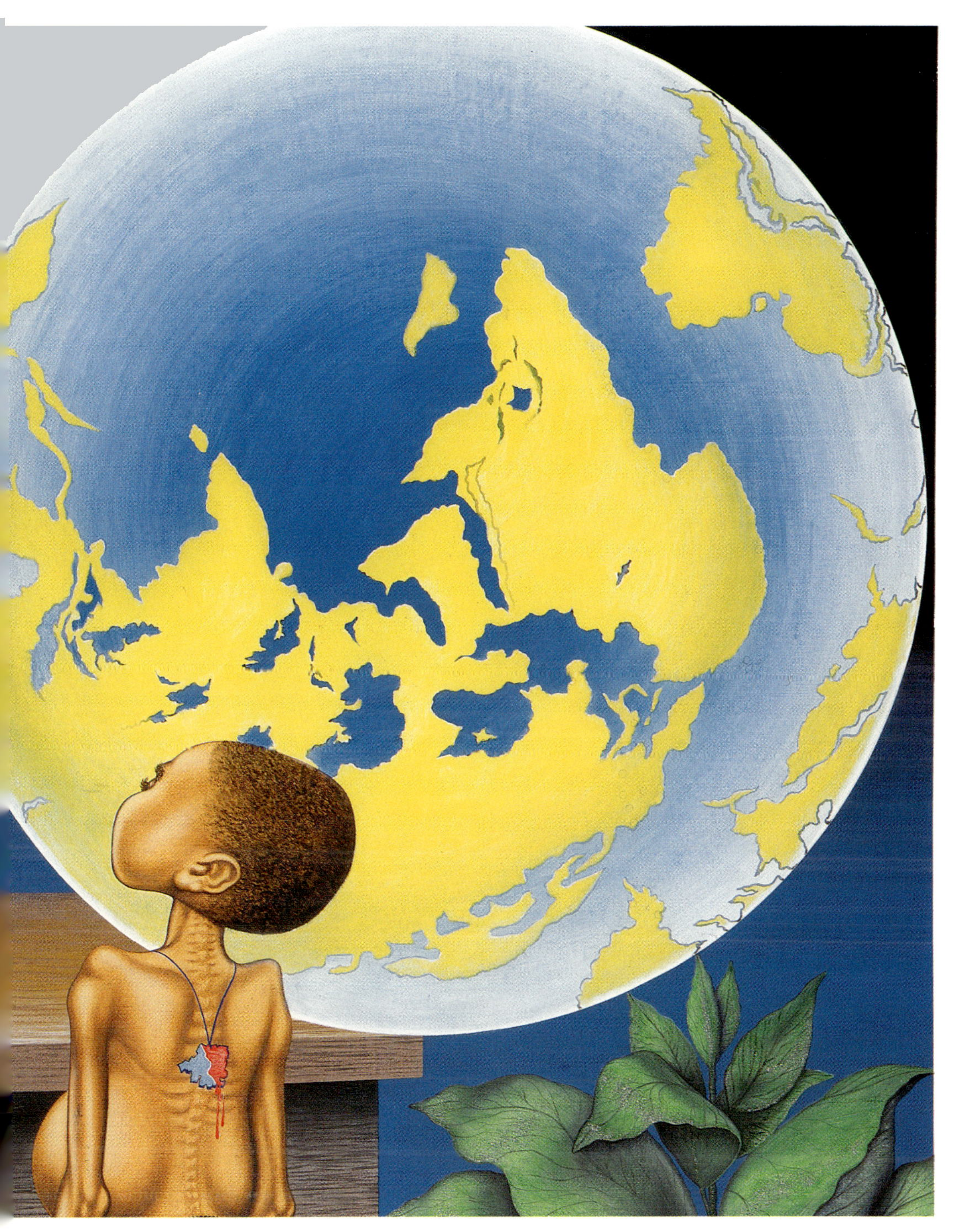

Djibril Sy

Visages d'Afrique
2000-2005
Colour photography
40 x 30 cm.

Images du Sénégal
2000-2005
Colour photography
30 x 40 cm.

Images du Sénégal
2000-2005
Colour photography
40 x 30 cm.

Kassak, Villages des tirailleurs
2002
Colour photography
30 x 40 cm.

Iles du Cap-Vert, Ville de Praïa
2003
Colour photography
30 x 40 cm.

Sousse, Rabat, Maroc
2000-2005
Colour photography
40 x 30 cm.

Images du Sénégal
2000-2005
Colour photography
30 x 40 cm.

Images du Sénégal
2000-2005
Colour photography
40 x 30 cm.

Images du Sénégal
2000-2005
Colour photography
40 x 30 cm.

Images du Sénégal
2000-2005
Colour photography
30 x 40 cm.

Images du Sénégal
2000-2005
Colour photography
30 x 40 cm.

Iles du Cap-Vert, Ville de Praïa
2003
Colour photography
30 x 40 cm.

Images du Sénégal
2000-2005
Colour photography
30 x 40 cm.

Images du Sénégal
2000-2005
Colour photography
40 x 30 cm.

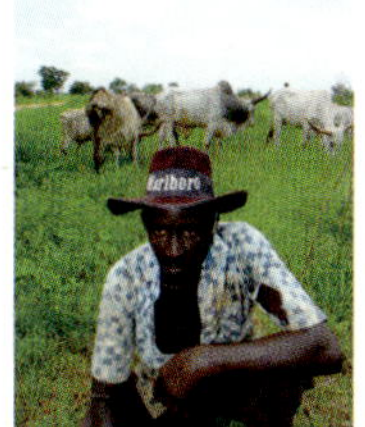
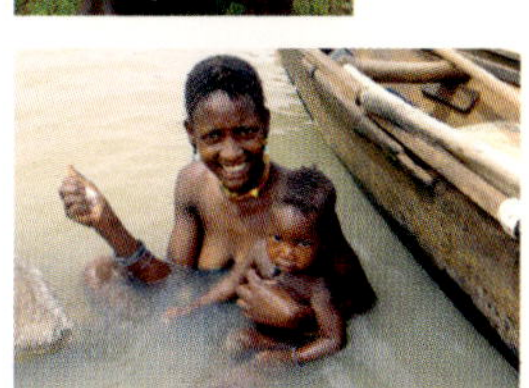
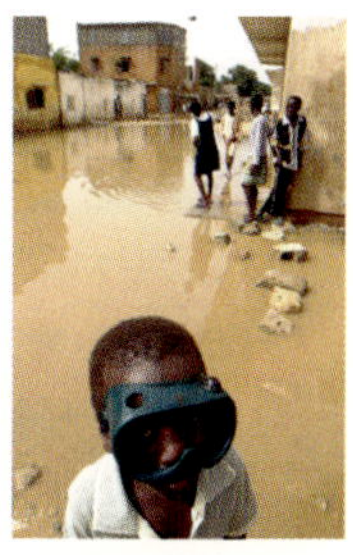
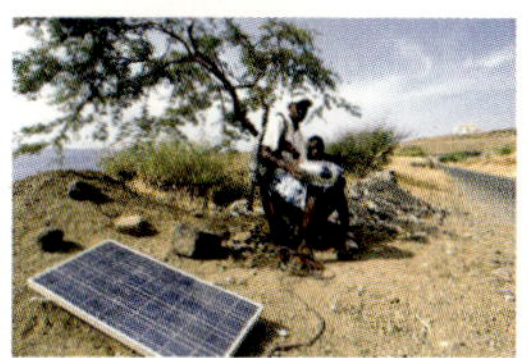
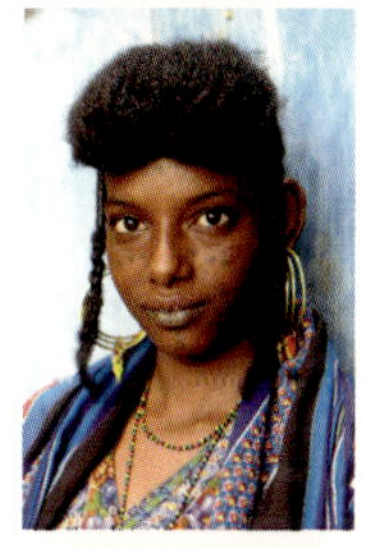
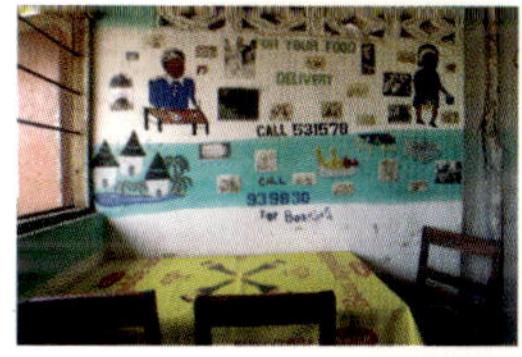
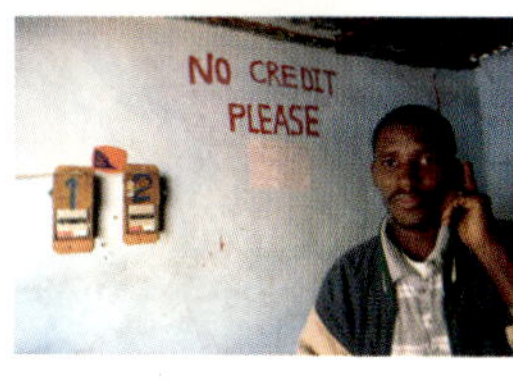
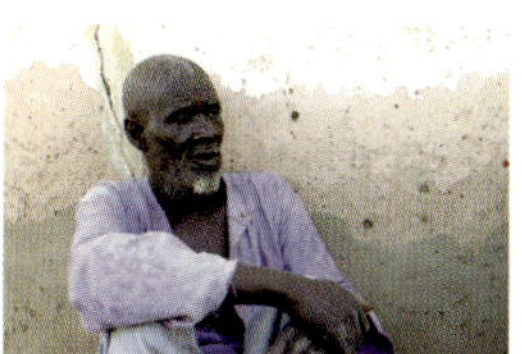
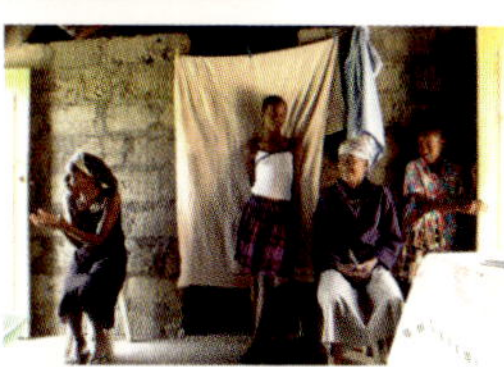
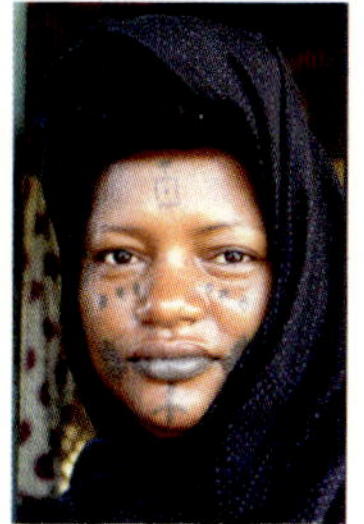
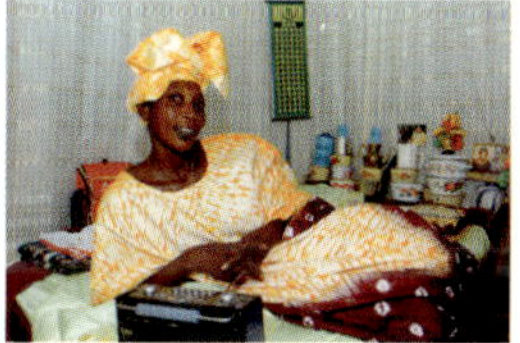
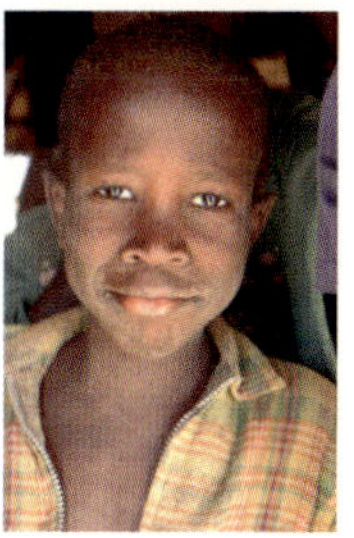
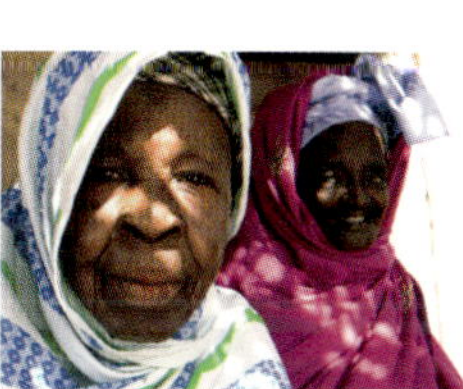

When I discovered photography, I was fascinated and I wanted to know why photography fascinated me and everyone else. I wanted to get to the bottom of it and in doing so fell in love with it.

Every image is a question and I am never satisfied with the answers I obtain. So I
ask the same question again but in a different way. I am profoundly satisfied with
the interest aroused by my question but I'm still waiting for an answer.

Djibril Sy

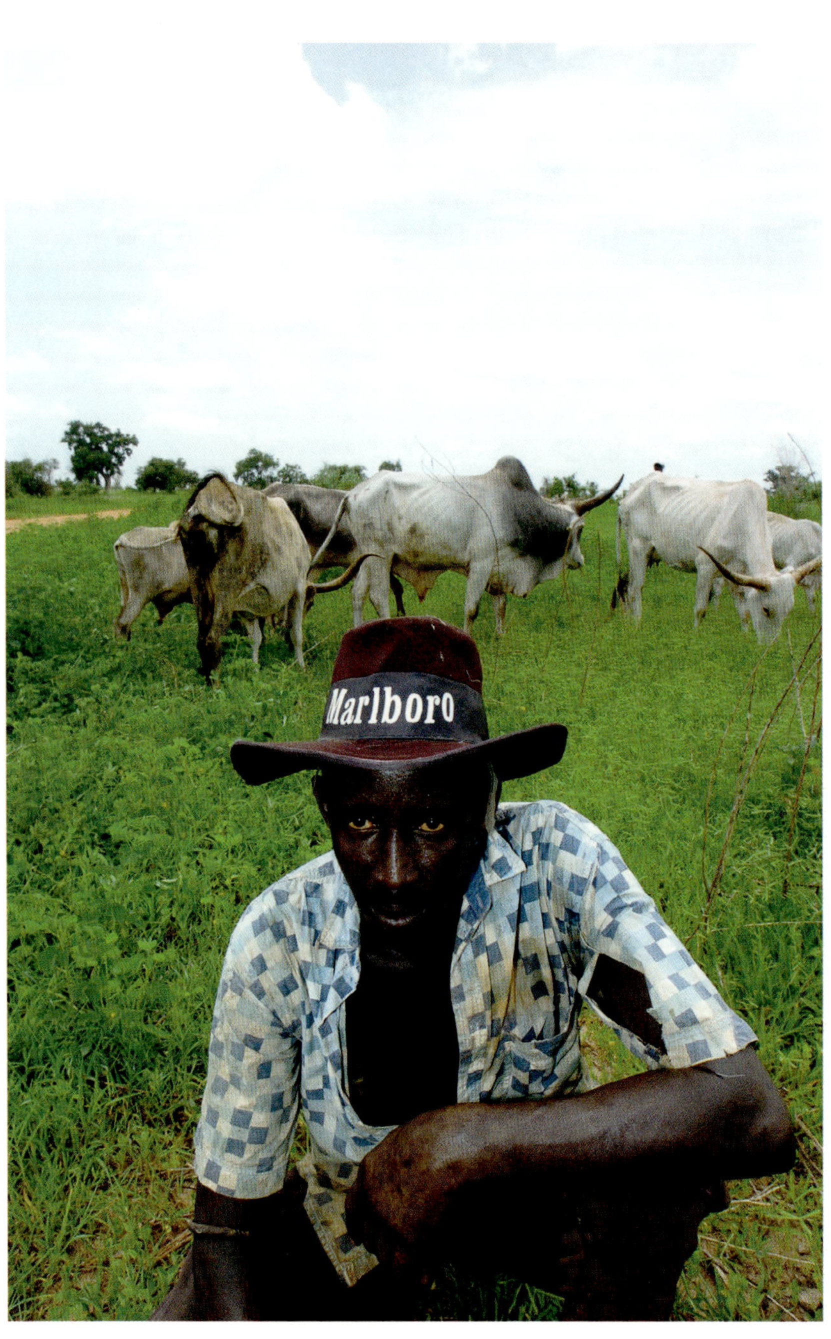

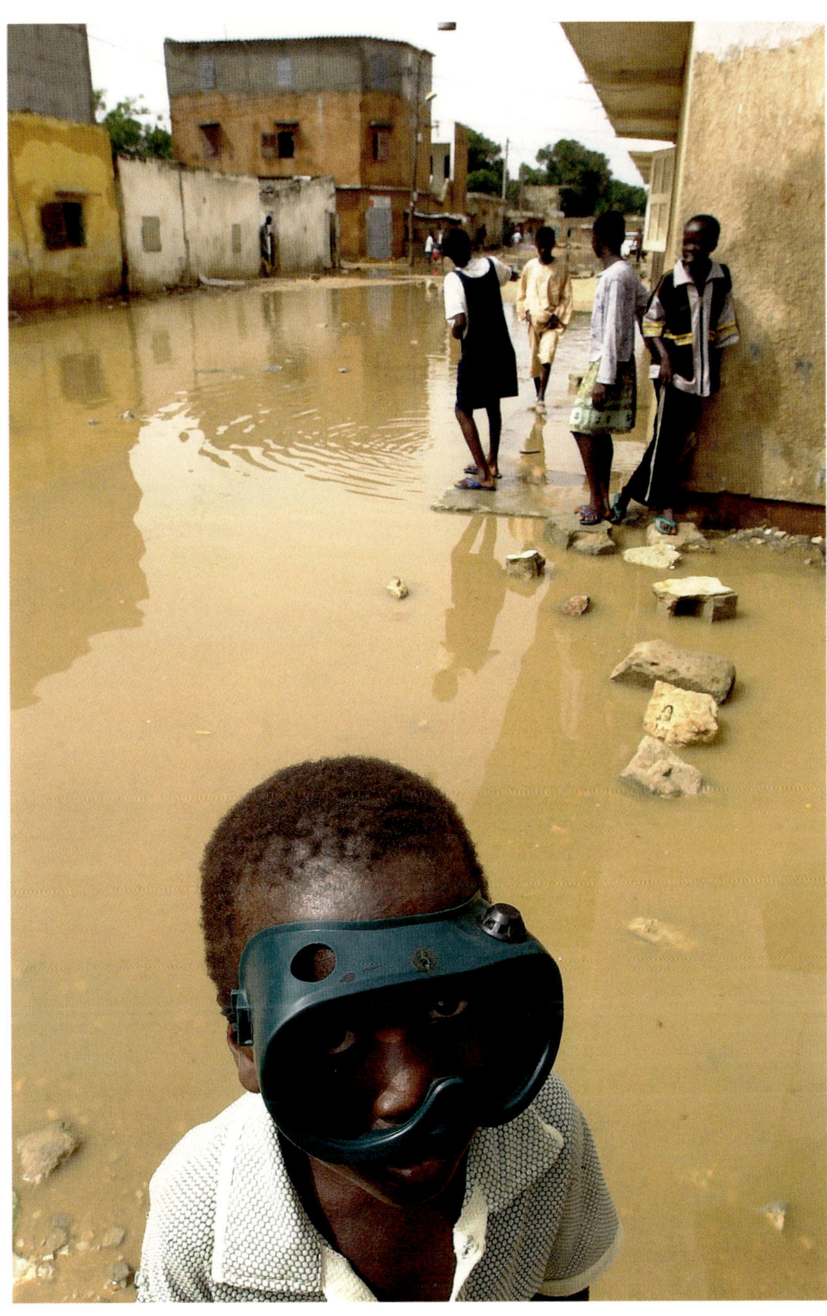

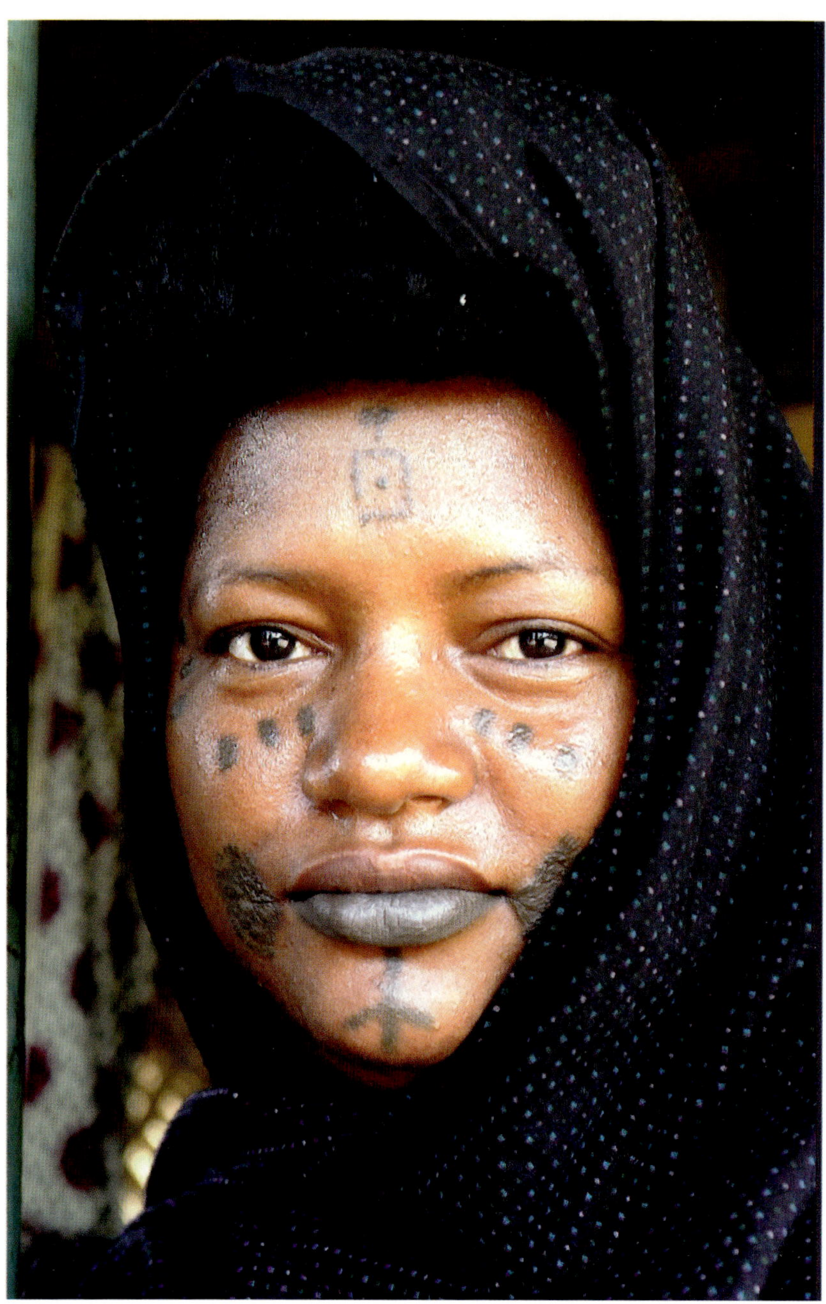

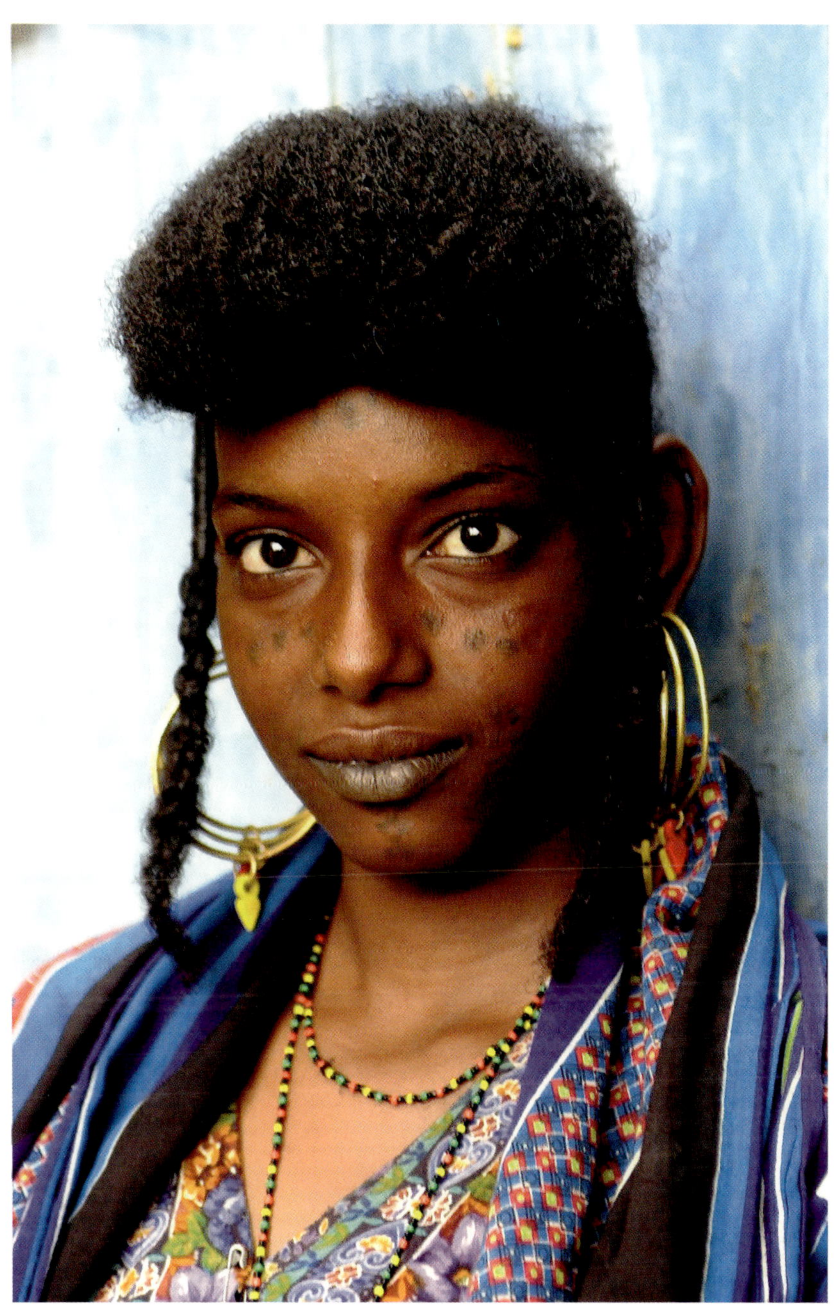

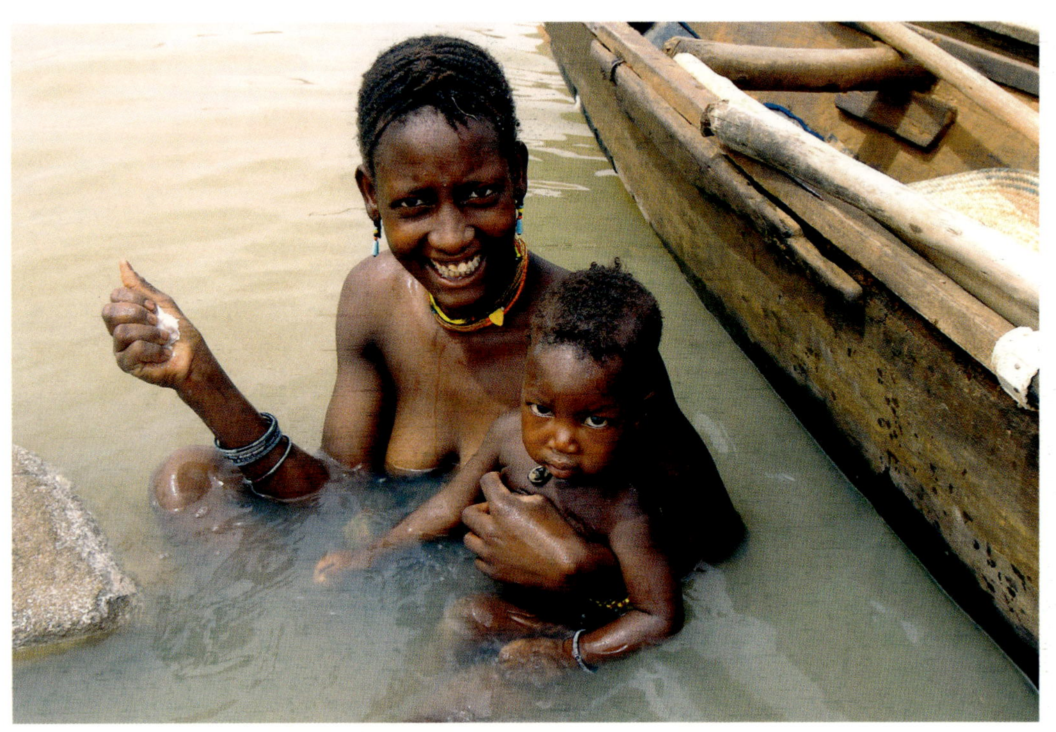

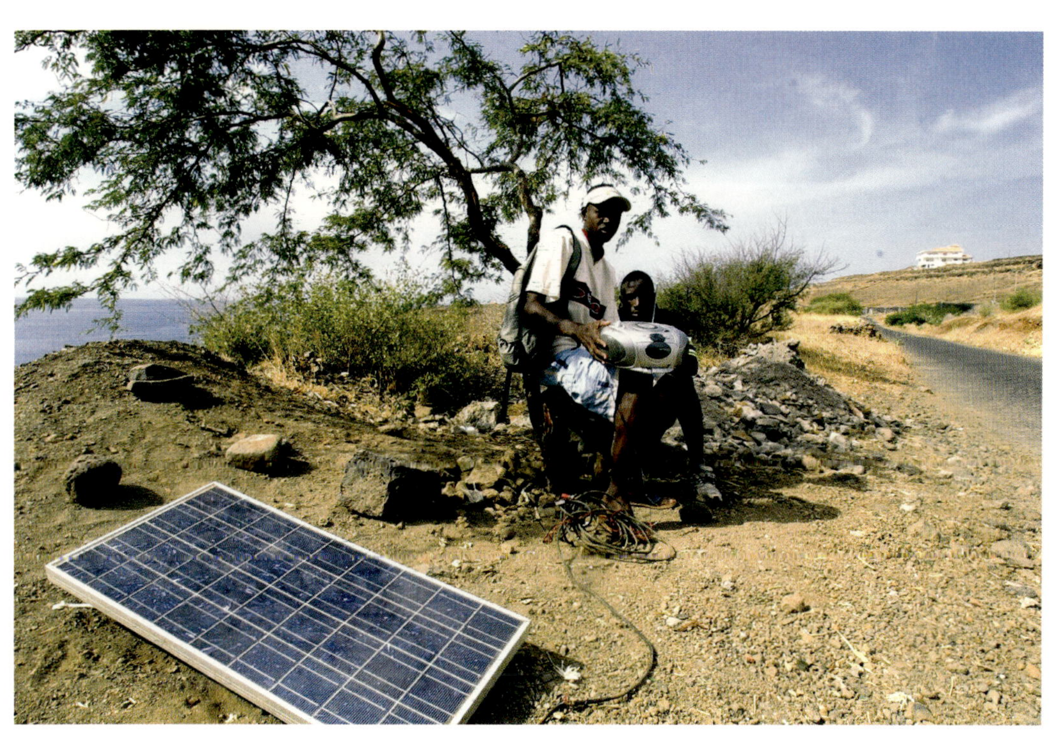

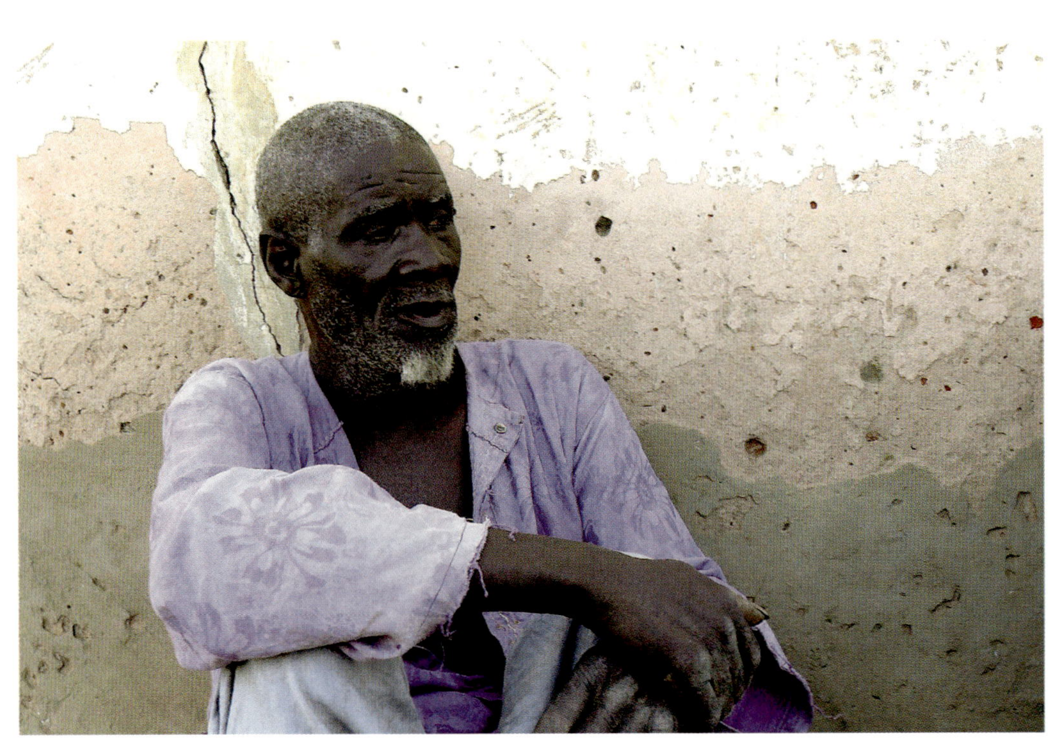

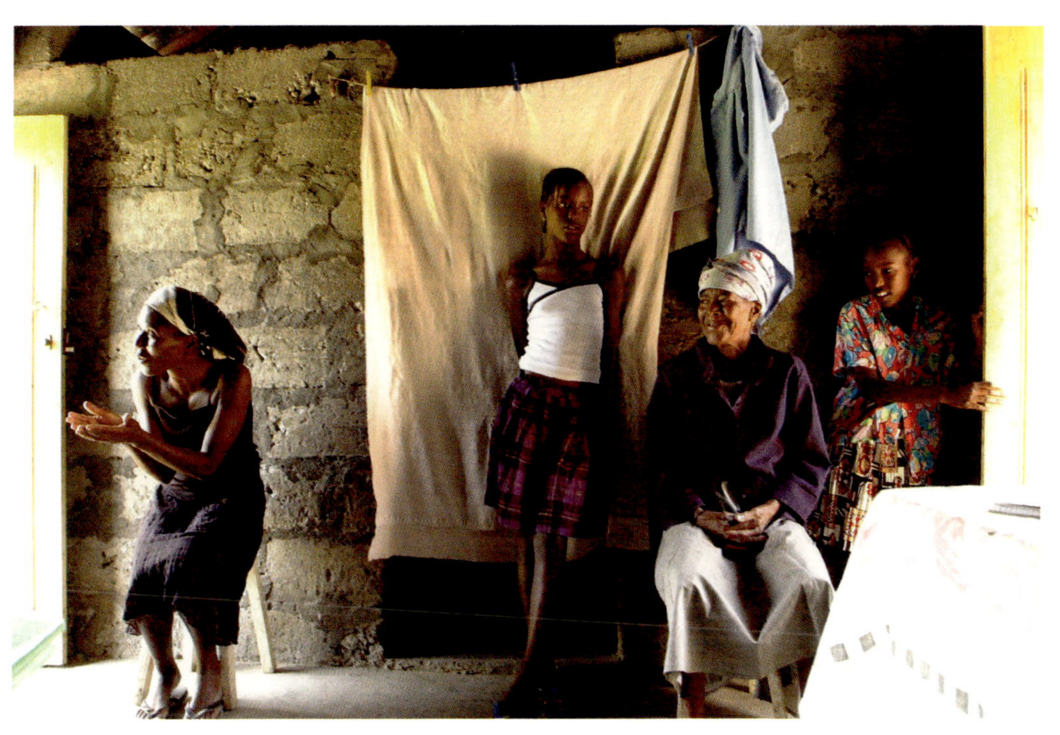

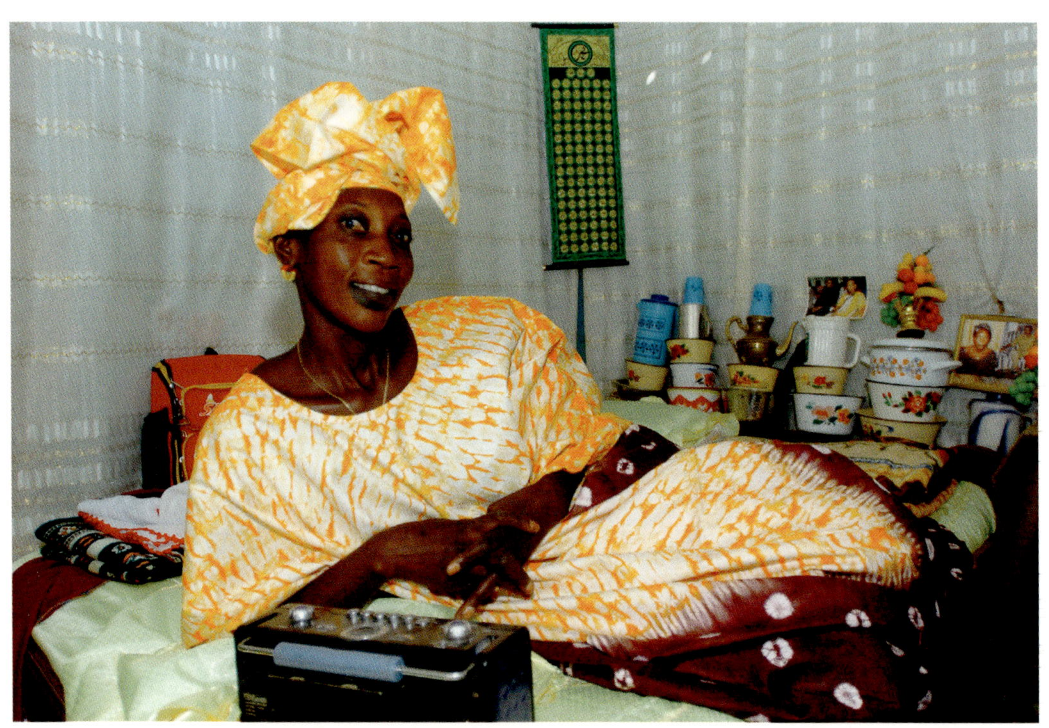

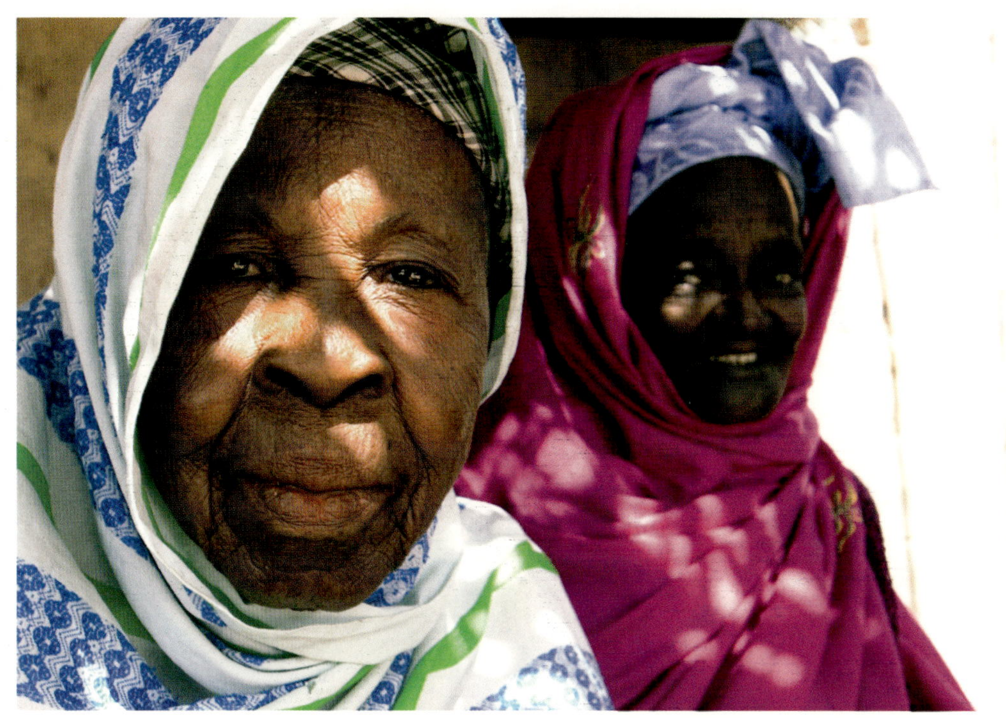

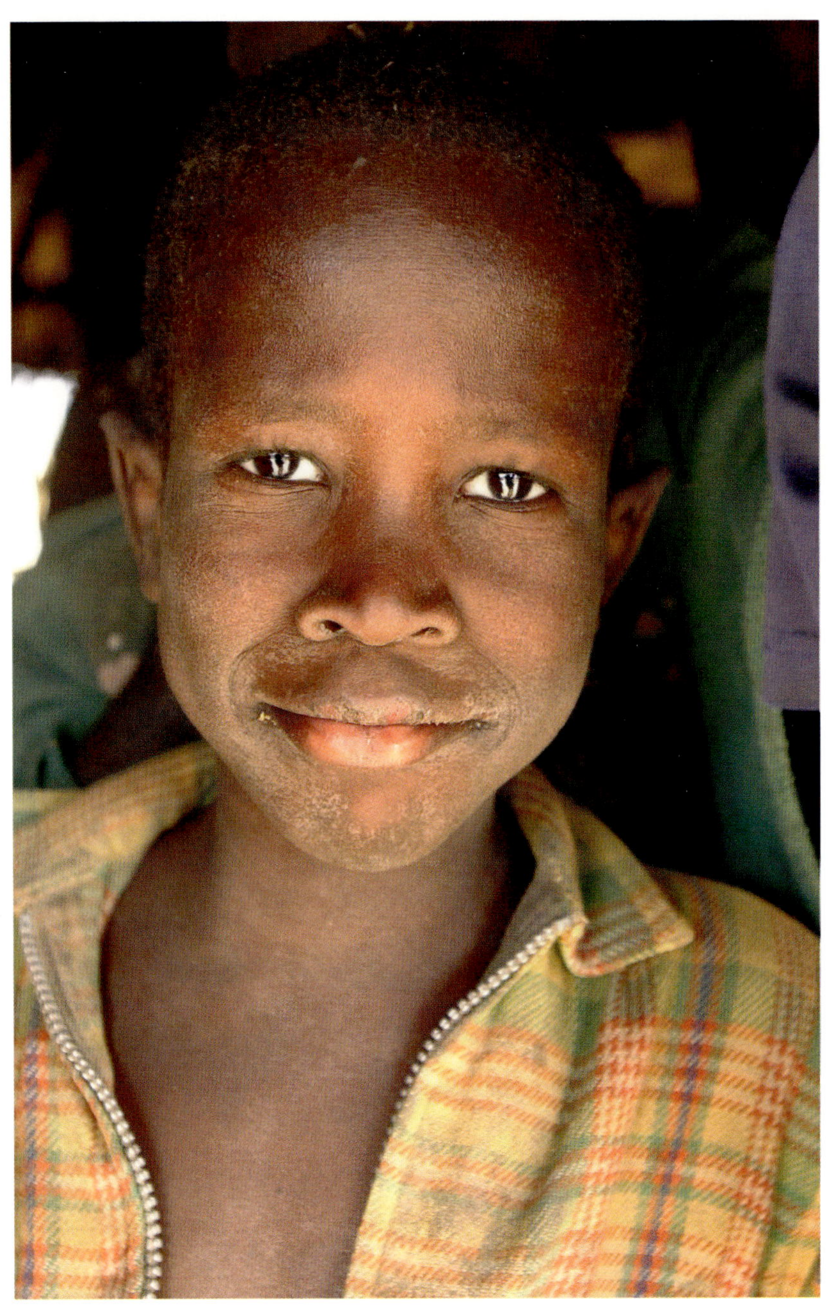

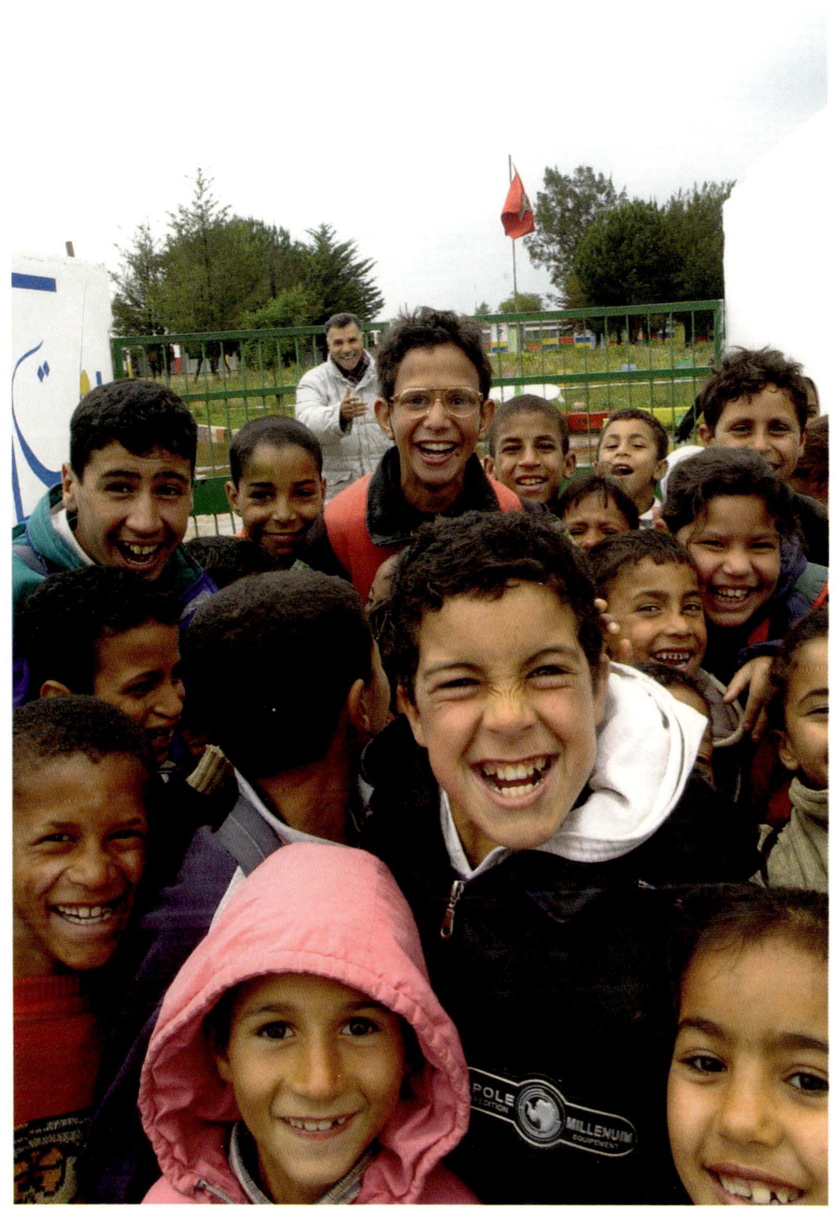

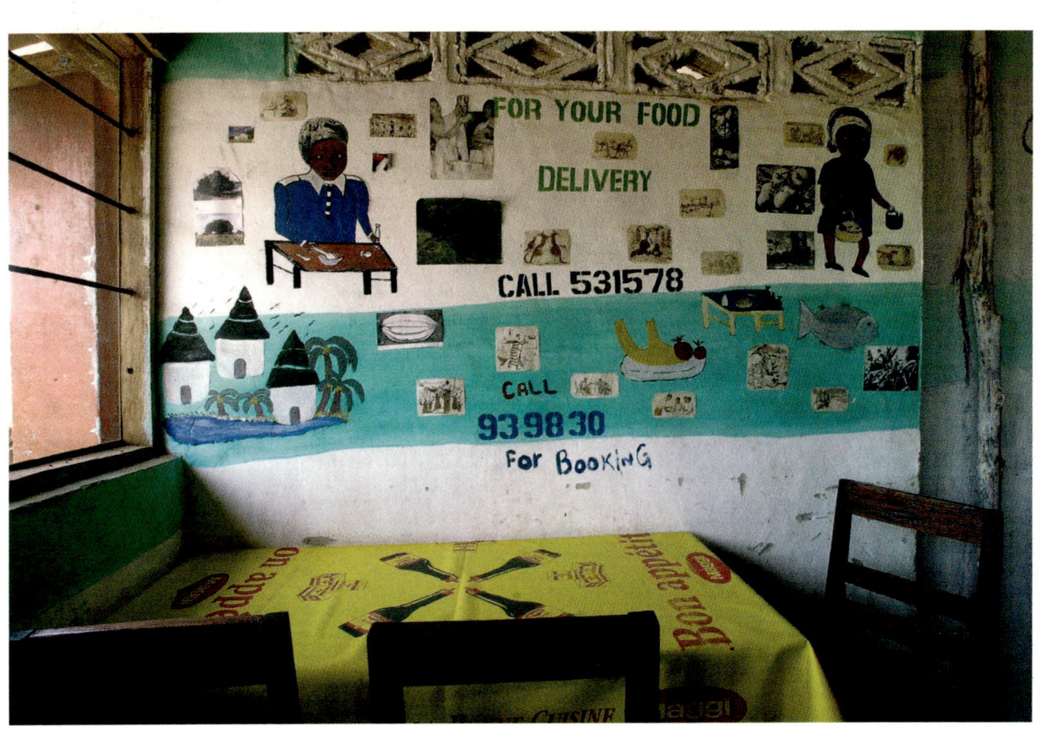

FOR YOUR FOOD
DELIVERY
CALL 531578
CALL
939830
For BookinG
Bon appétit
Maggi
Bon appétit
CUISINE

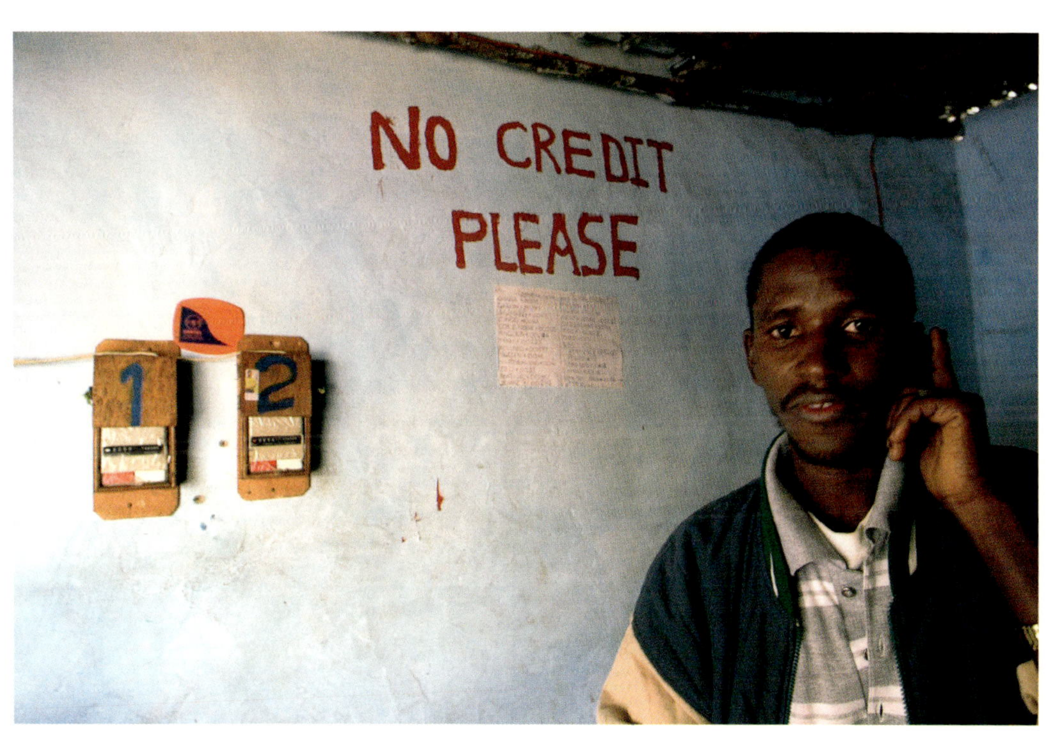
NO CREDIT
PLEASE
1
2

Emeka Udemba

The World is Your Home
2005
Acrylic, chalk and wood
on wall
Variable dimensions

Bath
2004
Video projection
6'

My interest has always focused on developing artistic strategies that examine
the unresolved dialectic between social classes, identities, economies, powers
and cultures. Through the strategic use of performances, installations, photography and drawings, I set out proposals through which existing structures might
be broken down (or not) in order to explore underlying forms of ideological
control. Conceiving information as knowledge that comes from everywhere
and ends nowhere, the works form an intricate network of semantic densities
devoid of straightforward exegesis, intensifying and reinventing the interaction
between work and viewer. These seemingly contradictory tasks of representing

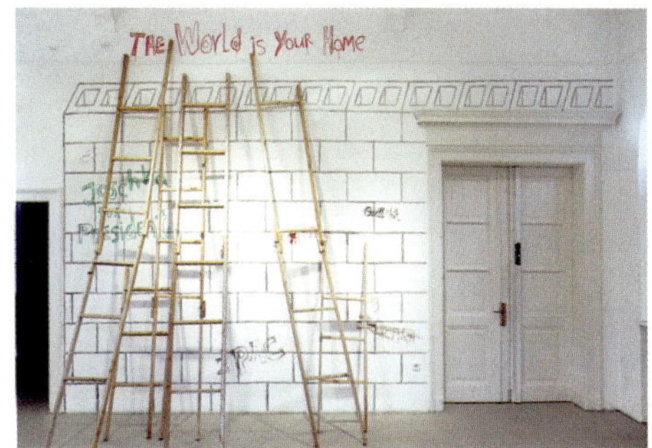

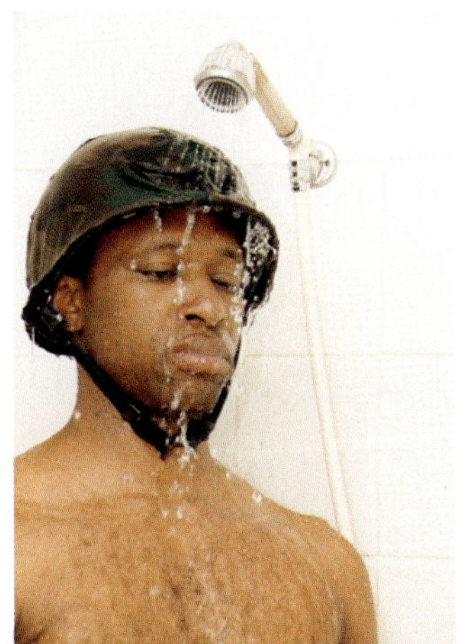

the formal and the metaphorical enable me to hybridise into significant new directions. Distanced from the dogmatic tendencies of formalist declarations regarding the truth of materials, the works create a space for the imagination where materials accomplish much more than simply asserting their physical presence. They do not only serve as codes. As forms, they invent and reinvent ways to describe human conditions; memories, ambitions and obsessions, all blended with powerful social, political and historical forces.

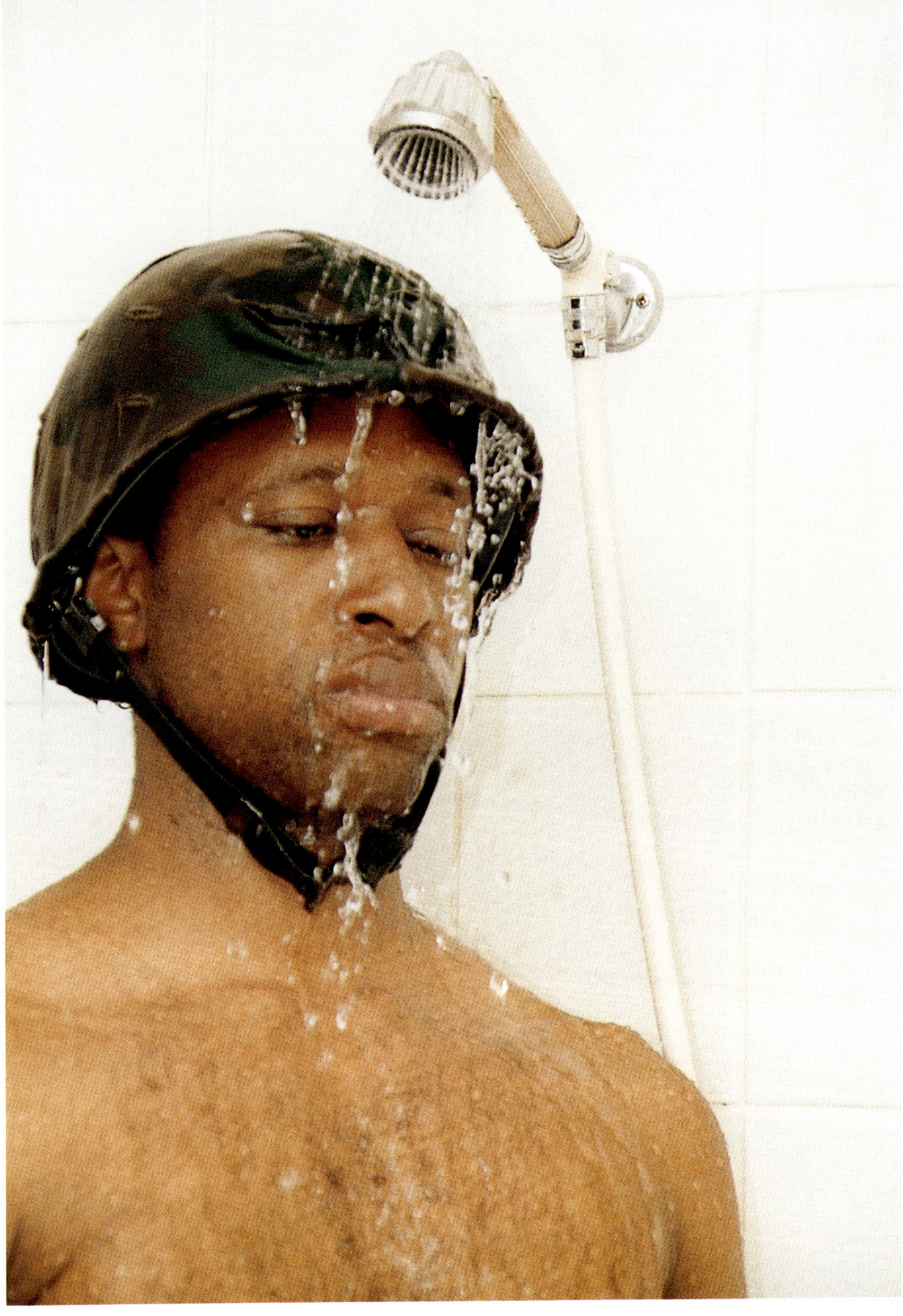

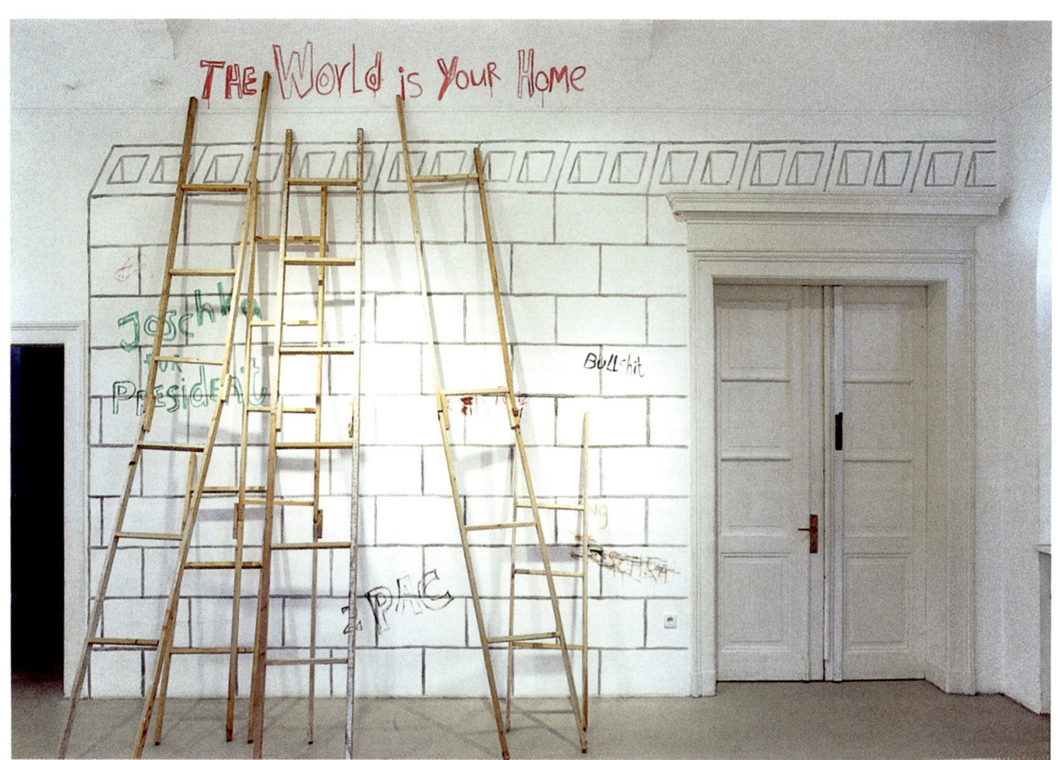
The World is Your Home
Joschka für President
Bullshit
2PAC

Ammar Bouras

Born in 1964. Lives and works in Alger.

Diploma
1989: Diplôme National des Beaux-Arts (DNBA, communication visuelle). Ecole Nationale des Beaux Arts, Algiers, Algeria.
1994: Diplôme d'Etudes Sup. en Arts Plastiques (DESA, Spécialité Peinture). Ecole Supérieure des Beaux Arts, Algiers, Algeria.

Stages
November 2001: Prohelvetia, Fondation suisse pour la culture, Switzerland.
April / June 2003: Ecole d'art d'Aix, Aix en Provence, France.
August / October 2003: Cité internationale des Arts, Paris, France.

Profesional Activity
Currently: Professor of Photography at Ecole Supérieure des Beaux Arts d'Alger.

Solo exhibitions

2005
L'être d'amour, Galerie Esma, Alger, Algeria.

2003
Je t'aime, N'hebek, I love you. Art book composed of nine screen printed images with 50 examples, d'art d'aix, Ecole supérieure d'art d'Aix in Provence, France.

2001
Stridences, Sangcommenttaire? Exposition-installation. Cercle Frantz Fanon, Alger, Algeria.

1999
Fenêtres, Fondation Asselah, Alger, Algeria.

1997
Espace Sofitel, Alger, Algeria.

1995
Journée de deuil, Teatri di Vita, Bologna, Italy.

Group exhibitions

2005:
Prix Barcelona 2005, FIAV, Spain.
Meeting Point, video installation, Stenersen Museum, Oslo, Norway.
Des Rives installation vidéo, Alger (Algeria), Corbas (France), Lyon (France).
Des artistes pour novembre, installation vidéo, La Citadelle, Alger (Algeria).

2004
et + si aff, vidéo. Distinction du jury FIAV « Festival d'Images et d'Art Vidéo » Bari, Italy.
Artistes dans la ville, Musée Mahmoud Saïd. Alexandria, Egypt.
L'autre Algérie, video proyection. Prohelvetia, Geneva, Switzerland.
Traverse video, video, Toulouse, France.

2003-2004
Voyages d'artistes, Algérie

2003
Espace EDF Electra, Paris, France.
Artistes d'Algérie, Médiathèque de Miramas. Miramas, France.
Projection vidéo. (16es Instants vidéo de Manosque) Manosque, France.
Alger - Marseille 8+3, Galerie porte-Avion et Château de Servières, Marseille, France.
Participation in Philippe Mouillon´s project Répliques, (Laboratoire).
Urban installation, Tunnel des Facultés , Alger (Algeria), Grenoble (France).
Participation in Denis Martinez´s project Jonction, Friche Belle de Mai, Marseille, France.
Le 20 e Siècle dans l'Art Algérien. Travelling Exhibition: Les Orangeries , Paris, France.
Musée Borelli , Marseille, France.
Projection vidéo. 31e Rencontre Cinéma de Digne-les-Bains, France.
D'une rive à l'autre, Cité Internationale des Arts, Paris, France.
Les Noces du loup, Docks du sud, Marseilles, France.
Alger Projection vidéo Festival (Object-if), Lausanne, Switzerland.

2002
Video projection Dans le
cadre du Festival (nuits
métis). La ciotat, France.

2001
Participation 2nd National
Visual Arts Fair, Constantine,
Algeria..

2000
Expression, Cultural Service
of Embassy of France
(Embassy of France, Alger,
Algeria).
Double Duo (Bouras - Zoubir
/ Ferroukhi - Sergoua) action
painting. Fondation Asselah,
Alger, Algeria.
Hommage à Anissa. Galerie
de la Fondation Asselah,
Alger, Algeria.
Art de vie, Organised by
Fondation Asselah, École sup.
des beaux-arts d'Alger.

1999
7'on Art Musée national des
beaux arts, Alger, Algeria.
Une œuvre, une aide, Espace
Sofitel, Alger, Algeria.

1998
Travelling exhibition,
organised by Foundation
Asselah, 12 villes, France.
Hôtel de ville, Skikda.
Foundation Asselah, Alger,
Algeria.
Union Bank, Alger, Algeria.
Solidarité d'une rive à l'autre,
Organisée par la CCAS,
Cannes, France.
Palais de la culture, Alger,
Algeria.
Peintres Algériens, organised
by Foundation Asselah,
Forum des Cholettes, France.

1997
*Souffrances et espoirs
d'Algérie*, Org.anised by
Foundation Asselah, Institut
d'arts visuels N.Orléans,
France.
Stages dans le cadre des
rencontres internationales
de la photographie, Arles,
France.

1996
Premier salon d'automne
des arts plastiques, Espace
Sofitel, Alger, Algeria.
Union Bank, Alger, Algeria.
Espace Sofitel, Alger, Algeria.
Esma Gallery, Alger, Algeria.

1994
14e salon des Arts
Modernes, Théâtre de
Verdure d'Alger, Algeria.
Biennial of youth
creators from Europe and
Mediterranean, Lisbon,
Portugal.

1992
Biennial of youth
creators from Europe and
Mediterranean, Valencia,
Spain.

Other exhibitions

2003
Art dans la Ville, Saint
Etienne, France.
Ce n'est qu'un regard.
Touring exhibition.
La Friche Belle de Mai,
Marseille, France.
Château de La Tour d'Aigues,
La Tour d'Aigues, France.
Immeuble Berluc, Forcalquier,
France.

2002
Hommage à Boudiaf,
Organisée par la fondation
Boudiaf (B. N, Alger), Algeria.
January 2002: *Homiste,
istighrabisme, ça ne reste
qu'un point de vue*, Galerie
Zehira, Alger, Algeria.

2001
Byoutelwit, Bastion 23,
Alger, Algeria.
ndependence Day, Galerie
Isma, Alger, Algeria.
La Chaise, Cercle Frantz
Fanon, Alger, Algeria.
Cenekunregard, Bastion 23,
Alger, Algeria.

2000
Exposition 0, Timimoune,
Algeria.

Frédéric Bruly Bouabre

Born circa 1923 in Zéprégué, Ivory Coast. Lives and works in Abidjan, Ivory Coast.

Solo exhibitions

2006
MAMCO.
Geneva, Switzerland.

2003
Musée Champollion,
Figeac, France.

2002
Dany Keller Galerie.
Munich, Germany.

1996
*Mondes: Alighiero e Boetti
et Frédéric Bruly Bouabré.*
American Center, Paris.

1995
*World Envisionned, Frédéric
Bruly Bouabré et Alighiero
e Boetti.* Dia Center for the
Arts, New York, USA.

1994
Ginza Art Space, Shiseido Co
Ltd., Tokyo, Japan.

1993
Frédéric Bruly Bouabré,
Portikus, Frankfurt,;
Kunsthalle, Berna; Haus der
Kulturen der Welt, Berlin,
Germany; Ludwig Museum,
Aachen, Germany.

Group exhibitions

2006
Made in Africa,
Museo Guggenheim,
Bilbao, Spain.

2005
Attirare l'attenzione, Centre
d'art contemporain Besançon,
France.
*African Art Now:
Masterpieces from the Jean
Pigozzi Collection,*
The National Museum of
African Art; Smithsonian
Institution, Washington, USA.;
Houston, USA.
Arts of Africa,
Grimaldi Forum, Monaco
Vive l'Afrique, Galerie du Jour,
Agnès b. Paris, France.
Trait d'Union 6 séquences,
Centre Régional d'Art
Contemporain Languedoc-
Roussillon (CRAC-LR)
Sète, France.

2004
*Africa Remix. Art
contemporain d'un continent,*
Museum Kunst Palast
Düsseldorf; Hayward Gallery,
London; Centre Georges
Pompidou, Paris; Mori Art
Museum, Tokyo.
Les Afriques Tri Postal.
Lille, France.
Je m'installe aux abattoirs! La
collection d'art contemporain
d'Agnès b. Les Abattoirs,
Toulouse, France.
L'Invention du Monde, Centre
Pompidou.
Paris, France.

2003
Transferts,
Palais des Beaux Arts.
Brussels, Belgium.
*Correspondances
Afriques,* Iwalewa-Haus.
Afrikanzentrum der
Universität Bayreuth,
Germany.

2002
Documenta 11: Platform 5,
Kassel, Germany.
Inauguration du Plateau,
Le plateau, Paris, France.

2001
egofugal 7. Istanbul Biennial,
Turkey
*Dessins Choisis d'Ethiopie
et d'ailleurs,* Forum Culturel
de Blanc-Mesnil, Le Blanc-
Mesnil, France.
*Voici, Cent Ans d'Art
Contemporain,* Palais
des Beaux arts de Bruxelles,
Belgium.
Dessins Choisis, Alliance
éthio-française.
Addis Ababa, Ethiopia.

2000
Zeitwenden, Kunstmuseum,
Bonn, Germany
Kunst Welten im Dialog,
Museum Ludwig,
Cologne, Germany
*Art spirite, médiumnique
et visionnaire, Messages
d'Outre-Monde.* Halle Saint
Pierre, Paris, France.

1999
Galerie du jour. Fiac.
Quai de Branly,
Paris, France.

1998
2nd Johannesburg Biennial,
South Africa.

1997
*Crossings, France / Hawaii
'97.* University of Hawaï art
Manoa. Art gallery. Honolulu,
Hawai.
Bienal de Kwangju, Kwangju,
Korea.
Galerie du jour. Fiac 1997,
Quai de Branly,
Paris, France
Geographiques FRAC Corse,
Corte, France
Galerie Jules Kewenig,
Frechem-Bachem, Germany.

1996
Galeria DV.
San Sebastián, Spain.
Bienal de Sao Paulo,
Ciccillo Matarazzo Pavillion,
São Paulo, Brazil.
Bienal de Sydney,
The Gunnery Sydney,
Australia.
By Night, Fondation Cartier
pour l'art contemporain, Paris,
France.
Neue Kunst aus Afrika,
Haus der Kulturen der Welt.
Berlin, Germany
Baz'art du jour,
Galerie du Jour Agnès B.,
Paris, France.
*Féminin/Masculin. Le sexe de
l'art,* MNAM Centre Georges
Pompidou,
Paris, France.

1995
9 X 1 1995, Galerie de
Marseille, France.
Galerie des Cinq Continents,
Musée des arts d'Afrique et
d'Océanie, Paris, France
Big City, Serpentine Gallery,
London, UK.
Dialogues de Paix,
Palais des Nations,
Geneva, Switzerland.
TransCulture, Bienal de
Venecia Palazzo Giustinian
Lolin, Fondazione Levi,
Venice, Italy.
Africanités, Galerie Frédéric
Roulette, Parls, France.
Entre Ciel et Terre, Galerie de
Marseille, Paris.

1994
*Identita e Rappresentazioni
Cartografiche.* Museo
Nazionale Preistorico
Etnografico Luigi Pigorini,
Rome, Italy.
Rencontres Africaines, Institut
du Monde Arabe, Paris,
France.

1993
Trésors de voyage,
Venice Biennial, Italy.
Art Against AIDS, Venice
Biennial, Italy.
Azur, Fondation Cartier
pour l'Art Contemporain, Jouy
en Josas, France.
*La Grande Vérité, les Astres
Africains,* Musée des
Beaux Arts, Nantes, France.
Chambre 763,
Hotel Carlton Palace
Hôtel Carlton Palace,
Paris, France.
Grapholies, Abidjan Biennial,
Ivory Coast.

1992
A visage découvert,
Fondation Cartier pour l'art
contemporain,
Jouy en Josas, France.
Oh! Cet écho!
Centre Culturel Suisse, Paris,
France.
Out of Africa,
Saatchi Collection,
London, UK.
L'art dans la cuisine,
Saint-Gallen, Switzerland.
Résistances,
The Watari-Um Foundation
for Contemporary art,
Tokyo, Japan.
FIAC Découvertes,
Galerie Alain GUTHARC.
Grand Palais, Paris, France.
África Hoy. Africa Now,
Centro Atlántico de Arte
Moderno, Las Palmas
de Gran Canaria, Spain;
Groninger Museum,
Groningen, Netherlands;
Centro Cultural de Arte
Contemporáneo, Mexico DF,
Mexico.

1989
Magiciens de la Terre,
M.N.A.M. Centre Georges
Pompidou et La Grande Halle
de la Villette, Paris, France.
WAAA, A Far African Art
Courtrai, Belgium.

Mbongeni Richman Buthelezi

Born in Johannesburg in 1965. Lives and works in Johannesburg, South Africa.
1986 -1989: Part-time student at African Institute of Art, Johannesburg.
1990 - 1992: Full-time course African Institute of Art, Johannesburg.
1993: Teacher Training Course, Johannesburg Art Foundation.
1997 -1998: University of Witwatersrand, Johannesburg.

Art Residencies
Guest Artist, Wiesbaden, Germany.
Kunst:Raum Sylt-Quelle, Rantum, Germany.
Atelierhaus Höherweg e.V., Düsseldorf, Germany.
Standard Bank National Art Festival.
Vermont Studio Center, New York, USA.
Guest Artist, Barbados Community College during the National Independence celebrations.
Art Omi International Artists Center, New York, USA.

Selected exhibitions

2006
Solo exhibition, Bellevue-Saal, Wiesbaden, Germany.
Solo exhibition, Johannesburg Art Gallery, Johannesburg, South Africa.
Rhythm & Jazz, Gallery Seippel, Cologne, Germany

2005
Solo exhibition, catalogue, SBK, Stichting Beeldende Kunst, Amsterdam, Holland.
Gallery Seippel, Sydney, Australia.
Catalogue, IBAC, Biennale Prague.
Solo exhibition, Galerie Seippel, Cologne, Germany.
Solo exhibition, People Kunst: Raum Sylt Quelle, Rantum, Sylt, Germany.

2004
Solo exhibition, Museum Goch, Germany,
Pretoria Art Museum, Pretoria, The DaimlerChrysler Collection in South Africa
Mural painting, Madeira.
Evidence, Art Space, Johannesburg, South Africa.

2003
Warren Siebrits Contemporary Gallery, Johannesburg, South Africa.
DEG, Deutsche Entwicklungs gesellschaft, Johannesburg.
Art Fair with Gallery Seippel, Cologne, Germany.
Tracing the Rainbow, catalogue, Gallery Seippel, Cologne.

2002
Solo exhibition, Gallery Seippel, Colonia, Germany, Project Room.
Tracing the Rainbow, catalogue, Kunst: Raum Sylt-Quelle, Rantum; Kulturverein Zehntscheuer, Rottenburg/Neckar, Germany.

2001
Solo exhibition, Atelier Haus Höherweg, Düsseldorf, Germany.
Solo exhibition, Spark Gallery, Johannesburg.

2000
Museum of Art, Houston, USA.
Royal State Theatre, London, UK.
The Drum, Birmingham, UK.
Pretoria Art Museum
Houston Museum of Art, USA.

1999
Museum for African Art, New York, USA.
Standard Bank Gallery, Johannesburg.

1998
Grahamstown National Arts Festival.

1997
50 Stories Exhibition, Carlton Center, Johannesburg.
Nondi Nisa Art Gallery, Johannesburg.

1995
Mofolo Art Center, Johannesburg
Electric Workshop, Johannesburg
Paper Prayers, Johannesburg.
Johannesburg Art Gallery.
Artist Proof Studio, Johannesburg.

1994
Boston University, New York, USA.
Van Rijn Gallery, Johannesburg
Sandton Gallery, Sandton /Johannesburg.
Berman Gallery, Johannesburg.
Print Exhibition, Staib Gallery, Johannesburg.

1993
Alliance Française,
Johannesburg.
Funda Center Auditorium,
Soweto/Johannesburg.
Development Bank
of Southern Africa,
Johannesburg.

1992
Africa Cultural Center,
Johannesburg.
Market Gallery,
Johannesburg.

1989 – 1992
Funda Center Auditorium,
Soweto/Johannesburg.

1989
Nasrec Showground,
Johannesburg.

1988
Gertrude Posel Gallery,
University of Witwatersrand,
Johannesburg.

Soly Cissé

Born in Dakar en 1969. Lives and works in Dakar, Senegal.

Training
1996: Diploma of the École Nationale des Beaux Arts of Dakar, Best of Promotion.
Practical training course in Belgium in ERG (Ecole de Recherche Graphique).
1995: Practical training course Scenography, Belgium (Brusells).
Centre Culturel Française of Belgium and Kolda, practical training course for the exhibition of photography.

Solo exhibitions

2005
ASTI, Italy.

2004
Musée des Arts et d´Historie, St-Brienc, Brittany, France.
Luigi Peci, Prato, Italy.

2003
Musèe Aventures Industrielles in APT, France.

2002
ARTEFACT, Point E Gallery, Dakar, Senegal.
MAM, Douala, Cameroon.
ATISS, Dakar, Senegal.

2001
ATISS, Dakar, Senegal.
2000ATISS, Dakar, Senegal.

1999
MC Cann Erickson, Paris, France.
Musée Rautenstrauch, Joest Museum, Cologne, Germany.

1997
ATISS Gallery.
Centre Culturel Français, Dakar, Senegal.

Group exhibitions

2004
Tenerife, Spain.
Hayward Gallery, London, England.
Museo Luigi Pecci, Prato, Italy.
Africa-Remix, Musée Kunst Plast, Düsseldorf, Germany.
Musée des Arts et d´Histoire St Bieus, Brittany, France.
Les Afriques, Musée des Arts derniers, Paris, France.

2003
L´Europe Fantôme, Espace Vertebra, Brusels, Belgium.
Plasticiens en movement, Espace de Makten, Brusells, Belgium.
Viterra Energy services Gmbh and KG Hünster, Germany.
Orangerie, Grugapark, Essen, Germany.
Art Conceptuel in Camouflage, Brusells, Belgium.

2002
Kuba kunsthalle, Wolfendüttel, Germany.
Biennial de Dakar (DAK´ART), Senegal.
Multicultural 2002, La Laguna, Tenerife, Spain.
Biennial of Dak´Art, Senegal.

2001
Havana Biennial, Cuba.

2000
Havana Biennial, Cuba.

1999
Céramiques Almadies, installation, Tanzhaus die Wersttat, Düsseldorf, Germany.

1998
ATISS Gallery, Biennial Dak´Art *Ouage-garage*, Centre Culturel Français of Dakar, Senegal.

1997
Jeux de la Francophonie, Madagascar.

Viyé Diba

Born in 1954 in Karantaba, Casamance. Lives and works in Dakar, Senegal.

Training
1986: 3rd Cycle of Urban Geography in the University of Nice, France
1985: Ecole Pilote Internatíonale d'Art et de Recherche (EPIAR), Ville Arson, Nice, France
1979 -1980 : Ecole Normale Supérieure d'Education Artistique (ENSEA), Dakar, Senegal.
1973 -1977: Institut Natíonale des Arts du Sénégal (INAS) of Dakar, Senegal

Foreign studies in the USA, Canada, France, Germany, etc.

Solo exhibitions

2005
MAM Galery,
Douala, Cameroon.

2001
Performance installation
*Les croyances religieuses
dans l'économie populaire
au Sénégal* in the Goethe
Institut, Dakar, Senegal.

1999
Contemporary African Art
Gallery, New York, USA.

1997
Fruits de la Passion Gallery,
Abidjan, Ivory Coast.

1995
Exhibition in *l'espace d'art
Les Moulins de Villancourt* in
Echirolles, France.

1994
Quatre Vents Gallery, Dakar,
Senegal.

1990
*Environnement: témoin
culturel*, Galerie Nationale
d'Art de Dakar, Senegal.

1998
Dak'Art 1998, Senegal.

Group exhibitions

2005
Biennial *Imagining the Book
II*. Alexandria, Egypt.

2004
Dak'Art 2004. Performance
installation *Messe Nue* in
l'espace de design Koch.B.
Stage in El max for
L'association Gudran,
Alexandria, Egypt.

2002
Dak'Art 2002,
Audiovisual *Ngor-Ouakam
Yoff* in Elton Mermoz Station
of Dakar, Senegal.

2001
Centre d'Art Contemporain,
Barcelona, Spain.
Havana Biennial, Cuba.

2000
Dak'Art 2002 Performance
installation *Mysteres
de la communication*,
Fondation Léopold Sédar
Senghor, Senegal.
L'Afrique a Jour,
Lille, France.

1997
Centre Art Contemporain,
Brussels, Belgium.

1997
2nd Johannesburg Biennial,
South Africa. Curator: Okwui
Enwensor.

1998
Waltraud Matt Gallery,
Liechtenstein.

1996
MAM Gallery,
Douala, Cameroon.

1996
Copenhague Container 96,
Danemark.

1995
Sto Gervais Gallery,
Geneva, Switzerland.
1st Johannesburg Biennial,
South Africa.
International workshop
of design, Dakar, Senegal.

1994
Découvertes 94,
Paris, France.

1993
*Biennale Africaine des
Arts Plastiques d'Abidjan*,
Ivory Coast.

1992
Centre Culturel Francais,
Dakar, Senegal.

1990
*Mairie du 7 eme
arrondissement a París*,
France.

1989
National Gallery
of Dakar, French Revolution
Bicentenary.

1985
All national art shows
of artist in Senegal.

Grants and Awards

*Chevalier des arts et lettres
de la République Francaise*,
2002.

*Chevalier de l'Ordre National
du Mérite*, Senegal, 1999.

*Grand Prix Léopold S.
Senghor*, Biennial of Dakar,
1998.

Citizen of honor of the County
of Prince George, Maryland,
USA, 1991.

**Workshop, work
placements and art
meetings**

2001
*Deuxieme rencontres
artistiques*, Bamako, Mali.

1998
Workshop in Liechtenstein
organized by Fondation
Aterrana Stiftun.

1995
Workshop Helsen in Geneva,
Switzerland.
*Premiere Rencontres
Artistiques*, Bamako, Mali.

1994
Workshop Helsen,
Gorée, Senegal.
Workshop and Exhibition
during the Rencontres
Artistiques Africaines
Ewolé in Lomé, Togo.

1993
Rencontres de Ouagadougou,
Burkina Fasso.

Modou Dieng

Born in Dakar, Senegal, in 1970. Currently lives and works in San Francisco, United States.

Training
San Francisco Art Institute M.F. A. Painting.
Ecole Nationale des Beaux –Arts, Senegal B.F.A., 1995.

Solo exhibitions

2003
Pascal Polar Gallery,
Brussels, Belgium.

2003
Expo sur la ville, Museum
Université Catholique,
Louvain la Neuve, Belgium.
In dialogue with the work
of Dutch artist Willem Van-
Genk, february-june 2003.

2000
Urban Steps,
IFAN Museum,
Dakar, Senegal.

1998
2x7 Modous,
IFAN Museum,
Dakar, Senegal.

1997
Saint-Louis Shows II, French
Cultural Center, Saint-Louis,
Senegal.

1996
Saint Louis Shows I, Wengalu
Gallery,
Dakar, Senegal.

Group exhibitions

2005
MouvemEant, Oaklandish
Gallery, Oakland,
California, USA.

2004
*Globalisations and the African
World*, Gettysburg College,
Pennsylvania.

2003
Art Paris, Carrousel du
Louvre, Polar Gallery,
Paris, France.

2003
Body of Work, Gallery Agniel,
Providence, IR, USA.

2002
International Exhibit, Biennale
Dak`Art`02,
Dakar, Senegal.
*A Continent Away: Multiple
Identities in Contemporary
African Art*. Brush Art Gallery
& Studios, Lowell, MA, USA.

2001
*Fushion: The Art of
Contemporary Africa*,
MOCADA (Museum of
Contemporary African
Diasporian Art),
Brooklyn, NY, USA.

2000
Urban Corner, performance,
Gardens IFAN Museum,
Biennale Dak´Art´00.

1998
Visual Arts Market, Biennale
Dak´Art ´98.
Espace ATISS, Biennale
Dak´Art´98.

1997
Artefact, Abidjan,
Côte d´Ivoire.

1996
Month of the Photograph,
Gallery 39, Dakar, Senegal.
Wengalu Gallery, Biennale
Dak´Art´96.
Espace ATISS, Biennale
Dak´Art´96.
Guy Gui Gallery, Biennale
Dak´Art´96.

1995
Exhibit *Art Horizon*,
Residence of
US Ambassador to Senegal,
Historical Museum
Gorée Island,
Wengalu Gallery, Dakar,
Senegal.

1994
Touring exhibition
in Salzburg & Vienna, Austria
with LOSITO.

**Professional experience
& Workshops**

2005
Curator show
Ephemeral Feminism,
Cruxible Steel Gallery,
San Francisco CA.

2000
Cover, *The Amos House
Collection*, compilation CD,
NY, USA.

1996-2000
Co-funder & Co.editor,
Orange Licht, Dakar Senegal.
Cultural Consultant, Africa
Consultants International,
Dakar.

1996
Artis, International Artist´s
Residency Workshop, Dublin,
Ireland.

1996
Mini-Symposium of Art,
Prison, Dakar.

1995
Interior and exterior
decoration for the film
Les Caprices d´un Fleuve,
Bernard Gireaudau,
Goree, Senegal.
Workshop *Art-Horizon*,
National Art School, Dakar.

Moustapha Dimé

Born in 1952 in Louga, Senegal. Died in Saint-Louis of Senegal in 1998.

1952-1966: Studies in Louga. Initiation in wood work's in contact with the local community "Lawbé".
1993: Establishes his studio in the Portuguese fort of Gorée Island, where he creates a workshop-school.
1992: Receives the Dakar Biennial of Arts First Prize ex-aequo.
19801982: Produces tapestries inspired by the "Bogolan" technique.
1980: Meets President Senghor who helps him to obtain bottoms for new voyages.
Goes to Mali where he is initiated in the "Bogolan" technique.
1977-1979: Ecole des Beaux-Arts de Dakar, advanced training course.
1977: Presents works in Dakar and in Louga, Senegal
1974: Travels to Mali, Burkina-Faso, Ivory Coast, Ghana, Togo, Nigeria.
1973: Stays in Gambia where he created bass reliefs.
1966-1970: Studies in the Craft Centre of Dakar.

Solo exhibitions

1997
Dany Keller Gallery, Munich, Germany.

1996
Dak'art 1996, Biennial of Arts, Dakar. Centre d'Art Contemporain, Brussels, Belgium.

1994
Theater of Merlan, Marseilles, France.

1993
39 Galery, Dakar, Senegal.

1992
Theater´s Gallery of Merlan, Marseilles, France.

1982
National Theatre Daniel Sorano, Dakar Cours Sainte Marie de Hann, Dakar, Senegal.

Group exhibitions

1999
Moustapha Dimé, Salle Saint-Jean, Hôtel deVille, Paris, France.

1997
Suites africaines, Couvent des Cordeliers, Paris, France.
Die anderen Modernen, Haus der Kultur Der Welt, Berlin, Germany; Biennial of Johannesburg, South Africa.

1996
Bogarde Gallery, Bruges, Belgium.
Symposium Helsen, Switzerland.

1995
De Warande Gallery, Turnhout, Belgium.
Symposium Helsen, Mariama Ba, Île de Gorée.
Biennial of Johannesburg, South Africa.

1995-1997
African Arts of our time, Segataya Museum, Tokyo, Japan.

1994
Tenq, Saint-Louis of Senegal.
Symposium Schwarzenberg, Austria.

1993
Biennial of Venice, Italy
Museum for African Art, New York, U.S.A.

1992
Vème Salon National des Artistes Plasticiens du Sénégal.
Dakar Ruptures II', National Gallery, Dakar, Senegal.
Rencontre Itinérance. Musée National des Arts d'Afrique et d'Océanie, Paris, France.
Biennial of Arts, Dakar. *Tenq*, Saint-Louis, Senegal.

1991
Sommet de l'OCI, Dakar.
Centre Culturel Français of Dakar: Young sculptors from Senegal.

1990
Carrefour des Arts de la Francophonie, Toulouse, France.
Takes part in the touring exhibition *Contemporary Art of Senegal*, Paris, France; Brussels, Belgium.

1989
Represents Senegal in *Premiers Jeux de la Francophonie*, Rabat, Morocco.

1986-1987
Ruptures, National Gallery, Dakar, Senegal.

1984
Arts plastiques et musique,
Centre Culturel Blaise
Senghor, Dakar, Senegal.

1981
Tenq, Dakar, Senegal.

Touhami Ennadre

Born in Casablanca, Morocco, in 1953. Lives and works in Paris, France.

Selected exhibitions

2006
The Carpenter´s Workshop
Gallery, London, United
Kindom.
Arte Fiera, Galerie Alain
Le Gaillard, Bologna, Italy.

2005
Galerie Alain le Gaillard,
Paris, France.
FIAC, Galerie Alain
Le Gaillard, Paris,
France.
*Occidente visto desde
Oriente*, Centre de Cultura
Contemporánea de
Barcelona; Fundación
Bancaja,Valencia, Spain.

2004
Shangai Biennial, *Techniques
of the Visible*, Shangai, China.
The Whitney Museum of
American Art, book signing
of *If You See Something Say
Something,* conversations on
art with Adam D. Weinberg
and the Whitney´s Alice Pratt
Brown Director, New York,
U.S.A.
*Speaking with hands.
Selected photographs from
the collection of Henry Buhl.*
Salomon R. Guggenheim
Museum, New York, U.S.A.
Periplo del Mediterraneo,
Museo dell´Academia
Ligustica di Belle Arti,
Genova, Italy.

2002
Documenta 11, *Platform 5,*
Kassel, Germany.
Museum Villa Stuck, *New
York, September 11*, Munich,
Germany.
Human Face, Artist Space,
New York, U.S.A.

2001
*The short century:
Independence and Liberation
Movements in Africa
1945-1994*, Museum of
Contemporary Art, Chicago;
P.S. 1, Contemporary Art
Center, New York, USA; Haus
der Kulturen der Welt, Berlin;
Museum Villa Stuck, Munich,
Germany.

2000
Biennale de Lyon d´Art
Contemporain,
Partage d´exotisme,
Lyon, France *Geist in
Stein– Lebensbilder einer
Kathedrale,* Diözesanmuseum
Obermünster, Germany.

1999
Black Light, Maison
Européenne de Photographie,
Paris, France.
Materia Prima,
Diözesanmuseum
Obermünster Regensburg,
Germany.

1998
Trasatlántico, Museo de Arte
Contemporáneo,
Las Palmas,
Gran Canaria, Spain.

1997
El individuo y su memoria, VI
Havana Biennial,
Havana, Cuba.
Die anderen Modernen,
Haus der Culturen der Welt,
Berlin, Germany.

1996
Staaliche
Antikensammlungen,
Glyptothek Herculeaneum ,
Munich, Germany.
Black Light, Dany Keller
Gallery, Munich, Germany.
Touhami Ennadre, Nederlands
Foto Institute, Rotterdam,
Holland, Nederlands.
*In/sight: African Photographs
1940 to the Present,*
Solomon R. Guggenheim
Museum, New York, U.S.A.

1995
*Three Contemporary African
Artists,* Tate Gallery, Liverpool,
United Kindom.
Haus der Kulturen der Welt,
L´Alhambra, Berlin, Germany.

1994
Touhami Ennadre,
Exit Art, 548 Broadway,
Rotterdam, Nederlands .

1993
Caisse Nationale des
Monuments Historiques et
des Sites, Notre Dame de
Paris, France.

1992
Trans Voices, Multimedia
Project, Posters exhibited in
New York and Paris Subway:
Centre Beaubourg, Paris,
France and American Center,
(Project by Whitney Museum
of American Art, New York,
USA.
Touhami Ennadre, Institute du
Monde Arabe,
Paris, France.

1990
Photographie en liberté,
Gulbekian Fondation and
Frankfurter Kunstverein,
Lisbon, Portugal, and
Frankfurt, Germany.

1988
*Splendeurs et misères du
corps,* Musée d´Art Moderne,
Paris and Museum für Kunst
und Geschichte, Freiburg,
Swizterland.
*Junge europäische
Photographies,* Frankfurter
Kunstverein,
Frankfurt, Germany.

1986
La photographie creative,
Bibliothèque Nationale, Paris,
France.

1985
Das Aktphoto, Museum
für Moderne Kunst,
Vienna, Austria.

1984
*Touhami Ennadre
—Photographie en France,*
Cité Internationales des Arts,
Paris, France.

1977
*Tendances actuelles de la
Photographie en France,*
Musée d´Art Moderne,
Paris, France.

Grants And Awards

1997
Villa Kujoyama, AFAA, Kyoto,
Japan.

1995
UNESCO Aschberg
Grant, Fondation Afrique
en Création.

1993
Grant Villa Médicis Hors
les Murs.

1989
Prix Leonardo da Vinci,
French Minister For
Foreing Affaire.

1987
Young European
Photographers Award of
Deutsche Leasing, Frankfurt,
Germany.

1984
Year Scholarship, Villa Arson,
CNAC, Nice, France.

1976
Prix de la Critique, Recontres
Internationales de la
Photographie, Arles, France.

Frances Goodman

Born in Johannesburg, South Africa in 1975. Lives and works in Johannesburg,
South Africa.

Academic Record and Residencies
2005: Recollets, Recollets International Accomodation and Exchange Centre, Paris, France.
2001: Irish Museum of Modern Art, Artist's Work Programme, Dublin,
 Ireland.

Postgraduate
2001 - 2003: HISK (Higher Institute for Fine Art), Antwerp, Belgium.
1999 - 2000: MA Fine Arts, Goldsmiths College, University of London, UK.
1998 -1999: Postgraduate Diploma, Goldsmiths College, University of London, UK.

Undergraduate
1994–1997: BA Fine Arts, Honours, University of the Witwatersrand, Johannesburg, South Africa.

Selected exhibitions

2005
Threat Zone, Triangle Project Space, San Antonio, Texas, USA.
[Prologue] reclaiming Europe from a new feminist perspective, Cornerhouse, Manchester, UK.
Art out of Place, Norwich Castle Museum & Art Gallery, Norwich, UK.
Double Check Re-Framing Space in Photography: The Other Space, Parallel Histories, Camera Austria, Kunsthaus, Graz, Austria.
Petite Mort, Solo Exhibition, Goodman Gallery, Johannesburg, South Africa.

2004
Wanting, Solo Exhibition, KULAK, University of Kortrijk, Belgium.
Double Check Re-Framing Space in Photography: The Other Space, Parallel Histories, Gallery of Contemporary Art, Celje, Slovenia.
David, Solo Exhibition, Gallery in the Round, SA National Festival of the Arts, Grahamstown, South Africa.
Goodman Gallery Booth, Basel Art Fair, Basel, Switzerland.
Your Heart is No Match for my Love, The Soap Factory, Minneapolis, USA.
Mo(NU)ment@Bornem, Weert, Hingene and Bornem (Klein-Brabant), Belgium.
Show Us What You're Made Of, The Premises, Johannesburg, South Africa.
After Hours, In/Out, Hisk, Antwerp, Belgium.

2003
Distance of Memory, Nairs House of Culture in Vulpera Tarasp, Nairs, Switzerland.
Opzij van het Kijken, Watou Art and Literature Festival, Watou, Belgium.
Something About Love, Casino, Luxembourg.
Intimate/Inanimate Moments, Solo Project, The Process Room, Irish Museum of Modern Art, Dublin, Ireland.
Open Studios, Higher Institute of Skone Kunst, Antwerp, Belgium.

2002
Viper, Basel New Media Festival, Basel, Swizerland.
Portrait, Sound Space, De Appel, Amsterdam, Netherlands.
Sensing Sculpture, Wolverhampton Art Gallery, Wolverhampton, UK.
Fluid, Bonnington Art Gallery, Nottingham, UK; Middlesborough Art Gallery, UK; Howard Gardens Gallery, Cardiff, Wales. *Unprincipled Passions*, John Hansard Gallery, Southampton, UK.

2001

Fluid, Wolverhampton Art Gallery, UK.
JUNCTURE, The Granary, Cape Town, South Africa.
Body: Rest and Motion, Oudtshoorn Festival, South Africa.
JUNCTURE, Studio Voltaire, London, UK.
Emotions and Relations, Sandton Civic Gallery, Johannesburg, South Africa.
Customised Jeans Exhibition, Cinch, London, UK.

2000

EAST International, Norwich School of Art and Design, Norwich, UK.
Goldsmiths MA Exhibition, Goldsmiths College, London, UK.
Two-person exhibition with Moshekwa Langa at the Goodman Gallery, Johannesburg, South Africa.

1999

Not Quite a Christmas Show, Goodman Gallery, Johannesburg, South Africa.
Celsius: (new) art from the (new) South Africa, IFA Gallery, Bonn, Germany.
Group Exhibition, the Lavender, London, UK.
The Paper Show, Goodman Gallery, Johannesburg, South Africa.

1998

Martienssen Prize Exhibition, Gertrude Posel Gallery, University of the Witwatersrand, Johannesburg, South Africa.
Fine Art End of Year Exhibition, Gertrude Posel Gallery, University of the Witwatersrand, Johannesburg, South Africa.
Closer than Bronze, Sandton Civic Gallery, Johannesburg, South Africa.
Women's Voice, touring various cities in Germany.

Curating

2000
JUNCTURE, The Granary, Cape Town; Studio Voltaire, London.

Lecturing

2001
Wolverhampton University, Wolverhampton, UK.

Awards and Merits

2004
Werkvbeurzen, Flemish Community, Belgium.

2002
Ernest Oppenheimer Memorial Trust, Scholarship, South Africa.

2002
Ernest Oppenheimer Memorial Trust, Scholarship, South Africa.

2000
Visiting Arts Award for *JUNCTURE*, Visiting Arts, UK.

1997

Martienssen Prize First Prize Winner, University of the Witwatersrand, South Africa.
University of the Witwatersrand, Anya Millman Travel Scholarship, South Africa.
University of the Witwatersrand Sculpture Merit Award, South Africa.

Romuald Hazoume

Born in 1962 in Porto Novo, Benin. Lives and works in Porto Novo, Benin.

Solo exhibitions

2005
La Bouche du Roi de R.H.,
article 14 de R.H. The Menil
Collection Houston, Texas;
CAISA, Helsinki Finland;
October Galllery London, UK.

2002
Romuald Hazoumé, Centre
Culturel Français, Turin, Italy.

2001
Romuald Hazoumé, Olivier
Houg Galery, Lyon, France.

2000
La Bouche du Roi, Centre
Culturel Français, Cotonou,
Benin.
Galerie Gut Gasteil, Prigglitz,
Austria.
Galerie Art et Public, Geneva,
Switzerland.

1999
Romuald Hazoumé Vor-Sicht,
Dany Keller Gallery, Munich,
Germany; Museum für
Konkrete Kunst, Ingolstadt,
Germany; The Project, New
York, USA.

1997
Romuald Hazoumé, Galerie
20X2, Arnhem, The
Netherlands.

1996
Romuald Hazoumé, Gelbe
Musik Galery, Berlin,
Germany; Dany Keller Galery
Munich, Germany; Firma
Harlekin Art Wiesbaden,
Germany.

1995
Voyage du côté de l'invisible,
Représentation de la
Communauté Européenne
Cotonou, Bénin.
Porto Novo, Benin.

1994
Je sais d'où je viens, Musée
de Honmé, F.I.F.
Limoges, France.

1992
Romuald Hazoumé, Musée du
Cloître, Eglise St Pierre Tulle,
France.

1991
Masques Bidons, II Centre
Culturel Français Bamako,
Mali; Centre Culturel
Français, Dakar, Senegal;
K.G. du Kunstmuseum,
Bonn, Germany; Museum
der Franziskaner de Werl,
Germany; Centre Culturel
Français d'Abidjan,
Ivory Coast.

1990
Impression Saharienne,
Centre Culturel Français,
Cotonou, Benin.
Masques Bidons, II National
Museum, Accra, Ghana;
Centre Culturel Français,
Lagos, Nigeria; *Africain
Forum*, Heidelberg, Germany.

1989
*Musique tribale pour sept
insectes*, Gardin Botanique,
Porto Novo, Benin.
Masques Bidons I Centre
Culturel Français, Cotonou,
Benin; Centre Culturel
Franco-Nigérien Niamey,
Niger.

Group exhibitions

2005
*African Art Now. Masterpièces
from Jean Pigozzi collection.*
Museum of Fine Art, Houston,
USA; The Grimaldi Forum,
Monaco; N.A. Art Smithsonian
Museum, Washington, USA.

2004
*Africa Remix, Contemporary
Art of a contintent*, Museum
Kunst Palast, Düsseldorf,
Hayward Gallery, London,
UK; (2005) Centre Georges
Pompidou, Paris, France; Mori
Art Museum, Tokyo, Japan
(2006).

2003
*Magic Makers Amour or the
fortification of pulpe*, Des
Moines Art Centers, IW, USA.
Musée Bellerive, Zurich,
Switzerland.
Musée d'ac de Lausanne,
Switzerland.
Fort Asperen Biennial,
Netherlands.

2002
Œil pour œil, African Marke,
Le Rectangle, Centre d'Art
Contemporain, Lyon, France.
Ivan Dougherty Gallery.
University of NSW, Sydney,
Australia.

2001
TRADE, Nederlands
Fotos Institut, Roterdam,
The Netherlands.
XXXV eme Prix International
d'Art Contemporain de
Monte-Carlo, Monaco.
Lost & Found,
New York, USA.
TRADE, Fotomuseum
Winterthur, Switzerland.

2000
Art Basel 2000, Galerie
ART& PUBLIC, Bâle,
Switzerland.
Biennale de Kwangju,
South Korea.
Sieben Hügel,
Martin-Gropius-Bau,
Berlin, Germany.
Partages d'exotismes,
5th Lyon Biennial, Lyon,
France.
*Dinge in der kunst des XX.
Jahrhunderts.* Haus der Kunst
Munich, Germany.
D'sign, Galerie Dany Keller,
Munich, Germany.
*This earth is a flower,
construction in Process VII,*
Bydgoszcz, Poland.

1999
Paradise 8,Exit Art,
New York, USA.
*Spaceship Earth,Art in
General,* New York, USA.
Liverpool Biennial, UK

1998
Triennale der Kleinplastik,
Stuttgart, Germany.
Breeduit, Van Reekum
Museum, Apeldoorn, The
Netherlands.
Warming, The project,
New-York, USA.
*The brigge construction
in Process VI,* The Bridge,
Melbourne, Australia.
Romuald Hazoumé,
The Art Gallery of New South
Wales, Sydney, Australia.
Kunstrai- Art Amsterdam,
Galerie 20x2, Arnhem,
Amsterdam, The Netherlands.
*Bénin-Bénin Gisteren-
Tussen-Morgen,* Van Reekum
Museum Apeldoorm,
The Netherlands.

1997
Workshop/Ondambo,
National Gallery of Namibia,
Windhoek, Namibia.
Lumière Noire, Centre d'Art
de Tanlay, Château de Tanlay,
France.
Havana Biennial, Cuba.
8 + 1, Centre Culturel
Français Cotonou, Benin.

1996
Art Cologne 96,
Cologne, Germany.
Galerie du jour agnès,
Paris, France.
Inclusion-Exklusion,
Steirischer Herbst 96,
Graz, Austria.
Kunst in der Landschaft III,
Gut Gasteil,
Prigglitz, Austria.
Neue Kunst aus Afrika, Haus
der Kulturen der Welt, Berlin,
Germany.
Géographies Tapissées,
Musee National des Arts
Africains et Océaniens, Paris,
France.
*An Inside story: African Art of
our time,* Tokoshima Modern
Art Museum, Tokoshima,
Japan; Himeji City Museum
of Art, Himeji, Japan;
Koriyama City Museum of Art,
Koriyama, Japan. Marujame
Inokuma-Genichiro Museum
of Contemporary Art, Japan;
The Museum of Fine Arts,
Gufu, Japan.

1995
Art Cologne 95,
Cologne, Germany.
orientATION, Istanbul
Biennial, Turkey.
*An Inside story : African Art
of our time,* Setagaya Art
Museum, Tokyo, Japan.
Afrika: Malerei heute,
Dany Keller Galerie, Munich,
Germany.
Africus, Johannesburg
Biennial, South Africa.

1994
Bivouac des artistes Niamey,
Andorre, Limoges, France.

1990
Festival Afrique / Antilles,
Bordeaux, France.
Dialogue France / Afrique,
Brazzaville, Congo.
Night of Art Helsinki, Finland.
Décor découverte - R.F.I.
Porto Novo, Benin.

1992
Out of Africa, Saatchi Gallery,
London, UK.

1993
*La grande Vérité, les Astres
Africains,* Musée des Beaux
Arts de Nantes, France.
Symposium Freiraum,
Forchtenstein, Austria.
Second sight, Northern
Centre for Contemporary
Art, Sunderland, UK; Newlyn
Orlon Gallery, Comwall, UK;
The Orchard Gallery, Dervy,
Ireland.

William Kentridge

Born in Johannesburg, South Africa, in 1955. Lives and works in Johannesburg, South Africa.

Solo exhibitions
since 2000

2005
William Kentridge: prints,
College of Wooster, Ohio,
USA (touring from Faulconer
Gallery, Grinell College).
William Kentridge, Musée
d'Art Contemporaine de
Montreal, Canada (touring
from Castello di Rivoli).
William Kentridge, Goodman
Gallery, Johannesburg, South
Africa.
William Kentridge,
Johannesburg Art Gallery,
Johannesburg, South Africa
(touring from Castello di
Rivoli).
Model Arts + Niland Gallery,
Sligo, Ireland.
Limerick City Gallery of Art,
Ireland (touring from Model
Arts + Niland Gallery).
Guggenheim Museum, Berlin,
Germany.
William Kentridge, Galeria Lia
Rumma, Naples, Italy.
William Kentridge, Miami
Art Central, (touring from
Castello di Rivoli), USA.

2004
William Kentridge, Castello
di Rivoli, Museo d'Arte
Contemporanea, Rivoli, Italy,
(touring K20/21, Düsseldorf,
Germany; Museum of
Contemporary Art, Sydney,
2004, Musée d'Art
Contemporain de Montréal,
Canada, 2005; Johannesburg
Art Gallery, South Africa,
2005).
William Kentridge, Art 3 and
la CRAC, Valence, France,
(touring to Musée Chateau
d'Annecy, Annecy, France,
2005).
William Kentridge, Marian
Goodman Gallery, New York,
USA, and Paris, France.
William Kentridge, Galleries,
Sydney, Australia.
William Kentridge, Grinell
College Faulconer Gallery,
Grinell, Iowa, USA (exhibition
of prints).
William Kentridge,
Metropolitan Museum, New
York, USA (works from the
collection of the museum).

2003
William Kentridge, Goodman
Gallery, Johannesburg, South
Africa.
*William Kentridge: Journey to
the Moon and 7 Fragments
for Georges Méliès,* Baltic Art
Center, Visby, Sweden.
*William Kentridge (exhibition
for award of Goslar Kaiserring
to William Kentridge),*
Möenchehaus Museum
Goslar, Goslar, Germany.

Group exhibitions

2005
Chabot Museum, Rotterdam,
Netherlands.
DreamingNow, The Rose
Art Museum of Brandeis
University, Waltham,
Massachusetts, USA.
The Experience of Art, 51st
Venice Biennale 2005, Italian
Pavilion, Italy.
Modern Times, Mönchehaus
Museum for Modern Art,
Goslar, Germany.
*Faces in the Crowd /
Volti nella Folla,* Castello
di Rivoli Museo d'Arte
Contremporanea, Rivoli,
Torino, Italy (touring from
Whitechapel Art Gallery,
London, UK).

2004
The Divine Comedy,
Vancouver Art Gallery,
Canada.
Monument to Now, Deste
Foundation, Athens, Greece.
Africa Remix, Museum Kunst
Palast, Dusseldorf, Germany;
Hayward Gallery, London, UK;
Centre Georges Pompidou,
Paris, France; Mori Art
Museum, Tokyo, Japan.
*New Identities: Contemporary
South African Art,* Museum
Bochum, Germany.
In Bed, MeranoArte, Meran
2nd Biennale: + Positive,
Toyota Museum of Art, Tokyo,
Japan.
Trouble, Le Grand Café,
Centre d'Art Contemporain,
Saint-Nazaire, France.
*Faces in the Crowd / Volti
nella Folla,* Whitechapel Art
Gallery, London, UK.

2003

Apparition: the action of appearing, Kettle's Yard, Cambridge, UK.
William Kentridge: Thinking In Water, Gallery at Dieu Donné Papermill, New York, USA.
Der Verlust des Anderen: Trauer und Traurigkeit in der zeitgenoessischen Kunst, Zentrum für zeitgenössische Kunst der Österreichischen Galerie Belvedere, Vienna, Austria.
Universes in Universe: Caravan, Sharjah Art Museum and Expo Centre Sharjah, Sharjah International Biennal, United Arab Emirates.
Banquet: Metabolism and Communication, ZKM Center for Art and Media Karlsruhe, Germany (touring to MediaLabMadrid, Centro Cultural Conde Duque, Madrid, Spain)
Coexistence: Contemporary Cultural Production in South Africa, Rose Art Museum, Brandeis University, Waltham, Massachusetts, USA (touring South African National Gallery, Cape Town, South Africa)
Transferts, Palais des Beaux-Arts, Brussels, Belgium
For the Record: Drawing Contemporary Life, Vancouver Art Gallery, Vancouver, Canada

2001

Hirshhorn Museum and Sculpture Garden Washington D.C., USA.
New Museum of Contemporary Art New York, USA.
William Kentridge Recent Editions, In association with David Krut Fine Art, Robert Brown Gallery, Wash. DC, & Gracie Mansion, New York., USA.
The Short Century, Museum Villa Stuck Berlin, Germany; Chicago, New York, USA; Vienna, Austria; Cape Town, South Africa.

2000

The Self is Something Else, Kunstsammlung Nordrhein-Westfalen Dusseldorf, Germany.
A Double View: Three Exhibitions, Tel Aviv Museum of Art, Israel.
Third Shanghai Biennial, Shanghai, China.
Vertical Painting, P.S.1, New York, USA.
Marian Goodman Gallery New York, USA.
Stephen Friedman Gallery London, UK.
Annandale Galleries Sydney, Australia.
Insistent Memory: The Architecture of Time in Video, Harn Museum of Art, University of Florida, USA.
La Beaute, Beauty in Fabula, Papal Palace Avignon, France.

Bodys Isek Kingelez

Born in 1948 in Kimbembele Ihunga, Democratic Republic of Congo. Lives and works in Kinshasa, Democratic Republic of Congo.

Solo exhibitions

2003
Bodys Isek Kingelez,
Centre Culturel Wolu-Culture,
La Médiatine, Brussels,
Belgium.

2002
Bodys Isek Kingelez,
Villa Stuck, Munich, Germany.

2000-2001
Bodys Isek Kingelez,
Kunstverein Hambourg,
Hamburg, Germany.

1996
D'autres Ajouts d'Eté, Bodys Isek Kingelez, Musée d'Art Moderne et Contemporain, Geneva, Switzerland.

1995
Bodys Isek Kingelez,
Fondation Cartier
pour l'Art Contemporain,
Paris, France.

1992
Bodys Isek Kingelez- Architekturvisionen aus Zaire, Haus der Kulturen der Welt, Berlin, Germany.

1990
Bodys Isek Kingelez,
Galerie Jean-Marc Patras,
Paris, France.

Group exhibitions

2005
Vive l'Afrique,
Galérie du Jour, Agnès b.,
Paris, France.

2005
Fantasmapolis, La ville contemporaine et ses imaginaires, Galérie Art & Essai, Université Rennes 2, Rennes, France.

2005
African Art Now : Masterpieces from the Jean Pigozzi Collection, Museum of Fine Arts Houston, USA.

2004-2005
Arti & Architettura 1900/ 2000, Genova Palazzo Ducale, Italy.

2004
Africa Remix, Art contemporain d'un continent, Museum Kunst Palast, Düsseldorf, Germany; Centre Georges Pompidou, Paris, France, Mori Art Museum, Tokyo, Japan.
Je m'installe aux abattoirs, La collection d'art contemporain d'agnès b. Les Abattoirs, Toulouse, France.
Les Afriques, Tri Postal, Lille, France.

2003
The American Effect, Global Perspectives on the United States, 1990-2003, Whitney Museum of American Art, New York, USA.
Transferts, Palais des Beaux-Arts, Brussels, Belgium.; Centre d'art contemporain de Woluwe, Saint Lambert, Brussels, Belgium.

2002-2003
Africanishe Reklamekunst, Iwalewa Haus der Universität Bayreuth, Bayreuth, Germany; München Stadtmuseum, Munich, Germany.

2002
Documenta XI,
Kassel, Germany;
Sao Paulo Biennial,
Sao Paulo, Brazil.

2001-2002
The Short Century, P.S.1 Contemporary Art Center and Museum of Modern Art, New York; travels to Museum of Contemporary Art Chicago, USA. House of World Cultures in the Martin-Gropius-Bau, Berlin, Germany; Museum Villa Stuck Munich, Germany. *DC: Thomas Bayrle / Bodys Isek Kingelez*, Museum Ludwig, Cologne, Germany.

2001
Africa: The Artist and the City, Centre de Cultura Contemporània de Barcelona, Spain.

2000
Contra la Arquitectura, Espai
d'Art Contemporani, Castelló,
Spain.
Zeitwenden, Künstlerhaus,
Vienna, Austria.
Out of Space,
Schnitt Ausstellungsraum im
Cologneischen Kunstverein,
Cologne, Germany.
Sydney Biennial, Australia.
Domiciles, Centre d'Art de
Tanlay, Tanlay, France;
Vision du Futur, Grand Palais,
Paris, France;
Musée International des
Arts Modestes (Commande
publique); Musée
International des Arts
Modestes, Sète, France.
Le monde est ma maison, Le
Parvis, Ibos, France.

1999-2000
Collezionismi, La Collezione
della Fonndation Cartier pour
l'Art Contemporain, Centro
Arte Contemporanea, Pallazo
delle Papesse, Siena, Italy.
*The 1999 Carnegie
International*, Carnegie
Museum of Art,
Pittsburgh, USA.
Mirror's Edge,
BildMuseet, Umea, Sweden;
Vancouver Art Gallery,
Vancouver, Canada.
Un Monde Réel,
Fondation Cartier
pour l'Art Contemporain,
Paris, France.
Kunst-Welten im Dialog,
Museum Ludwig,
 Cologne, Germany.
Zeitwenden,
Kunstmuseum Bonn,
Bonn, Germany.

1998-1999
Unfinished History, Walker
Art Center, Minneapolis, USA;
Museum of Contemporary Art
of Chicago, Chicago, USA.

1998
3ème Biennale de Dakar,
Dakar, Senegal.
Africa Africa,
Tobu Museum of Art,
Tokyo, Japan.

1997
Unmapping the Earth,
97 Kwangju Biennial,
Kwangju, South Korea.
*Projects 59: Architecture
as Metaphor*, Museum of
Modern Art,
New York, USA
*Trade Routes: history,
geography and culture.* 2nd
Johannesburg Biennial,
South Africa.
Veilleurs du monde, Cotonou,
Benin.
Àlbum, Fundació Joan Miro,
Barcelona, Spain.
A Dream of Urbanity,
Bankside Lofts, London, UK.

1996
*Rudiments d'un Musée
Possible*, Musée d'Art
Moderne Contemporain,
Geneva, Switzerland.
*Bomoi Mobimba - Toute
la Vie, 7 artistes zaïrois.*
Collection Lucien Bilinelli,
Palais des Beaux-Arts,
Charleroi, Belgium.
Neue Kunst Aus Afrika, Haus
der Kulturen der Welt, Berlin,
Germany.
*Wall and Space. Reality and
Utopia. Bodys Isek Kingelez.*
Architectural Visions,
Oksnehallen, Copenhaguen,
Denmark.

1995
*Dialogues de Paix , (Dans le
cadre de la commémoration
du Cinquantième Anniversaire
de l'ONU).* Palais des Nations,
Geneva, Switzerland.
Big City : Artists from Africa.
Serpentine Gallery,
London, UK.

1994
Crudo y Cocido.
Museo Nacional Centro
de Arte Reina Sofía,
Madrid, Spain.

1993
*La Grande Vérité,
Les Astres Africains.*
Musée des Beaux Arts,
Nantes, France.
*Home and the World
Architectural Sculpture
by two African artists.*
The Museum for African Art,
NewYork, USA.

1992
Out of Africa. Saatchi Gallery,
London, UK.

1991-1992
Africa Hoy, Africa Now,
Centro de Arte Moderno,
Las Palmas de Gran
Canaria, Spain, Groninger
Museum, Gröningen, The
Netherlands; Centro de Arte
Contemporáneo, Mexico DF,
Mexico.

1990
*WAAAAW
(A Far African Art),*
Courtrai, Belgium.

1989
Magiciens de la Terre, Centre
Georges Pompidou, La
Grande Halle de la Villette,
Paris, France.

Abdoulaye Konaté

Abdoulaye Konaté born in 1953 in Diré, Mali, lives in Bamako.
Studied in the *Institut National des Arts*, picture section, Bamako from 1972 until 1976
and at the *Instituto Superior de Artes Plásticas* in Havana, Cuba, from 1978 –1985.
Section Chief in the *Musée National du Mali à Bamako*, 1985-1997.
Palais de la Culture Director 1998-2002.
Rencontres photographiques Africaines de Bamako Director, 1998- 2002.
Responsible Mission for the *Ministère de la Culture du Mali*. For two years he was a jury member
for several national and international competitions.
He is currently *Directeur Général du Conservatoire des Arts et Métiers Multimédia Balla Fasseké
kouyaté*.

Solo exhibitions

2002
CCF, Bamako, Mali.

2001
Chapelle Jeanne d'Arc,
Thouars, France.

1994-1996
Centre Culturel Français,
Bamako, Mali.

1992
Musée National du Mali,
Bamako, Mali.
Musée de l'IFAN,
Dakar, Senegal.

1988
Go au Plateau Gallery,
Abidjan, Ivory Coast.
Paysages et Masques,
Tatou Gallery, Bamako, Mali.

1986
Musée National du Mali,
Bamako, Mali.

1984
Centre Culturel Français,
Bamako, Mali.

1983
*Salón Nacional de Pequeño
Formato*, Havana, Cuba.

1976
Maison du Peuple,
Diré, Mali.

Collectives exhibitions

2005
Centre Georges Pompidou,
Paris, France.

2004
Museum Kunst Palast,
Düsseldorf, Germany.
Musée de design et d'Arts
appliqués Contemporains,
Lausanne, Switzerland.
Le Palais des Beaux-Arts de
Bruxelles, Belgium.

2004
Hayward Gallery, South Bank
Centre, London, UK.

2003
La Maison des Arts à Paris,
France.

2002
Musée de Picardie,
Amiens, France.

2001
Galerie Palais de la Culture,
Semaine Nationale
des Arts.

2001
Salle Chemellier, Grand
Théâtre, Angers.

1998
International Biennial,
Johannesburg, South Africa
Sao Paulo Biennial, Brazil.
Kleinplastik, Triennial,
Stuttgart, Germany.

1997
Suites Africaines,
Couvent des Cordeliers,
Paris, France.
Modernities and Memories,
Venice Biennial, Italy.

1996
The Other Journey,
Kunsthalle, Krems, Austria.
Rencontres africaines, Laon.
Pluriel Gallery, Abidjan, Ivory
Coast.

1995
Rencontres africaines, Caixa
General de Deposito, Lisbon,
Portugal.
Maison de la Culture, Amiens,
France.
Setagaya Museum,
Tokyo, Japan.
Centre Culturel Français,
Cotonou, Benin.
Siège de la Communauté
Européenne,Cotonou, Benin.

1994
Otro País, Centro Atlántico de
Arte Moderno, Las Palmas,
Spain.Touring exhibition at
Fundació la Caixa, Palma de
Mallorca and at Palacio de la
Virreina, Barcelona.
Rencontres africaines, Institut
du Monde Arabe, Paris,
France.

1993
Grafolies Biennial, Abidjan,
Ivory Coast.

1992
International Arts Biennial,
Dakar, Senegal.

1991
Regard Croisés, Musée
National du Mali, Bamako,
Mali.
Siège World Bank, World
Bank, Washington, USA.
Association pour la Diffusion
de l'Art Plastique Africain
Contemporain (ADAPAC),
Paris, France.
Tsurumoto Room co.: LTD
Shibuyo Ku, Tokyo, Japan.

1990
ADEIAO, Musée National des
Arts d'Afrique et d'Océanie,
Paris, France
*Africa Fête go, Couleurs
dAfrique*, Saint Denis, France.

1989
Portraits de fanulle, Galerie
Jamana, Bamako, Mali.

1988
Wice Artspace, Paris, France.

1987
Centre Culturel Français,
Bamako, Mali.

1986
2nd Havana Biennial, Cuba.
*Artistes Maliens et
Soviétiques au Palais
de la Culture*, Palais de la
Culture, Bamako.
(with Stenka Jacques Samir
and Nafogo Coulaby).

1984
Havana Biennial,
L Gallery, Institut Supérieur
des Arts, Havana, Cuba.
25 Aniversario de la
Revolución, Karl Marx
Theater, La Habana, Cuba.
1st Havana Biennial, L
Gallery, Havana, Cuba.
Salón 13 de Marzo, Oriente
Gallery, Santiago de Cuba.
8 Biennale Artistique et
Culturelle du Mali.
Palais de la Culture, Bamako.
Exposition du petit Format, L
Gallery, Instituto Superior de
las Artes, Havana, Cuba.

Exposition pour la Paix,
Complejo Artístico Mella,
La Habana, Cuba.
8ème Anniversaire de
l'Association Nationale
des Artistes du Mali (INA),
Bamako.
4ème Salon de la jeune
Peinture d'Angers, Angers,
France.

1983
Salon 13 de Marzo,
L Gallery, Instituto Superior
de las Artes, Havana, Cuba

1978
Jeunes Peintres du Mali,
Institut National des Arts,
Bamako, Mali.

Medals

2002
*Chevalier de l'Ordre National
du Mali*

2002
*Chevalier de l'Ordre des Arts
et des Lettres, République
française.*

Awards

1996
Dakar Biennial Award,
Senegal.

1986
Mention of Honour at the
Conferences of University
Scientific Studies of ISA,
Havana, Cuba.

1985
First National Award of
Painting, *Salon 13 Marzo*
of University of La Habana,
Cuba.

1983
Diploma of recognition
of the *Instituto Superior de
las Artes de La Habana* on
the occasion of *Semana de la
Cultura Cubana*, Cuba.

1982
Honorary Diploma at the
Conferences of the *Instituto
Superior de las Artes* (ISA),
La Habana, Cuba.

1976
First Award of *Lion's Club
International*, Bamako, Mali.
Diploma of honor of the Fair
of Bamako, Mali.
Gold Diploma of Painting at
the *Semaine Artistique Locale
de Ségou*, Mali.

Mochekwa Langa

Born in South Africa, in 1975. Lives and works in Amsterdam, The Netherlands.

Solo exhibitions

2005
Moshekwa Langa, MAXXI-
Museo Nazionale delle Arti del
XXI secolo, Rome, Italy.
Backlash Blues, The Goodman
Gallery, Johannesburg,
South Africa.

2004
Present + tense, Kunstverein
Düsseldorf, Germany.

2003-2004
Interior Monologues,
Contemporary Atrs Center,
Cincinnati, U.S.A.

2002
Loss Draws & Co-Wives,
Galerie Ascan Crone-
Andreas Osarek,
Berlin, Germany.

2001
*Mountains of My Youth-A
Novel*, ARCO, Madrid, in The
Goodman Gallery,
Galerie Ghislaine Hussenot,
Paris, France.
Island Tourist Hotel, Galerie
Tanya Rumpff, Haarlem,
The Netherlands.

2000
Another time, Anoher place,
the Goodman Gallery,
Johanesburg, South Africa.
Moshekwa Langa, Galerie
Bernier/Eliades, Athens,
Greece.

1999
*Moshekwa Langa- Live and
in Person*, The Renaissance
Society, Chicago, U.S.A.
Moshekwa Langa, Centre
d´Art Contemporain, Geneva,
Switzerland.

1997
*Moshekwa Langa: Beware
of Imitations*, Galerie Frank
Hanel, Frankfurt, Germany.

1998
D.OR, Museum Boijmans van
Beuningen, Rotterdam,
The Netherlands.
Moshekwa Langa, Rembrandt
van Rijn Art Gallery,
Johannesburg, South Africa.

Group exhibitions

2005
Peabody Essex Museum,
Salem, Massachusetts, U.S.A.
Museo Clouste Gulbenkian,
Lisbon, Portugal.
AFRICA REMIX, Hayward
Gallery, London, UK; Centre
Georges Pompidou, Paris,
France; Mori Art Museum,
Tokyo, Japan.

2004
AFRICA REMIX, Museum
Kunst Palast, Dusseldorf,
Germany.
Fondazione Sandretto Re
Rebaudengo per l´Arte, Torino,
Italy.
Barbican Art Gallery, London,
U.K.
Cranbtook Art Museum,
Bloomfield Hills, Michigan,
U.S.A
*A Fiction of Authenticity:
Contemporary Africa Abroad*,
Contemporary Art Museum,
St. Louis, Missouri; Regina
Gouger; Miller Gallery; Purnell
Center for the Arts, Carnegie
Mellon University, Pittsburgh,
U.S.A.

2003-2004
*Moshekwa Langa: Drawings
and Installation Environments*,
Contemporary Arts Center,
Cincinnati, U.S.A.

2003
*Post Border Land-Afrikaanse
kunstenaars pakken uit in
Bagagehal*, Amsterdam, The
Netherlands.
*Somewhere Better than this
Place: Alternative Social
Experience in the Spaces
of Contmeporary Art*, The
contemporary Arts Center,
Cincinnati, USA.
*How Latitudes Become
Forms-Art in Global
Age*, Walker Art Center,
Minneapolis, USA.
*Black President: The Art and
Legacy of Fela Anikulapo-
Kuti*, New Museum of
Contmeporary Art, Nueva
York, USA.
*Looking Both Ways: Art of the
Contemporary Art Diaspora*,
Museum for African Art,
Nueva York, USA.
*Dreams and conflicts-
The Viewers Dictatorship:
Faultlines*, 50° Venice Biennial,
Italy.

2002
Art Basel, Miami Beach
(The Goodman Gallery,
Johannesburgo),
Miami, USA.
*The Short Century-
Independence and Liberation
Movements in Africa 1945-
1994*, Museum Villa Stuck,
Munich, Germany; House of
World Cultures in the Martin
Gropius-Bau, Berlin, Germany;
Museum of Contemporary Art
Chicago; P.S.1 Contemporary
Art Center, New York, USA.
Watching Ocean and Sky,
Public Art Development Trust
Livepool Biennial, Fourth Wall,
Liverpool, UK.

2001
*FNB Vita Art Prize Exhibition,
NSA*, Durban, South Africa
(First Price).
Juncture, The Granary, Cape
Town, South Africa.
*Africas: The Artist and the
City: a Journey and an
Exhibition*, Centro de Cultura
Contemporánea de Barcelona,
Barcelona, Spain.
The Place of Happiness,
the Watari Museum of
Contemporary Art, Tokyo,
Japan.

2000-2001
*Blick-Wechsel-Afrikanische
Videokunst*, ifa-Galerie Bonn;
ifa-Galerie Berlin, Germany.

2000
Mas and Space, Kwangiu
Korea Biennial.
Fun Five Fun Story, Guinness
Contemporary Art Project, Art
Gallery of New South Wales,
Sydney, Australia.
Paris pour escale, Musée d´Art
Moderne de la Ville de Paris,
France.
*Saman Taivaan Alla, "Vuosaari"
(Under the Same Sky)* Kiasma
(external proyect) European
Capital of Culture, Helsinki,
Finland.

1999
Traffic of Night in Paradise,
Frieshuis Amerika,
Amsterdam, The Netherlands
De dia, Liebaert Projects,
Kortrijk, Belgium.
Generation Z, P.S. 1
Contemporary Art Center,
New York, USA.
(Trans) Africa: Trafique, S. M.
A. K. extra muros, Kicherie
patiron, Sluizecken 30, Gent,
Belgium.
*New Worlds: Comtemporary
Art from Australia, Canada and
South Africa*, Canada Houese
Gallery, London, UK.
New Republics, Edmonton
Art Gallery, Edmonton,
Canadá; Australian Centre for
Contemporary Art, Melbourne,
Australia.
H & R Project, Brussels, (con
Peter Land), Belgium
*Celsius: (neue) Kust aus dem
(neuen) Südafrika*, ifa-Galerie,
Bonn, Germany.

1998-1999
*Aids World: between
resignation and hope*, Centre
dÁrt Contemporain, Geneva,
Switzerland; Centro d´Arte
Contemporanea, Ticino,
Bellinzona, Switzerland.

1998
XXXIV Bienal de Sao Paulo,
Parque Ibirapuera, Sao Paulo,
Brazil.
*Power Up: between
experience and expectation*,
Museum voor Moderne Kunst,
Amhem, Netherlands
FNB Vita Art Prize, Sandton
Civic Gallery, Johannesburg,
South Africa.
Memorias, Intimas, Marcas,
The Electric Workshop,
Johannesburg, South Africa
Transatlántico, Centro
Atlántico de Arte Moderno,
Islas Canarias, Spain.
Unlimited.nl, Galerie De Appel,
Amsterdam, Netherlands.
7th Kleinplastik Triennial
Sudwest LB Forum, am
Hauptbahnhof 2, Stuttgart,
Germany.

1997-1998
*The 2ⁿᵈ Johannesburg
Biennale-Trede Routes: History
and Geography*, National
Gallery, Cape Town, South
Africa.

1997
*Fin de siècle à Johannesbrug
1997*, Nantes, France
*The 5th Internacional
Istanbul Biennial (On life,
beauty, translations and other
dificulties…)*, Yerebatan
Cistern, Istanbul, Turkey.
*Atlas mapping: Artits as
cartographers*, Offenes
Kulturhaus, Linz, 1998;
Kunsthaus Bregenz, Bregenz
Austria.
*Cartographers: geo-gnostic
projection for the 21ˢᵗ century*,
Galerje Grada Zagreba,
Zagabria/Zagreb; Centre For
Contemporary Art, Zamek
Ujazdowski, Warsaw, Poland;
Art Pavillian "Muscarnok",
Budapest, Hungary.

Otobong Nkanga

Born in Kano, Nigeria, in 1974.
Lives and works in Amsterdam, The Netherlands, and Paris, France.

Education
1992-1994: Obafemi Awolowo University, (OAU) Ile – Ife, Osun State, Nigeria.
1995-2001: Ecole Nationale Superieure des Beaux – Arts (ENSBA) Paris, France.
2005: DasArts, De Amsterdamse School/Advanced Research in Theatre and Dance Studies,
The Netherlands.

Residencies/fellowships/stipends
2005: DasArts, Trustfund Stichting/Dutch Ministry of Education, Culture and Science.
2003: Dutch Ministry of Foreign Affairs/DCO/IC, The Netherlands.
Rijksakademie van beeldende kunsten/ Dutch Ministry of Education, Culture and Science,
The Netherlands.
2002: Ministère des Affaires Étrangères (AFAA) et Ministère de la Culture et de la
Communication (DAP), France. Rijksakademie van beeldende kunsten/Dutch Ministry of
Education, Culture and Science, Netherlands.
2000: Residency Programme, Houilles, France.

Solo exhibitions

2004
FOKUS 2, Kunstverein
Springhornhof, Neuenkirchen,
Germany.
(with Jens Haaning)
On Fragile Grounds, Window
Gallery and Objectif_
exhibitions as part of "CLOSE
READING #3", Antwerp,
Belgium.

2002
Classicism & Beyond,
Fotofest 2002, Project Row
Houses, Houston,
Texas, USA.

Group exhibitions

2006
One game – many worlds:
Football in inter-cultural
comparison, München
Stadtmuseum. Munich,
Germany.
Snap judgement, International
Center of Photography, New
York, USA.
Africa remix, Zeitgenössische
Kunst eines Kontinents, Mori
Art
Museum, Tokyo, Japan.

2005
Belonging, Sharjah
International Biennial 7,
Sharjah,
United Arab Emirates.
North /south lab, Tanzquartier,
Vienna, Austria.
Africa remix, Zeitgenössische
Kunst eines Kontinents,
Centre Georges Pompidou,
Paris, France,
Africa remix, Zeitgenössische
Kunst eines Kontinents,
Hayward Gallery, London.,
UK .

2004
Flying Circus Project,
TheatreWorks Ltd, Singapore.
Do you believe in reality?
Taipei Biennial, Taiwan.
26th Sao Paulo biennial, Sao
Paulo, Brazil.
Flash right, turn left, Artwalk,
Amsterdam, Netherlands.
Africa remix, Zeitgenössische
Kunst eines Kontinents
Museum Kunst Palast,
Düsseldorf, Germany
Peter Hermann Gallery,
Berlin, Germany.
Epifyten, De Klassieke hortus
als voerdingbodem voor
hedendaagse kunst Hortus
Botanicus, Amsterdam,
The Netherlands.

2003
Fractured Gaps, Open
Ateliers, Rijksakademie
van beeldende kunsten,
Amsterdam, The Netherlands.
El arte con la vida,
3th Havana Biennial,
Havana, Cuba.
International Performance
Manifestation, CEIA,
Belo Horizonte, Brazil.
Transferts, Palais des Beaux-
Arts, Brussels, Belgium
Shift and Wait, Collaborative
work with Le petit Jaunais
edition house for the
realisation of the series of
Lithographs in book form.
Maison de la Loire, Paris,
France.

2002
Awaiting Pleasures, Open
Ateliers, Rijksakademie
van beeldende kunsten,
Amsterdam, The Netherlands.
Classicism & beyond,
Fotofest 2002, Project Row
Houses, Houston, Texas,
USA.
Observatorio # 3,
Casa Camouflage,
Brussels, Belgium.
Dak'Art 2002, V Biennale
of African Contemporary Art,
Dakar, Senegal.
Rond point, La Halle
de Gombe, Kinshasa,
RD Congo.
Observatorio # 1, Casa
Camouflage, Brussels,
Belgium.
Made in Africa fotografia,
Biennale di Fotografia
Africana/ Sparzio Oberdan,
Milan, Italy.
En direct de bamako, Galerie
Photo Fnac Etoile, Paris,
France.
Dessins xxl, Le Lieu Unique,
Nantes, France.

2001
*Memoires intimes d'un
nouveau millenaire*, IV
Biennale de la Photographie
Africaine, Bamako, Mali.
Infamous labels No 10,
Bateau Phare in collaboration
with the Research program,
ENSBA, Paris, France.

2000
Festival de la Jeune Creation.
Houilles, France.
V Triennial Mondiales
d'estampes petit format,
Chamalieres, France.

1999
M.O.F., Galerie St Eustache,
Paris, France.
TOXIC, Chateau d'Oiron,
Oiron, France.

1998
Atelier Jean luc Vilmouth,
ENSBA, Paris, France.

1997
IV Triennial Mondiales
d'estampes petit format,
Chamalieres, France.
GERICAULT…POINT VUE
CONTEMPORAIN, Musee
des Beaux-Arts, Paris,
France.

Performances

2005
*Dream in one meter
square*, *Belonging*,
Sharjah International Biennial
7, Sharjah,
United Arab Emirates.
*Surgical Hits#03,
(The Needle)*, Tanzquartier,
Vienna, Austria.

2004
*Surgical Hits#02, (The
Needle)*, Theatre Works Ltd,
Singapore.
*Surgical Hits#01, (The
Needle)*, Kunst Palast
Museum, Düsseldorf,
Germany.
On fragile grounds, Window
Gallery and Objectif_
exhibitions as part of *CLOSE
READING #3*, Antwerp,
Belgium.

2003
Fractured Gaps, Group
performance involving 6
dancers, Open Ateliers,
Rijksakademie van beeldende
kunsten, Amsterdam, The
Netherlands.
Shift and Wait, International
Performance Manifestation,
CEIA, Belo Horizonte, Brazil.
State of Amnesia,
International Performance
Manifestation, CEIA, Belo
Horizonte, Brazil.
Perfect Measures, *Transferts*,
Palais des Beaux-Arts,
Brussels, Belgium.

2002
Sustained Suture,
Rijksakademie van beeldende
kunsten, Netherlands.
*The new acquisition of
Jennifer Mcbright*, *Classicism
& beyond*, Fotofest 2002,
9th International Biennial of
Photography, Project Row
Houses, Houston,
Texas, USA.
Bomboyi, Group performance
involving the Students of
the Ecole des Beaux-Arts
Kinshasa, Chooseone
Organisation, Paris, Rond
point, La Halle de Gombe,
Kinshasa, RDCongo.

2001
"Fiat Lux II", *Infamous
labels no 10*, Bateau Phare
in collaboration with the
Research program, ENSBA,
Paris, France.

1999
Fiat Lux I, M.O.F., Galerie St
Eustache, Paris, France.
The Dual Match (Footpitch),
TOXIC, Chateau d'Oiron,
Oiron, France.

Marie Blanche Ouedraogo

Born in 1971, in Ouagadougou. Lives and works in Ouagadougou, Burkina Faso.

Solo exhibitions

2006
Galerie Gondouwana,
Ouagadougou,
Burkina Faso.

2005
Restaurant Galerie
Baratapas, marche
de noël Ouagadougou,
Burkina Faso.

2004
Sur le panafricanisme, Centre
Soleil d Afrique, Bamako, Mali.
Ghana centre du bois,
ACCRA, Siège de l´anapap,
Ouagadougou,
Burkina Faso.

2003
Galerie Gondouwana,
Ouagadougou,
Burkina Faso.
Centre Culturel Français,
Ouagadougou,
Burkina Faso.
Art et Cinéma Restaurant
Galerie Baratapas,
Ouagadougou,
Burkina Faso.
Orangerie, Grugapark Essen,
Germany.
Viterra Energy Services
GmbH & Co.KG,
Münster, Germany.

2002
Porte ouverte a domicile,
Houston & Beverley hills,
USA.
Centre Culturel Français,
Ouagadougou,
Burkina Faso.
KuBa Kunsthalle,
Wolfenbüttel, USA

2001
Journée Porte Ouverte Ouidi,
Ouagadougou,
Burkina Faso.
Sparkasse
EssenRüttenscheid, Germany.
Wohnstift Augustinus, Essen,
Germany.
Citibank Krefeld, Germany.

2000
House of Deputies, Essen,
Germany.
Internationales Zentrum (IZ),
Duisburg, germany
Hessischer Landtag,
Wiesbaden, Germany.
Tanzhaus nrw die werkstatt,
Düsseldorf, Germany.

1999
Fondation Olorun
Ouagadougou,
Burkina Faso.
La Vénerie,
WatermaelBoitsfort /
Brussels, Germany
"Alte Papierfabrik" in
Ebertsheim, Germany.
Citibank Duisburg, Germany.

Group exhibitions

2006
Centre Culturel Français,
Ouagadougou,
Burkina Faso.
Place de la Nation,
Ouagadougou,
Burkina Faso.

2005
Galerie Princesse Yenega,
Paris, France.
Galerie Baratapas
Ouagadougou,
Burkina Faso.
Centre Culturel Français
Ouagadougou,
Burkina Faso.
Centre Web du Bois,
Accra, Ghana.

2004
Centre Soleil d´Afrique,
Bamako, Mali.
Centre du Bois,
Accra, Ghana.
Siege. Anapap,
Ouagadougou,
Burkina Faso
Musée International de la
Femme, Scontronne, Italy.

2003
Centre Culturel Français,
Ouaga, Burkina Faso.
Restaurant-Galerie
BaraTapas, Ouaga,
Burkina Faso.

2002
Foire iInternationale,
Lome, Togo.
Maison des Arts et Loisirs,
Laon, France.
Musée National Femmes
Bâtisseurs d'Afrique,
Ouaga, Burkina Faso.
Musée de Ouid, Benin.

2001
Rencontre Culturelle,
Limoges, France
Place de l Étoile Rouge,
Cotonou, Benin.
Galerie Nationale CNA,
Ouaga, Burkina Faso.
Francophonie à Tripoli,
Beyrouth, Sayda, Lebanon.

2000
Expo 2000, zaka,
Ouaga, Burkina Faso.
Galerie Jacques Cartier,
Chauny, France.

1999
Galerie Res Rey,
Grenoble, France.
Galerie Zaka Ouaga, Burkina
Faso.
National Center of Fine Art,
Cairo, Egypt.
Galerie Jacques Cartier,
Chauny, France.
Centre Culturel de Bale
Warteck, Switzerland.

1998
La Femme et L´Art, à la
Fondation Olorun,
Ouaga, Burkina Faso.
Des elles de femmes,
Centre Culturel Français,
Ouagadougou,
Burkina Faso.

1997
Art et solidarité,
Fondation Olorun,
Ouaga, Burkina Faso.
Journée du Tourisme Hôtel
Sofitel Sil Mandé,
Ouaga, Burkina Faso.
Galerie Arcane 21,
Sauve, France.

**Other professional
Experience**

2006
Workshops with Fondation
Jean Paul Blachere in
Ouagadougou, Burkina Faso.
Estage in bronze,
Ouagadougou, Burkina Faso.

2005
Stage design for Comédie
Française, Paris, France.
Centre Culturel Français,
Ouagadougou, Burkina Faso.

2004 Conference:
Contemporary Art in Burkina,
Ghana.

2003
Estage in Ouaga, Centre
Culturel Français, Burkina
Faso.

2002
Stage Lome, Togo.
Estage compienga, Ouaga,
Burkina Faso.

2001
Residecy in Tripoli, Lebanon.

1999
Residecy at the Centre
Culturel de Bale Warteck PP,
Switzerland.

Miguel Petchkovsky

Born in Angola, 1956. Lives and works in Amsterdam.
Gerrit rietveld fine art academie , Amsterdam, The Netherlands.

Cultural Activist
Member of The Union of Angolan Plastic Artists, UNAP.
Creative Director create Africa South.
Honorary member of the Nucleo De Art, Mozambique.
Adviser, magazine Eutopia, The Netherlands.

Selected exhibitions

2005

Hayward Gallery, Africa Remix, London. UK.

2004
Mais a Sul, Culturgest, Porto. Portugal.
Mais a Sul, Culurgest, Lisbon, Portugal.
Zimanoa, ABC Treehouse Gallery, Amsterdam. The Netherlands.
Africa Remix, Museum Kunst Palast, Dusseldorf, Germany.
Dare to exist, Museum Of Contemporary Art, Los Angeles, USA.
Images Never Seen on Television, SESC Vila Mariana, Sao Paulo, Brazil.
Du-Rex Art Gallery, Rio de Janeiro, Brazil.
Angola Yetu, Rotterdam City Hall, Rotterdam, The Netherlands.
Portugal, Cultureel Centrum De Werf, Aalst, Belgium.
III Design And Art Fair, Berlin 2004, Berlin, Germany.
Tangencya, Kwa Mulhe Museum, Ex-position, South Africa.
Tangencya, Old Court House Historic Museum, Glassificallon, South Africa.
Gymnasio Gallery, Lisbon, Portugal.
Porto Art Fair 2004, Porto, Portugal.

2003
Post Border Land, SBK, Amsterdam, The Netherlands.
Daqui/Dali/Para Alem, Gallery CMA, Lisbon, Portugal.
IV Porto Art Fair, Porto, Portugal.
Deslocamentos, Video Brazil Festival, Sao Paulo Brazil.
Africa Here And Now, SBK Art Gallery, Ernmen, The Netherlands.
Voices Of Women, Imagine IC, Amsterdam, The Netherlands.

2002
Crossing Boundarjes, Centre Soleil d Áfrique, Mali.
Image In & Out, Lille, France.
II Lusophone Art Biennial, S. Tomé, S. Tomé.
II Heritage Biennial, Lagos, Nigeria.
The Poetry of Form and Colour, Convento S. José Lagoa, Portugal.
4 Artist 4 Peace (Angola), Prince Claus Fund, De Hague, The Netherlands.
Interactive Electronic Festival, IEF Kwang Fong Gallery, Los Angeles, USA.
Jeu D'esprit, SBK Art Gallery, Amsterdam, The Netherlands.

2001
South, Video Project, Johannesburg/Maputo, South Africa/Mozambique.
Mens Momentanea, Gallery Barrack / Haus der Kulturen der Welt, Berlin, Germany.
Mens Momentanea, Espace Bertrange, Luxembourg, Luxembourg.
Art For A New Time, City of Düsseldorf, Germany.
Out Of Order, De Balie, Amsterdam, The Netherlands.
Black & White Copies, Etekwini Cultural Centre, Durban, South Africa.
Black & White Copies, NSA Art Gallery, Durban, South Africa.
World Wide Video Festival, Amsterdam, The Netherlands.
Stuti Aperti/Marco Fioramanti, Rome, Italy.
Improvisations, Aurtur Bual CMA, Gallery Amadora, Portugal.
Obegrensde Ontmoeting, Rotterdam Cultural City of Europe, The Netherlands.

2000
Afrique a Jour, Lille, France.
Body & Soul, Cultural Centre Petershagen, Germany.
Lapa Gallery, Lisbon, Portugal.
Echap Rain Project, Reijksakademie, Bamako, Mali.
Pieces Of My Time, Wanda Michalack Art Gallery, Amsterdam, The Netherlands.

1999
2000 Reasons,
The Millennium Collection,
The Hague, The Netherlands.
Made In The Netherlands,
Nieuwespoort, De Hague,
The Netherlands.
Percursos de Arte, Gallery
BES, Benfica, Portugal.
Translsce Project, Piterkov,
Trybunalsky, Poland.
Afinidades, Ginásio Art
Gallery, Lisbon, Portugal.
A Planetary Reply For The
World, Sao Paulo, Brazil.
De Balie, Amsterdam,
The Netherlands.

1998
Rational Emotions, Siemens
Art Gallery, Lisbon, Portugal.
Scena Studio, M Gallery,
Warsaw, Poland.
IV Urban Sculpture Biennial,
Amadora, Portugal.
B&S; Stadsgallereij, Heerlen,
The Netherlands.
Prince Claus Fund,
De Hagüe The Netherlands.
De Vluchtelingenweg,
De Balie, Amsterdam,
The Netherlands.

1997
Ujamaa IV, Museum of
Modern Art. De Zonnehof,
Amersfoort,
The Netherlands.
Scena StudioM Gallery,
Warsaw, Poland.
The manipulated mask,
Conference Green Light
For Africa, Utrecht, The
Netherlands.
Niza, The media in Africa,
Amsterdam, The Netherlands.
Retrospective, Fitares Art
Gallery, Lisbon, Portugal.

1996
Tribute to Artur Bual,
Municipal Art Gallery, Lisbon,
Portugal.
Ujamaaiv, Gate Foundation,
Amsterdam, The Netherlands.
Under different skies,
Copenhagen Triennial,
Denmark.
17éne Salon Internationale
de Puy, France.
Semntulo, CMA Art Gallery,
Amadora, Portugal.
Object & Subject, Hivos, The
Hague, The Netherlands.

1995-1994
The next second, Thami
M'Nyele, Amsterdam,
The Netherlands.
Tropen Institute, Amsterdam,
The Netherlands.
Txitelele, Maison Africaine,
Amsterdam The Netherlands.
Cultural Franco Mozambican
Centre, Maputo, Mozambique.
16éme Salon Internationale
de Puy, France.
SD Art Gallery, Warsaw,
Poland.
Destinos Inciertos,
Langenberg Art Galler,
Amsterdam, The Netherlands.
Txipema uw a Foto, Spectrum
Art Gallery, Amsterdam, The
Netherlands.
Cryptofoto, Criterium Gallery,
Amsterdam, The Netherlands.
Mahamba, Veredas Art
Gallery, Cintra, Portugal.
Ma ybuyee, Free Art Gallery,
Zandvoort, The Netherlands.

Guest lecturer

2002
Art in public space, Emmen,
The Netherlands.

2001
Cultural Studies, Leiden
University, Leiden,
The Netherlands.
Haus der Kulturen der Welt,
Berlin, Germany.
Technicon Natal, Fine Arts
Department Durban,
South Africa.
*Urban Archeology
Symposium*, Amadora City
Council, Amadora, Portugal.

2000
*Fontys Academie voor
Architectuur*, Stedenbouw,
Tilburg, The Netherlands.

1997-1999
Cultural Studies, Leiden,
The Netherlands.

1996-1998
Intercultural Communication,
Tropen Institute, Amsterdam,
The Netherlands.

1996-1997
Cultur and Conflict (ICC)
Breda, The Netherlands.

1995-2003
Various Workshops,
Mozambique, Mali, Poland,
Portugal, The Netherlands.
Video and Film Pioneiros IV,
Agricultura, Lucapa (35mm)
Placebo, Ó Pátria, Ylunga
(DVD).

Chéri Samba

Born in Kinto-Mvuila, Democratic Republic of Congo, in 1956. Lives and works in Kinshasa, DRC.

Solo exhibitions

2005
Les débuts de Chéri Samba,
Kunstverein. Braunschweig,
Germany.

2004
*J'aime Chéri Samba. A
selection of paintings from the
exhibition at the Fondation
Cartier*, Paris, France; Texas
Southern University. Houston,
USA.

2003
*Chéri Samba moto na
Tervuren*. Musée Royal de
l'Afrique. Tervuren, Belgium.
Chéri Samba Populärmalerei,
Galerie Peter Herrmann.
Berlin, Germany.

2000
*Chéri Samba une fois encore
à Kinshasa* Centre Culturel
du Zoo. Kinshasa, Democratic
Republic of Congo.

1999
Ludwig Forum für
internationale Kunst. Aachen,
Germany

1998
Institut für
Auslandsbeziehungen (ifa).
Stuttgart, Germany.

1997
Musée National des Arts
d'Afrique et d'Océanie. Paris,
France.
Übersee Museum. Bremen,
Germany.

1992
Opere recenti Studio Rafaelli.
Trente, Italy

1993
Galerie Apunto, Amsterdam,
Netherlands.

1994
Le Grand Maître de l'Ecole
de Kinshasa/ Democratic
Republic of Congo. Galerie
Extravagances - Centre
d'Art et de Plaisanterie
Montbéliard, France.
Annina Nosei Gallery.
New York, U.S.A.

1995
Arndt und Partner Gallery,
Berlin, Germany.

1992
Kunsthalle, Basel; Bâle,
Switzerland.
Chéri Samba/Matrix 117.
Wadsworth Atheneum
Hartford, Connecticut, USA.
Stadtmuseum München.
Munich, Germany.

1991
Portikus, Francfort, Germany.
ICA -Institute of Contemporary
Arts. London, UK.
Formas de dissidencià .
Fundació Miró.
Barcelona, Spain.
Museum of Contemporary
Art. Chicago, USA.
*Chéri Samba, le peintre
populaire du Zaïre*. Provinciaal
Museum voor Moderne Kunst.
Ostende, Belgium.

1990
Galerie N.O.M.A.D.E . Paris,
France.

1988
3ème festival de Saint
Herblain. Château de Saint
Herblain. Nantes, France.

1984
Centre Culturel Français.
Lubumbashi, Democratic
Republic of Congo.

1981
Centre Wallonie, Brussels,
Belgium.

1980
Centre Culturel Français.
Kinshasa, Democratic
Republic of Congo

1975 -1978
*La grande exposition publique
de Chéri Samba*. Façade
de son atelier. Kinshasa,
Democratic Republic of
Congo.

Group exhibitions

2005
Vive l'Afrique. Galérie du Jou,
Agnès b. Paris, France.
*African Art Now:
Masterpieces from the Jean
Pigozzi Collection*. Museum
of Fine Arts Houston.
Houston, USA.
*Africa Remix. Art
contemporain d'un continent*.
Museum Kunst Palast,
Düsseldorf, Germany;
Hayward Gallery London;
Centre Georges Pompidou
Paris; Mori Art Museum,
Tokyo, Japan.

2004
Le Salon de Mai. Atheliers
Berthier, Opera National
de Paris, France.
Peinture populaire congolaise,
ADEIAO, Centre d'Etudes
Africaines. Maison des
Sciences de l'Homme, Paris,
France.
*La collection d'art
contemporain d'Agnès b*. Les
Abattoirs Toulouse, France.
Les Afriques, Tri Postal Lille,
France.

2003
Der Rest der Welt, Neuffer
am Park Pirmasens, Germany.
Kin moto na Bruxelles,
Hôtel de Ville.

Brussels, Bergium.
Africanishe Reklamekunst,
Iwalewa Haus der Universität
Bayreuth; München
Stadtmuseum, Germany.
*Africa Apart: Afrikanische
Künstlerinnen und Künstler
konfrontieren AIDS*,
Neue Gesellschaft für
Bildende Kunst (NBGK),
Berlin, Germany.

2002
Money and Value, Swiss
National Exposition,
EXPO 02, Bâle, Swizterland;
Sao Paulo Biennial, Brazil.
Kin Service, Espace Croisé
Contemporary Art Centre
Roubaix, France.
Painting on the Move,
Kunsthalle Bâle, Switzerland.

2001
*Les Grands Maîtres de
Kinshasa*, USA.
Kinshasa, DRC.
*La Cité dans la Peinture
populaire de Kinshasa*, Centre
Wallonie, Brussels, Belgium;
Centre Culturel Kuntwala.
Kinshasa, DRC.
In Fumo Arte, Fumetto
Galeria d'Arte Moderna e
Contemporanea. Bergamo,
Italy.
El Tiempo de África. Sala
Plaza de España Madrid,
Spain.
AN/SICHTEN, Museum für
Völkerkunde. Vienna, Austria.

1999 - 2000
Kustwelten im Dialog,
Museum Ludwig, Cologne,
Germany.
Expériences du divers,
Galerie Art & Essai Université
Rennes, Rennes, France.

1998
Dak'Art, Dakar, Senegal.
*Africa, Africa: Vibrant New Art
from a Dynamic Continent*,
Tobu Museum, Tokyo, Japan.
*Patchwork in Progress
1A: Marcel Broodthears &*

Chéri Samba,. Musée d'Art
Moderne et Contemporain.
Geneva, Switzerland.

1997
Pour un Clin d'Œil, Halle de
la Gombe Centre Culturel
Français. Kinshasa, D.R.C.

1996
Neue Kunst aus Afrika. Haus
Kulturen der Welt, Berlin,
Germany.
*African art towards the
year 2000*, Rundetårn.
Copenhagen, Denmark.
Inklusion/Exklusion,
Steirischer Herbst. Gratz,
Austria.
10ème anniversaire du
Centre Wallonie, Brusseles.
Kinshasa, D.R.C.
*Bomoi Mobimba. Toute la vie.
7 artistes Zaïrois, collection
Lucien Bilinelli*, Palais des
Beaux Arts, Charleroi,
Belgium.
L'Aquarium, Hirshhorn
Museum & Sculpture Garden
Washington, USA.
*An Inside Story: African Art
of our Time Beyond Art*,
Setagaya Art Museum Tokyo;
The Tokushima Modern Art
Museum, Tokushima; Himeji
City Museum of Art, Himeji;
Koriyama City Museum of
Art, Koriyama; Marugame
Inokuma-Genichiro; Museum
of Contemporary Art,
Marugame The Museum of
Fine Arts, Gifu, Japan.

1995
*Chacun son Destin, Johan
Muyle et Cheri Samba,* Foire
d'Art Actuel, Heysel Galerie
Bilinelli, Brussels, Belgium.
*Afrikanische Kunst aus
der Sammlung Han Koray*,
Völkerkundemuseum
der Universität, Zürich,
Switzerland.

Djibril Sy

Born in 1950 in Dakar, Senegal, where he is based and works.

Professional Experience
2001-2005: Photographer-reporter for *PANAPRESS,* Pan African Information Agency.
1996-2000: Journalist and photographer for *Quotidien Dakar Soir.*
1996-1996: Professor of photography *École Nationale des Arts,* Dakar, Senegal.
1979-1979: Official Photographer of the Dakar City Hall, Senegal.
1977-1977: Freelance photographer for R.I. Mauritania.
1975-1975: Photography assistant at the *École des Beaux Arts*, Dakar, Senegal.

Selected exhibitions

2003
1st Fuji African Press Award.

2001
Centro Atlántico de Arte
Contemporáneo de Las
Palmas, Spain.

1999
Mairie de Willisaw en
Lucerne, Switzerland.

1997
Work placement in Zurich,
Switzerland.

1996
Work placement in London,
UK.

1995
Africa 95 (London and
Leeds) RV, UK and Germany.
TENG *Africa 95* Saint Louis
du Senegal, Senegal.

1993
Mois de la photographie
de Paris, France.
Biennale de photographie
de Bamako, Mali.

1992
Mois de la photo de Dakar,
Senegal.

Publications

Jeune Afrique.
L'Express.
Le Point.
Figaro.
Le Monde.
Bilan.

Emeka Udemba

Born 1968 in Enugu, Nigeria. Lives and works in Kirchzarten, Germany.
1987-1991: Studied Art Education at the University of Lagos / College of Education Lagos.

Residencies
2006: Laab Residency, Cite Internationale des Arts, Parias. 2005, Le Pavillon,
Palais de Tokyo, Paria.
2001: Schleswig Holstenisches Kunstlerhaus.

Selected exhibitions

2005
Uber Schonheit, Haus
der kulturen der Welt, Berlin,
Germany.
Forderkreis zeitgenossischer
Kunst, Euskirchen, Germany.
Galerie im Wiehrebahnof,
Freiburg, Germany.
4 Photographer, Niavaran
Cultural Centre, Teheran, Iran.
Final cut, Palais de Tokyo,
Paris, France.
Istituto Nazionale per la
Grafica, Rome, Italy.
Founded and Curator, Lagos
Open, an experimental
Contemporary Art project, in
Lagos, Nigeria.

2004
Espacio C, Camago, Spain.
Kornhaus Forum, Bern,
Germany.
Rendezvous, Cite
Internationale des Arts, Paris,
France.
Photography, National de
Nantes, Nantes, France.
World meeting of artists,
Caracas Venezuela.

2003
Goethe Institut, Lagos,
Nigeria.
2nd Video Recycling Festival,
Berlin, Germany.
Visa, Ifa Galerie Bonn,
Germany.
Ifa Galerie Stuttgart,
Germany.
L'Europa fantome, Brussels,
Belgium.
Africa for Africa, Palais
des Beaux Arts, Brussels,
Belgium.
Galerie Barnoud, Dijon,
France.
Photo Biennale, Bamako,
Mali.
Havana Biennial, Cuba.

2002
National Museum Onikan,
Lagos, Nigeria.
Dakar Art Biennial, Dakar,
Senegal.
Ars Electronica, Linz,
Germany.

2001
Kunstverein Rottenburg,
Stuttgart, Germany.
Utopia and Realities, Osorio,
Spain.

2000
Heimat kunst, haus der
Kulturen der Welt, Berlin.
Project Queich, Landau,
Germany.
Expo 2000, Hannover,
Germany.
Galerie Hilt, Basel,
Switzerland.
Kunsthalle Gundlingen, Basel,
Switzerland.

Acknowledgements

All the artists and lenders

CAAC. The Pigozzi Collection, Geneva
Fonds du Musée Bruly Bouabré, Ivory Coast
Museum Goch, Goch
André Magnin, Paris
Yaya Savané, Abidjan
Galerie Seippel, Cologne

And all those who one way or another
have supported this project

Yolande Bacot, Parc de la Villette, Paris
Philippe Boutte
Geneviève Breerette
David Brody
Hassey Cissé
Yaya Cissé
Souadou Diabate
Toumani Diabate
Dieumbe Dimé
Paul Faber, Royal Tropical Institute, Amsterdam
Lorna Ferguson
José Luis Gallero
Goodman Gallery, Johannesburg
Patricia Hoorelbeke, Acción contra el Hambre, Bamako
Olivier Longué, Acción contra el Hambre, Madrid
Baber Maiga
Dr. Mann, director Museum Goch, Goch
Anne McIlleron
Gabriel Malou
Thierry Métais, Acción contra el Hambre, Bamako
Tumelo Mosaka
Obie and Lynn Oberholzer
Idrissa Ouedraogo
Panavision, Dakar
Hamadou & Atou Pele Cissé
Mar Sánchez Ramón
Mireia Sentís
Ralf Seippel
Sekou Touré
Mamadou Touré Béhan
Karine Vayer, Parc de la Villette, Paris
Sue Williamson

Special thanks to
Samuel Sidibé, Director, Musée National du Mali, Bamako.

Obra Social Caja Madrid
Carlos María Martínez Martínez, General Manager

La Casa Encendida
José Guirao Cabrera, Director

Cultural Department Coordinator
Ignacio Cabrero Rodríguez

Exhibitions Coordination
Yara Sonseca Mas
María Nieto García
Vanessa Casas Calvo

There & Back. Africa
Curated by
Danielle Tilkin

Exhibition

Design
Estudio Joaquín Gallego

Installation
TEMA S.A.

Transport
Tti

Insurance
Mapfre

Audiovisual equipment
Salas Audio Vídeo

Catalogue

Texts
Danielle Tilkin
Boniface Mongo-Mboussa
and the artists

Design
Base

Printing and photomechanics
T.F. Artes Gráficas, S.A.

Translations
Polisemia, S.L.

© of the publication, La Casa Encendida
© of the texts, the authors
© of the translations, the authors
© of the photographs, the authors

ISBN: 84-95321-81-5
ISBN-13: 978-84-95321-81-7
Legal Deposit M-13343-2006